Wicca Witc

MW01534920

6 Books in 1:

Beginner's Guide to Learn the Secrets of Witchcraft with Wiccan Spells, Moon Rituals, and Tools Like Tarots. Become a Modern Witch Using Meditation, Cards, Herbal, Candle and Crystal Magic

Astrology and Numerology Academy

WICCA BOOK OF SPELLS

WITCHCRAFT

Introduction

Wicca is a belief system which celebrates life and nature. It focuses on the changing cycles of the year, as well as changing cycles of our own life. While our culture promotes development and progress, fast living and constantly pushes us to work more, buy more and have more, It stands for a peaceful and harmonious way of life in which people make an effort to slow down and notice the world around them.

During the last 100 years, our focus on "progress" degraded the earth to such an extent, that not only have water, soil and air become toxic, but the over-exploitation of natural resources and release of vast amounts of agricultural chemicals into the environment, had resulted in a global climate change, the consequences of which we are only beginning to experience.

Wiccans believe that the Divine is present in nature, and so nature should be honored and respected. Everything from animals and plants to trees and rocks are elements of the sacred. By damaging our natural environment, we are eating away at our own life support systems.

The way of life revolves around the Wheel of the Year which is marked by festivals on each solstice and equinox. These are very important times as it is believed that as seasons change, the creative power of Nature is vitalized and can be tapped for magical purposes.

Rituals are an important element of Wicca practice. They are linked to the seasons and moon phases. Moon is central in all Wicca festivals because the Wicca calendar is based on lunar year. Moon phases, and the Full Moon in particular, are seen as auspicious times when doing magic comes easy.

Many Wiccans embrace magic as part of their practice. Magic helps you get things done, on the basis on your inner power. It teaches you how to plug into a wider wisdom that seems to know what's right for you and use magic to cause changes to occur in accordance with your desires.

We live in a fast-paced, hectic world where information overload, toxic environment and stressful lifestyle make us sick, frustrated and permanently exhausted. We are obsessed with being young, beautiful, successful, and perfect. Instead, we are strung out, disillusioned and often angry.

In stark contrast to modern lifestyle, the lifestyle is soothing and healing. Living according to its principles and embracing its uplifting, nature-focused beliefs will help you find inner peace and make sense of this hectic world of ours.

Wiccans draw strength and inspiration from the elements, the heavenly bodies and all the creatures on the earth. In a world dominated by a cult of wealth and power, It can help you rediscover the spiritual connection to nature and teach you how to tune in to your inner self.

Chapter 1: What Is Wicca

What is Wicca? Is it devil worship, Satanism, evil magic, or necromancy? These are essential misconceptions that need to be cleared before diving into the ethics and other details about It.

Wicca is a Neopaganism religion, and practicing magic is the central element of it. It is a religion with several different covens and traditions. It is a group of like-minded witches who practice magic and worship the Goddess and God. Wiccans belong in different organizations of covens, which are groups of witches who practice together, usually under the leadership of a High Priestess, Priest, or both. Covens can vary in size, and general covens tend to be small. In some traditions, the correct size is 13, which is a number generally associated with the occult and witches. However, you do not need to be connected to a coven to be a Wiccan. You can be a Wiccan without being associated with any coven or Wiccan organization.

Next, it is essential to understand what pagan means. The word pagan was first used in ancient Rome to indicate someone who was not a Christian. The phrase has changed in the following centuries to refer to people who practice magic. This association continues to this day.

Is Wicca a Religion?

The short answer to the question, "Is Wicca a religion?" is yes. The long answer is that it is a Neopaganism religion with 1.5 million practitioners in the United States. Some fewer people identify as Wiccan in the United Kingdom and around 150,000 witches in Australia. The US, the UK, and Australia are the only nations that have a significant number of practitioners of Wicca. One of the criticisms of Wicca as a religion is that many covens are not associated with a larger network of practitioners; however, some covens do have such an organization, especially covens in the Gardnerian tradition of Wicca.

Just like in Christianity, Wicca is divided into different traditions. There are several traditions in Wicca, which includes Dianic, Gardnerian, Alexandrian, Algard, and Seax Wicca. Covens can be associated with any of these traditions or none at all.

Many people are opposed to Wicca, especially Evangelical Christians, because they believe that it embodies Satanism and that Wiccans worship Satan as they call on evil spirits.

Wiccan Ethics

Wiccans do not have a strict set of rules or laws like Christianity. Instead, Wiccan ethics center around not harming other people and not practicing black magic like necromancy or domination magic (see below).

Wiccan Rede

Wiccan ethics are based on the Wiccan Rede. The Wiccan Rede is occasionally confusing because it is both a two-line poem and a 24 line poem. The first Wiccan Rede is the Short Rede, which is a two-line statement about Wiccan ethics. The Long Rede is a 24-line poem on the same subject, except it goes into greater detail. The Long Rede's last two lines are the Short Rede.

Essentially, the Wiccan Rede is a statement that you can love anyone unless they lie to you, and as a Wiccan, you shouldn't harm anyone intentionally in any way. That would include casting black magic at someone or engaging in something designed to hurt or take something away from someone.

Black Magic

The one thing that is universal in Wicca is that practicing black magic is forbidden. Black magic is a kind of magic designed to take something away, attack, or engage in dark magic like necromancy or mental domination. Black magic is the opposite of Wiccan or white magic. While Wiccans attempt not to hurt anyone with their magic, warlocks try to take advantage, lie, and cheat people.

Prejudice

One thing that every Wiccan encounter, even if you try not to reveal you are a Wiccan, is prejudice. Wiccans are often called evil or Satanic and everything that is not associated with Wicca at all but is a stereotype of a witch. Generally, the people who are prejudiced and attack Wiccans are Evangelical Christians, who associate all witchcraft with evil and Satanism. However, the only real similarity is that both religions are neopagan, but many people will not associate or understand that Wicca is not evil. You will inevitably encounter such situations, and it is crucial to be prepared for them.

History of Wicca

Many of the traditions of Wicca come from more ancient Pagan belief systems and practices, however, the advent of Wicca and its founding philosophies originated in England and was introduced in the mid-1950s by a British civil servant by the name of Gerald Gardner.

A basic idea of Wicca is that it is considered what some might term Neo-Paganism, however, some distinct qualities and characteristics set it apart from the traditional denominations of the paganism practiced in more ancient cultures.

Before Gardner's introduction of Wicca to the public in 1954, the concepts of Wicca could be traced back to a woman named Margaret Murray who was a renowned folklorist, anthropologist and

Egyptologist, who studied the traditions and cultures of a wide range of religious practices, combining a field study of these sects and describing in her own words the concept of witchcraft.

Murray wrote a large set of books about medieval religious practices, specifically those centered on witch-cults in Europe.

Her works inspired readers to rekindle the pagan arts by creating their covens, structuring their worship around the descriptions from Murray's books. All of this was going on in the early 1920s in Great Britain and Europe and likely led to Gerald Gardner's more structured philosophy called Wicca.

Gardener's book entitled Witchcraft Today demonstrated the origin of the word Wicca and what it means to the craft. In his book, it is spelled with only one 'c', as in "wica", and it wasn't until the 1960's that the second 'c' was added. Gardner mentions that the word 'wica' is a Gaelic, or Scots-English word meaning "wise people". He had always had an interest in the occult and eventually became initiated into a coven of his own in the late 1930s. Eventually, he formed his coven in the late '40s, buying land and establishing it as a center for the study of folklore. It became his occult headquarters and where he would bring to light the Wiccan way through his writing and practice.

A great connection existed between Gardner and the famed occultist Aleister Crowley. The two men met in the late 1940s and had much to discuss their personal beliefs and magic.

Gardner's work and writing out of his rituals of Wicca for publication were strongly influenced by Crowley's work, which had dated back to the earlier part of the century.

Gardner published his works, one of them is a novel entitled, High Magic's Aid, which became one of his first standard tomes to describe the practice of Wicca.

It was his Book of Shadows, however, that became the most highly regarded and sought after. Gardner's Book of Shadows was his collection of spells, rituals and other information about the craft. To this day, it is one of the most central books for the practice of Wicca, or at least for learning from the original Wiccan, Gardner himself.

Fortunately, Wicca was then, and remains to be, an ever-evolving practice and does not adhere to a strict set of rules.

It happens to be a very flexible religion. It offers that people follow a simple set of ideas and concepts and that there is freedom within those ideas to explore and form a deeper understanding.

Initiates of Gardner's coven were given the Book of Shadows to copy out and use, and that was one of the ways they belonged to the coven, sharing the same spells and rituals to carry forward and practice. Gardner met Doreen Valiente in the early 1950s before Wicca had it coming out.

She contacted him after seeing an article in a magazine about covens, witches, their practices, and what that reality was like. Under Gardner's guidance, she was able to revise The Book of Shadows for Gardner to offer it as a favorite book for others outside of the coven and also prominent Wiccan circles, similar to how Crowley had marketed his beliefs and findings.

Valiente became a Wiccan leader of her coven and was a prominent figure and scholar in the world of steadily growing Wiccans. The story of Wicca, when you look at it like that, seems like no more than a trifle in the annals of history, but when you look a little deeper, it had a profound impact on the world of magic.

Leading up to Gardner's exposure of his new religion, there were several ways that people were still looking to practice the ancient Pagan arts. Witchcraft was an incredibly taboo practice and it was highly frowned upon for centuries after the witch trials.

The study of the past by Margaret Murray helped people to find a new appreciation and understanding for the beauty of this magic, and if it wasn't for her work and that of other occult philosophers, Wicca might not have been born. To be honest, it has always existed in some form or fashion and it has carried many other names. The big umbrella term for it would be Pagan, and that word houses a whole cornucopia of possible sects and denominations, practices and rituals. So then, it begs the question: what makes Wicca different?

Based on nature worship of the pagan religions, modern-day Wicca approaches connection to the divine through rituals and practices, festivals of the solstices, observances of deities, specifically a male and female god form, herbalism, a code of ethics and a belief in reincarnation and an afterlife. Some say that it is a modern-day interpretation of those pagan religions and traditions, which existed before Christianity. It has its origins in Europe, but in today's world will also incorporate concepts from other religious practices like Shamanism and pre-Christian Egyptian religion. It has been noted that there are strong similarities to Druidism, as well, despite there being a lack of evidence about how the Druids truly worshipped.

A majority of Wiccans are duotheistic, meaning they worship a male god and a female goddess, or the Horned God and Mother Goddess, or Mother Earth. It is not always the case, and even the early forms of Wicca, back in Gardner's day, were not strict. Most of the time, it was

31

determined on a coven by coven basis, what deities would be worshiped by the group and how to perform certain rituals. Some other forms of Wiccan practice involve, and are not limited to, atheism, pantheism, and polytheism.

This opens the playing field to anyone wishing to establish a Wiccan practice, involving all of the other ethics and rituals into their work while getting the chance to determine how they want to worship.

The basics remain the same, but the deities or what gets worshipped changes. Apart from these components outlined in the earliest forms of Wicca, there is a devout appreciation for the Earth and all of her inhabitants which is why Wicca tends to be called a nature-based religion.

The use of herbs and plants in spell work and rituals is celebrated regularly, and also includes a devotion to the seasons of the Earth cycles and Moon cycles, bringing focus to all living rhythms.

The history of Wicca may feel recent; however, it comes from a long and green history of pagans, druids, witches, warlocks, and all of the individuals and covens along the way who had a sincere devotion to the presence of Earth magic and all of its gifts.

Giving attention to the origins of Wicca is an essential beginning to your study, and as you embrace the methods of how Wicca can be practiced, like those before you, you can build upon it to make it work for you the way that feels best. There are only guidelines and no strict rules. Wicca is meant to evolve with the individual, and whether you are practicing alone or in a group, the Wicca of the past will always be a part of the Wicca of the present. Your Wicca.

Wiccan Beliefs

Beliefs and worldview play an important role in any magical model. Wicca has taken an arduous journey through the past century weaving in and out of the public eye and developing into a worldwide religion. As it travels, just like any religion, it adopts many beliefs and evolves to match its adherents' desires. There are so many distinct sects that literally anyone can find a suitable Wiccan group to be a part of. The subtle beliefs and political views may differ, but overall, the Gardnerian structure remains the most popular base to build a Wiccan community upon. These beliefs all stem from Gardner's initial structure, borrowing from ceremonial magic and pagan communion with natural forces. The moment that Gardner publicized his teaching was the moment Wicca broke free from the shadows and became a part of our world.

Today, so many people identify as Wiccan, or as a witch, and this may mean many things to many people. For the most part, when we speak of Wicca, we are referring to a basic overview of principles and beliefs. The horned god and moon goddess are the central devotional figures in Wicca, but many communities argue over whether or not these are actual kinds of intelligence or Jungian archetypes at work in the human psyche. These choices are left to the individual to decide how they wish to work with these powerful currents. Overall, there is a set base of core beliefs, but let us be open-minded as we approach them.

We will examine some of these core values of Wicca touching on duo theism, polytheism, monotheism, atheism, magic, witchcraft, elements, and death. All of these ideas can be found in the Wiccan sphere, some more popular than others, but overall can be found in various forms throughout the religion. Let's explore some of these popular topics and touch base on the core beliefs of Wicca.

Belief in God

The belief in a higher power comes along with most religions; it is a dividing factor and a unifying one. Wicca is widely recognized as a dualistic religion, having two main deities that encompass the religion. These deities are the Moon Goddess and Horned God. These deities are recognized as the masculine and feminine forces that move within all living things on earth. Wicca also adheres to a notion that there is an even greater power, or source, where all things stem from. This source is thought to be omnipotent in all things.

The god and goddess of Wicca can take various forms and are thought to be found in all living things as masculine or feminine properties, humans having a balance of both of these energies. As humans, we need to balance the masculine and feminine, working to maintain these forces inside of us. Building a relationship with the god and goddess acts to accomplish this on a spiritual level.

In Wicca, it is widely regarded that the omnipotent source is all-encompassing and that all other spirits are divisions of the god and goddess. To grasp this oneness of the universe, we must acknowledge and respect the gods in all their forms, especially in nature.

Magic

Wiccan magic can mean a lot of different things. There are many practices and acts that can be considered magical, and these powerful practices are key to the Wiccan religion. Among these practices, we see divination, spell casting, astrology, meditation, prayer, and many other methods of manipulating reality.

Overall magic strives to improve your life through the communion with nature or manipulating invisible forces for your personal goals and growth. Some consider selfish or evil magic to be black magic, while good or selfless magic is called white magic. These labels are troublesome and often create rifts among spiritual communities. We can safely say that it is rare to find anyone who is completely selfless in their magical endeavors. There is no problem with getting what you desire through magic, so do not let these labels deter you.

Witchcraft

Witchcraft is technically considered a type of magic whose emphasis is on earthly magic, such as natural magic and herbal magic. The witch in all her forms lives in these practices, living on the fringe of society and acting as healer and destroyer. Often associated with women, witchcraft can be practiced by men as well.

Working with herbs, elemental magic, full moon ceremonies, and many sublunary practices are at the core of modern witchcraft. We see this power manifesting in the breaking of taboos, the uprising of communal politics, and feminist revolution. The witch does not like being controlled or told she cannot do what her free will desires. Witches have always been persecuted throughout history, regardless of their contributions to society and its evolution.

The Five Elements

The five elements are found in many cultures around the world. Air, earth, fire, water, and ether or spirit are the primary elements found in

Wicca. These elements are thought to be what all things are made of. Modern science has disproven this concept as a literal philosophy, but symbolically, these elements are still very powerful. When we work with the elements, we are effectively connecting with separated equal parts of a whole. These elements are found in everything on earth, some having certain qualities in abundance than others. Balancing our elemental influence as humans is key to a balanced life.

Death

Wiccans do not fear death or preach of its haunting imminent threat to our lives. Wiccans believe that life is not linear but a cycle or continuum. Death is not the end of our lives but simply a migration to another world or returning to the source. Death is often celebrated, and death-related ceremonies are popular in Wiccan communities.

Ancestral magic is popular among some Wiccan communities as well. These practices entail leaving offerings for our ancestors and working with them through necromantic practices. This magic is very powerful and is a great first step for beginners on a magical path.

Initiation

Initiation is a key element to any magical structure. Initiation is loosely defined as a means where you are accepted into spiritual practice by the spirits or gods you are working with. You do not get to decide if you are initiated; only the gods can do this. When you are initiated into a magical teaching, the chosen deity of those teachings will initiate you.

Gardner's original structure held that one must enter through various rites of passage to be initiated into a Wiccan coven or group. Gardner taught that these rites must be performed perfectly to initiate one into the religion. These initiation rituals have been practiced since Gardner's passing and keep the lineage with his original rites and structure. As we've mentioned, Gardner claimed to have been shown these rites as a member of a coven he joined that he also claimed to be a lineage of pre-Christian pagan systems of initiation. Many Wiccans today do not believe this origin story to be true, instead just keeping the lineage history as starting with Gardner's first rites.

Gardner said that it takes a year and one day from the time someone begins practicing the craft to the instance of initiation, but many people claimed he broke this rule often for favored students. For a general overview of these rites, there are three distinct degrees; the first degree is starting your practice, the second degree is familiarization with ritual tools and rites, and the third degree is participation in the Great Rite. The Great Rite is a sexual initiation performed physically or symbolically with magical tools. There is much controversy over many people abusing the vulnerable nature of the great rite. Gardner claimed that these rites must be performed in the nude, but many covens today disregard this idea, choosing robes or even casual everyday clothing.

Initiation is the first step of becoming an adept magician and not just a beginner. Many purists believe that initiation must be done in the midst of a Wiccan group with a high priest and Priestess present, but many seekers have successfully self-initiated into the Wiccan rites all by themselves. We see self-initiation gaining popularity with access to these powerful practices through the internet and other technologies. Some people may not have a local Wiccan group or find that their local group is not welcoming. Under these circumstances, you must opt for self-initiation. Some people may just feel like lone wolves, preferring a rogue magical practice; this is perfectly fine and works well for many Wiccans.

We can see that magic and Wicca work symbiotically to form a balanced and powerful religion. Wicca draws inspiration from many different practices from Victorian ceremonial magic to the pagan culture's use of natural magic. This basic structure remains as Wiccan communities continue to form around the world, although many sects have differing opinions on the subtle nuances of ceremony or political beliefs. We find that this path has one ultimate goal: the communion with the horned god and goddess, the chosen deities of the Wiccan religion. These forces are divine masculinity and divine femininity, respectively. Once the god and goddess initiate us, we are true Wiccans and can move our practice beyond earthly bounds, being able to reveal the secrets of the universe to ourselves and even share them with others if we so choose.

What Does a Spell Really Mean?

Spells are usually confused with a lot of other related words like charms and incantations. This is particularly annoying because a lot of websites and information repositories have interchanged the meanings of these terms.

A spell, by definition, is usually a form of word used as an incantation or magical charm for a desired outcome. This means that spells consist of words that are impregnated with powers. Alternatively, a spell can entail the desire to birth change in the lives of other people or even in your life. When casting a spell, you also include your energies, belief and intent in order to make it a reality. Even though this sounds simple, in order to actually cast spells, you need to concentrate your focus and energies in the right proportion. You may likely not experience any results when you don't mix the process of casting spells with energy. Also, there are certain mental conditions that have to be in check to successfully cast spells. If you cast a spell when you are angry or if you make a mistake in the process of casting spells, it is sure to go wrong, and sometimes the result may be catastrophic. Generally speaking, spells sometimes do their own thing so some results of spells are not the intended results. The universe is in the habit of occasionally interrupting the process of casting spells and most of the time it is in control of what happens so your intent is not usually what you get when you cast spells.

Anyone who is under the influence of a spell is really out of control. His actions and thoughts are controlled by the person who cast the spell or by the spell.

While spells have gotten some negative attention from a lot of people, they can be a way of making things better for the person doing the casting. For example, when you know how to cast spells, there are a lot of benefits that you stand to acquire with this knowledge. You can go all out and create the ideal life you've always wanted for yourself, your friends and your family. With the power available to you, when you begin to learn how to cast spells, you can be of help to the earth and the universe by extension. With the right mind and application, you can serve the purposes of mankind with this power. But you have to remember that you'll be laden with enormous responsibility when you have great power. What, then, is stopping you from using this enormous power that lives within you?

Just Believe…

These two words may be the most important words you'll hear on your journey to learning how to cast spells. Spell casting is something that anyone, irrespective of who they may be, can venture into, but the outcomes of the spells carried out by these people are informative. There is a place of commitment, energy, focus and will in casting a spell as they go a long way to determine how effective your spell will be. Without consistency of character and commitment, the object of your desires will not readily be manifested.

For example, it is a senseless venture casting a spell to enable you to find a job when you have not actually applied for any. No! Spells don't work that way. Without any intentional commitment to the object of your desire, the universe can do very little to help you achieve your aim.

Like we said earlier, there is a place of belief when casting your spell. If you harbor any negativity before or during the process of casting your spells, it will really show in your results. If you have rounded up the spell as ineffective, it is almost certain that you will back up the process with minimal energy; your thoughts will also become negative and the end result will be non-effective or even catastrophic. So it is in your best interest to make sure that you keep your thoughts positive so that your spell can be reinforced.

And then there is this prevalent thought that once you've cast a spell there is no need to remember it. Even though this may be true for some kinds of spell, it does not apply to every spell. You may like to follow your innate feelings on this one. When you feel a need to keep an eye on your spell, do so. Another benefit of carrying this out is that it increases your energy.

Visualizing Your Spells

The practice of visualizing your spells is very important. You'll do yourself good when you are able to come up with an imprinted picture of what you desire in your mind before engaging the process. Making use of the job example again; when you attend a job interview to fill a space in a certain company where you want to work, you should visualize yourself already occupying the position you want to occupy when you cast your spell. When engaged effectively, this singular process will be the turning point in your life as it is almost always certain that you will get the job. Visualize yourself already in the position that you are applying for and try to see in your mind's eye your name and details on the office stationery. The aim of this exercise is to put your consciousness on that path you want and set the pace for your body to follow.

Components of a Spell

A spell's components are the real-life necessities and some of the tangible realities that should be in check in order to cast the spell successfully. Each spell's description is an indication of the necessities you must adhere to so that your spell works for you. They include some verbal (V), somatic (S), or material (M) components of the spell. When one or more of the conditions are not met, then it is sheer futility trying to cast your spell because it won't work.

The Verbal Component

For most spells, the use of mystic words and sounds are what gives life to them. It is important to note that words are not really the source of the power, but then the right use of these words, certain resonance and pitch are necessary to produce the desired effect. There are some spells that do not require the use of words and sounds, for example those that are cast on their target to keep them silent.

The Somatic Component

In addition to the use of words to cast a spell, there are other physical requirements like some sets of gestures that are required to successfully cast a spell. Any spell that requires this component in order to work will not work if no gesture is made.

The Material Component

When your knowledge of spell casting increases, you'll get to know that there are some spells that must be cast with the use of certain material objects. For example, a Spellcasting focus and a Component Pouch are two materials used in casting spells.

When a spell indicates that a material requirement is used by the spell, the person casting the spell must make this necessary requirement for each casting of the spell available. The person needs to possess a hand free to hold a Spellcasting focus or to make use of the spell's material components, but then the person can also make use of the same hand that he uses to carry out the process.

The Timing of a Spell

Observing the Right Times to Cast a Spell

Just as stated in the Bible (Ecclesiastes 3:1), there is a season for everything that happens under the sun. For communities that primarily depend on agrarian means of livelihood, the farmers are have mastered the times and seasons for harvesting, planting, weeding etc. by the study of signs provided by nature. In like manner, some people have interpreted the Bible passage above to mean that there are seasons that are efficacious for spiritual activities also. This is in synchrony with the belief that the energies of the planets, moon, and the sun are in harmony with a common goal. Considerations include the following:

The Moon Phase

New moons indicate new beginnings and fresh starts and Venus is known to be the planet of love. This means that if you are interested in casting a spell to attract a new lover, this spell should be carried out on the Friday of a new moon.

It is obvious that you may not always be well disposed to cast a spell during the right time so it is important to at least get the phase and date correct.

The Moon's Phases

Although the moon can be separated into eight unique phases, a lot of spell casters channel their energies into the five most famous ones. They include:

- The New Moon

- The Dark Moon

- The Full Moon

- The Waxing Moon

- The Waning Moon

The Dark Moon- This phase takes place when the moon is completely absent from the night sky. This time is the right time for paybacks, throwing curses and bringing down your enemies.

The New Moon- The new moon starts when the first sliver of the moon can be seen in the sky during the night just when the dark moon phase is gone. This is a good time to start the birth of something.

The Waxing Moon- The waxing moon is a period that falls in between the full moon and the new moon. During this period, the moon assumes a characteristic reverse C shape so that the dark side of it is positioned at the left while the light side of it is positioned at the left. This phase is suitable for casting spells that draw things to us.

The Full Moon- This phase is observed when the moon is round and totally lit up. During this period, you can cast any type of spell that you want.

The Waning Moon- The waning moon is marked with a period that falls between new moon and full moon. During this period, the moon always appears as C shape so that the dark side is positioned at the right side of the moon and the light side is positioned at the left side of the moon. During this period, it is ideal to cast spells that take things away from us.

In antiquated times, certain folks called signs for the parts of the body that they controlled instead of the signs themselves. A lot of countrymen devoted a great deal of consideration to the part of the body that the moon occupies prior to engaging in anything that had a touch of nature or magic. For instance, it is not allowed to pull out a tooth when the moon is positioned in the head (Aries) because it entails a high risk of bleeding.

The Head (Aries) - Birthing an action, initiating new beginnings, challenging things, casting certain spells on people, dominating and controlling situations and people, breaking bad habits.

The Neck (Taurus) - Planning on long-term goals, handling money matters, putting up preserves, engaging in public speaking, handling dental work.

The Arms (Gemini) - Juggling tasks, travel, protection, intellectual pursuits.

The Chest (Cancer) - Attending to home and family matters, signing agreements, weddings.

The Heart (Leo) - Children, self-confidence, love, creativity, protection, ideal for carrying out large purchases and engaging in what you desire to last.

The Bowels (Virgo) - Getting a job, analyzing, organizing, buying medicine, breaking bad habits, healing pets, healing.

The Kidneys (Libra) - Contracts, partnerships of all kinds, creativity, writing, socializing, diplomacy, marriage.

The Genitals (Scorpio) - Buying antiques, psychic development, seduction, divination, investigation, lust, research.

The Thighs (Sagittarius) - Spiritual pursuits, liberty starting an exercise or a diet program, expanding the mind.

The Knees (Capricorn) - Protection, self-control, pursuing ambitions, focusing on your career, organizing.

The Legs (Aquarius) - Originality, volunteering, socializing, art, friendship.

The Ankles (Pisces) - Psychic development, banishing negativity.

Almost everyone on this planet is conversant with the fact that there are seven days in a week, but not everyone knows that there are seven planets in the solar system that are associated with classical astrology. Each day of the week comes with its own correspondences because of these associations.

The Sun (Sunday) - Achievement, success, wealth, career, authority figures.

The Moon (Monday) - Dreams, intuition, spirit work, psychic-ism.

Mars (Tuesday) - Power, dealing with enemies, wars.

Mercury (Wednesday) - Wisdom, healing, communication, commerce.

Jupiter (Thursday) - Happiness, luck, expansion.

Venus (Friday) - Marriage, romance, friendship, love.

Saturn (Saturday) - Transformation and psychic attack, protection.

As a plus to these traditional suggestions, a lot of spell casters are engaged in personal spells. For instance, Fridays are the usual days when people get paid, hence there is a tendency to associate Fridays with wealth and money and many engage in spells of that nature on Fridays.

Also if you are looking at getting a job as a writer, you may like to cast your spell on Wednesday because Mercury is the god of communication.

Chapter 2: Rules of Wicca

As a religious group, Wicca began in the middle of the twentieth century around 1950, although its basis goes back centuries to Pagan practices and beliefs. In the beginning, it was a secret society that one could join by being initiated and taking an oath. However, as years passed, people began to move on and form their own groups and using what they had been taught along with new traditions. The original traditions carried elements of British legend, learnings from Kabbalah, and some Eastern mysticism. Wiccan has no set governing body or set of rules. No particular Wicca Bible exists that gives followers a set of guidelines for universal use. So practices will vary from one group or individual to another. But there are some beliefs and ideals that are common to almost all of the modern followers of Wicca.

Harm No One

This is a theme that is common in all Wiccan beliefs. Most followers keep to the belief that anything done in the practice of Wicca should not cause harm to anyone or anything.

Respect the Beliefs of Other People

In the practice of Wicca, people hold the belief that every person must find their own path in life and must be allowed to follow that path. Beliefs can be shared with other people but must never be forced upon other people.

Be Responsible for Yourself

Every individual is responsible for their own personal actions in life. Whether you are doing magic or just going about your daily activities you must be prepared to take responsibility for whatever you do.

Remember the Holidays

Wiccan Holidays are based on the cycles of the seasons and the rotation of the earth. Wicca celebrates eight major days of power, called Sabbats, and the Esbats which are celebrated monthly.

Honor Your Ancestry

No matter what our ancestors should be spoken of reverently and with honor. Many Wiccans feel that their ancestors guide them and watch over them because many Wiccans commune with those in the spirit world.

Life After Death and Karma

Many Wiccans believe in karma and life after death. There is a belief that whatever we do in this life will be visited on us in our next life. This is similar to the Eastern belief that however you live this life will determine what you return as in your next life and how your next life will be. In addition, usually, Wiccans do not believe in hell, heaven, or the concept of sin.

The Divine is Present in Nature

Wiccans believe that nature should be respected and honored because the Divine is present in and lives in elements of nature. Rocks, trees, plants, and animals contain elements of the sacred. This is similar to the Native American belief that life flows through all things, from the tree to the rock to the person to the animal, and if one part of the chain is broken or damaged, then the life cannot flow as well as it should. This is why many people who practice Wiccan are quite passionate about taking care of the environment. Also, the Divine is both male and female and is present in all people. Interacting with the gods is not a function of a select group of people because all people are sacred beings.

There are also the Principles of Belief that were set down by the Council of American Witches in the mid-1970s. They were a loosely organized group that did not stay together for very long, but they were able to give us a list of thirteen beliefs that many Wiccans follow to one degree or another. These are not meant to be hard and fast rules. They include practicing rites to mark the Holidays, being responsible to the environment, the natural potential of all people to have superpowers, the lack of animosity toward other religions and their beliefs, and the belief that people should improve their overall health by seeking what they need in nature.

There are certain laws often referred to the Rules of the Craft that present guidelines for the behavior of the follower. Most Wiccan will follow one or more of these and it is up to the individual follower to choose the one set of laws that are most in line with their personal beliefs and follow it. This would also be an entry into the front of the Book of Shadows.

The Witches Rede

This rule contains one line that almost all Wiccans follow even if this is not their guiding rule, and that is to harm no one. This is also the reason why many followers will close a spell with words like 'to harm no one' or 'to benefit the good of all.

The Charge of the Goddess

In Wicca, this is an inspirational text designed to honor the Goddess in ceremonies held in the Sacred Circle. It asks for the help of the Goddess to guide and teach the followers.

Seven Hermetic Principles

These are considered to be the seven ancient rules for one to learn to master oneself. This is done by pursuing knowledge that pertains to mysteries of a spiritual nature.

The Delphic Maxims

These are thought to have been delivered to man by Apollo himself and give guidelines for living a pious life, such as obeying the law, learning self-control, seek wisdom, and practice discipline in all things.

The Rule of Three

This rule states that the things you do will come back to you not once but three times.

Law of Power

This rule states that the power of a witch must only be used for their own good and for the protection of themselves and others if necessary.

The power is a gift from God and the Goddess and must be treated as sacred.

Wiccan Tools

Before you get too far along in your magical practice, you must have certain magical tools to help guide you in controlling and guiding the magical energies of the universe. A Wiccan should always have their tools consecrated and ready to go in case of emergencies.

Consecrating Magic Tools

The first thing you need to know to use any item is to consecrate it. Consecrating an item is a prerequisite for using it in your spells. If the item is not prepared correctly, then the item will not bond properly with your magical energy, and it may become a drain to the spell instead of its intended purpose. Therefore, it is very important to take the time to consecrate your magical tools. When you consecrate your items, you bond with them, and they align themselves to your magical energy. Because of the connection between you and your tools, your magic will become more powerful when you use them. Also, note that you may not need each item in this book. You should try to find which ones speak to you.

Follow the steps below to consecrate your items:

1.Create a magic circle with white chalk or table salt.

2.Draw or place a physical pentacle in the middle of the circle.

3.Put each of the tools on the pentacle, usually in the middle of the pentacle.

4.Put a drop of water and salt on the item.

5.Allow a cloud of incense to pass over the item.

6.Say the following invocation:

Oh, Inana! Oh, Dumuzi!

Bless this tool with your divine hands!

Bless this tool with your honor and glory!

Major Tools

The list of items in this book is divided into two. The first part has major tools that you will use more often in your spells. This includes crystal balls, wands, and chalices or cups, among others. The following are major items that are generally useful.

Altar

The first tool that you should have is an altar. An altar is a piece of furniture or a box that you place items on such as candles, pictures, clay idols, and other small items for the worship of the deity. The altar should be consecrated to the Moon Goddess and the Horned God, or if you want it to be more specific, it can be connected to any of the historical gods or goddesses. Using an altar can increase the magic behind your spells.

Crystal Ball

Crystal balls are another powerful magical tool. Crystal balls are used for scrying or casting divination spells. Crystal balls are very useful for revealing hidden things. Like many of these tools, you can bond to them to give them more power. You typically use a crystal ball as the item you focus on during the spell, or you can gaze into it to scry with it.

Cup

Cups or chalices are powerful magic items that are associated with the element of water, and it is also tied to the suit of Cups in a tarot deck. You can use your cup to carry water or a potion. A spell may call for you to sprinkle water on an item. If you encounter this, you should use your cup or chalice to carry the liquid in.

Pentacle

A pentacle is associated with both the element of earth and the tarot card suit Pentacles. Also known as a paten, the pentacle is a very powerful item. You can have an object with a pentacle on it, or you can draw a pentacle on the ground with table salt or chalk. The advantage of drawing it is that you can make it exactly the size of your magic circle. Pentacles are associated with strength and protection

Sword

Swords are associated with the element of fire and the tarot card suit of Swords. It is also known as an athame or ritual knife. An athame is a knife with a black handle. Swords are controversial in Wicca as many Wiccans feel that there is no room in the religion for any form of weapon. The athame is more common than actual swords. Swords are a powerful suit, as it is closely associated with fire, which is raw and chaotic power.

Wand

The last of the major tools are wands. Wands are associated with the element of air. It is also associated with the tarot card suit Wands. A wand can be a very powerful magical tool. Because of its association with air, wands are typically very light object like a stick or a length of metal. Wands are often adorned with gems and other magic items.

These items can amplify the wand's energy so that you can perform more powerful magic with it.

Minor Tools

The minor tools are a list of various items that you can easily incorporate into your magical practice. These items include cauldrons and jewelry. While not as powerful as the major items, the minor items are very useful when used correctly. Below are a variety of magical tools that you may want to use.

Besom

Besoms are brooms that witches use in ceremonies and rituals. The myth of witches riding broomsticks has its origin in besoms. Besoms are used in ritual seasonal dances as a phallic object, or it might be used in a hand-fasting ceremony, which is a neopagan ritual that binds two people in a marriage-like union. The witch will have the couple jump over the besom to finish the hand-fasting ritual.

Boline

Boline is a ritual knife with a white handle. The blades of these knives are often curved. Unlike the athame used in major rituals, the boline is used for common tasks like cutting herbs or carving runes into a candle. The boline is used when the task is too messy or dirty to use your athame.

Cauldron

A cauldron is a pot, generally made of cast iron, used by a witch to brew potions. The cauldron is a classic symbol of a witch, and it is a very useful tool. Many spells will call for brewing a concoction that is drunk by the target of the spell or even the witch who brewed it. Not everything brewed in a cauldron is meant for drinking. Sometimes, a cauldron is used to make pastes and salves. Cauldrons are connected to the element of water for obvious reasons.

Censer

A censer is a metal dish where incense is burned. You can also place other burned items on the censer. For example, a spell may ask you to burn a picture of someone. After you do so, you should place the ashes on the censer.

Cingulum

The cingulum is a ritual cord that initiates use to show what rank they are in a coven, or a larger one can be spread out in a circle to mark the boundaries of a magic circle.

Incense

Incense is an item that, when burned, releases fragrances and clouds of smoke. Incense has been used throughout history as a ritual gift to various gods and goddesses, including the historical goddesses and gods. Incense can be used either for the smoke or the fragrance.

Jewelry

Another item that you can use is jewelry. Jewelry is very powerful magic items that are worn to activate their often continuous powers. Jewelry can be used to store some of your magical energy so that you can summon it quickly, or it can be used for protective magic and warding yourself of black magic or harm.

Smudge Stick

Smudge sticks are bundles of various herbs that are bound together, generally with string. Wiccans use smudge sticks to drive off evil or malicious spirits, demons, or ghosts. Smudge sticks are also used to create protections for homes or other spaces.

Stang

The final tool, the stang is a long wooden staff. The staff should have a natural fork in it or two antlers attached to it. The stang is associated with the Horned God because of the antlers. Stangs are very useful because they can be used as a mobile altar. This lets you easily carry an altar with you so that you can cast many types of magic away from home.

Chapter 3: The Basic Principles and PRACTICES of Wicca

What They Believe, Do and Teach

It is no exaggeration that if you ask five or ten Wiccans about Wicca, you are bound to have completely different responses or at least minor variations. The reasons for this aren't farfetched: there is no Wiccan guidebook or Holy book, and there is no strict regulatory body to curb the growing differences. More so, Wicca emphasizes individuality over group worship. This, therefore, underscores its esoteric nature and the growing diversification to which it is continually subjected. Based on this, there are many conflicting beliefs and practices plaguing Wicca as a neopagan religion. The consequence of this is double-sided. While diversification makes Wicca an interesting topic of research and discourse, it also makes the differences difficult to reconcile, and this has slowed down its acceptance among non-Wiccans.

The Sovereignty of the Goddess and the God

Every Wiccan group is founded on the belief in the existence and sovereignty of the Moon Goddess. Although not all covens are duotheistic, almost all of them believe in the existence of the Goddess and her male counterpart. Both deities are believed to be responsible for life and fertility. Special days of the year are designated to the worship of the Goddess and the God respectively. These are the Wiccan festivals which are, together, known as the Wheel of the year.

In addition to the Goddess and God, Wiccans believe in other deities, which are considered smaller in authority and honor. These are referred to as the deities of the respective Wiccan traditions. Some of them are Cerridwen, Herne, Apollo, Athena, Isis, and so on. In most covens, the particular small deity of worship is known only to the coven members. Whatever the small deity of worship is, one fact remains unmistakable about Wiccan groups. They all believe in the power of the divine, hence they emphasize the need to personally attain the state of constant connection to the supernatural.

Only Initiates are Allowed in the Deep Circles

To be upfront enough, Wicca is not discriminatory, but it draws the lines between initiates and non-initiates. As much as it allows nonmembers ample room to be partakers of public festivals and minor activities, it doesn't allow them access to the core rituals of the group. For example, the particular small deity which a particular coven believes in is revealed to its initiates only. Wicca is occultic in nature and therefore values initiation. Initiation often involves a thorough process but must begin with the potential Wiccans making up their minds to be a member. This stage is never forced or hurried. The covens allow such persons access to minor practices and public festivals for a period of time in order to help them decide whether or not they would really love to be part. Once this stage has been completed and the decision to join has been made, the first initiation follows.

The first initiation is a rebirth of the individual, the process of which initiates dedicate themselves to the cause and activities of the group in order to show themselves as worthy members. Upon successfully completing the first stage, they are made to undergo the second initiation. After becoming a full member, a Wiccan can study and practice well enough to progress through the ranks otherwise known as degrees. Only those who have reached the Third Degree are capable enough to become High Priestesses or Priests. Self-initiation is only allowed for those who wish to practice Wicca in solitary.

Magic is a Tool for Self-expression

Magic, sometimes alternately spelled 'magick', is another basic practice in Wicca. It is interesting to mention that Wiccans do not consider magic a supernatural ability, but a mere body of spell work with which an individual harnesses their inner strengths to redirect the natural energy around to suit their intentions. This requires spells, crystals, wand, candles, study and the likes. Magic appears to be literally practiced in Wicca. In other words, any Wiccan can engage in magic in as much as they possess the skills required, but there are certain regulations that bind its practice. First off, magic is only practiced within a sacred circle, and rules such as the Law of Threefold Return, which is also known as the Rule of Three, and the Wiccan Rede are to prevent Wiccans from using their magical powers to the detriment of others. These rules, however, are part of the efforts to differentiate the Wiccan practice of magic from the sometimes harmful magic practiced by other groups. Wiccan magic is often done during rituals as a group, and could also be individually practiced.

The Spirit World is Real

The reality of the supernatural world is emphasized in Wiccan practice. Literally, all Wiccan groups believe that there exists a metaphysical world with which we can interact. This involves communication with the dead, certain spirits, and sometimes powerful demons all of which serve as spirit guides. Communication with such metaphysical powers is made possible via a series of methods including astrology, tarots, and runes. This also relates strongly to the belief in ancestry. It is the belief in Wicca that those who are long dead are actively watching over the living. In other words, the ancestors are powerful enough to oversee, protect and influence the lives and activities of those living. This, according to Wiccans, makes it a necessity to constantly commune with the ancestors.

There is Life after Now

One of the guiding principles of Wicca is that there is life after death and that whatever one does in the present life comes back to influence one's experience in the next one. This principle is not to be mistaken with the Christian and Islamic belief in Heaven, Hell, eternity and sin. On the contrary, Wicca does not believe in such concepts. Rather, it emphasizes that life continues afterlife. Put differently, after the current life, there is another life. It also emphasizes that karma is real and that whatever one does now, whether good or otherwise, will be revisited on one later on. This payback principle is enshrined in the Law of Threefold Return. It is in order to enjoy a peaceful and fruitful afterlife that Wicca preaches harmlessness. The Wiccan Rede is a summary of this belief: harm no one. As a result of this, everyone must be willing to accept responsibility for their actions and inactions. Whatever the consequences of your acts are, whether positive or otherwise, Wiccans believe that you must be willing to take responsibility for such actions.

The Divine is Present in Nature

There is a pantheistic connotation in this Wiccan principle. Most, if not all, Wiccan groups believe that the Divine is present in every natural thing. They hold that although the Goddess and God are supreme deities, they manifest in humans, animals, plants, insects, and every other natural thing in the environment. Hence, they revere every natural element, believing that every natural element is sacred since the Divine is present in them. This buttresses why they emphasize the possibility of communing with supernatural beings. They hold that everyone irrespective of their ranks can communicate with the Divine and not just the priests alone.

Festivals are Based on Nature

To further buttress the value which Wicca places on nature, it must be mentioned that all Wiccan festivals and celebrations are based on the rotation of the earth in relation to the Sun. Based on the resulting seasons, Wicca holds eight major annual celebrations which are known as Sabbats, as well as other monthly festivals called Esbats.

Respect and Tolerance of other Religions

It is a rare phenomenon to find Wiccans in altercations with individuals of other faiths based on beliefs. The major secret behind this is the Wiccan tolerance for other faiths. More so, they do not proselytize their practices or preach to others to become part of their faith. This is because they believe in the personal journey to spiritual discovery. An individual who would become a Wiccan would do so based on personal conviction and not by the influence of any kind nor inheritance.

The beliefs and practices of Wicca are definitely inexhaustible, owing to the diversification that has rocked it over the years. Based on this, it is almost impossible for even Wiccans and scholars of Wicca to agree on a comprehensive body of beliefs and guide system that binds all Wiccan groups. Some common examples of the diversification are whether Wicca is monotheistic or duotheistic, and whether self-initiation is allowed or not. These differences, among others, remain unresolved and they account for the slow acceptance the faith continues to endure. This situation, notwithstanding, does not completely mean that there are no common grounds whatsoever in Wicca. On the contrary, there are a number of them.

Chapter 4 Different Ways of Casting a Spell

A witch can cast a spell in different ways, depending on their level of expertise. Some of the ways can be more effective, but difficult to master. Some may have higher risk and require stronger guidance from the deities. Below are some of the different ways of casting a spell:

Casting Through Metals and Crystals

For beginners, spells using metals and crystals are the safest. It is an indirect way of casting a spell and it has a lesser risk of ricocheting. Metals and crystals are home to mythical spirits. These spirits charges the magical objects and unless they will listen to the witch, the spell would not have an effect. However, the mythical spirits easily charges the metals and crystals, especially if the deities are in your favor.

Also, metals and crystals do not need any contact with the subject of the spell. The subject does not have to eat or inhale any. Thus, it could not harm him in any way, unless the spell is wrong or evil.

The most common crystals used in magic are moonstone, amethyst, quartz, amber, emerald, ruby, sapphire and diamond.

The most common metals used in magic are gold, silver and copper.

Casting using Potions

Potions require some magical and health expertise, especially if the potion needs to be ingested. Experts suggest that if you do not have enough experience with concocting potions, do not cast any spell using it.

Herbs and essential oils can be used in making potions. Other ingredients, like crystal powders, metal powders and even parts of animals may be required in making the potion. Also, the spells should be specific whether the potion needs to be ingested, applied topically or splashed.

Direct Casting

Casting without any magical objects can also be done, but it is also one of the most dangerous of all the ways. It requires a lot of expertise and focus. A slight mistake in the spell can make it work differently compared to your intention.

Experts suggest using a wand when direct casting. The wand can charge the spell and make it more powerful. Also, the wand can block any repercussions when you make mistakes in your spell.

Casting by Offering/Ritual

Another way of casting a spell is by making an offering or a ritual. It is a difficult way of casting a spell, and could also be dangerous. Casting by offering or by ritual is almost the same as summoning the spirit to do the spell for you.

Experts say that you have to win the favor of the deities before you try to do this type of spells. The spirit that you may summon would claim more than what you offered and could cause harm to you or the subject of your spell. Some spirits are also mischievous and may play with your spell, before making it favorable for you.

How Real Witches Cast Spells

Casting spells is, unsurprisingly, not like the movies. There's no 'Abracadabra,' 'Hocus Pocus' or flashing lights and sound effects, because this is magick, not magic. There is a difference, and it's not just the matter of a single letter. 'Magic' is illusion, tricks, entertainment, Hollywood stuff. 'Magick' is what witches do. It's real but subtle change, and above all, it's positive change, putting your energy out into the Universe to swing things your way, and when it happens, it will seem like coincidence.

Spells don't go against science and don't seek to achieve the impossible, so no real witch will ever cast a spell to make 70lbs of ugly fat melt away without conscious effort on your part, or make your hair grow 10 inches in a matter of days. You can't turn an ugly duckling into a swan with a spell, but Nature can, and that's the basis of spell craft. You work with Nature, the Elements and the Universe to bring about the changes you want.

One common misconception about spells is that the incantation must be said in exactly the right way, and that things must be done in the right order, within a specified timeline, otherwise disaster strikes. The reality is that it's not really what you say that matters.

If you get the words wrong, it's a human mistake, and the deities recognize that. The spell won't fail because of it. What is important when casting a spell is the intent, the focus, and the purity of thought? If the words you speak are honest and come from the heart, the spell will work, even if you make a mistake.

Magick works on every level, but you also have to work with it. You can cast a spell for success, and it will give you an edge at the exam, or that important job interview or audition – but only if you put the work in as well. It's no good casting a success spell and then going off on holiday instead of revising for your exam or preparing for the interview or audition.

That illustrates a lack of intent and a lack of focus, and if you treat spell casting is a quick fix to help you coast through life without putting in some effort on your own behalf, the magick will not work for you.

As with all witchcraft rituals, spell casting is first and foremost about preparation. The first thing you need is a thorough understanding and grounding in the philosophy of witchcraft. Without this, you should not even consider working with magick. As has been noted, it's not about tricks, it's about understanding Nature, the Elements and the deities, and working with those entities to create and channel the energy and power necessary to cast successful spells and create magick.

In order to cast successful spells, you have to know yourself and know and acknowledge to the Universe what your real intention is, what you want to change about yourself. Casting the spell puts that knowledge 'out there,' and energizes and motivates the caster. Change starts within yourself – there is nothing you cannot do, so you need to banish the word 'can't' from your vocabulary and believe in the power of your spells.

Witchcraft and spell craft are based on positivity, focus, and intent. Before you cast a spell, you need to meditate to clear your mind and release any negative thoughts and energy. With a clear, focused mind, you can concentrate on your intent, and imagine your spell working. Visualize every detail in your mind, and believe that it will happen. Have faith in your own powers and energy and the powers of the Universe that you are able to call on through your Craft.

Remember the dogma 'Harm None.' Your spell should be something positive that brings good to yourself, those you love, and the wider world. If there is any negativity, manipulation or bad thinking attached to your spell, it will not work.

The objects you use in spells do not have magical powers, but they do help to focus your mind on the intent of the spell. For example, if you are casting a spell for love, roses and hearts and pink candles may be used. Pink is the spell candle color for love, and hearts and flowers are universal symbols of love, so these objects help to concentrate your mind on the purpose of the spell.

This concentration assists the flow of the energy and power that are needed in order for the spell to succeed. It's also helpful to familiarize yourself with the sequence of the spell before you cast it. Constantly referring to guidelines will take the focus away from the spell itself, since it will disrupt your concentration.

Another point to remember is that a spell doesn't necessarily have incantations and objects. The simple act of putting a leaf on a different tree, or making special oil counts as a spell in some cases.

Spell craft is as much about feelings and preparation as it is about the mechanics of the actual spell. Take time to prepare yourself for the spell, mentally, physically and practically.

Make sure that everything you need is where you need it so that you don't need to interrupt the ritual once it is under way. Remember you will also need the tools you normally use for casting a circle since the spell-like all witchcraft rituals and practices – should be cast within the sacred circle to ensure the protection and assistance of the Elements and the deities and the strength of the magick.

Where you cast your spell is also important. If you are casting the spell outdoors, make sure the place you have chosen is safe, and that you won't be interrupted during your work – because spell casting is work, and it needs to be carried out in the right way if you are to stay safe and the spell is to be effective.

As a beginner, you may prefer to conduct your early spells in the presence of a more experienced witch, or even a friend who is sympathetic to your beliefs. Just remember that spell casting – like everything else connected with witchcraft – is natural, not mystical. Anybody can do it, and like any other skill, your ability will improve with practice.

Chapter 5: Timing Your Spells and Correspondences

Figuring out the best time to cast a spell does not have to be hard. If you want to cast a spell, then do it. There are a lot of witches who believe that spells become more powerful if they are done at certain phases of the moon or on certain days of the week. This is because of the various planetary energies that people believe are available at certain times, and it is those energies that can add strength to the spell.

There are several options for spell timing, and you don't need to time your spell to work with all these options. Any of them would be helpful. You could layer them if you want, but it isn't necessary.

Using the Moon

If you want to use the moon's energy to add power to your spells, here are some rules you should follow.

For spells that are meant to draw something in or to bind something, cast them during the three days after a new moon when it is waxing. The most powerful time for these spells would be during the full moon.

If you want to do a banishing spell or push something away from you, cast the spell any time during the three days after the full moon when it is waning. The best time would be the night or day of the dark moon before it appears.

The moon will enter into different signs every day or so. You can check out some online lunar calendars to create one for your time zone and location.

70

Zodiac Signs

Aquarius: January 21 – February 20

The Air element and Saturn rule this sign. If the sun is in Aquarius, then the new moon will also be in Aquarius. If the sun is in Leo, then the full moon will be in Aquarius.

This isn't a great time for magic. You should choose to focus on organizations or groups that you are a part of or would like to support. This is a great time to bring in new members or friends to your group to uncover or reveal secrets or mysteries and works that need to remain hidden. This is also a good time to do dreamwork or strengthen group ties or friendships.

Pisces: February 21 – March 20

This sign is ruled by the Water element and the planets Neptune and Jupiter. If the new moon is in Pisces, the sun will be in Pisces, and if the sun is in Virgo, the full moon is going to be in Pisces.

This time is best for dream, astral, and journey magic that is aimed at expanding consciousness. All divination and psychic work will be supported. It is good to expand your boundaries and your personal growth.

Aries: March 21 – April 20

This sign is ruled by the Fire element and the planet Mars. With the sun in Aries, the new moon will be in Aries, too. When the sun is in Libra, the full moon will be in Aries.

This moon is the best time to begin new business ventures or projects, especially if you need some extra courage or a push. It is a good idea to do blessing or cleansing work or to buy magical tools that have a blade. Any spells that are related to self-improvement, personal strength, or courage are best done this time. Spells that protect military members' work are also great during this time.

Taurus: April 21 – May 20

This sign is ruled by the Earth element and the planet Venus. A Taurus sun means that the new moon will also be in Taurus. A Scorpio sun means that the full moon will be in Taurus.

Any spells that concern the arts, like supporting new galleries, theatres, and auditions are a good idea when the moon reaches Taurus. Spells related to submitting manuscripts and wishing for successful performances and exhibitions are also better performed at this time. This energy is often connected with security, stability, and the household. Spells that work toward cooperation between business partners and having peace in the family will be supported. Taurus energy will encourage material comfort and prosperity, protection from theft or damage, loss of material things, and creating new habits toward improving oneself. Love spells will be supported during this time, but it will be better if you are working toward strengthening existing relationships or finding your life partner.

Gemini: May 21 – June 20

This sign is ruled by the Air element and the planet Mercury. With a Gemini sun, the new moon will also be in Gemini. With a Sagittarius sun, the full moon will be in Gemini.

With the moon in Gemini, it is best to work on spells about prophecy and divination, getting into your school of choice, success in school, increasing web traffic, luck in communication, gambling, and wishing spells. Spells on getting a positive reception of term papers, articles, and manuscripts are also a good idea.

Cancer: June 21- July 20

The Water element and the Moon rule this sign. When it is a Cancer sun, then the sun will be in Cancer, too. When it is a Capricorn sun, then the full moon will be in Cancer.

You can do spells that are meant to improve respect and love within a family, get rid of barriers for more harmony in the family, heal pain from past wrongs, and protect and purify the home. During this time, spells on psychic development, divination, blessings, cleansing, calming emotional turmoil, along with garden and kitchen witchery are also supported.

Leo: July 21 – August 20

The Fire element and the Sun rule this sign. With a Leo new moon, the sun will be in Leo, too. If the sun is in Aquarius, then there will be a Leo full moon.

This is great for spells related to your companion animals, hobbies, and success in sports by getting rid of barriers. It is also best for fighting obsessions, increasing passion and sex, and encouraging a good reception in theatre performances, productions, and concerts.

Virgo: August 21 – September 20

This sign is ruled by the Earth element and the planet Mercury. If the new moon is in Virgo, you will have a Virgo sun as well. With a Pisces sun, then the full moon will be in Virgo.

You should use this time to dedicate, consecrate, cleanse, make, or buy any altars and ritual tools. It is a good time to cleanse and purify your work area or home. Spells related to employment in the service or health field are supported at this time. It is also a great time to do magic related to finding domestic help and getting organized.

Libra: September 21 – October 20

This sign is ruled by the Air element and the planet Venus. If the new moon is in Libra, the sun will also be in Libra. With an Aries sun, the full moon is in Libra.

All spells that are related to contractual partnerships and marriage will be supported during this time. All matters dealing with justice or the legal system, including criminal court matters, divorces, leases, and contracts are supported. Spells done during the waxing moon will strengthen a marriage or romantic relationship. If done during the waning moon, it will disrupt a marriage or romantic relationship. Spells that make sure people get what is coming to them are best performed during this time.

Scorpio: October 21 – November 20

This sign is ruled by the Water element and the planets Pluto and Mars. With a Scorpio new moon, the sun will also be in Scorpio. If you have a Taurus sun, then you will have a Scorpio full moon.

This is the best time to cast spells about obsession, along with protection and self-defense spells. During the waning of the moon is the best time to do exorcisms. Use the waning moon to banish negativity. Spells for increasing courage and transformation are stronger during this time, along with spells related to passion, human fertility, lust, sex, inheritance, rebirth, and death.

Sagittarius: November 21 – December 20

This sign is ruled by the Fire element and the planet Jupiter. If the new moon is in Sagittarius, the sun will also be in Sagittarius. With a Gemini sun, the full moon will be in Sagittarius.

This is the best time to do spells that support making good impressions on professors, getting into the college you want, or supporting your studies. Any spells that deal with any long-distance travel, divination, connecting to Gods, spirits, higher purposes, or any religious activity are better done during this time.

Capricorn: December 21 – January 20

This sign is ruled by the Earth element and the planet Saturn. If there is a Capricorn new moon, then the sun will be in Capricorn, too. If the sun is in Cancer, then you will have a Capricorn full moon.

Any spells that relate to the relationship you have with your dad, fatherhood, or male fertility are all supported during this time. Any banishment spell while the moon is waning is supported. Spells for success and any career or business ventures are also supported.

Void of Course

This refers to the point when the moon leaves one sign and will end once it enters the next. Normally, it isn't a good idea to cast spells during this phase, even though some people do disagree. Some believe that any efforts put into it will be wasted during this time phase, and some believe everything will end in a disaster.

Weekdays

The moon rules Monday. It is the best time for spells about love, receptivity, dreams, and reconciliation (during waxing). Monday is also best for banishing strife, celebrating the stages of a woman's life, regulating cycles, banishing infertility (during waning), and increasing female fertility.

The planet Mars rules Tuesday. It is the best day for spells about driving away military threat, breaking negative spells, binding enemies, banishing fears (during waning), achieving military honors, protecting military personnel, and developing courage (during waxing).

The planet Mercury rules Wednesday. It is the best time for spells about getting rid of illness, getting rid of bad luck, getting rid of a writer's block, getting rid of barriers in communications (during waning), healing, wishing for safety in travels, increasing luck, and divination. It is also good for spells to influence others by communicating, increase communication (during waxing), and encourage positive responses to a written article, manuscript, or written paper.

The planet Jupiter rules Thursday. It is the best time for spells about supporting ambition, dealing with problems with people in authority, achieving business goals, getting rid of problems at your job, getting rid of impotence and male infertility, seeking for justice (during waning), asking for a promotion or raise, looking for a new job, increasing male fertility, and increasing wealth (during waxing).

The planet Venus rules Friday. This is the best day to do spells that deals with increasing beauty, finding new friends, finding ways to travel, increasing happiness, increasing romance, increasing lust and general love (during waxing), getting rid of barriers in love and relationships, and getting rid of sadness (during waning).

The planet Saturn rules Saturday. This is the best day to do spells that deal with getting rid of poverty, getting rid of infertility in livestock and crops, getting rid of negativity, increasing fertility in livestock and crops, increasing prosperity, bringing harvests, blessing the home, purifying, cleansing, and communicating with spirits (during waxing). Spells on astral magic, astral travel, psychic defense, and psychic attacks (during waning), and séances are also best done during this time.

The Sun rules Sunday. This is the best day to do spells that deal with finding new associates to further your career, making new friends, encouraging peace, achieving recognition for accomplishments, bringing in prosperity and wealth, preventing war, finding lost things, removing barriers to further your career, going to auditions (during waning), and getting a promotion, raise, or new job (during waxing).

Equinoxes and Solstices

- Winter Solstice: This is the best time for spells about the hearth, home, new beginnings, and family connections.

- Autumnal Equinox: This is the best time for spells about contracts, harvest, and endings.

- Summer Solstice: This is the best time for spells about energy, male fertility, contracts, and weddings.

- Vernal Equinox: This is the best time for spells about home, family, love, fertility, new beginnings, spring cleaning, and "out with the old and in with the new" concept.

Using a Clock

One method used in conjuring is timing your spells according to a clock. This is using an old analog clock with a face and hands. Digital clocks won't work.

Spells that bind or draw things to you should be done when the clock's hands are making their way up. Spells that bind or banish things from you and anything you need reversed needs to be done while the hands are on their way down. It is up for good, down for bad.

Midnight is significant and represents the balance between evil and good. Helpful spells are best done during the half-hour that is leading to the stroke of midnight, while spells that harm need to be done during the first half of the hour right after midnight.

Planetary Hours

You could also decide to perform your spells during a specific planetary hour. People do this if there aren't any foreseeable helpful solar or lunar influences, or you could cast your spell on a corresponding hour during a day of your choosing to help add more planetary energy into your magic.

To calculate planetary hours, you can find tools on the internet, or you can use the next bit of information.

These hours are calculated from sun-up of one day to the sun-up the following day. To calculate the hours, you need to have this information:

- The time the sun rises on any particular day in your location

- The time the sun sets on that same day

- The time the sun rises on the following day

You are going to find how long the day's hours are and how long the night's hours are. You have to find how many minutes there are from the time the sun rises on a certain day to the time the sun sets on that same day and then divide that number by 12. This is your day hours. Now, you have to figure out the number of minutes between sundown and sunrise the following morning and then divide it by 12. This will give you your night hours.

When working with these hours, the first hour starts when the sun rises and will correspond to that planetary day. The first hour on Monday corresponds with the moon. Tuesday's is Mars, Wednesday's is Mercury, Thursday's is Jupiter, Friday's is Venus, Saturday's is Saturn, and Sunday's is the Sun. Now, you have to use how long your planetary hours are. Next, add the minutes from that first hour, and this will give you the second hour and so forth.

The earliest practitioners of Witchcraft categorized this in a way that meant something to them. They would compare things to other items in the world, as well as their medicinal and magical uses. These are what gave us our modern correspondences.

These tables of correspondences can help Witches today. They give us the ability to look things up to figure out what energy it corresponds to so that we can match our spells and intent. Some correspondence tables will vary, depending on the tradition.

- Elements

  o Water – West, feminine, purification, cleansing, healing

  o Earth – North, rebirth, coins, feminine, pentacles, life, death

  o Fire – South, wands, fertility, masculine

  o Air – East, swords, mind, masculine, wisdom, life, communication

- Wood

  o Hazel – dowsing, divination, protection

  o Birch – creativity, rebirth, fertility

  o Holly – luck, protection

  o Rowan – astral travel, success, personal power

  o Oak – success, protection, good fortune, money, fertility

  o Ash – universal magic

  o Hawthorn – defense, cleansing, protection

  o Alder – spiritual decisions, intuitive abilities

  o Willow – healing, nurturing, protection, knowledge

- Flowers

o Violet – dedication, loyalty, luck

o Daffodil – love, fertility, Spring

o Narcissus – inner peace, harmony, tranquility

o Dandelion – purification, cleansing, healing

o Lily – renewal, abundance, fertility, rebirth

o Echinacea – prosperity

o Hyacinth – ease grief, peaceful sleep

o Goldenseal – business dealings, gain, money

o Hibiscus – lust, passion, love, prophetic dreams

- Colors

o Silver – reflections, Moon work, truth

o Red – courage, lust, health, sex

o White – purity, the Divine, truth

o Pink – innocence, friendship, love

o Black – negativity, banishment

o Orange – new opportunities, attraction, encouragement

o Brown – earthwork

o Gold – business endeavors, Sun spells, prosperity

o Purple – power, ambition, royalty

o Yellow – persuasion, protection, happiness

o Dark Blue – empathy, willingness, psychic abilities

- o Green – money, prosperity, forgiveness, fertility, compassion, empathy

- o Light Blue – healing, patience, understanding

- Herbs

  - o Thyme – Water. Use for courage, psychic abilities, and getting rid of negativity

  - o Apple Blossoms – Water. Use for divination and love

  - o Sage – Air. Use for purification, prosperity, wisdom, and smudging

  - o Basil – Fire. Use for fidelity, female reproduction health, and love

  - o Rosemary – Fire. Uses are pretty much universal

  - o Catnip – Water. Use for love and psychic bonds

  - o Peppermint – Fire. Use for love, purification, and clearing out negativity

  - o Chamomile – Water. Use for love, good luck, purification, and protection.

  - o Pennyroyal – Use for prosperity, money, and protection. (pregnant women should not take this internally)

  - o Hyssop – Fire. Use for banishing negativity, self-defense, and purification

  - o Oregano – Use for protecting yourself and ward against negativity

  - o Lavender – Air. Use for sleep, calming dreams, headaches, purification, and love

Gemstones and Crystals

1. Turquoise – Water. Use for wisdom, intuition, and healing.

2. Agate – Earth, third eye chakra. Use for depression, mental health, and energy

3. Tiger's Eye – Fire. Use for protection, courage, and self-confidence

4. Amber – Throat chakra, Sun, and Fire. Use for strength, clarity, protection, and confidence

5. Sapphire – Throat chakra, Libra, Water. Use to bring spirit guides and prophecy

6. Amethyst – Crown chakra, Pisces, Water, Pisces. Use for intuitive powers, cleansing, the mind, and consecration

7. Quartz – all the elements, the Heart chakra. Use for all types of spells and rituals

8. Bloodstone – Sun, Mars, and Fire. Use for bodily matters, the health of blood

9. Opal – all four elements. Use for spiritual and emotional health and protection.

10. Carnelian – Earth. Use for treating infertility, impotency, grounding, and shielding

11. Obsidian – Fire. Use for intuition, energy work, and the subconscious

12. Garnet – Root chakra, Persephone, and Fire. Use for meditation, reproductive health, intuitive skills, and lunar rituals

13. Moonstone – Diana, Selene, Hecate, and Moon. Use for wisdom, female reproduction, Goddess-centric work, and intuition

14. Hematite – Sun, Saturn, and Fire. Use for inflammation, healing, protection, willpower, confidence, and blood disorders

15. Lapis Lazuli – Third Eye chakra, and Water. Use for meditation, lifting spirits, trance work, consciousness, and connecting to the Goddess or God

16. Jasper – Earth. Use for good fortune, centering, luck, and grounding

17. Jade – Earth. Use for balancing, healing of internal organs, and love

Chapter 6: Basic Spells

The last chapter gave you a basic idea of how to create and cast spells. The simple steps to casting a circle and invoking the energies and intentions of your craft will help you gain clarity and awareness with your work and your purpose. This chapter is a fun and easy collection of five, simple spells that you can use to get you started in your practice. You can use these spells as they are written but feel free to modify them to your liking and personal needs and preferences.

One item of note that you may find in your study and practice of Wicca is the Power of Three. Often in spells, you will notice an incantation "by the power of 3" or "3 times3" and this number correlates to a Wiccan rule of thumb that states whatever energy you are putting into the Universe will come back to you 3 fold, so make sure you are working with good intentions and not malice towards anyone. It goes hand-in-hand with the Wiccan Rede.

Banishing Spell

A banishing spell should always follow the Wiccan Rede that states, "If ye harm none, do as ye will." The intentions behind every spell you do should never be malicious or cause energetic harm to another. If you are needing to banish a person, do so lovingly or compassionately and allow the intention of your spell to do the work for you.

You will need the following:

- A sheet of paper

- A pen

- A fire safe bowl or container to put burning paper in

- Matches or a lighter

- *A few banishing herbs that you can choose from the following list:* Angelica, broom, cedar, cumin, lilac, oak, onion, pine, rosemary, sage, salt, thistle, yarrow

- A small bag, or bowl to put your herbs in on your altar. If they can be made into a bouquet, you can arrange them that way as well, otherwise, you can set them in the pouch or bowl.

Steps:

- Cast your circle.

On the piece of paper, write what you are wanting to banish. Be clear and specific. You may be desiring to banish the unwanted energy left by your in-laws in your house or you may be trying to banish a person from bothering you all of the time. It could be you are also wanting to banish your anxiety, or nightmares. Whatever it is, state it clearly on the paper with the pen. (Using ink is better than pencil but you can use pencil if you have no pen around). Have your herbs handy and you can use them to sprinkle over the sheet of paper in the bowl after you have read your words aloud or you can keep them ready to set on your altar after your spell.

Read what you wrote on your paper aloud. Saying it three times in a row is a good practice. You can then set it in the bowl first and sprinkle it with banishing herbs before setting it on fire and letting it burn. You can also use the herbs afterward instead of burning them with the paper.

As it burns, say the following words:

- By the power of 3 times three,

- I invoke the spirits and guides to come to me,

- Banish this negativity,

- From my home, my life, so mote it be!

Once the paper has burned, take the ashes and you can sprinkle them outside in the garbage or anywhere far away from you and outside of your home. You can even toss them in the street to make sure they are not on your property. You can then sprinkle the banishing herbs on top of the ashes to seal the deal. Go back indoors and close your circle and light a candle of protection on your altar. Smudge the area and yourself for extra clearing and cleansing.

Third Eye Opener- Psychic Spell

Part of the journey of practicing Wicca is to open yourself to your psychic and clairvoyant abilities. The more open you are, the better you can communicate with the energy of all things around you and invoke more powerful intentions. Your third eye is the place of your visions, dreams, and psychic abilities and this herbal spell can help you open it and keep it open.

You will need the following:

- *As many of these* dried *herbs as you like:* mugwort, acacia, honeysuckle, peppermint, rosemary, thyme, cloves, yarrow, dandelion, lilac, lavender, calendula

- A purple pouch with a drawstring (you can sew it or buy it an it can be small)

- A purple marker

- A purple candle and/or a silver candle

- Matches or a lighter

Steps:

1. Cast your circle and invoke the deities of your choice.

2. With the purple marker, draw an eye on the purple, drawstring bag.

Fill the bag with the herbs.

3. Light the candle (s) and state the following:

I open my eye, for the better to see,

May these herbs awaken me.

By the power of 3 times three,

Third eye open, so mote it be!

4. Rub the bag of herbs on your third eye and let the candles burn. Sleep with it under your pillow at night.

5. You can also add a crystal or stone to the bag that is useful for divination and psychic ability.

6. Close your circle as usual.

Protection Spell

Protection is a useful way to keep yourself from attracting unwanted energies to you. It may be that you want to protect yourself from other people's energy, or you want to protect your whole house. Either way, the herbs and intentions in this spell can help with that.

You will need the following:

- Anise

- Basil

- Bay Leaf

- Black Pepper

- Cayenne

- Cloves

- Fennel

- Garlic

- Rosemary

- Salt

- Mortar & Pestle or food processor

- Bottle with cork or lid

- Black Candle

- Matches/ lighter

Steps:

1. ***Grind together the following herbs so they are mixed together like a powder:*** Anise, basil, bay leaf, black pepper, cayenne, cloves, fennel, garlic, rosemary, salt.

2. Put them in a bottle.

3. Cast a circle and "charge" your bottle of herbs with the intention of protective energy. Once you feel like you have set the intention firmly and clearly, you can end the invocation.

**NOTE: Charging is a way for you to clearly send the energy of a specific intention into something. You can simply hold the bottle between your hands and speak aloud your intentions with whatever you are charging, making a declaration of what the object's purpose is.

4. Close the circle.

5. Sprinkle herbs around the perimeter of your house. You can also wear them in a pouch around your neck, or sleep with them under your pillow. If you want, you can do a light sprinkling in the corners of your house as well.

6. Store what isn't used on your altar and use whenever needed.

7. Light a black candle of protection if you feel like you need that extra energy.

Money Spell

Who doesn't want a little extra money? When you need to draw abundance into your life, you need a little money spell to set things right. Casting a money spell has a way of helping you align with the energies of abundance and prosperity you are looking for in your life.

You will need the following:

- 3 green candles in candle holders

- 3 dollar bills (you can use coins as well, but bills work best)

- **Herbs:** basil, cinnamon, clove, ginger, nutmeg, mint, dill, patchouli (you don't have to use all of these herbs- you can use one, or create a blend of your choice.)

Steps:

1. Cast your circle.

2. Place the three dollar bills on your altar and sprinkle your herbs on top of each bill.

3. Place a green candle on top of each bill.

4. Repeat the following words for each candle you light:

Money, money, come to me,

In abundance, three times three.

May I be enriched in the best of ways,

Harming none along the way

This I accept, so mote it be!

Bring me money, three times three!

5. Close your circle.

6. Let the candles burn until they go out on their own.

Love Spell

We are all looking for love and a little love spell can help you open your heart to letting love in, as well as calling it to you. The love spells that are available in the world today are numerous and all very different. You can come up with so many different types of love spell and this one is a fun one to get you out under the stars.

You will need the following:

- Pink and/or red candles

- Lighter or matches

- Rose Petals

- Jasmine/ Rose/or Lavender incense

- Rose quartz crystal

- Sheet of paper

- Pen

**NOTE: This spell is to be performed at night when stars are visible in the sky.

Steps:

1. Cast a circle of protection and intention.

2. Light the candle on your altar and the incense as well.

3. On the sheet of paper, write down all of the qualities you are hoping for in a partner. Be as specific as possible. Read the list out loud in front of your altar. Fold the paper and set it underneath the candle holder.

4. Leave the candle and incense burning (make sure it is in a safe place) and take your rose petals and rose quartz outside.

5. Find a star that you are attracted to and hold your hand out, palm up, with the rose petals and rose quartz in it.

6. Imagine starlight from that star beaming down to your hand and charging and infusing the petals and the crystal. Think about the qualities that you wrote down on the paper as you continue to visualize.

7. Say the following words:

    Star of love, burning bright,

    Aid me in my spell tonight.

    Unite my true love to me,

    As I will, then shall it be.

8. Take the petals and the crystal back inside to your altar and say the following words as you sprinkle the petals around the base of the candle:

Hear me as I call to you,

Come to me, my love so true.

9. Set the rose quartz on top of the petals in front of the candle and allow the candle to burn. If you need to extinguish the candle overnight, you can relight it in the morning.

All of these spells are an excellent way to get you started on your journey with crafting rituals to help you align with your intentions. As you advance in your work, keep playing with new versions of what you would like to do as you cast.

Chapter 7: Candle Magic Spells

In Wiccan belief, a spell's power is enhanced using candles of various colors. Since Wiccans of different covens have slightly varied techniques in executing candle spells, it is of utmost importance to try out the many theories about utilizing colored candles within spells.

For spell rituals, using beeswax candles are always recommended. To further increase a candle spell's effectiveness, magical carvings and additional oils are used. However, it is recommended that only one candle is utilized for each spell and allow it to burn itself out completely.

One of the most common intents in casting Wiccan candle spells is to improve financial status. If you're one of those people who want to improve their financial situation, the candle spells below would surely help.

Simple Health Blessing

This next spell does not, in any way, represent a definite medical cure for any ailment. What this next spell does is bestow a blessing of good health to the recipient, which acts as a preventive measure against any kind of disease.

For this spell you'll need the following:

- A stick of cinnamon

- A white-colored candle

- Apple juice

Always remember that in most Wiccan traditions, the use of natural ingredients is highly recommended. Therefore, organic apple juice is preferred in this case. Pour the natural apple juice into a small glass and with a cinnamon stick, stir it four times.

Light the candle up and while getting a few sips of the apple juice.

After getting a few sips, recite the following incantations verbatim:

"Aradia blesses my body and my soul, Wellness, and health is my goal."

Drink the rest of the apple juice in the glass and then snuff the candle out. This spell is the best cast whenever you feel an ailment is about to come down on you or each day when you wake up to stay in good shape.

Clear an Argument Spell

Keeping a good relationship with our fellow man is always important if you want to have a peaceful life. However, we are not perfect human beings and it is perfectly normal to resent somebody for something they have done towards us. This spell lets you clear up any lingering resentment towards an individual and rekindle your lost friendship.

To case this spell, you'll need the following:

- A yellow-colored candle

- A paper envelope

- A dried or non-dried bay leaf

Write your full name on one side of the envelope and your friend's complete name on the other.

Place the bay leaf inside the envelope and seal it.

Light the candle up and hold one corner of the envelope against the candle's flame until it catches on fire.

Hold the burning envelope until the very last second before it burns your fingers and places it inside a small fire-proof bowl or cauldron. Let the candle burn out itself out.

Candle Healing Spell

This particular spell is the full version of the simple candle healing spell. This spell is used in conjunction with conventional medical treatments and medicine to heal a wide range of ailments.

To case this spell, you'll need the following:

- Letter of intent written on white paper.

- Petals from a white-colored flower.

- Spring or Natural Water.

- Salt

- Sage bundle

- A small bowl

- Mint

- Lavender Oil

- Honey

- White-colored candle

On a white paper, jot down all of your intentions towards the recipient of the healing spell. Make it a point to include how you want the recipient of the spell to feel.

In addition, write down the specific ailment affecting a specific body part that you want to be removed from the person.

Below is a good example of what you should write on a piece of paper:

"With your healing hand oh Goddess Aradia, wrap Mother Teresa's arms in a blanket of your healing light, removing all wounds and soothing her pain."

Choose a symbol to represent that person and carve it into the white candle.

After carving the symbol on the candle, hold the candle as you ask the god or goddess of your belief to increase the healing energy that you are projecting to the recipient. Envision the recipient as being happy and looking healthier than ever and concentrate on that intent for as long as possible.

Light up the sage bundle.

To clear any negative vibes from the person you are trying to help, pass the letter of intent, candle, and bowl through the smoke created by the burning sage.

Put the letter in the bottom of the bowl.

Starting from the middle part of the candle, rub honey on the candle going towards the top half. Once you've covered the top half, start from the middle again but this time work your way down to the bottom half of the candle.

Put the candle on top of the written letter.

Sprinkle a ring of salt around the white candle and add a little bit of mint and sage.

Put the white petals of the flower on the surface of the natural water.

Light up the candle and envision the person being surrounded by a white light.

Concentrate on the candle's flame as you chant a small incantation stating your intent to send a white healing light, blessings, and love towards the recipient of the spell. Don't forget to include the recipient's complete name in the incantation.

Let the candle burn itself out. If you want the spell to be applied in a span of days, snuff the flame of the candle out after reciting the incantation then relight and recite it again on the next day. Repeat this process depending on how many days you want the spell to be applied.

Bury the remainder of the materials of the spell once you are done and have achieved the desired result.

Light of Joy Candle Spell

This next spell is categorized as a household-type candle spell designed to remove any tension among household members that are bringing in negativity in the family. This particular spell not only applies to homes but also roommates as well.

To successfully cast this spell, you'll need the following:

- Sandalwood incense

- Fresh basil

- Four candles of different colors

- A big piece of quartz crystal

- One pink-colored candle

It is recommended that you perform this spell in the center of the house. However, if the center of your house is not accessible, you can perform this on a table or an altar.

Arrange all the candles in a circular manner.

- Put the quartz crystal in the middle of the circle that you just created with your candles.

- Pile all the basil leaves on top of the quartz crystal.

- Light all the candles up.

Light the incense and carry it through all the rooms in the house. Making sure that the smoke from the incense is well spread.

Put the incense back with the candles and let them burn out by themselves. Days after you've successfully cast the spell, you'll slowly feel the tension being lifted away from your home.

Chapter 8 : The Power of the Moon

First, let us remember that the human body is made up of 60% water. The Earth is also covered by 70% water. So, why wouldn't the Moon's energy affect us when the Moon alone is able to create high tides? We are one with the Earth. The Earth is part of us. We are the Moon, sky, and oceans. This energy is always around us, whether we pay attention to it or not. Did you know that the Moon does not actually create its own light. Instead, it is illuminated by the reflection of the light of the Sun. Yet you can see the power of the Moon, and it can be felt in many different ways.

You may already know that you enjoy sitting outside and gazing up at the Moon on a clear night. You may also find that you are mesmerized by its beauty and image how another person is sitting somewhere else is able to see the exact same thing that you are seeing.

But did you realize that this celestial body is able to affect your daily actions and choices? Most everybody has heard old farmers talking about how it is important to plant your crops according to the cycle of the Moon. And we all know how people say a Full Moon brings out all the crazy people.

If you don't believe me, all you have to do is ask a police officer or look through some hospital records. More mayhem and crime seems to happen during a Full Moon.

The thing is, it's not just crazy people who come out during the Full Moon. Babies tend to be born more often during a Full Moon. Plus, it is believed that romance will bloom on a clear night under the light of the Full Moon.

Everything living on Earth is greatly affected by the cycles of the Moon. While there are scientists who have tried to debunk this idea, there are many more anecdotes and legends that hand around about the "madness" that occurs during the Full Moon. The thing is, it's not just the Full Moon that is able to affect our actions, energy levels, and moods. Every single phase has a unique effect on us and everything in nature.

This is why it is so important that you align your energy to the energy of the Moon. You may find that during certain phases, you are naturally pulled into organizing things, evaluating your life, or taking inventory of things you have.

While the Full Moon can create chaos and craziness, the New Moon is not as showy. It is a time that is more relaxing, and you may be naturally drawn to setting intentions or seeing what you have accomplished.

Humans were more affected by the Moon during ancient times because they didn't have electricity or our modern amenities. A lot of the women would start their menstrual cycle when the Moon was in her dark phase. This is when they would retreat into their "red tent" or "moon lodge." The men were left to take care of themselves, the chores, and the children.

If modern women have the chance to take a few days off each month during their period where they didn't have to worry about their responsibilities, perimenopause and menopause wouldn't hit them so hard. Unfortunately, we no longer have Moon lodges, and bosses and families look at women as the only person who can take care of household chores.

Moods and the Moon

It has already been mentioned that on the night of the Full Moon, more things go haywire in the human world. But, if you're still not quite on board with the Moon affecting our moods, let alone when women give birth or have their menstrual cycle, I would like to present to you a real life situation.

One man was admitted to a psychiatric ward in 2005 because of violent mood swings. His mood would swing violently from one extreme to the other and would sometimes cause suicidal fantasies or hearing things that weren't actually there. His sleep pattern was also erratic and would swing from insomnia to sleeping 12+ hours each night.

His doctor kept meticulous records of his mood and sleep patterns to try to make sense of it all. The doctor found that the man's mood and sleep patterns seemed to track with the rise and fall of the oceans. Typically, if there was a high tide, the man's sleep duration would be short. This particular man was simply given pills and light therapy to control his mood, and nothing else was done about this hunch the doctor had.

12 years after that, Thomas Wehr, a renowned psychiatrist, published a paper that described 17 patients who suffered from rapid-cycling bipolar disorder. This was a form of illness marked by a person switching between mania and depression more quickly than most. They also showed an uncanny regularity in their moods, like the last person we talked about.

Since the beginning of time, humans have believed that the Moon controls our moods. We get the word lunacy from the Latin word lunaticus, which means moonstruck. Pliny the Elder, a Roman naturalist, and Aristotle, a Greek philosopher, both believed that epilepsy and madness were caused by the Moon. While studies on the Moon affecting births, criminal activity, and violence are inconclusive, there is definite evidence that the Moon affects our sleep cycle.

A 2013 study, which was highly-controlled, found that people slept 20 minutes longer and took five more minutes to fall asleep around the Full Moon, even though they were never exposed to Moonlight. Their brain activity, though, suggested that their time in deep sleep had a drop of 30%.

If you deep dive into the studies performed on humans to see how they respond to the Moon, you are going to come across the same thing, "We aren't certain that the Moon is to blame." Scientists may not be able to fully accept the fact that humans are indeed affected by the Moon; they can't ignore this phenomenon. Otherwise, they wouldn't have come up with the hypothesis that they study.

High Tides and the Moon

Now, the Moon doesn't just affect the birth of babies, crime, menstrual cycles, and organization. It also has an effect on the Earth in the form of tides. Both the Moon and the Sun influences the tides, but the Moon plays a bigger role. The Moon is much closer to the Earth than the Sun is, and the tidal effect that the Moon has is twice as strong as the Sun's.

We are going to dive into a bit of science for a moment. The Sun and Moon have a gravitational force that affects the Water in our oceans, which causes it to bulge on opposite sides of Earth. Since the Earth rotates, the two bulges act like "waves" that continuously undulate around Earth. At mid-ocean, these waves are a little under a yard high when you compare them to the water level of the troughs between them.

The acts of the tides are one of the most reliable phenomena that happen in the world, and we understand that they move in and out about twice each day, but this isn't exact. Why is that so?

Well, a single day on Earth is how long it takes Earth to spin around once on its axis in relation to the Sun. This is what is referred to as a solar day and takes 24 hours. However, for the Earth to reach the same position in relation to the Moon, it takes 24 hours and an extra 50 minutes, which is what is called a lunar day. The reason for this is that the Moon revolves around Earth in the same direction that Earth moves. This is why it takes Earth 50 minutes to catch up.

Since the Moon's tidal force is twice as strong as the Sun's, the movement of the tides follows lunar days. This means that it takes half of a lunar day, about 12 hours and 25 minutes, to go from one high tide to the next. This is why we have high and low tides about twice each day.

Animals and the Moon

In Southern California, about twice a month from March to August, people will gather on the beaches to watch a spectacle each evening. This is when grunions lunge themselves onto the shore as far as they can to mate. Their mating ritual is timed to the tides, as well as the hatchings that happen about ten days later. The larvae emerge every two weeks from the eggs, and this coincides with the peak high tides. This is because the baby grunions need the tides to wash them back out to sea.

The person choreographing this grunion mating dance and birth is none other than the Moon. Science tells us the Moon affects the tides, but it is a lot harder to imagine that the Moon also affects living creatures, especially for those who live in cities that are filled with artificial lights.

All throughout the animal kingdom, the absence or presence of Moonlight, and its predictable changes can shape many important activities. Among those things are communication, reproduction, and foraging. Research has found that Moonlight can influence the growth of fish, the navigation of dung beetles, the behavior of lion prey, as well as birdsong.

Lions in the Serengeti are considered night stalkers. The most successful ambush animals, which can include humans, happen during the darker Moon phases. But how their prey responds to the change in predator threats as the light during the night changes during the month has always been a mystery.

The lion's prey, buffalo, gazelles, zebras, and wildebeests, are plant eaters. They have to forage a lot to meet their food needs, even if that means going out at night. Some new studies have found how their foraging changes depending on the lunar cycle.

The common wildebeest tends to be the most attuned to the lunar cycle. They create their entire night based on what phase the Moon is in. At the darkest parts of the month, they would stay in areas they deemed as safe. When the nights became brighter, wildebeests were willing to venture into areas where lion might be.

Now, the African buffalo is the most daunting prey of the lion, and they are also the least likely to change how they act throughout the lunar cycle. But, when the nights were darker, they were more likely to create herds to make grazing safer.

Zebras and gazelles changed up their evening routines based on the lunar cycle. Unlike other pretty, they reacted more directly to the change in the Moon. Gazelles did more once the Moon came up. Zebras would sometimes start moving about and doing things before the Moon came up. This may seem risky, but being unpredictable could play a part in the zebra's defense.

The Moon doesn't just affect nocturnal creatures. For example, the white-browed sparrow weavers live in families. All year, they sing together in order to defend their home. But, when it's breeding season, the males will perform solos at dawn.

During the mating season on the morning after a Full Moon, the male birds would wake up ten minutes earlier to start singing than if there had been a New Moon. The extra light of the Full Moon helps to kick start their singing.

It's not that hard to look throughout nature to see things that are affected by the Moon. With all of these correlations, why wouldn't you want to make sure your magic matches up with the cycle of the Moon? Your body already does.

Chapter 9: Special Moons

Other than the various phases of the Moon, there are other specialty Moons that can offer you more power. The main two specialty Moons that witches look for are the Blue Moon and eclipses. These times of the year are rare, especially the Blue Moon, as it offers you extra power for your magic.

Lunar Eclipses

Before we jump into the magical powers of the lunar eclipse, let's look at the science behind an eclipse.

The Moon, by itself, doesn't give off any light. The light that we are able to see is the sunlight reflecting off the surface of the Moon. A lunar eclipse happens when the Earth's shadow blocks the sunlight, which makes it look temporarily dark. Unlike with solar eclipses, which only specific areas of the world can see, a lunar eclipse can be seen by any area that is dark enough when it happens.

The shadow of the Earth is called its umbra. Specifically, the umbra is the darkest part of the shadow of the Earth. The outer edge of the shadow is called the penumbra.

There are several different types of lunar eclipses. The first is the penumbral lunar eclipse. This is where the Moon passes through the outer shadow of the Earth, which creates partial darkness of a part of the Moon. You can have a total penumbral lunar eclipse. This is where the Moon is completely shadowed b the penumbra, but it never reaches the umbra.

Then there is a partial lunar eclipse. This is where the umbra of the Earth shadows a significant portion of the Moon, but doesn't cover it completely.

Then there is a total lunar eclipse. This is where the Moon is completely covered by the umbra and fully shadowed. However, since there is light refracted through the atmosphere of the Earth, the Moon will look a bit reddish.

Then there is a selenelion. This is a horizontal eclipse, and only occurs if the sun and the Moon are visible when it happens.

0 – is when the eclipse is very dark and is pretty much invisible.

1 – is when the eclipse is dark and either dark brown or grey in color.

2 – is when the eclipse is brick-red. There will be an umbral shadow that has a yellow edge.

4 – is when the eclipse is copper-red. There will be an umbral shadow with a bluish edge.

Another very specific type of lunar eclipse that witches love is called the Blood Moon. On the Danjon Scale, the Blood Moon is considered level three. The Blood Moon is when an eclipse happens when the Moon is in its closest position to the Earth, which is called perigee. Whenever the Full Moon happens at perigee, you will likely hear the phrase "Super Full Moon."

Despite the name, there isn't anything ominous about the Blood Moon. This Moon is seen as more witchy because it looks red. Within the scientific community, this color-changing phenomenon is referred to as Rayleigh Scattering.

Raleigh scattering helps to describe how the sunlight appears to change colors as it moves through the atmosphere of the Earth. The atmosphere works like a filtration system for the sunlight. While sunlight is considered to be "white" light, we know that it really contains the full visible spectrum of colors that are seen whenever light passes through a prism. This is the reason why we sometimes see rainbows whenever it rains because the water vapor acts like tiny prisms.

Having a basic understanding of this scientific wisdom is very helpful when it comes to your magic practice. It explains the mechanisms that help to fuel our work during a lunar eclipse. If we don't understand how the material world works, it is possible that we could fall prey to superstitions and fear-mongering that surrounds these natural occurrences. Witches don't allow fear to control them. Knowledge is power.

So here is a quick little science lesson for you. Depending on the sun's angle, and the amount of Earth's gasses, water vapor, and volcanic dust that is moving through the atmosphere, these things shift the wavelength of the sun's light. The colors on the red end of the spectrum will have longer wavelengths, and their frequencies are lower than the other colors. The colors on the violet end have higher frequencies and shorter wavelengths. The Rayleigh scattering effects is the reason that sunrises and sunsets look orange and red in color.

So, the Blood Moon looks red because it only has a small amount of light to reflect back onto the Earth's surface. Since red is least altered during the filtration process, you only get to see the color that was able to survive the trip. This means that the Moon reflects red back onto the Earth.

There are many legends and folklore surrounding lunar eclipses.

Christopher Columbus used his almanac to figure out that there would be a lunar eclipse in February. He used this piece of information to scare some natives of Jamaican into offering shelter and food to him and his men. He told the chieftain that God was angry with the natives didn't want to help him. He told them that God was going to turn the Moon blood red, and then take it away to show his displeasure. The Moon did disappear, and this created a lot of terror for the locals. Right before the eclipse ended, Columbus told them that God would forgive the natives as long as they made sure that the sailors were fed. The Moon came back, and Columbus and his mean got to eat very well until the next ship arrived.

In Benin, Africa, a tribe there views the lunar eclipse as a time of battle between the Moon and the sun. They dance and chant during this time to encourage their reconciliations into the sky. They used the period as a way to sort through quarrels that they are having, much like the sun and Moon resolving their feud once the eclipse ends.

In Norse mythology, a monster called Managarmr, the Moon Hound eats the Moon and stains the sky in blood during Ragnarok. Managarmr is the son of a giantess and Fenrir, the grey wolf.

There are some practitioners who view the eclipse as being the equivalent of a full lunar cycle packed into a single event. After all, the Moon does look like it is going from waning, waxing, and reappearing during the eclipse.

There are some modern traditions that consider the eclipse as a metaphysical bonus round. Basically, any spell work that is done during this time is amplified and has extra power. So what kind of magic is best done during an eclipse? Eclipses only take place during the Full Moon, so keep your intentions turned towards spiritual development and personal growth.

113

Most Wiccans see the lunar energy during an eclipse to be more potent. There are several different ways to look at this energy. It could be, as mentioned earlier, that you get all of the energy from each phase in one single night, but there is another way you can look at it. You can look at the energies of the sun, Earth, and Moon in alignment. The Moon is reflecting the energy of the Earth and sun back on to the Earth. The Moon and sun will be in opposite Zodiac signs during an eclipse.

Also, if there is a lunar eclipse taking place somewhere, you can still harness its power even if you can't physically see it. It is all in your intention.

But why, exactly, do Witches care so much about all of these special lunar eclipses like the Blood Moon?

The simplest answer is that when the Moon is close to the Earth, it has a strong pull on the tides. The interaction between the sunlight, its passage through the atmosphere, and its reflection off of the Moon that is created by the eclipses moves the Moon's energy into the "red" end of the light spectrum. All of this relates to the element of Earth, the root chakra, and our animalistic survival needs.

The long explanation; when I said "tides," I was referring to more than the ocean. In Wicca, and other Pagan traditions, it is understood that the ocean is simply a metaphor for our mysteries and depths. The Moon affects how water flows, and this same power ebbs and flows through all of us with our emotions, moods, instincts, and intuitions.

Let's look at this metaphorically. The sun represents our outer persona, the conscious thoughts we make, our energy, our will, and how we project the power in the world to make the life we live. The Earth represents the body, our home, our material world, and our sustenance.

114

The Moon represents our intuition, our subconscious mind, and our shadow illusions that can change our true will. These things are in a near perfect line where the material self is shifted, and the conscious self is changed to show and energize our deepest desires.

This is a lot of crazy cosmic drama. So when a Blood Moon occurs, take a look into the Zodiac signs to see what special conditions are being enhanced and use that information.

The way that the lunar eclipse will affect you depends on the astrological sign that the eclipse occurs in. It is important that we don't forget that the stars surrounding the Moon set the stage for all of these solar system movements. To figure out what drama the Moon will intensify, you need to look at the Zodiac.

Each Full Moon happens because the Moon is 180 degrees opposite the sun. This creates a gateway effect for everybody on the Earth, where we are in the middle of polar opposites. Knowing the spectrum that we are placed in during the eclipse helps us to work with the eclipse.

So, if the eclipse happens when the sun is in Aquarius, then the Full Moon will happen on the opposite end in Leo, which is what happened on January 20, 2019. These two signs are fixed in Air and Fire. Aquarius' dreamy thought process is empowered by the bold action of Leo that helps to support our egos.

There are 12 possible mixtures of Zodiac signs within eclipses. You will have to figure out this for each eclipse before it happens in order to use its power. Since an eclipse will put the Earthly, material spin on your conscious and subconscious dreams, it creates a very strong gateway through which you can use to bring your hidden desires to heart.

Lunar Love Spell

If the lunar eclipse falls in Leo, this spell will be more powerful.

You are going to need:

- Gold candle

- Picture of whatever you are trying to attract or something that symbolizes it

- Sage or favorite incense

- Pen

- Essential oil – choose your favorite or mix them before you cast the spell

- Paper

Start by clearing your space and altar by burning some sage or incense. Take the time to cast a circle, call on the elements, and any guides that you want to protect and help you with your spell.

Once you know exactly what you want, write it down with as many details as you can using the pen and paper that you have. You want to really feel everything that you are writing down. As you write it, make sure you visualize it, too. After everything is written down, now write: "thank you for bringing (the things you want) into my life now." Your guides and the Universe like to be recognized.

When you have finished writing, anoint your candle with your mixture of oils. Do this by pulling the oil from the bottom up the candle and out toward you. You should also anoint the picture or symbolic representation of what you want in your life.

Now, burn the paper that has your intentions written on it. Keep everything safe by burning it in a fire-proof bowl. Put the ashes of the paper and place them in a potted plant and mix it into the dirt. This will help your intentions come to life.

Each day, for one week, light a candle. Make sure the symbolic representation of your intention is kept with you whenever you light the candle, and acknowledge your guides and thank them.

Blood Moon Spell

For this spell, all you will need is a calm mind and yourself. It is a good idea to meditate before you begin.

To start, you need to take a ritual bath. Sit in the bath and visualize all of your negative energy being washed away. Then, when you drain all of the water out of the tub, believe that all of that negativity is being drained away.

When the eclipse is getting ready to happen, step outside, and find a place where you can view the Moon clearly. Once is Moon is completely eclipsed, say: "I summon the Triple Goddess in all her names, forms, and faces. I summon the Maiden, Mother, and Crone and ask them kindly to grant me a wish. I wish (state what you want and be as explicit as you can). I thank you, great Triple Goddess. As I will so mote it be. Blessed be."

Go back inside and know that your wish has been heard.

Lunar Spell for Freedom, Gratitude, and Strength

This is a great spell whenever you are finding it hard to detach yourself from things that are no longer serving you.

You are going to need:

- Musical instrument

- An altar

- A black or white candle

Begin by casting a circle and summoning the elements, God, and Goddess, and whoever else you would like to call in for this spell. Some good Goddesses to call in for this spell are Nyx, Kali, Nyphthys, and Hekate.

You don't have to go outside to do this spell, but you can if you want. It is going to feel amazing. Begin by lighting the candle. Pick up the musical instrument, even if it is something you have had to improvise. The important thing is that you feel comfortable. Allow the energy of the eclipse to guide you as you play the instrument. While you are playing, say: "In the light of the lunar eclipse, I summon thee oh (your chose guide), to stay with me. The power of the Moon, together with the sun, is providing me with strength for my journey has begun. I, (say your name), am here to honor my Goddess, my God, and my ancestors for everything they have made for me. I am free from my habits (think about old habits you want to release). I am free from my addictions (again, think about any addictions you want to release). I am free from my problems (think about the problems). Under the shadow, I begin a new path full of blessings and motivation. The sun

119

will guide me, and the Moon will light my inspiration. I thank thee! I thank thee! I thank thee!"

Allow the candle to burn out. You can have fun at this time in whatever way you want. Once the candle is out, close your circle and thank your guides.

Magic of the Blue Moon

In today's time, a Blue Moon refers to the occasions when there are two Full Moons in a single month. The majority of the time, there is only one Full Moon is a month, but sometimes a second Full Moon can fall into a month. The only month of the year that can't have a Blue Moon is February. Some Blue Moons, according to this definition, that has happened or will happen occurred on July 31st in 2015, the first Full Moon was July 2nd; January 31st in 2018, where the first Full Moon occurred on January 2nd; March 31st of 2018, where the first Full Moon occurred in March 2nd; and October 31st of 2020, where the first Full Moon will occur on October 1st.

The Sky & Telescope magazine, in 1946, erroneously referred to a Blue Moon as a month that has an extra Full Moon. This is the definition that caught on and is what most people believe.

Before this, a Blue Moon referred to having an extra Full Moon during any season. Season refers to a span of time between solstices and equinoxes. Most of the time, each season will have three Full Moons, but sometimes there will be a fourth. Since every Full Moon has its own name associated with its season, an extra Moon can mean that the names line up wrong, so the additional Moon gets a different name, so it is referred to as a Blue Moon. Blue Moons, in this definition, are the third Full Moon during a season that will have four Full Moons.

These Blue Moons tend to happen once every 2.7 years. Some Blue Moon dates, following this definition, are May 21, 2016, May 18, 2019, August 22, 2021, and August 19. 2024.

Blue Moons, according to the first definition, tend to happen more often than the other types of Blue Moon. When you hear somebody talk about a Blue Moon, there is a good chance they are referring to the first definition. However, this definition is dependent on an arbitrarily imposed month lengths while the second goes with the natural cycle. For most Wiccans, Pagans, astronomers, and astrologers, they follow the second definition that follows the seasons is the most useful. That being said, it tends to be harder to track, and most people will just follow the first definition.

The Blue Moon is twice as powerful as the regular Full Moon. This is a good time to perform anything that needs an extra kick. Any spells, intentions, or rituals performed during this moon are great for long-term results because it really sets things in motion and helps you to read your end result.

You can harness the magic of the Blue Moon to invoke spiritual energy, improve vibrations, and set intentions. Blue Moons are also a good time for truth seeking, meditation, love spells, divination work, protection, wishes, and banishing. The Goddesses most associated with a Blue Moon are Hathor, Artemis, Luna, Isis, Astarte, Diana, and Selene.

Shakespeare was the one who came up with "Blue Moon." Depending on the type of culture you grew up in, the Blue Moon could be tricky and mysterious. Other people think that his time is lucky. But the fun thing to look at is what some of the old wives' used to say about it. Let's take a quick look at some Blue Moon superstitions:

1. Working spells for fertility during the day before, of, and after the Blue Moon gives them more power.

2. Pick berries and flowers during a Blue Moon for abundance and love. You can also dry and label these to use in the future.

3. Native Americans view a Blue Moon as a time of change.

4. The energy of the Blue Moon can help you with your goals, which include finding a job, figuring out legal problems, exciting travel, and improving finances. You can also place objects that represent any of these goals on your altar under the Moon.

5. If a Blue Moon happens during an eclipse, when you do good deeds, you will get that back in your life. This is also the best time to resolve feuds.

6. Turning a coin that is in your pocket during a Blue Moon will give you more luck and fortune.

7. Teachers of the Islamic faith suggest praying for a person's well being during a Blue Moon.

As you can see, a lot of this works into Wicca, and you can use some of the old wisdom to improve your practice. Now, let's take a look at some Blue Moon magic that you can have ready the next time a Blue Moon rises.

Cleansing Ritual

To get ready for your ritual, you will want to cleanse yourself. You can do this however you would like. You can take a simple shower or bath, or you can do something more special.

You are going to need:

- Paper

- White candle

- Matches or lighter

- Pen

- Black thread

Decide of you are going to do this inside or outside. Doing it outside has an amazing effect on this spell. If you do it inside, try to do it close to a window that can be opened up as it will sometimes get a bit smoky.

Once you are clean and have everything ready, spend some time focusing on your breathing. Release things that could be bothering you so that you can give your ritual all of your attention. Now, light your candle. Take some time to watch as the flame moves.

If you want, this would be the time to call the elements and your chosen deities.

Now, take your paper and do some free writing. Write down anything that has been troubling you as of late. Pour all of your feelings out on the piece of paper. There is no need to worry about if it is legible, spelled correctly, or makes sense. Just write things down. The paper can hold these things. You can use as many sheets as you need.

Once you are done writing, roll the paper up into a tight scroll. If you want to use some related herbs, place them in the center of the paper before rolling it up. Tie the black thread around it to keep it tight.

Get to where you are under the light of the Moon. If you are outside, you don't need to move. Inside, you can stand next to a window and poke out your arm or face. Take some deep breaths, and while you are exhaling, feel all of these worries slipping away.

Light the paper and watch while it burns. While it is burning, picture all the darkness flowing out of you and into the Earth, anything else that helps you picture yourself releasing your worries. At this point, you can do whatever feels right to you. You can chant, dance, sing, drum, play music, or whatever feels right to you.

If at any point the paper stops burning, light it again and let it burn out completely. The ashes or small bits that are left on the plate can be buried or given to a plant.

It is now time to end the ritual. Do this by thanking and saying goodbye to any elements or deities that you called. You can add in any closing words that you want at this point. If you can, allow the candle to burn out as you meditate in the afterglow of your ritual.

Blue Moon Beauty Spell

This is a great spell if you have been focusing on your flaws. This will help you to feel confident and see yourself as a beautiful person.

You are going to need:

- Any black crystal

- Purple candle

- Bowl of water

- Lavender oil

Begin by lighting your candle and dropping some of the lavender oil into the bowl of water. Place the crystal into the water. Take some time and center yourself. Take some deep breaths, and meditate for a few minutes. When you feel ready, say:

"I am filled with beauty, from head to toe. This beauty remains forever. It will only continue to grow. I will fight forever to protect it. It is a fire within me that will forever remain free."

Say this as many times as you need to. It will continue to intensify the more you say it. Believe the words you are saying. Once you feel ready, take the crystal out of the water. Keep this crystal with you and use it for self-love. Let the candle burn out.

Blue Moon Money Spell

A Blue Moon is a great time to perform money spells. It helps you to set intentions for wealth and good fortune while also opening you up to prosperity and abundance. If you really want to harness the power of the Moon, you can time your casting to just after midnight before the Moon reaches its peak.

You are going to need:

- Dried bay leaf

- Matches

- Statue of your chosen lunar deity

- Pen

At midnight on the night of the Blue Moon, place the statue on your altar. Take some time to think about the money that you want. Hold the bay leaf in the palm of your hand and begin to visualize different ways of getting that money. Try to think up at least five ways that you could get this kind of money. Really think about the amount of money you want and think about how it makes you feel.

Now, on the bay leaf, write down the amount of money that you want. Hold the leaf again and breathe. Now light a match and burn the leaf as you focus on the money. As the smoke begins to rise, ask out loud for the money.

Blue Moon Happiness Spell

If you are looking to add happiness into your life and make others around you happy, then this is the perfect spell to do.

You are going to need:

- Clear quartz

- Bowl of water

- Orange candle

- Citrus oil

Begin by lighting your candle. Drop some of the citrus oil into the water. There is no exact amount, just as much as you think you need to. Put your quartz into the water. Now, take a moment to clear out your energy, so take a few deep breaths and allow yourself to become present in the moment. Once you feel sufficiently cleared and centered, say:

"There is a bright light surrounding me and all of my loved ones. We are protected; we are blessed. Nothing can stop us."

While you are doing this, picture the light of the Moon surrounding you and everyone you care about. Visualize it as much and as deeply as you can. Once you feel ready, take the quartz out of the water and then hold it whenever you need to feel happy. Let the candle burn out.

Moonlit Walk

This is a very simple ritual that you can do during a Blue Moon. Take a walk beneath the Blue Moon and allow all of its vibrations to wash over you. This could also be used as the start of a ritual or spell to help cleanse you.

Chapter 10: The Power of Crystals

You have probably held a crystal in your hand at some point in your life and looked at it from every angle. You might have even felt a mysterious power that these stones hold. They speak a silent living, creative, infinite power that lies in the Earth. Crystals have been respected for hundreds of years and have been used in jewelry and talismans since ancient times. Mineral stones and crystals have been used for many magical purposes, bringing energy into your physical space, and for healing. Let's learn the basics of crystals.

What Are Crystals?

In many "new age" and Wiccan circles, the word "crystal" talks about a large variety of minerals, and many of them aren't even true crystals. All of them fall under the crystal umbrella.

A simple definition of a mineral is "any inorganic substance that gets formed in the Earth's underground geological processes naturally." Each mineral will have its own energy signature and chemical composition.

Most minerals are made of molecules that fit together in repeating patterns that give them their geometric forms that we think of when we hear "crystal." When crystals form, it is called crystallization. Crystals form with liquids cool and begin to harden. Specific molecules in this liquid will band together while they try to stabilize themselves. This happens in a repeating and uniform pattern that creates the crystal.

Crystals can be formed from magma, or liquid rock as it cools. If it cools very slowly, crystals will form. Very valuable crystals like rubies, emeralds, and diamonds form this way.

The most common crystal is the clear quartz. This is what a true crystal ball will be made of. Amethyst and rose quartz follow the clear quartz as the most abundant. Bloodstone, jade, and lapis lazuli are popular stones that are used in magic. These crystals are actually a combination of minerals and aren't considered to be true crystals. Some crystals like jet and amber are actually organic substances that have been fossilized. In order to keep things simple, many people who work with these gifts use the words "stones" and "crystals" interchangeably.

How Crystals Form

As stated above, crystals are a solid whose components like ions, molecules, or atoms get arranged in a very organized structure that forms a lattice that goes in every direction. Macroscopic crystals are normally identified by their shapes and consist of flat faces with specific orientations.

The process of growing crystals through mechanisms is called solidification or crystallization. The word crystal comes from the Ancient Greek word kruos, which means "icy cold, frost," and from crustallos that means both "rock crystal" and "ice."

Most of the minerals do occur in nature as crystals. Each crystal will have an internal pattern of atoms that have a certain way they lock new atoms into patterns that repeat over and over again. The resulting crystal's shape like a hexagon or cube will mirror the internal make up of the atoms. While a crystal grows, changes in chemical composition and temperature could create some interesting variations. Students aren't going to find that perfect mineral crystal in their backyard. This is due to the fact that for a crystal to form perfect geometric surfaces and forms, crystals have to have the perfect growing conditions and enough room to grow. If many crystals grow close to each other, they might mesh together to create a conglomerated mass. This is what happens to many rocks like granite that is created from many tiny crystals. Specimens that you see in museums are grown in environments that give them the room to grow, so they form the perfect geometric shapes.

The way atoms arrange themselves inside will determine the mineral's physical and chemical properties, and this includes its color. Light will interact with various atoms to make different colors. Most minerals are colorless if found in their pure state, but impurities in the atomic structure could cause a change in color. Quartz is normally void of color but it can be found in colors from brown to pink to the deepest purple found in amethyst. It just depends on the type and number of impurities within the structure. When quartz is in its normal colorless shape, it will look like ice. The Ancient Greeks thought that clear quartz was actual ice that was frozen to the extent that it couldn't melt.

Scientists normally describe a crystal as "growing," even if they really aren't alive. Under the Earth's surface, they bristle and branch into trillions of atoms that connect into three-dimensional patterns. Every crystal will begin small but will grow larger as more atoms are added. Some will grow from water that is rich in minerals that have dissolved. They could grow from vapor and melted rock. Because of the influences of various pressures and temperatures, atoms can combine to form wonderful arrays of crystal shapes. It is because of all the perfection of symmetry and form that has drawn scientists to look at and study minerals. Symmetry can be found everywhere in nature – the beautiful wings on a butterfly, the petals of a sunflower, a snowflake, and minerals aren't an exception. These repeated patterns happen within the basic structure and will reflect this pattern of the crystal's faces. You can see the symmetry of a crystal with your eye, but if the crystal is too small, you will have to look through a

131

microscope or magnifying glass. Seeing the patterns of crystals might be hard at first, but as you get more experienced, the more symmetry in the crystals, you will be able to recognize. Some minerals don't have crystals that are well formed and are a bit hard for experts to classify.

Crystals' Powers

Even though they are classified as inorganic, crystals are understood by most healers and Witches to be living because they give healing energy to plants, animals, and people. Specific crystals like tourmaline and quarts exhibit a power that scientists call "the piezoelectric effect." When pressure is applied to these stones, like being tapped with a hammer or squeezing them, they will give off an electric charge. Crystals like quartz exhibit a pyroelectricity. This means they release an electric charge when they get exposed to a temperature change.

Crystals are made up of minerals that are in a structured, geometric pattern. They have been classified according to their internal structures. It is their geometrical structure that gives them the healing and magical properties.

The crystal's power comes from its internal geometry. To be able to completely understand this, you have to understand sacred geometry. This is a philosophical and mathematical field that looks at the proportions and geometrical shapes within the Universe. These can be found anywhere in the world. It can be found in man-made buildings and nature. According to this, every geometric shape will vibrate with its own frequency, and this gives them their specific energetic properties. The symbols vary and are numerous: the pentacle, the triskele, the flower of life, and the Fibonacci spiral, just to name a few.

Because gemstones are arranged naturally in a geometric pattern, sacred geometry will also apply to them. This theory is the core of crystal magic. This is why we build grids using geometric shapes.

Now that you know about sacred geometry, it will help you understand how and why crystals work. Every crystal will vibrate at a frequency that is unique to its internal structure. These vibrations will affect the crystal's energy in ways that science can't explain. Because we are energy, we can be affected by crystals. Because crystals vibrate at high frequencies, they naturally store information. This is why quartz and selenite are used in electronic devices. With intentions, we can program and charge crystals so that they can help us manifest our goals. They are batteries that help power our intentions. This makes them perfect for use in magic.

There are actually only a few crystals that are popular enough to be used in magic and healing that has shown these effects during scientific studies. Normal science hasn't discovered what alternative healing practitioners have always known, and that is each crystal gives off its own energy that will interact with the energy and everything that is around it.

Witches, along with Wiccans, know that a stone or crystal's power is the same power that is in natural phenomena like a flowing river or the wind. Everything, whether invisible or visible is nothing but energy. All of that energy is connected. Because intention or thought is also energy, this too can be harnessed and sent into the Universe through the crystals that we work with. By doing this, the stones, and crystals become energy conduits. They can bring healing to us or send positive

133

energy into the spiritual realm to manifest change in the lives of others as well as ourselves.

Magic and Rituals

Wiccans use stones and crystals to line their sacred circle before they start their ritual. They can be used to honor deities with certain stones that are sacred to certain Goddesses and Gods. Certain magical tools like pentacles and wands are sometimes decorated with crystals, and they are used in all sorts of magical jewelry.

Stone and crystals are used for all sorts of things, from manifesting love and wealth to divination to healing. Just like in ancient times, they are still being used for talismans, amulets, other charms for luck, along with protections and scrying. Crystals can add power to your spells, whether they are the main focus or as a helper ingredient of the spell.

Amethyst gets used a lot as a boost for all kinds of spells. Clear quartz is usually kept on an altar to help sharpen focus, especially if it is a very complex spell. You could also charge a certain crystal for certain purposes and carry it with you wherever you go, such as a citrine to attract money or red jasper for courage.

Crystal magic is a great way to work with colors naturally. Crystals aren't dyed like cloth or candles. Vibrant colors will resonate with various aspects of our existence, like money, health, and love, but according to their own vibrations. Pink that is found in rose quartz is great for loving vibrations, and this makes it great for bringing love to you. Green resonates with abundance and this makes bloodstone and jade great for spells that involve prosperity.

Fun Facts

- There are some living organisms that can produce crystals.

- Crystals are popular in jewelry since they come in a variety of colors and the sparkle and shine.

- Many computer screens use liquid crystals in their display.

- Diamonds are one huge molecule that is created from any atoms in one single element.

- The science of studying crystals and how they are formed is called crystallography.

Chapter 11: The Magic Within You

Enhancing Your Personal Power

To continue strengthening your magical powers, you'll want to develop a routine that allows you to practice magic regularly. You might choose a single day of the week during which you'll have time to focus on magical studies and spellcasting, but for optimal results, you'll want to incorporate magic into your life on a daily basis.

You might not have time to perform a spell every single day, but you can carve out ten or twenty minutes every day to read, research, cleanse your tools, build your altar, or pray to the deities of your choice.

Choose one area that is of particular interest to you--crystal magic, candle magic, herbal magic, divination, astrology, whatever piques your curiosity--and dive in deep. Learn all there is to know about the subject. It won't be long before you start to notice patterns, correspondences, and synchronicities on your own, even without the benefit of an authority to guide you towards these discoveries.

Treat your mind and physical body with reverence. That doesn't mean you can't enjoy a night of drinking and debauchery now and then, or spend a day on your couch imitating a sloth when you're feeling run down. But stay conscious of the fact that your body and mind need balance, just like everything else in the universe--too much of anything, whether good or bad, can be detrimental to your empowerment as a witch.

Work on meditation and lucid dreaming to enhance your intuitive gifts. The more clear-headed and psychically aware you are, the easier it will be to customize and design spells for yourself. You'll also get a better feel for the types of magic that are really working for you, and those that are mostly a waste of your time and energy.

Spend as much time in nature as you can. You will feel the true power of the deities and elementals in these spaces, and learn to believe in miracles, because they are visible in the natural world every single day.

Every tree, every cloud, every river, every blade of grass, every rock, every animal that has managed to stay wild in the face of growing civilization, is an example of magic at work in the real world. Let the realm of nature be your church; don't ever stay away too long, lest you lose sight of your faith.

Designing Custom Spells

You might even try your first few spells without magical tools or ingredients at all; instead, simply use an original incantation, physical gestures, visualization, intent, and focus to try and get the job done. You may be surprised at what you can accomplish with these elements. When you add candles, crystals, herbs, tools, and more, all these items will do is fortify your spell work.

But without the foundation that stems from your core identity, these items will be like icing without a cake: hollow, saccharine, and ultimately useless.

Keep track of your efforts in a grimoire or journal. Every witch carries a unique personal energy; most of us will encounter certain tools or ingredients that clash with our identities, and others that resonate with extraordinary power.

Whenever possible, avoid using the items that do not mesh with your energetic frequency, and incorporate the items that do work for you into as many spells as possible. Keeping a diary of your spellcasting successes and failures is the fastest and most foolproof way to discover what these items are, and how they can be useful to you.

As you build your repertoire of custom spells, don't be afraid to experiment, and be playful. The absolute worst thing that can happen is that the spell won't be as successful as you'd hoped--and if that happens, it's hardly the end of the world, is it? With every failed spell, you learn a lesson, and with every successful spell, you gain confidence and empowerment. As far as I can see, that's a win-win situation.

The only things you stand to lose are your inhibitions, your sense of cynicism, and feelings of powerlessness. So take chances--the potential rewards far outweigh the risks.

How Can I Tell If My Magic Is Working?

Recognizing the impact of your magical workings can be tricky, especially for novice witches. Depictions of magic in movies and television can be wildly misleading, giving the impression that a successful spell will result in immediate changes, punctuated with a bang or a fireworks display.

137

In reality, some spells take quite a long time to effect change, and the results can be subtle, counterintuitive, invisible, or otherwise difficult to detect.

When we worry that our magic isn't working, it can be tough to maintain resolve and continue practicing regularly. Spellcasting takes a lot of energy, and the tools it requires can be expensive, so it's understandable to be concerned that your efforts may have been wasted.

Many experienced witches maintain, though, that the more time you spend questioning the results of a spell, the less likely it is to effect real change. For a spell to work, you have to believe wholeheartedly that your willpower has already impacted the matter at hand, and treat the issue like a closed book. Rumination will not help--in fact, it may have just the opposite effect.

Here are some common clues that your magic is, in fact, working. If you're having these experiences, don't lose hope--these are signs that the spirits are warming up to you, and are interested in what you have to say.

Feeling an Immediate Sense of Calm

If you're able to maintain focus and raised energy throughout a casting, you should feel an immediate energy shift when the spell is finished. This shift may occur in the space surrounding you, within your physical body, in your mind, or in all three areas simultaneously. Most witches describe this as a sense of calm, tranquility, peace, or serenity.

Some actually feel their body temperature drop slightly; others might feel their heartbeat or pulse slow down. Others still might get an adrenaline rush or a feeling like butterflies in their stomachs.

Natural Energy

Particularly after a spell that banishes bad habits, toxic relationships, or negative energies, you might awaken the following day with a natural bounce in your step, even without the benefit of caffeine. You might feel like a weight has been lifted from your shoulders or a sense that you see the world through a brighter, clearer lens than you did the day before. You also might feel ready to tackle items on your to-do list that you've been dreading or putting off for weeks.

Extreme Lethargy

Some witches feel a burst of energy after completing a spell successfully, but others may feel extremely drained for a few days after casting. Both symptoms are potential signs that the spell worked as intended. Feeling drained may be more likely if the spell called for more energy than a solitary witch could channel on their own.

This symptom is also common following invocation, evocations, summoning's, banishments, or divination practices. It means that your body has served as a vessel for immortal energy. You'll need to rest and recuperate for a few days, at least. But ultimately, you should see positive results reflected in the world around you after you've healed from the experience.

Unusual Cravings, Impulses, and Desires

Sometimes, in the aftermath of a successful spell, you might wonder if you are pregnant, possessed, or just losing your mind. You might crave foods that you've never enjoyed before. You might feel attracted to people, aesthetics, or places that previously disgusted you. Your tastes may change drastically, and you may feel inspired to partake in activities that never appealed to you before. These changes may not take place immediately or quickly, but if and when they hit you, try to take them as a sign that the divine spirits are steering you in a new direction. This is a gift; be grateful.

Life Becomes Unpredictable and Full of Surprises

If your routine becomes peppered more and more often with unexpected incidents and exciting changes, this may be a sign that the spirit world is tinkering with your reality. Sometimes, these changes may not seem positive initially. As far as the universe is concerned, though, all change is good change. Destruction makes way for creation; death makes space for rebirth. Whatever changes come, try to maintain faith and trust in the natural balance.

Noticing Synchronicities and Omens

If you start to notice unusual patterns in your day to day life, this may be a sign that the spirit world is watching over you, or even trying to communicate with you, guiding you towards your desired fate.

This might mean encountering the same number over and over, seeing strange shapes in clouds and other natural formations, or noticing a type of wild animal that seems to be following you around.

Other omens include: the moon face showing unusual colors, like red or pink; strange weather patterns, like snow falling under a bright sun; plants blooming or dying suddenly with no explanation; interpersonal coincidences, like picking up the phone to call someone at the moment that they dial you, or meeting people who share your name or birthday; prophetic dreams, or clear messages delivered while dreaming; and perfect shapes and symbols appearing in nature.

Magic as the Key to Inner Peace

No witch is ever finished learning about magic. Even so, your growth as a witch shouldn't become a source of anxiety or cause feelings of incompetence. Whatever your skill level, or degree of experience, you should find that magic, when practiced regularly, brings you a deep sense of inner peace, balance, and acceptance.

It will allow you to feel connected to the world on a level that is greater than social importance. Even through periods of melancholy, loss, or grief, you'll be consistently reminded that you belong to the universe as a whole; that you'll always have a father in the sun and sky and trees; that you'll always have a mother in the moon and earth and sea; that you'll always have friends in the element of nature. Honor these blessings and the universe will honor you in return.

Frequently Asked Questions

This chapter is dedicated to answering any common questions on Wicca, herbal magic, crystal magic, and candle magic that most beginners have when first starting off their journey.

Wicca Magic

Q: What is the difference between a Witch and a Wiccan?

A: Wiccan is a religion, while witchcraft is a practice. Many people believe that Wiccan is a religion of those who are in tune with nature and worship Goddesses and Gods but do not seek to harness the 'power' and 'energy' of the elements; in other words, they don't cast spells as witches do. All Wiccans are witches who are all in tune with nature but choose to not work with the universe to bring changes into their lives. But, not all witches are Wiccans, many witches don't worship Goddesses and Gods and choose to harness the energies of the universe.

Q: Is witchcraft associated with 'the Devil'?

A: This is one of the most popular questions and misconceptions about witchcraft, although many witches perform rituals during the night and many wear dark robes in movies, they are, however, not associated with 'the Devil' or 'Satan,' in fact, many Wiccan's do not believe in the Devil.

Q: Is a pentagram a symbol of Satan or the Devil?

A: It is not unless placed incorrectly. A pentagram is a five-pointed star that can be enclosed in a circle. If it's standing on two points, with one point up, then it represents protection from evil. When the pentagram is upside down, two points pointing up, and one point pointing down, it becomes a symbol that is used by the church of Satan.

Q: Are there any rules to witchcraft?

A: There are none. You don't have to worship anyone specifically or follow a guide book on how to be a witch; many practitioners build their own path based on their beliefs. But there is one code that all witches know of *'If it harm none, do what you will,'* which signifies that if your practice harms a living thing, then the concept of 'karma' will be applied to you.

Q: Is it possible for a Christian to follow the path of Witchcraft and Wicca?

A: Many people will say yes, while others say no. It is not definite since all religions and people have their own opinions. Many Wiccans and witches follow the Christian path and are freely open to the teachings of Jesus, but may Christians consider witchcraft to be associated with the devil. On the solitary, you should be free to follow any path that you desire, or whatever feels right to you. The actions and your connection to spirituality are what matters, not the name that you give your practice. Always follow your intuition and guide yourself.

Candle Magic FAQ

Q: What should I do with the leftover empty glass after my glass candle has finished burning?

A: You can always recycle it and use it as jars for herbs or other witchy ingredients, or you can simply discard it, but make sure that the leftover candle wax and wick (if any remains) be buried in nature.

Q: How long does it take for a candle spell to work?

A: The time cannot be predicted, for it varies from different casters and their intentions and ingredients used. Easier spells, such as house blessings and emotional healing, could work immediately while hard ones such as love, employment, and success might take some time seeing as the spell influences other people too. The mindset, actions, ingredients, and intentions greatly influence the outcome.

Q: Do I need an altar to cast candle spells?

A: No, an altar is not needed, but it can be helpful. If you choose to not use an altar, make sure to cleanse your work area before proceeding with the spell.

Q: When casting spells, can I move my candle from one room to another?

A: Yes, you can! It is perfectly fine to change the location of their candles especially when you are not around to supervise the candle. Be careful when moving candles around, for they can get very hot. This is why many practitioners should have candle holders available for them in case the candle requires burning to the end which can take a couple of hours.

Crystal Magic FAQ

Q: Should I pay attention to the size of a crystal when buying them?

A: It is not important, but sometimes size can make a big difference. Every stone is unique and size can contribute to that specific symbolic meaning. For example, a small pebble in the corner to protect your home from bad energy might become forgotten while a big chunk of black tourmaline by the front door will never go unnoticed.

Q: Can more than one gemstone necklace be worn at a time?

A: Yes, many gemstones radiate on the same energy and vibrational level so they can work great together, but do not wear more than three. It is also recommended that they are worn on different lengths; not only it makes it look cuter, but they are also not messing with each other's energies. Some gemstones should only be worn alone so make sure you read about their individual guidelines before wearing them.

Conclusion

Thank you so much for making it through to the end of this series! Let's hope it has been informative, easy to understand, and able to help you accomplish all of your magical goals, whatever those goals may be.

After all that we've covered in these pages, the next step that I'd urge you to take is to begin crafting your own spells, potions, and rituals, to create a magical routine that fits you and your unique beliefs like a glove. There is no doubt in my mind that the most powerful spells in existence are those that involve a unique and personal touch.

One of the best things about Wicca is that your interpretations, views, and beliefs are highly flexible. When you are just starting out, you are encouraged to read and learn as much as possible, and so your initial beliefs are bound to be shaped by the guides you read.

Over time, when you begin to embrace Wicca in your daily life, you might have certain epiphanies that re-shape your approach to the practicing this religion. What you believe on day one, might be **very** different to your beliefs on day 100, which could be a world apart from your views on day 1,000. It can be a lifelong journey, and even after decades you will still find yourself learning new things. This is one of the many benefits of keeping your own Book of Shadows—you can literally track how your Wiccan journey has evolved over time.

Remember: nobody can tell you how to practice Wicca, and the religion can mean anything you want it to mean to you. While I have presented the information in this guide as "correct", I am in no way suggesting that it is the only way to practice Wicca. If you read other guides, there may be conflicting information. And when you read another guide to the topic, you will likely come across even more conflicting information!

That's just the way Wicca is. Even if you encounter some different opinions—even those completely opposed to what you have read in this guide!—it doesn't mean one guide is right, and another is wrong: it just means the many different authors have interpreted different aspects of the religion differently.

I will leave you with that thought, as it is now time for you to start your own journey, and interpret the information presented to you in your own way. I have included a number of tables of correspondence at the end of this guide, which you should find helpful at some point in time. I have also included a number of suggested sources for further reading, as in the early days it is important for you to absorb as much information as possible on the subject.

Introduction

Welcome to the wide world of Wicca, a set of beliefs, rituals, and traditions that has swept across the Western world since the mid-twentieth century. Immerse yourself in a system of belief that connects us back to nature and to the spiritual realm, all while undertaking self-care and personal empowerment. We are all interconnected—with each other, with the earth and the physical realm, with the spiritual energy that flows throughout the universe. Take advantage of such knowledge to build a life of intention and fulfillment.

In order to begin understanding what Wicca is and what the religion can mean to you, it is also important to understand just what Wicca is not. The reason this is important is that there is a lot of misinformation that exists in the world about Wicca. In an attempt to preserve your relationship to nature as you go through the journey into Wicca, it is crucial that you separate the white noise from the truth of Wicca.

Wicca is not a cult. This is a critical point that you need to understand if you are going to have a relationship with the world as a Wiccan. Also, the practice of witchcraft does not mean you have joined a cult either.

Essentially, to become Wiccan means to hold all life in high regard. Since Wiccans can and do practice spell magic, this is what this book will essentially be about. The main goal of this book is to introduce you to beginner's spells and magic that you can use in your everyday life as a Wiccan witch. There are spells that are meant to be performed by covens, but for the purposes of this guide, I will not include them.

I will focus on the magic that you can accomplish as an individual. If you are still trying to find your way in the Wicca religion and are still practicing your hand at spells, then this book is definitely what you have been looking for.

To be Wiccan does not necessitate that you have to be a part of a coven. There are quite a few Wiccans that practice their religion and magic on their own. This is what this guide focuses on—your personal journey into the world of Wicca and witchcraft.

Wicca is an amazing journey that heightens your relationship with the world but, like with any religion, it is founded on some basic principles and rules.

Wicca is, at its very core, an inclusive belief system that emphasizes our relationships with the natural and spiritual realms. Anyone who wishes to channel their energy into a positive and powerful life of intention and achievement can begin by practicing Wicca today!

Chapter 1 Overview of Wicca

Wicca is a way of life, often called a religion. It lays the groundwork for people to live and work harmoniously with the world around them. When you live life the Wiccan way, you are living in a way that encourages togetherness with the godly and with everything that has been brought into existence from the Divine.

When you choose to live life the Wiccan way, you agree to live in profound awe and appreciation of the world around you. You are expressing gratitude for the world that you experience from the sunrise and sunset to the growing and harvesting of plants and the natural lifecycles of the animals around you. Everything that is a part of your natural world becomes sacred to you as you see it as being a sacred gift afforded to you by the world surrounding you.

This particular belief system predates Christianity, and it originates in Ireland, Scotland and Wales. There, the ancient ancestors learned how to live together in unity with the world around them, honoring the Divine in everything and cherishing all that was. Much of the information that is used in modern Wicca stems from these ancient traditions, although there is plenty of modern information and twists that have been incorporated into the tradition since.

It is important to understand that Wicca has multiple "types" of belief systems to it. Plenty of off-shoots of the original traditions have developed, allowing for many different types of belief systems to be incorporated into their lifestyle. This way, regardless of what your beliefs are, you will likely find someone in the Wiccan faith who believes similarly to you, allowing you to connect with others who can help you advance your own practices and learn more about yourself and this intricate belief system.

We are but a part of the Earth, no greater and no less than any other creature that crawls, flies, or swims. Thus, it is our duty to care for, heal, and protect every being that exists. To be Wiccan is to give selflessly, to take on the role of a teacher, and to go on a continuous quest for improvement.

To be Wiccan is to recognize power in everything and every creature that you behold. As Wiccan, it is for you to see the divine power in whatever face it chooses to manifest itself. That face can be in the form of the naked tree branches shivering in the autumn wind or in the promise held by each petal of a budding flower in spring.

The medieval church made great efforts to demonize the image of the Wiccan faith. But if anything else, to be Wiccan means to become a promoter of peace and to lead by example by living a violence-free lifestyle. Our goal is to co-exist in harmony with all creatures in this Earth and with the divine powers that surround us.

As Wiccan, it is important for you to understand that we do not acknowledge the idea of an absolute evil such as Satan. Unlike believers of other religions, Wiccans are not driven by fear of "punishment in the afterlife" or "eternal damnation." Instead, Wiccans are encouraged to be kind to others and to "behave" in this life simply because it is the right thing to do.

Another misconception that is as old as time is the idea of Wicca as a cult. Increasing our numbers and manipulating people's heads to gain power has never been the Wiccan way. On the contrary, to be Wiccan is all about embracing diversity. As Wiccans, we always respect and uphold the individual's right to choose the way he wants to live his life.

Does this mean that there are no rules that govern the Wiccan faith?

As a religion, Wicca functions with a basic set of rules. The first among these set of principles is the Wiccan Rede which states that as long as you harm none, you are free to do as you choose. It is because of this rule that Wiccans are discouraged to use magick to intentionally harm another living being.

To be Wiccan means to be in sync with the universe. Thus, you will be able to tap into the infinite pool of universal wisdom and gain access to the knowledge of magick. That privilege is accompanied by a great responsibility. As Wiccan, you are encouraged to use magick exclusively for doing good.

According to the Law of Threefold Return, whatever energy you send out into the world, whether it's negative or positive, will return to you and when it does, it shall be three times stronger. It is important to note that this rule is by no means a way to reassure obedience by striking fear. The universe does not seek to punish anyone. This is simply a natural reaction. Think of the universe as a vast ocean of energy which connects and encompasses the individual energies of all living beings, including you.

When you send out ripples of energy, be it in the form of an action or an intention, it will be released into that vast ocean and will touch everything and everyone. But just like ocean waves, that energy will eventually return to touch you as well.

In the '70's, there was a rise in horrible criminal activities done by members of satanic cults. Sadly, the media wrongly associated these activities with Wiccans and these misconceptions were spread among the public. Feeling the threat, the Council of Witches formed the 13 Principles of Wiccan Belief to regulate Wiccan practice.

Up until today, a great number of covens use this model when creating mandates. The main idea behind these principles is that we are to care for nature just as we must allow nature to care for us. Within us lies an innate power which we must control and wield so that we are able to live in harmony with nature and with all beings.

Each of us consists of internal and external dimensions, inner and outer realities, and it is our duty to nurture both dimensions. As Wiccan, you must appreciate the universe's creative power which is revealed through the merging of the masculine and the feminine energies. To Wiccans, sex is symbolic of life and a source of energy which can be powerful when used in magick.

Additionally, it is necessary to note that different covens are run by different rules created by their committees. Such rules serve to guide you in the prudent use of magick. Each coven is ruled by the High Priestess or the High Priest. To become a member of a coven is to agree to live according to these rules.

You also have the option to become a solitary practitioner. Whichever path you choose, remember that the goodness in your heart, your conscience, and the purity of your intention is a far greater guide than any rule set in stone.

What is Magick?

Belief in magick is an essential part of the Wiccan religion. In the simplest sense, magick means harnessing the energy of the universe to make something happen. Everything in this universe is made up of energy. You are made up of energy. And all of our energies are interconnected by what is called the Universal Energy that flows freely and endlessly around us. Everyone was born with the ability to tap into and wield these energies to create a certain effect.

As Wiccan, you must believe that it is your birthright to access this illimitable supply of energy so that you may improve your life and those of others. Tapping into this energy and using it is done through magick and spellcasting. Each time you cast a spell; you are borrowing energy from the divine essence of the universe. You can understand now why spellcasting should be a sacred act and is not to be taken lightly. It is not for you to abuse the powers of the universe. Practicing Wiccans utilize magick for meaningful endeavors such as to help a friend recover from an illness or from grief, to attract love for others of for oneself, to heal the Earth, or to invite happiness into one's life.

Wicca Core Beliefs and Philosophies

Wicca can be described as a broad religion as it has the happiness of including a lot of different perspectives, realities and beliefs. There are, however, several major core beliefs that are practiced by a majority of Wiccans as a way to establish a grounding basis for understanding the magic you are working with when you are practicing.

These concepts are taken into account, no matter what coven you are in, or what deity you are worshipping. The concepts outlined in this chapter are main platform, or foundation, of what Wicca is and how it explains itself to anyone wishing to follow this path.

Nature is Divine

A majority of Wiccans will tell you that nature is divine. It is like a backbone to the entire practice and there are so many ways that this core belief manifests itself in these rituals. We are all members of this Earth: every rock, tree, leaf, plant, animal, bird, insect, and person, not to mention hundreds of thousands of other species and landscapes.

The Earth is or sacred home and we are a sacred part of it. It is where all life energy is stored and recreated and we are a part of those cycles and systems. To worship nature is to worship the very essence of all things. And you will find that all Wiccan holidays and festivals that are celebrated are derived from a worship of nature. Each festival is marked by a solstice or equinox. All esbats are marked by the cycle of the moon. And just about every ingredient in the rituals and spells of these festivities comes from nature somehow.

There is also a celebration in nature of the unity of opposing forces. There is always a balance of the light and the dark and nature-worship provides the opportunity to look at life from that place of balance and serenity. It is the presence of the male and female in all things; the yin and the yang. That is nature.

The practice of devoting space and love to nature is a part of the Wiccan creed and even though it is not a demand that you follow that practice, it comes naturally when you consider all of the other core beliefs.

Many of the tools that you will use for your rituals and spells are derived from nature. You will find yourself gathering herbs or pieces of wood for making a wand. You may be harvesting certain plants to hang around your house for a certain holiday, or dressing your altar in the perfumes and trinkets of the forest floor. All of nature comes into Wicca and it is a powerful process to fully connect with the divine in nature.

Karma, The Afterlife and Reincarnation

Karma is an echo of what you may find in the Threefold Law (see below) which basically states that what you do in this life carries over into your next one. To make such a suggestion, one must believe in the concept of reincarnation, which creates an open doorway for your spiritual being and essence to return to another life, after your last one, to continue to learn lessons and acquire knowledge for the evolution of all things.

According to Wicca, this is what will always be and has always been, and so in order to adopt the principles of Wicca, you must look into the reality of who you were before, and who you are going to be next. It might be that you are already familiar with some of your past life experiences and you already know what lessons you are trying to learn from those lives. In other cases, for some, you gain new knowledge as you go and are not always privy to what you are supposed to be learning. The concept of Karma asks that you remind yourself what you need to heal from your former lives so that you can ascend further into your true power and magic. And while you are at it, in this life you are living now, be sure that what you do is something you want to take with you into the next life.

Although there is the concept of reincarnation, there is also the concept of the afterlife, sometimes referred to as Summerland, and it is here that you rest between lives to prepare for the next one, to gather your strength and reflect on the journey before to create the best journey forward.

All of these concepts help the Wiccan to bridge the gap between Earth and Spirit and that the balance of the divine is always present, no matter what life you are living, or what stage of travel you are in between worlds.

Ancestors

It is not uncommon to call upon the ancestors in the practice of Wiccan rituals and casting. Many Wiccans believe that our ancestors are always with us, guiding us and showing us the way and should be honored for their own commitment to forging ahead and living life.

Wiccans celebrate deities of various kinds and it is normal to include your ancestors in your practice just as frequently, as they are a part of the cycle of the self and have many lessons to teach as you grow and honor your own path. The concept of honoring the ancestors in not specific to Wicca and is a cross-cultural truth, present in most religious practices.

A great deal of worship for the ancestors comes from a need to embrace the past as well as what your ancestors continue to do for you in the future.

Wheel of the Year

All of the cycles of the year are celebrated in Wicca. Every solstice has a celebration, or Sabbat, and every equinox, too. The rituals and spells that accompany these times are a sacred honoring and celebration committed to the end of something to hail the beginning of something new. In the calendar of the year, there are endless deaths and rebirths that can occur and as a Wiccan, you will find harmony and abundance with every passing season because of that very truth: life begets death which begets more life.

In all of the seasons there are also moon cycles that are celebrated throughout the ritual of Esbats. The cycles of the moon organize the seasons and every waning moon leads to an ending, into a darkening, while every waxing moon leads to a powerful fullness that has its own magic and ritual associated with it.

All of the rhythms and cycles are a part of Wiccan work and it will be a part of this world forever. The concept of worshiping the divine in nature goes closely with the wheel of the year and should be counted as a major component of Wiccan worship.

Personal Responsibility and Responsibility

This concept agrees with the Wiccan Rede and the Threefold Law. You are responsible for every action you take. Wicca asks that you are wise to your power because it might be more than you realize, especially when you are working with the sacred divine energies of all things and all life.

When you are practicing Wicca, you are becoming responsible for more than just yourself; you are using the energy of all life to celebrate and support the life you lead and everything you choose can have an impact on another. It is a wonderful way for you to be honest with the truth of karma as well, because whatever you are responsible for in this life, goes with you forward into the next.

You are incredibly powerful, and Wicca helps you to embrace your internal power and life force energy; it also asks you to be responsible with your power and to harm none and do right by your actions and rituals.

The Wiccan Rede: Harm None

The Wiccan Rede simply states that you should do nothing in your practice that could cause harm to another individual. The basic concept of the golden rule of thumb, that you would do unto others, but it is also asking you to be very cautious in your practice and to consider how you are wording your spells and rituals.

The practice of Wicca is meant to be of benefit to the greater good of all life and so a lot of it has to do with intentions. When you are practicing you might find that you need to state that you are wanting to harm none and that you will uphold the good of all living things on Earth, so it be in your power.

You will find this credo in all of the Wiccan books you find and it has held steady and true for some time. It holds you to your personal responsibility and power and that you have to be the one to make the right choice when using the gift of magic.

Equality

Coercion is not an element of the Wiccan faith. Proselytizing is frowned upon and an aura of acceptance for all backgrounds and spiritual purposes is embraced. Wiccans generally believe that there needs to be an equality in all matters and that all people have a right to walk their own spiritual path; the one that is right for them.

The concept of equality should go without saying in all religions, but unfortunately this is often not the case. This is one way that Wicca is so unique; it offers a way to receive wisdom and abundance through worship of the divine without suggesting that it can only be done a certain way.

Wicca equals equality and the practicing of this artful religion requires an open heart and an open mind to anyone who is in need of a spiritual community and path.

Rule of Three

The Threefold Law, aka Rule of Three, is used in many Wiccan traditions. Not everyone supports this law, however it comes up often and should be noted, or practiced if it suits you. This concept states that whatever spell or magical act is being performed, the resulting energy created from that act will go into the Universe, and come back to the practitioner three times.

You may or may not be familiar with this concept, and it has origins in other cultural practices, especially those of Eastern religions that believe in the law of karma. Wicca is what gives it the concept of three times, the number bearing importance to the reality of the power you are wielding.

It might not happen in the way that you think, for example if you wish harm on someone else, you may have three separate instances of bad fortune as a result, or it could feel like the impact of the return is 3 times greater than it normally would be, like expecting to get paid $100 and getting paid $300.

The Threefold Law is just another way to help you keep a balance with your practice and ensure that you harm none, and that includes harming yourself with the energy of three coming back to you.

Elements in All Things

In Wiccan belief, there are five elements: earth, air, fire, water, ether, or spirit. During rituals and ceremonies and especially in the casting or consecrating of a circle, the five elements are called into balance the energies of the ritual or spell. Not all Wiccans practice with five elements and just use the 4 main ones, conserving spirit as represented by the deity that they worship.

These elements are the fundamental building blocks of all things on Earth and in the Universe. They are responsible for the great eternal cycle of life through creation and destruction, the birth-death-rebirth cycle. These forces of nature that are sacred to Wiccans are always a part of practice because they are the literal life force that binds all matter and all spirit.

161

These elements have been studied throughout time and were part of philosophies dating back to the early Greeks, who were also worshippers of deities and religions of nature. These concepts are found across continents throughout many religions and beliefs including in Egypt and Babylonia, Hinduism and Buddhism, and many more.

The elements are definitely a tool that must be used in your Wiccan practice and as you get further along in your understanding of your spell work and rituals, you will find how important and powerful they can truly be.

Chapter 2 The Benefits of Wicca

Wicca has many aspects as a spiritual practice. There's no way to practice magic, and there's no way to practice magic. People practice magic from all sects, cultures, and for a variety of reasons. That being said, there are a variety of fundamental characteristics that can help those who work. Here are the twelve advantages of wick:

Anyone Can Be A Wicca – Wicca is often associated with the Wicca faith, but one doesn't have to be Wiccan to practice Wicca. Those from all religious backgrounds practice sorcery, and so do non-religious people.

There Are No Rules – Yes, there are spell books, manuals, resources, and a variety of things that people recommend, but the ritual is yours, and it can be as complicated or as simple as you like.

You Can Do It From Anywhere – A lot of Wiccans have named holy places and altars to practice spells, but in fact, they can be practiced anywhere. All you need is you, your goal, and a place where you can concentrate.

Time In Nature – One of the most significant benefits of Wicca is that it helps you spend more time outdoors, interacting with nature, meditating, and having a more significant appreciation for your environment. It also gives you time to unplug the phone.

Knowledge – Wicca requires a lot of training, and you never really stop learning. You will learn a lot about plants and their medicinal properties, the phases of the moon, nature, flowers, trees, animals, crystals, yoga, chakras, natural healing, tea, mythology, history, and the magic of all these things. You should know more about yourself, too!

Knowing What You Want – Spellwork needs you to be explicit about your goal, and that can give you a lot of insight into what you want in life. As a consequence, it can help you take more action to move towards these issues.

Time To De-Stress – Wicca is, at its core, a spiritual practice focused on nature. As Earth's children, few things can make our minds easier than connecting with nature and the elements. It also lets you meditate and think regularly.

There Are Many Paths – Since there is no way to practice magic, you should find the path that most people identify with. You could be a green wick, a sea wick, or a hedge wick. You should meet in a coven or on your own. You can obey the spell books or create rituals of your own.

Reasons To Celebrate – There are many holy days in which some Wiccan celebrate, including the summer and winter solstices, the spring and autumn equinoxes, Samhain, Beltane, and others. People celebrate in different ways, but they often involve cooking a special feast, ceremonies, nature walks, reflection, remembering ancestors, bonfires, and appreciation.

Inspiration – A lot of wicks share their inspiration, positivity, and joy with others, and social media make it easy to consume all that wisdom.

It's Inclusive – One reason I think that Wiccan resonates with so many people is that it's welcoming. This empowers women and does not discriminate against LGBT people. This gives people space to explore faith in a judgment-free environment that also encourages compassion, self-care, harmony, and healing.

It Promotes Healthy Habits – Drinking tea, cooking with herbs, spending time outside, reading and dreaming, meditation, being honest about what you want, communicating with the environment, taking care of the earth, taking care of animals, reading books, and sharing your feelings are all things that you can do more if you practice Wicca.

Chapter 3: Step by Step Guide to Rituals

Practicing magik is easy. All you need is a few tools, a place to set up an altar, and clear intentions. The following step-by-step guide will help you on your path to opening yourself up to the most basic form of rituals, spells and meditations. You don't have to follow these rules in order to cast; you can use them as a foundation to work from and get ideas to create your own powerful rituals and spells.

A lot of Wicca is intuition and connection to your higher self and your own divine wisdom and authority. Let yourself be a guide as you determine the best ways to invoke the right power, energy and intention to bring more abundance and prosperity into your life.

As you get started, look around your house for some of these tools. You don't have to rush out to the store and buy a bunch of new items to make your altar or prepare your spells. So much of what you will use you can find around your house until something better, or more intentional, comes along.

Your Tool Kit

A witch's basic tool kit requires only a few things which you can find in the list below. There are other items that you can consider optional while you are getting started until you are able to build up your tool chest of magical properties and elements.

- Candle(s)/ candle holder

- Matches/ lighter

- Salt

- Stones/ crystals (optional)

- Incense/ or smudge stick (preferably sage)

166

- Dish of clean water in a glass, or wooden bowl (not plastic)

These very basic tools are all you really need to get started. As you play around more and advance, you can add things that bear meaning to your ritual or spell that you are casting. Some Wiccans like to keep figures of their preferred deities to have present, or to place on the altar you create. You can also bring more herbs into the ritual as you see fit, but ultimately, all you need to start with are the items on the list above.

You don't need an altar to use these tools. You can even carry them with you to places out in nature or wherever you are casting magik and can consider it your traveling toolbox for making magik.

The candle brings fire to your ceremony, one of the elements that you will need to call into your circle. The matches and the lighter are to light both the candle(s) and the incense. Salt is a powerful protective agent. Some people cast their circles by making a salt circle around their bodies and their tools, but you can also just keep it with you in a box or a tin to have it as a representation of the Earth energy and also as a symbol of protection.

The stones and crystals, although optional, can come in handy and are very helpful for magnifying and intensifying energy; so whatever ritual or spell you are performing, your chosen stones/crystals can help enhance that experience and bring more energy to it. All stones and crystals have their own unique properties and so finding the ones that resonate most with you will be a significant part of your journey.

The incense/ smudge stick is used to purify the energy around you and cleanse the aura of the room and your own auras. You can use it before, during, and after your ritual to help you feel balanced and attuned to your spells.

Candles

Candles play a major part in any ritual. We have all used the light of candles since we learned how to create our own lasting light and the candle is a great symbol of life in the practice of Wicca.

The act of lighting a candle is a powerful energetic vibration of intention and opens a doorway for you to connect more deeply with the powerful magik you are wanting to invoke. Using candles in all of your ritual and spell work is a good way to bring that energy and focus forward.

Sometimes, you may want to have a candle in a container so that you can burn it overnight or until it burns out. Letting the sacred flame of your spell work continue to burn is a way of energetically stating that your intentions will stay alive until the next candle is lit.

You will also want to find candles that might correlate with your spells based on their colors. Here is a list of what each candle color might represent in a spell you are working:

White – Purity, unity, peace, cleansing, innocence, balance, healing, magik involving young children, spirituality, aura balancing

Yellow – Success, happiness, joy, pleasure, concentration, learning, solar/sun magik, confidence, travel, memory, imagination, flexibility, air element

Orange – Opportunity, creativity, joy, investments, legal matters, justice, self-expression, overcoming addictions, success in business, ambition, vitality, fun

Pink – Feminine energy, compassion, love, romance, domestic bliss, partnerships, friendships, protection of children, nurturing, self-improvement

Red – Vitality, passion, courage, sexual potency, fertility, survival, fire element, independence, conflict, competition, war, danger

Purple – Contact with spirits, independence, wisdom, influence, breaking habits, changing luck, banishing evil energy or dark forces, spiritual power

Blue – Focus, forgiveness, communication, truth, fidelity, good fortune, astral projection, water element, sincerity, patience, domestic harmony, lifting bad/low vibrations

Green – Physical and emotional healing, luck, growth, acceptance, marriage, prosperity, abundance, dispel/counteract jealousy or greed, tree and plant magik

Brown – Earth magik and earth element, stability, material goods or wealth, construction, real estate/ house magik, house blessings, animal, and pet magik

Black – Protection, safety, repelling black magik, reversing hexes, defense, banishing negative vibrations, grounding, wisdom, scrying, pride

Silver – Psychic awareness, lucid dreams and dream states, meditation, communication, feminine energies, victory, stability, moon magik, luck with gambling

Gold – Masculine energies, prosperity, abundance, sun/solar energy, positive vibrations, divination, great fortune, attraction, luxury, health, justice

You don't have to use colorful candles to cast spells or practice rituals. Any kind of candle will work and you can use them in whatever way feels safest and best. Using the colored candles will offer an extra boost of energy and intention to your spell and craft work. Color magik and candle magik are both very potent and powerful energies and when combined together they make for a great force of light and alignment with your intentions in your practice.

Smudging

Smudging is an ancient ceremonial practice and involves the burning of sacred herbs that create a pungent and aromatic smoke that cleanses and purifies. Using a smudge stick, or bundle of dried herbs, in your ceremonies is of great benefit and should be practiced as often as you like.

When you use a smudge stick in your spells and rituals, you are energetically purifying the space around you and protecting your energy from unwanted energies that may be drawn to you. You can use the smoke of your smudge stick to draw a wide circle around the space you will be casting in. You can also use salt in the same way but often the mess is harder to clean up, unless you are outside.

Smudging is a beautiful ceremonial tool and you can do it before, during, and after your incantations and rituals. Some of the most popular smudge sticks are:

- Sage

- Cedar

- Sweet grass

- Lavender

- Juniper

- Mugwort

- Palo Santo (sacred wood, not herbs)

Any of these would work in your ceremonies and craft works. You can even make your own. All you need is the herb of your choice. Tie it in a bundle with string while it is freshly cut. Hang it to dry upside down. Use when needed.

Stones and Crystals

Stones and crystals, each have unique qualities and characteristics. Some of them are good for protection and grounding while others are best for enhancing connection with spirit and opening the third eye.

Working with a variety of stones and crystals is highly recommended since they all have very different vibrations and meanings. There are hundreds and thousands of various stones and so you may have to enjoy doing a little digging and research to find the best fit for your personal needs.

Try an experiment to find the right stones and crystals: Find a local shop in your area that specializes in selling stones and crystals. While in the shop, use your dominant magick hand (it might not be your dominant writing hand) and hover over the stones you feel drawn to. Let your intuition be your guide. If you feel "pulled" toward a stone, pick it up and notice how it feels. If you can sense a strong energy in it through the palm of your hand, then that stone or crystal is resonating with your vibration and will be good for you to work with.

Everything in your tool kit is a way for you to gain more connection to the greater energies and spirits of the world around you. As you work with these tools, look for the ways that they make you feel energetically attuned to what you are working on. Sometimes, you may resonate more with the fire element and may desire more candlelight in your practice; other times, you may have a need to bring more Earthly items from nature into your casting or take yourself out into the woods to do your rituals.

All of the elements play a major role in your Wicca work and so developing relationships with these tools is of vital importance. The work you do with the energy of nature brings a deeper and closer connection to yourself and all of the energies that are here to help you and guide you on your path. Work on building the tool kit that feels like you and enjoy practicing your rituals with your sacred and magical elements.

Setting Up Your Altar

An Altar is a space of devotion to something. It can be anything you want it to be and creating your altar is the artistic expression of your magik and your practice. We all need a place in our homes that reflects our most important desires and passions as well as our thoughts and expectations. An altar is a perfect way to create a physical manifestation of your spiritual journey.

There are no rules to setting up your altar and often times, it will change with you as you grow and evolve. It takes on the life you are living as you add and subtract things from it based on the intentions and practices you are doing.

Altars are a reflection of who you are and what you are praying to and so while you develop your own altar, be clear about how it shows off what you are choosing to align with at all times. It needs to be a place that has a flow and an energy of harmony and balance. It may be necessary for you to tend to your altar daily or frequently to maintain its energy and ability to attract abundance into your life.

Your altar should be in a place in your home where it cannot be disturbed easily by others and can be easily seen by you so that you are always alive to it. Many people put altars where anyone can see them and that is perfectly okay; it doesn't need to be hidden; it only needs space to exist undisturbed by anyone but you.

The altar of your choice can be on a bookshelf, in a cabinet, on top of your dresser, hanging on the wall, etc. It is up to you to choose the right place for your altar to exist. Once you have found the proper location, you can acquire the items you need to create it and decorate it.

Often times, people will use a cloth to lay out on the surface of wherever it will sit. It could be something small, like a scarf or a handkerchief or it could be something more meaningful, like a piece of heirloom lace from your Grandmother. You don't have to use a cloth at all, but if you choose to, make sure it is something that reflects the overall energy of your altar.

Next, you can start bringing in objects to help you align with your spiritual path and purpose. Many people place sculptures or figurines of their favored gods and goddesses, others may use paintings, pictures, or photographs to set out as an homage to a particular deity. Anything goes really and it all depends on what you like and what you are wanting to focus on.

Another approach is to just use the items from your tool kit. You can place these items on the altar and dedicate this space to your sacred rituals so that your tools are always resting on your altar. Essentially, building an altar for your magical tools. Bringing focus to these items through the display on an altar will remind you of the importance of working with this magik and will help you continue to honor your Wiccan practice. When you are opening your energies to work with your tools, you can start by lighting candles on your altar, burning some incense or smudging the altar and starting your rituals in this way.

Your altar is basically a display of your internal magical self. It is a reflection of your power and your curiosity to ask questions about the great unknown and to worship the energy of all things in this world. Bring to your altar anything that is resonating with you at the time. You may decide to decorate it with fresh cut flowers and let them wilt and dry to illustrate the idea of life and death.

You may also want to collect items from your nature walks to devote the altar to Mother Earth. It can also be a place that changes with every Wiccan holiday celebration making your altar a devotion to the seasons and rhythms of the Earth.

Don't be afraid to alter your altar. It can transform with you as you grow and it will need to be tended to the way you tend to yourself. Treat it like a living thing and as an expression of yourself. Whatever water you keep on your altar, if any, needs to be clean and pure; don't let it get dirty and stagnant as that will be a sign showing you that you are neglecting your altar and your spiritual practice.

Tend to it and allow it to be a consistently transforming part of your life that invokes a deeper spiritual reflection of your journey.

Asking the Gods/Goddesses for Support

Whether you are looking for guidance from the gods and goddesses of Pagan ritual or not, letting yourself be open to their assistance and guidance is a good way to bond with the energies of all things as you work with your Wiccan practices. You may not have a particular deity that you work with or devote your altar to but as you are preparing your rituals, it is a good idea to let the universal energies know that

174

you are ready to tap in and find help if it is offered as you cast your spells and perform your rituals.

All you have to do is say the following words as you light the candles on your altar and burn your incense:

"I am opening the lights of all life to the energy of all things. I ask for guidance, support, and protection from the Great Mother and Father and all offerings from the spirits and deities of all life. I am open to receive your love, light, and warmth as I progress in my ritual. So mote it be."

You can change the wording to be anything that feels right for you based on what energies you want to call in to help. You may be more inclined to practice fairy magic or to work with the animal kingdom of spirit guides. You may also desire to connect with your ancestors as you begin your rituals and spell castings. All of these ways of connecting to that work will help you, so make sure it is in alignment with how your individual Wiccan practice is for you.

Change the wording of the above message to reflect your practice but keep the message the same. Stating that you are open to receive help and guidance is a very powerful tool of connection. Maintaining a desire to only work with the energies of light and love is an important factor because it declares that you are wanting to work with the higher vibrations and that you don't want to call on anything harmful or low energy like a trickster spirit or energy who may not be as helpful as other energies will be.

Opening yourself to all of this will help you concentrate even better on what your intentions are and what you are wanting to accomplish with your spells. Relax, ask for support, and give thanks to all the energies that come to provide you with help along your path.

Casting Your Circle

You don't have to use your altarpiece to cast your circle. You may be out in the woods when you need to cast and will be far away from your altar. It might be also that you just utilize your altar to store your magical tools between casting and won't need to involve it in your Wicca work; however, you may find that you feel more grounded in your practices if you start by connecting with the energy of your altar before casting your circle. It is really up to you how you choose to work with your own energy and magical tools.

Why do you cast a circle and what does it even mean? When you are invoking the energies all around you and connect your own energy to the spiritual plane, you need to have an opening and closing of intention and protection. It is a helpful way for you to have clarity and focus while you are performing rituals and casting spells but it also serves as an intentional centering of your energy and attachment to your spiritual self. Casting is almost like a meditation to get you engaged with your work.

The meaning of casting a circle in your preparation is also to align you with the four directions and the four elements. Each way you travel is represented by your circle and each element of the life spark is represented to connect you to your full purpose and potential. It is a meaningful acknowledgment of your journey when you cast a circle and it brings into focus that which helps you succeed on your path: the directions and the elements.

Remember to create a space that feels healthy and balanced for you while you practice. It is best to do it away from where others will interrupt or disturb you. The following steps will help you cast your circle of intention and protection.

1. If you are working near your altar and you want to include it into your ritual, you can begin by lighting candles on the altar and lighting your smudge stick to cleanse the energy of the altar and your body.

2. Facing the north, say the following words: "I call upon the energy of the north. Welcome to this circle of light. And so it is."

3. Facing the east, say the following words: "I call upon the energy of the east. Welcome to this circle of light. And so it is."

4. Facing the south, say the following words: "I call upon the energy of the south. Welcome to this circle of light. And so it is."

Facing the west, say the following words: "I call upon the energy of the west. Welcome to this circle of light. And so it is."

**NOTE:* You have creative freedom to change the wording of these phrases. They are a simplified version of what you can say to announce the calling of the four directions into your circle and you may find as you advance and feel more creative with your practice that you will want to add some information to how you call upon the directions.

5. Once you have called on the directions, you can now invite the elements to wherever you are sitting. You may keep your

elements placed on the altar or you may wish to set them out on the table you are sitting at or on the ground if you are sitting at that level. You can use specific tools and objects for this part and if you can, lay the corresponding element in the directional position it is aligned with. For example, for your earth element, place your dish of salt or soil to the north.

6. Set your earth element in the position of the north (wherever you are sitting) and say the following words: "I call upon the energy of earth as I cast my circle of protection and power. Welcome to this circle of light. And so it is."

7. Repeat Step 7 as you did with the directions in Steps 2-5, laying out an object or representation for each element. East is air; south is fire; west is water. You can use a smoking incense or smudge stick for air or you can place bird feathers in this position. A candle works for the position of the south and fire, and a dish of clean, clear water works for the west.

8. Alternatives for these items would be crystals or stones that would resonate with the directional energies; a stone or crystal for each direction representing the elements.

The final step of the circle casting can be a personal declaration, like the following: *"I awaken to the energies of the four directions and the four elements and cast this circle of protect and light with their help and guidance as I work with their energies. So mote it be."*

NOTE: The phrases 'So mote it be' and 'and so it is' are saying the exact same thing. It is the energy of stating 'and this is real'. Saying it at the end of an intentional phrase is a very powerful energetic assignment for whatever magick you are performing. Either one works well and can be used interchangeably.

You are now on your way to delving more deeply into the ritual and spell casting that you are choosing. Get comfortable with how you like to cast your circle and repeat it the same way every time. Casting a circle of power and protection is a ritual in and of itself and your personal circle casting should be unique to you. Build your own version of casting a circle from the steps above and have fun with it!

Spells, Rituals, Intentions

The next step in the process of a typical spell or ritual is the actual spell work or ritual work that aligns you with your intentions. Remember: it is important to have clear intentions before going in, so before you cast your circle, ask yourself: what is my magical purpose today?

Once you have clarity about what you are wanting to achieve or focus on, you may want to design your ritual or spell from your own personal idea of how it should go or you can use already existing spells and craft work that feel natural and good for what you are wanting to accomplish. There are tons of spells online, in books, all over, that can help you choose the best way for you to align with your craft work.

Much of what you will be doing in this step is clearly detailing and stating your intentions to create the energy of life around it. It may include herbs and other items that support your intention. If you are celebrating a holiday or a specific god or goddess, you will be working with those items and energies specifically to enhance your ritual or spell.

Words are important and you may need to write down ahead of time the words you want to share once you have opened a circle. Preparing for your ritual or spell is just as important as executing it. Prior to opening your circle, write down the words for your spell on a piece of paper. Gather the herbs you wish to include in your circle, or the relics and objects that will be meaningful to you.

There are so many unique possibilities for how you can invoke your own powerful magik and let it be known to the energies of all that surrounds you. The following steps are simple ideas and clues for how you can get started with creating your ritual and spell. Remember that practicing Wicca is a creative and artistic experience and there really isn't a wrong way to do it. You can use the following steps to help get you started with building a spell and/or ritual.

1. Set your intention. Write it on paper, on leaves, on stones or pieces of wood to burn, on anything magical.

2. Gather your ingredients. You may be working with herbal remedies that support your intention. Make a bouquet of them to dry on your altar. Collect the stones, crystals and any other earth elements that feel appropriate and place them where they feel best. You may want to collect sacred water from a waterfall or a river that feels magical to you.

3. After casting your circle of protection and power, you can now begin your ritual with your objects and intentions. Using your

written intentions as a declaration is a wonderful way to open yourself up to the energy of what you are wanting to accomplish. Don't just write it on the paper or the leaves; read it aloud so that you can feel the words come out of your mouth with sound and release the words into your circle.

4. Use your candles, incense and crystals, or other ritual objects to set intentions and make declarations as well. For example: if you are using fire magic, you may have chosen a certain number of colored candles that correspond with the energy you are wanting to invoke. As you light each candle you can say, *"As I light this candle, I welcome the power of fire to bless my ritual and invoke the passion of firelight to aid me on my path."*

**NOTE: Everything you do carries energy and intention, so even when you are lighting a candle, make declarations about what you are doing out loud so that the energy is clear in your ritual.

5. Use the same concept from Step 4 with your other ritual or spell casting elements. For example: if you have sacred river water to add to your ritual, as you pour it into a chalice or a bowl you can say something like: *"As this water flows into this cup, let it flow through me with intention and energy to fulfill my purpose. And so it is!"*

6. *After incorporating all of your ingredients for your spell you can recite, or speak aloud, your words of intention and incantation. Let's say you are casting a spell for prosperity. All you have to say is:* "Here on this day, I summon the life force

181

energy of prosperity. The candle will burn night and day to align me with the fortune I seek. Water will flow in this chalice until prosperity comes to me. Smoke I will burn every day and night to welcome the gift of abundance. Salt I will shake onto these coins to gain more of what I seek. Prosperity! And so it is!"

Any spells and rituals that you do will be fun, unique, and specific to the cause of the work you are doing. Once you have a basic feeling for how to open a circle and bring forth your intentions in your magical practice, you will find the freedom to explore more of the possibilities of finding and creating your own spells and rituals.

Even if you find popular spells online or in other books, you can always build onto or alter these spells to fit your needs. No harm will come to you if you make some changes to already existing spells. Wicca is a creative practice and all it needs is your devotion to the light of your truth and your inner knowing as you walk the path of Wicca.

Closing Your Circle

Closing your circle is as simple as opening it. All you have to do is pay respect and gratitude to the elements and to the directions. You may want to face each direction again to ask the directions to comfort you on your path as you allow your spell to take effect.

You can also connect with the elements you have in your space and carefully return them to their altar space as a way of creating closure with them. Here are a few steps to help you close your circle, as you opened it:

1. Thank each element by addressing it directly. *Ex:* Thank you to the earth that grounds me (sprinkle salt or soil into your hands

and rub them together, letting the salt/soil fall away natural). Thank you to the air that blows me forward on my journey (snuff out the smudge stick). Thank you to the fire the lights my way (blow out candle). Thank you to the water that cleanses and purifies (dip fingers in water and flick on your altar or on your own face).

2. Stand up or point your energy in the direction of each of the four directions to thank them for their presence, similar to the way you did it with the elements in Step 1. All you have to do is offer gratitude and move through each direction, closing the circle the way it started.

3. Alternative: You can combine Steps 1 and 2 and close the circle by thanking each direction and the corresponding element simultaneously.

4. A final thank you can be expressed to the Great Mother and the Father or whichever gods/goddesses you have invoked for your ritual.

5. The final words: "And so it is!" or "So mote it be!"

Accepting Your True Power

Wicca is a beautiful, fun and magical way to connect with your true power and the energy of all life around you. It has a way of asking you to be present and to identify your whole being and the nature of what you are seeking with a mindful appreciation of nature and all of her energies.

One of the most profound lessons of Wicca and other Pagan practices is that it is a way for you to creatively explore yourself and your inner power as you transform and grow. The best way for you to approach rituals and casting spells is to trust your own inner knowing about how the spell should go and what ways it can unfold.

You will find a wide range of variations for one specific intention or spell, because there isn't a wrong way to cast. As long as you are upholding the Wiccan Rede, then anything goes, essentially. As you continue to work with your own spell work and rituals, remember to honor your power above all else. Devotions to the Earth Mother and all of the other gods and goddesses are equally important to the devotion of your own magical powers and truths.

Have fun inventing your own spells and create your own *grimoire*! A grimoire is simply a book of magic spells and invocations and you can make your own at any time as you see fit. Every spell you cast can be written down, step by step in your own book of magic that is specific to you and the traditions or beliefs you choose to follow. Working on your own grimoire is a special way of devoting yourself to your path of magic and having a reference to your own book of spell work can help you in the future when you want to repeat or enhance spells that you have already created and performed.

It is very traditional for a witch to make his or her own grimoire and so while you are opening yourself to your Wiccan experience, get a notebook and begin a journal of your recipes and incantations so that you can refer to and use them later. It is a helpful way to trust in your own magick and true power.

Chapter 4: Love and Relationship Spells

Spell for New Friendships

Whether you've just moved to a new area and don't know many people yet, or your social life simply needs an overhaul, this quick spell brings new people into your life to form friendships with if you so choose.

It's best done during a waxing moon, but if you've got an upcoming social encounter that you'd like to put some magical energy into, by all means, don't hold off just because the moon is waning.

You will need:

- 1 small rose quartz, clear quartz, carnelian, or lapis lazuli stone

- 1 yellow spell or votive candle

- Lavender essential oil

Instructions:

- Anoint the candle with the oil.

Place the stone in your dominant hand, palm upward, and lay your other palm on top.

Clasp your hands together, close your eyes, and visualize yourself surrounded by positive people who are fun and comforting to be around.

When you've captured this feeling, take a deep breath, exhale, and open your eyes.

Place the stone in front of the candle and then light the wick as you say these words:

"Friendships new and true, let our kindred souls unite. "

Carry the stone with you whenever you leave the house, and leave it where you will see it when you are home.

Charm for Attracting Quality Relationships

As a culinary spice, coriander has a warm, fragrant, slightly nutty flavor. But not everyone knows that coriander is actually the seed of the herb known as cilantro.

Interestingly, the seed and the leaf taste nothing alike. This dual nature is reflected in the magical uses of coriander, which include both attracting love and guarding against unwanted energies.

The seed is used in love spells, aphrodisiac potions, and for making peace between quarreling people, as well as for exorcism and protection of the home. And because it's readily available in the spice aisle of most grocery stores, it's a great herb to work with for beginning kitchen Witches.

This spell draws on both the attractive and protective qualities of coriander for a balanced approach to attracting new potential partners into your life.

This is particularly good for those who seem to have no trouble attracting admirers, but plenty of trouble in the relationships that develop. With the energy of coriander, people who are ultimately no good for you will not make it into your sphere of awareness, while people who present a positive, healthy, compatible match will have a clear path to you.

Adding rose quartz to the mix enhances the positive vibration of the spell. Be sure to get whole seeds rather than coriander powder, since you'll be carrying the herb with you.

You will need:

- 13 whole coriander seeds

- 1 small rose quartz

- 1 small drawstring bag or piece of cloth

- 1 red or pink ribbon

- 1 work candle (for atmosphere—optional)

- Instructions:

- Light the candle, if using.

Arrange the coriander seeds in a circle around the rose quartz.

Close your eyes and visualize the feeling of being completely at peace with a partner who loves you for exactly who you are.

When you have a lock on this feeling, open your eyes, focus on the rose quartz, and say the following (or similar) words:

"I draw to be nothing less than healthy, balanced love."

Now collect the coriander seeds, placing them one at a time into the drawstring bag or cloth. (It's best to start with the seed at the southern-most part of the circle and move clockwise.)

Add the rose quartz, close the bag or cloth, and secure with the ribbon.

Bring the charm with you whenever you're feeling like taking a chance on love—especially when you go out in public.

Romance Attraction Smudge

This is a fun, simple ritual for enhancing the atmosphere in your home or any space where you'd like to encourage romance!

You will need:

- 1 red candle

- A sprig of dried lavender or lavender-only smudge stick

- Rose essential oil (optional)

- 1 feather (optional)

Instructions:

Anoint the candle with a drop or two of the rose oil, if using. Wipe away any excess oil from your fingers, and then light the candle.

Ignite the lavender sprig or smudge stick from the candle flame as you say the following (or similar) words:

"Loving lavender, creative fire,
charge this space with love's desire."

Starting at a point in the northern part in the room, move in a clockwise circle, fanning the lavender smoke with the feather (if using) or your hand, so that it spreads throughout the room as much as possible. If you like, you can repeat the words of power above as a chant as you go.

Leave the lavender to burn out on its own in a fire-proof dish, if possible—otherwise, you can extinguish it gently in a potted plant or bowl of sand.

Stellar First Date Confidence Charm

If you're the type who gets nervous before meeting a potential love interest for the first time, this spell is for you.

Simply carry the charm with you in your pocket or purse—you may want to enclose it in a drawstring bag or cloth if you're carrying it with other items to keep it intact.

Keep in mind that the focus here is on your own confidence and sense of self-love *no matter what the* other person is like. If you have a good time, no matter what the outcome, then the spell has been a success.

You will need:

- One pink or white ribbon, about seven inches

- One little piece of carnelian or tiger's eye

- Sea salt

- One work candle (optional)

189

- One little drawstring bag or piece of cloth (optional)

Instructions:

Light the candle, if using.

Layout the ribbon on your altar or workspace.

Create a circle of sea salt around the ribbon—this will concentrate the energy of the spell around the charm.

Place the stone on the ribbon, and say the following (or similar) words:

"My confidence radiates from within I am comfortable in my own skin. This meeting of souls will be a pleasure. I charm this stone for extra measure."

"

Tie the ribbon gently around the stone and secure it with a knot.

Now go out and have fun meeting someone new!

Ritual Bath for a Blind Date

Whether you're on a blind date set up by a friend, or taking the plunge in the world of online dating, it can be nerve-wracking to meet someone new.

This spell makes it nearly impossible not to have a good time, by sublimating nervousness and promoting self-confidence, which will improve the energy of the encounter no matter what the outcome. Indeed, you will enjoy yourself even if it's clear by the end that there won't be a second date!

Himalayan salt is a wonderful relaxant, but it can be potent and induce sleepiness, especially if you don't use it regularly. Therefore, if you're taking this bath right before the date, you may want to opt for the sea salt.

The herbs can be sprinkled loosely if you have a mesh catch-all drain for your tub. Otherwise, place them in a teabag or a thin washcloth to keep them from spreading out into the water.

You will need:

- One tsp. to one tbsp. hibiscus

- One tsp. to one tbsp. chamomile

- One tsp. to one. tbsp. coltsfoot or red clover

- Two to three tbsp. Himalayan salt or sea salt

- Five drops of lavender essential oil

- One citrine, aventurine, or tiger's eye

- Candle(s) for atmosphere

Instructions:

Run the bath until the tub is a quarter of the way full, and add the salt.

When the tub is halfway full, place the crystal of your choice in the water, and add the oil.

When the bath is almost full, add the herbs.

191

Light the candle(s), turn off any artificial lighting in the bathroom, and climb in.

Relax and consciously release any anxiety you may be feeling about meeting this new person. Also, release any attachments you may be feeling to the desired outcome.

Stay in the bath for at least 20 minutes. If you can, remain in the tub while draining the water, as the energy of the herbs and crystal tends to have a stronger effect that way.

Bring the crystal with you on the date, and have a good time!

Relationship Potential Divine "Forecast"

For single people, getting to know a new potential love interest can be exciting, but also confusing.

Even though you may seem to "click" with this person, you're still operating in an atmosphere where there's far more unknown information than known. It can be hard to avoid wondering whether it will work out in the way you're hoping for, and easy to get caught up in over-analyzing even the smallest of details.

Perhaps you're wondering if the person is "too good to be true," or worried that you might jump into something too quickly. Or you may just be trying to talk yourself out of a potentially great relationship simply because it will require you to leave your comfort zone. Maybe it's a little bit of all of the above?

The problem, of course, is that over-thinking it actually gets in the way of your ability to see the situation clearly and can create more confusion, rather than less. This spell can help you get a sense of whether your new prospect has enough romantic potential to be worth putting further mental energy into.

You may get a simple, definitive *yes* or *no*, but you may also get more information that helps you come to your own decision about it or a signal that for now you just need to stay open and detached from any particular outcome. Whatever your "forecast" turns out to be, this spell will get the energy moving from a place of stuckness toward a place of resolution, by helping you get out of your own way!

Any of the three crystals below work well for this spell, but if you happen to have all of these and are looking to choose one, here are some finer energetic points to consider for your particular situation:

• *Malachite* is particularly appropriate if your current confusion or concern stems primarily from a prior relationship experience.

• *Quartz* is a good all-purpose intuition booster and helps clear out inner turmoil.

• *Amethyst* helps to dispel illusions and keep "obsessive thinking" in check.

You will need:

• One little to average-sized amethyst, quartz crystal, or malachite

• One little strand of paper

• One scented candle (optional)

Instructions:

Light the candle, if using.

Spend some time getting grounded and centered. Let go of any actual thoughts around the person for the time being.

Write the person's name on the strip of paper, and ask for any and all illusions you may have about the person to be cleared away. (Don't ask specific questions, or your mental energy will muddy up the spell.)

You may want to say the following (or similar) words:

"Infinite intelligence of the Universe,
please light the path that I am meant to see,
with regard to [name of person] and me."

Fold the paper enough times so that it more or less fits underneath the crystal, and place it on your altar with the crystal on top.

When you go to bed, place the crystal (and paper) underneath your pillow. You will likely receive further information in your dreams, but don't worry if this doesn't happen—information of some kind will come to you in your waking life within the next 48 hours.

Choosing Peace in Tough Situations

At some point in our lives, we all face enormous challenges that we know we can do nothing to control. It may be that a loved one is facing

194

a serious illness, or it may even be a major world event causing chaos in your life.

It's always fine to work magic for whatever influence you may be able to have on the outcome of a situation, but this can be difficult to do from a place of empowerment when you're feeling personally affected, which can negate the energy of the spell.

In times like these, you need to take care of yourself first before you can help anyone else.

 This spell is best worked for an hour or so before going to bed. If you prefer to let spell candles burn all the way down on their own, you'll need to place it in a sink before going to sleep!

Otherwise, you can gently extinguish the candle and repeat the spell on successive nights until the candle is spent.

This spell is really meant to be personalized as much as you wish. Put on meditative music, brew chamomile tea, stretch your limbs, take a hot bath, and/or do anything else that helps you relax. The more energetically "prepped" you are for this spell, the more powerful it will be.

You will need:

- Peace of Mind Oil blend

- 1 white candle

- Meditative music (optional)

Instructions:

Put on the music, if using, and take any other measures to calm yourself as much as you can.

Sit quietly and take a few deep breaths. Anoint your pulse points and the candle with the oil.

Close your eyes and take a few more deep breaths, clearing your mind as much as possible.

When you feel ready, open your eyes and light the candle, while saying the following (or similar) words:

I release this burden to my higher power and turn my attention to balance and rest. So, let it be.

Sit and gaze at the candle flame for several moments, keeping your mind as quiet as possible and your focus on the light.

"Spare Key" Spell for Spiritual Connection

Although we usually think of other people in the context of "relationship," we also have a relationship with our "higher power"— or whatever your personal term is for the force that moves through you when working magic. This spell focuses on strengthening that relationship, which is ultimately the foundation from which all human relationships stem.

While it may be becoming less common in today's world, it has long been the custom of many households to keep a spare key just outside the home, whether under the doormat, in a potted plant, or some other hidden location. This is done as both a backup in the case of lost keys and as a way of allowing relatives or friends access when the homeowner is away.

This spell draws on the energies of wisdom and trust that are inherent to this custom, as a way of honoring the benevolent forces working for you in the unseen realms.

By blessing and burying a key outside near your home (or in a potted plant indoors, if necessary) you are signaling to your higher power—whether it be a deity, a guardian spirit, or simply the benevolent energy of the Universe—that you welcome their presence and assistance in your home and in your life, no matter where you may be at any given moment.

It is also a way of reminding yourself that should you temporarily lose your connection to your spiritual center, you will always be able to find your way back in.

Depending on whether the crime is a factor in your neighborhood, you may feel comfortable using an actual spare key to your home, but any metal key will work for this spell.

Some people like to use a gold key to represent God and/or a silver key to represent the Goddess (using two keys is perfectly fine).

You will need:

- 1 key

- 1 white candle

Instructions:

Hold the key in your hands while meditating quietly for several minutes.

Focus on that feeling of being truly connected to your true self and your higher power.

When you feel ready, light the candle and say the following (or similar) words:

"[Name of deity/spirit/higher power], you are welcome now and always in my home and my heart. Let this key represent your access, and mine, to my highest self, from this day forward."

Pass the key through the candle flame very quickly three times (in order to protect your fingers, don't give it any time to become hot).

Then bury it at least 6 inches down into the earth outside your home, or in the soil of a large potted plant.

Chapter 5 : Herbal Magic: Rituals and Spells

There are thousands and thousands of magical rituals and spells that you can incorporate into your herbal magic practice. This chapter will give you some highlights of things that you can do to utilize herbs for casting spells, brewing potions and a variety of other things as well. In the last chapter, you read about more of the healing brews and potions, but always remember that they are no less magical than the recipes you are about to read. All of your herbal craft work has a magic to it and these rituals and spells are just another exciting layer to your Wicca Herbal Magic practice.

Magical Tea Infusion for Any Kind of Potion or Brew

So many of these potions are really just a simple tea. The last chapter had a few examples of some healing tea potions to help you in times of sickness and health and you can infuse more magic into any of those brews with this simple Tea Infusion Ritual. Use it daily, for any tea you want to brew. The magical energy that you use to charge all of your spells and remedies will bring you a fulfilling enrichment from the inside out.

Instructions for Making and Enjoying a Magical Tea (Infusion)

Follow these steps to empower your tea:

1. While steeping the potion, envision yourself covered light (choose the color based on what magical effect you are needing. Ex: green for healing; pink for love; orange for power, etc.)

2. While pouring and drinking the potion, visualize that same colored light coming from the liquid.

3. After drinking, see the light radiating from within you, flowing through your whole body and then out into the world around you

4. See it reach towards the sky (as above) and go down into the earth (so below), extending your will and desire into the universe.

5. You can say a mantra or affirmation for your Tea Spell while you drink and envision the light.

Making a Magical Tincture

You have already read instructions for making a tincture in Chapter 3, and this spell and ritual will help you infuse your tinctures with a charge of energy and magical intention or purpose. Every time you shake your jar of herbal alcohol potion (twice daily for one month) you will infuse it with the magic energy you need through this tincture charging spell.

Spell and Ritual to Charge Your Tinctures

You will need the following:

- 1 green candle- represents herbal spirits

- 1 white candle- honoring spirit and magic

- 1 candle to charge the tincture- the color chosen depends on the spell you are working

- mixing bowl – glass or stainless steel, no plastic

- Herbs and alcohol for the tincture (or alcohol substitute)

- 2 Mason jars

- Cheesecloth

1. Create a triangle with your candles on your altar, or wherever you are performing your ritual. Put the white candle at the top point of the triangle, farthest from you and the green and other candle at the base points of the triangle. The white candle point directs energy from you and out into the Universe.

2. Place the bowl in the center of the triangle of candles on your altar. Your herbs and alcohol (or substitute) should be near to where you are working, but not yet in the bowl.

3. As you light the white candle, state the following: "For the power of the spirit"

4. As you light the white candle, state the following: "For the herbal spirits"

5. Depending on the final colored candle and your needs for this tincture spell, light the candle and state your purpose as you did with the other two candles.

6. With each herb you are using for your tincture, you will pre-measure your ingredients before you start your ritual. After lighting the candles, you will take each herb measurement, one at a time, and as you place it in the bowl on the altar you will offer a blessing of gratitude and state your need for that particular herb.

7. You will repeat this ritual for each herb you put into the bowl, one by one. As you add each herb, stir the mixture clockwise to incorporate them together. Clockwise is the direction for increasing or bringing something to you in this practice. Counterclockwise would be the decreasing or removal of excess of something in your life.

8. After all, herbs are added and stirred, place your hand over the bowl and state your magical purpose and intention.

9. Depending on your need, and likely corresponding to the color candle you have chosen for your specific spell, imagine and visualize that color of light coming out of your hands and into

the herb mixture on the altar, charging it with colorful light. (Ex: love = pink light; money = green light, etc.)

10. Away from the lit candles, pour your herbs into your mason jar and add the alcohol. Secure the jars with lid.

11. Taking the mixing bowl off of the altar, put the jar of herb and alcohol mixture in its place in the center of the candle triangle. Leave the jar in this place until the candles have all finished burning.

12. Once the candles have burned out, you can move your sacred tincture to a darker place to cure. It can be somewhere on your altar covered with a cloth, or in a cupboard.

13. As you shake the tincture, focus on your energy on all planes, body, mind, spirit. You can come up with your own chant to say as you shake, but here is one example of what you might say, every time you shake your jar: "Herbal potion, magic brew, I shake your powers, releasing true. Giving power, making light, magic set, in tincture right."

14. You will need to shake the jar twice a day for at least a month and will want to repeat your words and visualize your intentions as you do.

15. After the month has passed, you can strain your liquid through the cheesecloth and remove all of the herbal plant fibers. You can then dilute it with distilled water, if desired, and keep bottled and store for magical use!

Spell and Ritual to Charge Your Bath

There are a variety of herbs that you can use to make a ritual bath. A majority of the herbs that you will put in your bath will most likely need to be in a sachet, or a larger tea bag so that they don't clog your drain when you let the water out of the bath. You can also add larger blossoms and petals to the water, essentially making a giant infusion to relax your body in.

Ritual baths are incredibly healing to the body and the spirit and if you are working with magic and herbal remedy, then this spell will hell you to charge the herbs and charms for your bath experience so that you are floating on the highest vibration of magic possible.

You will need the following:

- An assortment of herbs (depends on your spell work)

- Sea or Epsom Salt

- Sachet to hold herbs

- Essential oils (optional)

- Mixing bowl

- Candles (choose the colors based on your spell's needs)

- Flower petals and heads (dry or fresh)

- Smudge stick

On your altar, set your candles either in a triangle or arch. Make the point of the triangle or arch farthest from you. (You can also do this ritual on the kitchen table if your altar isn't big enough).

1. Place the mixing bowl in the center of the candles on your altar.

2. Light each candle, invoking the energy of the candle magic you are asking for in your spell. It will depend on your intentions and your purpose as well as the color of the candle you have chosen.

3. Once the candles are lit, slowly add your herbs to the mixing bowl, one by one. Each time you add a new herb, stir the mixture. You will want to stir clockwise to add to or gain something from your ritual bath, and counterclockwise to purge, remove or release something as you bathe. It depends on your spell.

4. You can add fresh or dried herbs, salt, magical powder, essential oils, and anything else appropriate to your spell, stirring in the correct direction with a sacred tool, each time you add something new.

5. After you have mixed everything together, light your smudge stick and allow it to smoke. Once it has smoke flowing, swirl the smoke into the mixing bowl in the direction you have chosen it needs to go and say the following words:

"Herbal mixture, green goddess light, come into my bath tonight. Mix with water, purify. Sacred magic, lift my light."

Play around with words and phrases that are pertinent to your spell. **You can also bring your smudge stick into the bath with you later to smudge the water before getting in.

1. Place your hands over the mixture in the bowl and visualize the color of light that is appropriate to your spell, coming through your hands and into the mixture. State any words that will invoke the energy needed in your sacred bath ritual.

2. Once charged, you can begin to put the herbal mixture into the sachets, tying them off and preparing them for the bath.

3. Remove the bowl from the altar and place the sachets in the center of the candles on the altar or workspace. You can leave them there for as long as you feel it is needed, or until the candles burn out.

4. Your bath sachets are now charged with your magic and you can perform the ritual. As you draw your bath, stir your water in the same direction you stirred your herbs in the mixing bowl and incant some words to let the water know your intentions and purpose. As the water spins in the tub, add your sacred herbs to the water to allow them time to steep.

5. Light some candles and smudge the tub. You can smudge before you draw the bath or after; it is up to you.

6. Add some fresh or dried rose petals, or other flower heads to the bath. You can also add some drop of charged essential oils (you can use the same candlelight work and visualization charging on your bottles of essential oils).

7. While in your bath, let the herbs work their magic on your spirit. Visualize what you are trying to invoke or manifest through this spell and let yourself relax into the possibilities.

8. When you drain the water, ask it to carry your magic forward into the universe and to bring your intentions into life and all reality.

Herbal Love Potion Spell

Who doesn't want some extra love in their life? Everyone is looking for a little love and when you work with the energies and herbs that can promote those relationships, emotions, and experiences, you are giving a serious boost to your love experience.

With any spell, it all comes down to specifics and exactly what you are trying to invoke or manifest. Love spells can be anything from drawing your true love to you, to increasing sexual passions, to promoting a deeper bond and marriage partnership.

Every spell needs your specific intentions and purposes and so it will be up to you to modify any ritual, potion, brew or energy to be comparable to what your desires are.

For this Herbal love potion spell, it will be a simple energetic approach to allowing an increase of love power in your life. Whether it is to enhance your already existing relationships or to open yourself to new ones, this spell is designed to increase the energy of love's passion and flow into your life.

You will need the following:

- Roses

- Rose petals

- Lavender

- Cinnamon

- Jasmine

- Peppermint

- Chamomile

- Rosemary

**NOTE: Herbs may be fresh or dry

- Mixing bowl

- Pink and Gold candles (3-5)

- Incense (cinnamon, jasmine, or rose)

This simple infusion is like any other tea you might make, but in order to charge and infuse it with your intentions, there are a few extra steps to help you make it a truly magical love potion. For the ingredients, be creative with how much of each you want to use. Depending on your personality and personal likes, you may want more jasmine in your infusion than roses. You'll probably only need a pinch of cinnamon and a smaller dose of the chamomile and lavender because of their strong sedative qualities.

1. Begin this ritual the same way you started your last one (see Spell and Ritual to Charge Your Bath), by setting your candles on your altar or workspace, either in a triangle or arch, with the top or point farthest away from you.

2. Place your mixing bowl in the center of the candle arrangement and light the candles stating: "Magic fire, candlelight, I invoke your power and wisdom right. Love is life and mine is true, I choose to love and bring it through."

3. Once the candles are lit, light your incense on the altar. You can make a statement at this time to invoke the powers of love through the aromatics you are burning.

4. Ready to add the herbs, you can start adding each one by one. Communicate what each herb or flower means to you in the light of love. Each one may have a different essence and energy for you, and it is different for everyone. Let your intuition guide your thoughts and words and speak the magic of each herb as you add it.

5. Every time you add a new element to the bowl, stir it clockwise, to increase love and making it bigger in your life.

6. Once your magical love herbs are all mixed together in the bowl, send your purpose and intentions into the love potion. You can use creative visualizations, spoken words, and you can even invoke the deity and goddess of love, Venus to help empower your potion.

7. Let the mixture sit by the candlelight until the candle burn out. You may wish to relight some of your love incense to keep the energy potent and aromatic.

8. While you wait for your love potion to charge by candle magic, eat some love foods, like pomegranates, apples, figs, and berries. Envision the love power you are wanting to invoke while you eat these treats.

9. After the candles have burned out, you can now use the herbs to make an herbal infusion to drink. You may want to save some of those love foods to enjoy while you sip your tea.

10. Adjust the quantities as preferred and add the love potion to boiling water and allow to steep for up to 10 and no more than 15 minutes before drinking.

11. Enjoy by a warm fire or in the loving sunlight, or even under the goddess moon.

12. You may also like to use these same herbs to create a sacred ritual love bath. You can blend the sacred bath and the love potion infusion into one magical night of love power to enhance your magical intentions.

Sun and Moon Charging Ritual

So much of the Wiccan practice is celebrating the cycles and rhythms of Mother Nature and all of the powerful energies aligned with those cycles. A great deal of the magic work that you do has an energy of intention that relates to the night and the day, the power of the sun and the moon.

A variety of spells and rituals are performed around these important cycles and energies and can have a potent energetic charge to any spell work or magical practice. The following ritual offers instructions on how to use the energy of the sun and/or the moon to charge your herbal potions, spells, and brews.

You will need the following:

- Herbs of your choice (fresh or dry- depending on the spell)

- Glass, wood, or steel mixing bowl (alternative: sacred cloth for rituals)

- Smudge stick

- Dry, safe place outdoors

- Moonlit night

- Sunny day

The process of this ritual is similar to other rituals. You may want to cast a circle of protection outside around your outdoor workspace or altar to create an intention. You can also use magical herbs and powders to sprinkle a circle around your workspace.

1. Bring the ingredients you need outside to the spot where you will be working.

2. Place the bowl there and you may light a candle and the smudge stick

3. Smudge the area around your temporary outdoor altar space, working in a clockwise direction, since you are wanting to charge your herbs, or add the sun or moon power to them. This would be a good time to sprinkle your magic or protective herbs around the space.

4. Add the herbs of your choice to the bowl or cloth, on at a time if you are using more than one, stirring clockwise with each addition. You can burn your smudge stick at intervals as you stir as well. (If you are using a sacred cloth instead of a bowl for your herbs to lay out in the light, you can use your hand to spread the herbs around in a clockwise fashion, or sweeping motions)

5. As you add each herb, you can say some spell work words to invoke the energies of the herbs and declare your intention to charge them with the light of the sun or moon (you can choose both sun and moon and do an overnight into afternoon spell).

6. Place your hands over the herbs once they are incorporated together and envision the silver light of moonlight going into them, or the golden light of sunshine (or both depending on your spell).

7. If you feel a need to cover the herbs so they are not disturbed by animals or rain, try to find a glass lid that the light can get through and if possible, avoid plastics.

8. Leave the herbs on the outdoor altar for as long as you need the moonlight or the sunlight or both. It is advisable to let them charge for at least 5 hours and not more than 10, depending on the time of year and the daylight/ moonlight hours available.

9. Once you have finished with the charging ritual, you can close the circle, paying respects and gratitude to the sun and moon and bring your herbal potion back inside to be jarred and stored.

10. If you feel a need to refresh the moonlight/sunlight charge on this jar of herbs, you can just place the jar back outside in a second ritual as you see the need.

All of these rituals and spells can be modified, recreated and built upon based on your own practice and magical needs. All spells and rituals are a creative craft and art form, so don't be afraid to step outside of the box and peer through the kaleidoscope. There are so many possibilities for what you can do. Enjoy the fun of crafting your spells and rituals and watch your life transform in meaningful ways to help support the happiness, healing, and joy that comes from a magical life!

Chapter 6: Spells for Wealth

When witches cast spells for wealth, it may not always be spells for money, because real wealth can't always be measured in financial terms. And even if wealth comes your way, what is the true price? Asking for spells for wealth falls under the 'Be careful what you wish for' banner. Is it really in your best interests? You need to think these things through before you decide to cast spells for wealth.

And always remember this: Harm None. Another point to remember that your wealth spell should be cast for need, not for greed. Don't ask for wealth unless you really need it, or the magick won't work. With that in mind, here are some simple wealth spells that work.

Herbs of Prosperity

You may think having a pot of herbs in the home is nothing to do with spells, but consider this. First, you need to know which herbs have magickal properties, and what they are, and then you have to focus intent on the herb, and believe it will bring you wealth. So, have a small pot of basil, parsley, rosemary or thyme to bring prosperity to your home. Or more than one!

Bowl of Change

Place a bowl of change by the front door to keep money in your pocket. Add foreign coins and old, out of circulation coins to bring money into the home.

Mandrake Money

This is one for people with retail businesses. Wrap a large denomination note around a piece of mandrake root and secure with an elastic band. Keep it in your cash register and wait for your turnover to double. It will happen soon.

Abundance Candle Spell

Use the energy and power of the candle flame to draw wealth to you with this simple spell. You need:

- A green candle

- Cinnamon oil

- Vanilla oil

- A coin of large denomination

Carve the word 'Wealth' along the length of the candle with a sharp object – a craft knife, scalpel or toothpick would do it. Now use the oils to anoint the carved word. Place the coin in the candle holder, and then set the candle on top of it. Light the candle, and allow it to burn completely away.

When the candle has burned out, take the wax covered coin and keep it in a safe place to bring wealth to you.

The Self-Love Spell

This spell focuses on self-love and self-importance. It is very easy to accomplish, and it only takes about ten minutes. It is the perfect spell to start with if you want to continue on the path of love spells.

Ingredients needed:

- One birthday candle (pink or red is preferred, but since this spell is about you, specifically, use whatever candle calls to you)

- Essential oil (orange, rose, jasmine, or sandalwood)

- One rose quartz crystal

- One agate slice

- A pinch of Himalayan pink salt

Step 1: Use a paintbrush to anoint the birthday candle with the essential oil, brushing in upward strokes.

Step 2: Use the lighter to melt the bottom of the candle, then place it in the middle of your agate slice, upright.

Step 3: Place your rose quartz close to your candle to promote and enforce your intention of self-love

Step 4: Light the candle. Sprinkle the Himalayan pink salt in a circle around the candle to offer an extra layer of protection.

Step 5: Meditate in front of your burning candle. Think about everything about yourself that you love. Feel that self-love with every fiber of your being. If you find yourself thinking about a negative situation that happened, try to turn it into a positive one. For example, if you start to think about something you said to a coworker that you felt was embarrassing, try to flip it around by thinking: "Yes, that was embarrassing, but everyone does embarrassing things sometimes, and that is what makes us human. These feelings are normal, and I still

217

love myself. Accidentally saying something embarrassing does not make me any less loved or important."

Step 6: Allow the candle to burn out completely as you meditate in silence. This takes anywhere from ten to fifteen minutes. Allow positive feelings to engulf you.

Invitation of Love Spell

This spell will help to attract love into your life and to let the universe know that you are ready to love and to be loved.

Ingredients:

- Three white candles

- Rosemary (a small piece is fine)

- One rose quartz crystal

- Incense (vanilla preferably)

- One small, red box (a gift box is perfect)

- Pink or red felt-tip or pen

- Patchouli essential oil

- Three candle holders

- An item that you personally feel represents love

Step 1: Find a place, either outdoors or indoors, that you feel safe and relaxed. Make sure it is relatively quiet, so you do not get distracted. A garden, forest, or even a favorite room in your place of living is perfect.

Step 2. Spend some time meditating to clear your mind of any distracting thoughts. When you feel ready, anoint all three candles with the patchouli oil.

Step 3: Place the candles in the candle holders and the holders directly on the floor or ground. It does not matter what position you put them in. Begin to chant:

"Love is in my life and has come to me.

I am in love, and they are in love with me."

Step 4: Place the rose quartz in the box, along with the item that you chose earlier. You can even write out a list of qualities you look for in a lover and use the list as your item. The box, with the items inside, focuses your intent and represents what love means to you.

Step 5: Hold your box in your hands. Allow yourself to be overwhelmed by feelings of love as you imagine what you will feel

219

when the happiness awaiting you is finally yours. Imagine yourself in love. Take the time to meditate on these thoughts.

Step 6: Think of some affirmations that have to do with your desires. For example, "I will be loved" works well. Light your candles and chant the affirmation you chose repeatedly.

Step 7: Purposely deliver your intentions into the universe by saying, "so mote it be." Snuff your candles out, then close the box shut. Do not open it until the love you asked for arrives into your life. After your desires are fulfilled, then you may remove the crystal and keep it nearby as a reminder of what the universe provided.

Fire Flowers Spell

This spell is intended for those who have severed ties with a lover, or even just a relationship with anyone that caused distress and feel as if they are isolated from any sort of love in their life. It also works for those who are looking to uncloudy a pathway to a brand-new relationship.

Ingredients:

- Pencil and Paper

- A cauldron or any container that is fireproof

- One pink candle

- A candle holder or a safe dish

- Three dried white flowers (for example daisies, lilies, daffodils)

- The essential oil of your choice

- Incense (rose preferably)

Step 1: Choose a quiet, undisturbed place to cast this spell. Use a lighter or a match to light the incense, and let the smoke cloud the area.

Step 2: Place the candle in its holder or on a safe dish and light the candle.

Step 3: Gently remove the petals from one of your chosen flowers, one at a time. As you do this, chant the following words:

"I am (inhale at this time)

Full of power (exhale)

A powerful love (inhale)

That burns like fire (exhale)"

Step 4: Begin to remove the petals from the other two flowers, and say the incantation again once for each flower. When you are done, place the petals in your cauldron or the incense burner.

Step 5: Take a slow, deep breath. Clear your mind of distracting thoughts. When you are focused, use the pencil to write your full name on the piece of paper.

Step 6: Use the candle's flame to light a corner of the paper on fire. Place the paper in the burner or cauldron so that it can burn undisturbed.

Step 7: Allow the paper and the candle to burn completely. When the paper turns to ashes, and the candle wick is burned out, bury the flower petals and ashes, preferably in a flowerpot or a garden. Do the same with the candle, but keep it separated from the other items. Say thanks to the universe and the deities.

Wealth Attraction Bath

This bath cocktail can be used at any time, but it's most effective if you use it just before something important that could bring money your way. For example, just ahead of a business meeting, job promotion or financial opportunity. You need:

- A couple of tablespoons of sea salt

- 3 drops of basil oil

- 3 drops of cinnamon oil

- 3 drops of pine oil

- A small amount of dried patchouli

- A small bottle, such as a travelling bottle for toiletries

Run your bath and add the oil and herbs. Soak for at least 15 minutes, and visualize the outcomes you want from the meeting or event, and how you want it to bring wealth to you. Before you drain the bathwater, fill the bottle and take it with you.

Law of Abundance Spell

This spell needs to be cast on the night of a full moon. Take a check from your check book and leave the date line empty. On the payee line, write your full name. In the amount box, write 'Paid in Full,' and on the line where the words should be written, write the same thing. On the signature line, write 'Law of Abundance.' Place the check somewhere safe and special to you. You are not actually asking for something, just for anything that may be due to you, which is why it works – 'need not greed.'

Lavender Money Spell

For this spell, you need a conjure bag, which is a red flannel bag used for magickal purposes. If you want to make one, you can find directions online, or you can get a witch to make one for you. The magick will probably be stronger if you make your own though.

Once you have your conjure bag, you need seven money items of different denominations, depending on your home currency. Your money will increase by seven times, or even seven times seven.

Mint Prosperity Spell

This spell needs to be cast in a sacred circle, in which you'll need to have a mint plant and your wallet. Once the circle is cast and the quarters called, take the mint to the Earth Quarter and draw a pentagram over it with your hand. Return the mint to the altar and rub it over your wallet. Now place a mint leaf in the wallet and carry it with you to attract prosperity.

All of these spells will work for you if you need wealth. It's perfectly natural to wish for wealth, and if you practice witchcraft, the next progression is to think you can cast a spell for wealth. However, do you need that wealth, or is greed telling you that you need it? If you are just wanting to build your bank balance, and don't really need more money, the wealth spells just won't work for you. You really need to understand that, and also understand that wealth isn't always measured by money.

Chapter 7: The basic and advance practice of candle magic

Candle magic is perhaps the least difficult type of spell casting, and all things considered, it doesn't require a ton of extravagant ritual or complex apparatuses. As it were, anybody with a light can do magic.

Recollect when you made a desire before you extinguished the candles on your birthday cake. A similar thought applies to flame enchantment, just rather than simply seeking after your desire to work out as expected, you're announcing your expectation. Things being what they are, the birthday candle ritual depends on three key supernatural standards:

- Decide on a goal.

- Visualize the end result.

- Focus your intent, or will, to manifest that result.

Types of Candles

Candles come in all shapes and sizes. You will find a wide variety among different occultist shops, body shops, or even grocery stores. It helps, however, to buy from shops that specialize in magickal intent so that if you have any questions, there will be somebody there who likely knows what they are talking about, compared to an average grocery store clerk.

The majority of witches and those who practice magick rituals will tell you that the size of the candle is not important, but if the candle is too big and takes three days to burn out, you may not want to use those in a spell that requires the candle to burn all the way down naturally, which is a requirement in most spells. Therefore, a giant, bulky candle can actually be counterproductive.

The main types of candles are tea lights, votive, tapers, columns, encased pillars, and free-standing pillars. All of these types can be used interchangeably, but the best kinds of candles to use in spells that require them to be burned all the way are votive and tapers. This is because their wicks are typically short, and they are generally the easiest to control. One of the most popular candle types are the menorah candles, which are about four inches in length and are sold in bulk at easily accessed places, such as the grocery store. They are white, thin, and unscented, which make them perfect for most kinds of spell work.

In a few cases, a spell or ritual may need a specific kind of candle, such as a candle shaped like a certain figure to represent a specific person or a seven-day candle. Below is a short list containing the intent of a few commonly used candles in these cases.

- *Female figure:* This is used to attract or repel someone specific but can also be used to represent someone close to you who identifies as female.

- *Male figure:* This is used to attract or repel someone specific but can also be used to represent someone close to you who identifies as male.

226

- *Couple:* Candles shaped like a couple are used to bring a married couple closer together.

- *Genitalia:* This one is pretty straight forward. It is used for arousal, passion, sexual desire, and fertility.

- *Buddha:* Good fortune, abundance, and luck

- *Devil:* A devil-shaped candle is used for temptations, whether to encourage or banish them.

- *The Cat:* This is used specifically for money spells, luck, or even protection.

- *Skull:* This candle shape is used to repel unwanted feelings or thoughts. It is also used for healing spells or cleansing.

- *Knob Candle:* The seven knobs that make up the body of this candle represent seven wishes.

It is highly suggested that you use a candle that has never been used for spell work. Don't just pick up a candle that you burned for your nighttime bath and use it in a money spell because you do not have anything else. If you do not feel like going out and buying a new candle that day, you should save your spell work for another day. According to most magickal beliefs, a candle, once lit, absorbs the vibrations caused by the many items around it. It is believed that this may lead to a negative or ineffective magickal outcome, so you must exercise caution.

Colors and What They Mean to a Wiccan

In our world, colors have many purposes. They are used in art to express a certain intention or mood, to stimulate the mind with subtle or winding patterns, or even to organize. To a Wiccan, colors play a vital role in spell casting and intent. Each color has a role and intention for our everyday lives. Certain days, feelings, and even numbers have a connection to a certain color.

Candles, with their superb symbolic qualities, allow us to work directly with the magickal properties that they possess. For hundreds of years, humans have associated different colors with certain qualities or events. For example, passion and love have always been associated with the color red, as it is the color of blood and the heart. The color green is ever-present during the growing season of the earth and, therefore, has long been associated with abundance and prosperity.

In order to accurately cast the spells highlighted in this book, you will need to choose your candle's color carefully, and, ideally, perform the spells on the day of the week in which the intent is clear. Utilizing these color and time correspondences in your magick reinforces the intent of your spell and makes it more potent.

Red: Red is a symbol of vitality, passion, intense emotions, fertility, desire, sexuality, and strength.

White: White represents purity, healing, the beginning of a phase, the ridding of malicious spirits, peace, and innocence.

Pink: Pink is the color of love, friendship, affection, reconciliation, and harmony.

228

Purple: Purple represents spirituality, wisdom, idealism, devotion, and spiritual strength, insight, and emotion.

Black: This color rids negativity. It represents protection, stability, dignity, and the end (but also seed to a new beginning).

Blue: Blue symbolizes healing, truth, wisdom, protection, spirit, and patience.

Brown: Brown represents solidarity, grounding, strength, endurance, and unity with nature.

Yellow: This color symbolizes happiness, achievement, inspiration, knowledge, completeness, and imagination.

Green: The color green represents abundance, wealth, growth, prosperity, employment, balance, and renewal.

Gold: Gold represents integrity, inner strength, self-realization, intuition, and understanding.

Silver: Silver is the color of intuition, vision, purity, healing, capacity, memory, and intelligence.

Orange: This color represents energy, stimulation, vitality, communication, happiness, and attraction.

Grey: Grey symbolizes contemplation, stability, reserve, and neutrality.

The Intent behind the Days of the Week

Monday: Monday is ruled by the moon, and deals with fertility, insight, wisdom, beauty, illusion, emotions, and dreams. The colors best used on this day are blue, white, and silver.

Tuesday: Tuesday is ruled by Mars, and deals with victory, success, courage, defense, logic, vitality, conviction. It is a good day to cast problem-solving spells. The colors best used on this day are black, red, and orange.

Wednesday: Wednesday is ruled by Mercury, and deals with luck, change, fortune, creativity, education, insight, and self-improvement. The colors best used on this day are orange, purple, and grey.

Thursday: Thursday is ruled by Jupiter, and deals with prosperity, wealth, healing, abundance, and protection. The best colors to use on this day are purple, green, and blue.

Friday: Friday is ruled by Venus, and deals with love, fertility, birth, romance, passion, friendship, and pregnancy. The best colors to use on this day are green, pink, and blue.

Saturday: Saturday is ruled by Saturn, and deals with wisdom, change, cleansing, motivation, and spirituality. The best colors to use on this day are black, purple, and brown.

Sunday: Sunday is ruled by the Sun, and deals with promotion, success, fame, prosperity, and wealth. It is a good day to cast money spells. The best colors to use this day are gold, yellow, green, and orange.

Now that the days and the colors have been covered, it is time to choose a candle. To choose the color, it is best to correlate your intentions with the color you pick and the day that you cast the spell. For example, if you want to cast a spell that will multiply your wealth, you will want to use gold, yellow, or green candle and cast a spell on a Sunday.

The potency of your desired spell entirely depends on how you choose to organize it. The closer you cast the spell to the intended day and with the right color, the more potent it will be. This is why it is of dire importance to choose your candle with deep thought and preparation.

Candle Magic Spell for Drawing Money

This spell is an easy and fun way to manifest more money in your life. It will bring together some of the other magical items you have learned about and will involve the use of a few additional items as well.

You will need the following:

- 3 green spell candles + holders

- Matches or a lighter

- Vervain essential oil

- Dried mint, crumbled into small pieces

- Dried basil, crumbled into small pieces

- A piece of parchment paper

- A carving tool, to carve a symbol into the wax (a pin, a needle, or knife)

- Several coins of various shapes, sizes, and country of origin

Steps for the Candle Magic Spell for Drawing Money

1. Cast a circle as desired.

2. At the altar, set your 3 green candles in an arc or semi-circle so that the top of the arc is away from you on the altar.

3. One at a time, pick up a candle and perform the following:

- Carve any symbols of prosperity that you like or that are a part of your practice into the wax, anywhere on the candle and all over the candle (you can look at runes and Celtic symbols if you aren't sure where to start). Rub off any wax that naturally sheds from carving.

- Rub essential oil on the candle (you can use your own blend and have it diluted in a carrier oil if that is desired).

- On the parchment paper, sprinkle the dried herbs so that they are all mixed together.

- Roll the anointed candle on the herbs and collect them on the outside of the candle.

- Say the following words or something similar, as you go through these steps for each candle:

"Candle magic born with me,

Help me to manifest my destiny.

I ask for money, riches, and wealth,

To come to me in the right good health.

This candle green will burn my truth,

To call to me abundance, forsooth.

The powers that be will hear my call,

To become richer now, and that is all.

233

And so it is"

4. With each candle carved and anointed, they can all be in their holders in the semi-circle as you sprinkle the coins in front of them, saying the following words:

"Money brought, and money sent,

I ask for riches by divine rite lent.

With open arms, I ask of thee,

To send me money, three times three!

So mote it be!"

5. Light the candles, and let them burn all the way to the end of the wick until they each go out.

6. If you have any remaining herbs from your candle rolling, you can now use them to light as incense on top of a charcoal disk in your cauldron.

7. Close the circle and bury the coins in the ground of your yard or garden.

This money spell can be modified to your own liking, but you can get a better picture of a fun way to use candles in your rituals and spells, using some other magical items and supplies.

Candle Magic Spell to Celebrate Imbolc

Imbolc is a time of year to celebrate the dawn of the Maiden (Triple Goddess) and the coming of Spring. It is a ritual typically celebrated with a lot of candles and the color white. You can modify this spell to your liking.

You will need the following:

- 10 white spell candles + holders

- Jasmine essential oil + carrier oil if desired (or Spring blend of your liking)

- White flowers of any kind

- Matches or lighter

- Hyacinth incense or a fragrance of first spring flowers

Steps for Candle Magic Spell to Celebrate Imbolc:

1. Cast your circle as desired.

2. Anoint each of your white candles with essential oil while you ponder the magic of the Maiden Goddess. You can even speak to her directly as you consecrate your candles.

3. Set them in their holders, and place them all over your altar space. You can also place them in other areas around the altar, as long as they are in places where they are seen and safe.

4. Light your incense of choice and lay the white flowers around. Try to place a few flowers near or next to each of your candles so that each one has a flower spray near it.

5. If you have flowers left over, you can set them anywhere that feels right. You can also just use flower petals if it is easier or more affordable than whole bunches of flowers.

6. Begin to light the candles and speak the following words, or something similar, as you do:

"Oh, Maiden Goddess of beauty bright,

Welcome back from Winter's night.

I ask you now to join me here,

By candlelight and flowers dear.

I welcome thee with all my heart and soul,

To bridge the gap between the dark and light worlds.

The time has come for Spring to be sprung,

Welcome, oh Maiden, may your powers be done!

And so it is."

7. Enjoy some delicious foods, herbal teas, or other brews as you sit by the candlelight and welcome the dawn of Spring with the Maiden divine.

Any spell can be enhanced with a little candle magic. Fire brightens your cause and purpose and joins every element together into one instrument of magic. Continue working with all the different colors, crafts, and variations of how to make magic with candles, and let them deliver your message to the Great Divine.

Most candle spells require the candle's flame to burn all the way down naturally, on its own, without being disturbed. However, it is hardly a good idea to leave a flame unattended, even in the form of a candle. Staying with the candle as it burns down could take hours, depending on the kind of candle one uses, and most do not have the time to spare. If you absolutely must leave your candle, simply place it in a safe place away from any flammable objects. An empty tub or sink are examples of safe places to leave the candle while you go about your daily business. It is also important to note that many oils used for anointing can be highly flammable and must be used with care. Some spells require the candles to be snuffed out, and it is easy for one to forget that there is oil on their fingers as they try to pinch the candle out. Handle these oils with extra caution.

As you explore and practice the magickal qualities of candles, you will soon take note that if you exercise the appropriate cautions and keep your focus, as well as a sincere intent, with harm to none, of course, you will begin to see your spell work flourish with success.

Chapter 8: Casting Circles

Casting circles is one of the basic skills used in witchcraft. It often the first thing that beginners will learn. The idea of casting circles is a bit complex, even if the techniques tend to be simple.

Casting a circle or circle-casting is the practice of creating a temporary space to perform a ritual or magic. By definition, it is round. While circle-casting is most commonly used by Wiccans, other Witches from different religions cast circles as well. The circle is a temporary temple, an area away from the ordinary world that can hold the magic you are working.

Typically, a circle is cast at the beginning of a rite by the high priestess and/or priest. Solitary practitioners are able to cast circles as well. After the spell work is done and the ritual is completed, the circle is released.

The circle is not a physical, but psychic boundary. It is not felt or seen by your regular senses. However, a circle can be detected energetically. It is also believed that this circle extends throughout all worlds and not just within our physical plane.

Why Should I Cast a Circle?

There are many different things that can interfere with your magic. Chaotic entities that feed your power, people with contrary wills, distractions from the world, are a few things that can interfere. Having a circle casting is one way to help shut out these influences and keep yourself focused. A magical trance can be psychically vulnerable, so a lot of witches will cast a circle to help protect their minds.

The outer barrier isn't the only important barrier of the circle. The inner barrier is just as important. Magical energy often bounces around and scatters throughout the Universe. The point of performing magic and rituals is to concentrate your energy on a purpose. Having a circle will allow you to gather more energy and hold onto it. If you call upon certain deities or spirits, a circle will offer them a cozy place to be during your rite.

So, you could say that a circle is meant to keep disturbances out and energy in. While this is very much a simplification, it is an easy way to look at it. It can also be viewed as a tool to improve the strength of your magic.

Do I Have to Cast a Circle?

You do not have to cast a circle. Not every tradition uses a circle. Egyptian, Norse, and other folk and shamanic magic practitioners work will without one. It is simply a useful technology and not a hard-and-fast rule.

How Big and What Shape Should My Circle Be?

The traditional size for a Wiccan circle is nine feet in diameter. Nine, or three times three, is a very important thing in Wicca. In many traditions, and within most covens, they will have a ritual nine-foot cord. They fold it in half and anchor it in the center and walk around in a circle to trace the circle's edge

Now, that's not to say you have to have a nine-foot circle. This is simply a suggestion. You can tailor your circle to the space you have available. You can make it too small, though.

To figure out if it is too small, gather your spell tools and yourself in the space you were thinking about using. If the circle you cast is so small that you could accidentally penetrate its edges while gesturing or reaching for something, then it is too small. Now, if the circle is being cast for a coven, the circle should be big enough so that everybody can maintain a comfortable distance from one another.

If, like most solitary practitioners, you only have a bedroom or study of some sort to work your magic in, a nine-foot circle is definitely not practical. It is better to have a smaller circle than a large circle that extends through furniture and walls. You typically don't want anything more in your circle than you, your altar, and tools for your spell work.

Casting Your Circle

It is always good to check and double check to make sure that you have everything with you before you cast your circle. Have your altar set up, your book of shadows with you, all of your spell and ritual tools, and anything else you may need in your space before you start casting your circle. Most people do not want to walk through their circle to get something once it has been cast. That said, if an emergency arises and you do need to leave quickly, then do so. Nothing catastrophic is going to happen if you leave your circle before closing your circle. A child and pet can also walk through your circle, and it won't disrupt anything.

Also, some people will draw a "door" if they need to leave their circle before their spellwork is finished using a wand or athame. You can also pretend that there is a "curtain" there that you walk through. When you reenter your circle, simply walk around the edge in a clockwise circle to help strengthen it again.

One last note before we jump into the circle casting methods, there are two words that you need to learn that may show up in some spells. The first is deosil. Deosil means clockwise. The second is widdershins. Widdershins means counterclockwise.

Simple Circle Cast

To begin, you will need to mark your circle. You first need to figure out where you want your circle to be. It doesn't matter if you are using the space where your altar is, doing it outside, or in your bedroom, you want to make sure it is somewhere you aren't going to be disturbed.

While you don't have to, some people will physically mark their circles with something meaningful. You can use a cord, crystals, or candles to mark your circle. You can also use crystals that correspond with the cardinal point.

Next, you will need to conjure up some energy that is going to protect and surround you and your work. Place yourself in the middle of what will be your circle. Allow yourself to relax and take a few deep breaths. Imagine that the top of your head is starting to open up like a funnel to take in a divine, white light. This is the crown of your head is will always have a strong connection with the Divine. You can open this up and amplify it whenever you want.

Bring your arms out so that your palms are facing out. Every time you take a breath in, picture yourself pulling all of that light into your crown, and every time you breathe out, push the light out through your palms to surround you with a protective shield. As your space fills with all of this energy, you may notice that you start to buzz or tingle, develop goosebumps, or feel uplifted.

Using the arm you write with, stretch it out to the side and point to the edge of your circle. Spin, three times, in a clockwise direction as you

241

mentally mark your circle using this divine light. Bring both hands above your head and say: "I ask that the God and Goddess bless this circle so that I might be free and protected within this space. So mote it be."

Your circle is now cast; you can start to perform your ritual or cast spells. To close this circle, simply spin counterclockwise and feel the protective light dissipate.

Advanced Circle Casting

You'll need a compass and four candles. The four candles can be all white, or you can have one blue, one red, one yellow, and one green.

To start, take your compass and find the four cardinal points. Put the candles at each of these points. If you have the colored candles, the green one goes at North, yellow at East, red at South, and blue and West.

Begin at the North candle, light it, and repeat: "Guardians of the North, element of Earth, I call upon thee to be present during this ritual. Please join me now and bless this circle."

Move to the East candle, light it, and repeat: "Guardians of the East, element of Air, I call upon thee to be present during this ritual. Please join me now and bless this circle."

Move to the South candle, light it, and repeat: "Guardians of the South, element of Fire, I call upon thee to be present during this ritual. Please join me now and bless this circle."

Move to the West candle, light it, and repeat: "Guardians of the West, element of Water, I call upon thee to be present during this ritual. Please join me now and bless this circle."

Take your wand or athame and point it towards the edge of your circle. Walk in a clockwise direction three times and picture a white light rushing into the crown of your and being pushed out through your arm and through your tool, to the edge of your circle.

Take your place in the middle of the circle and feel your circle being filled with divine light. Say: "God and Goddess, guardian angels, and spiritual guides, please be present with me during this ritual. Bless this circle and keep me protected. No unwanted entities are welcome here; only pure, divine beings are invited into this space. This circle is cast. So mote it be."

You can now start your ritual and spellwork. When closing the circle, make sure you blow out your candles in the opposite order you lit them and thank the elements for being present.

Circle Casting

This is a rather simple circle casting, but you are going to need three, four, six, or nine things of a certain object. You can pick whichever number and whichever item resonates with you, but each other should be objects that are similar. For example, you could use four houseplants, nine candles, three rocks, or six seashells. If you have any sacred items, feel free to use those.

To cast your circle, start by holding your objects in your hands and create the intention for them as you move around your circle and place them to mark off the edge of your circle. If you are using candles, you will want to make sure that you have them placed on something safe so that you can light them safely without them catching something on Fire.

If you feel there are some words you would like to say as you do this, you can do it now, but this circle casting does not require that. Once you have placed all of your items, you are free to do your spell or ritual work.

To close this circle, all you need to do is pick your items in the opposite direction that you placed them.

Closing Your Circle

Once all of the work has been done, you will need to close your circle. When you release your circle, it gives the energies within a chance to dissipate and the room to return to its pre-ritual state. There are many different ways to close your circle, like ringing a bell, performing the casting in reverse, or picturing the walls dissolving. Gathering up your tools and putting them away will also help to scatter out the energy.

If you forget to close your circle, or you simply don't close it well, the circle will eventually fade on its own in a few minutes or hours. If you regularly use that area for your ritual work, then it may slow down the dissipation. That doesn't mean you should make it a habit to just walk away. You should always close your circle.

Chapter 9: Meditation and Dreams

It is scientifically proven that meditation is good for everyone. It connects you to your mind, body, and spirit on all levels and helps you attain a higher state of awareness while it promotes physical health. Meditation is often linked to spirituality and its many practices and you may not think it would be involved in the Wiccan practice, but it is one of the main attributes.

In almost every spell and ritual I perform, there is a moment of meditation. I have to meditate in order to connect with my inner knowing and the divine source energy I am working with. It only takes a few moments and it brings me into deeper closeness with the energy of all things, providing me with the ultimate balance.

Meditation isn't something you have to teach yourself how to do well; it comes naturally during your craftwork and if you are simply open to being with yourself and your Magick, then you are in meditation. Overall, meditation is just a natural part of communing with your own soul as well as the soulful energy present in all things in life.

The purpose of learning to be a witch is to enhance your life. You can do this with magic. You can find yourself entirely engulfed in a new and more adventurous lifestyle. Enhancing your life with magic takes a lot of practice.

Magic is not something that comes easily to most people. It takes getting out of your head to achieve anything. Life enhancement is a big part of the Wiccan culture, and that is what draws a lot of people to it.

However, despite a lot of people being drawn to this religion, there are a lot of people that leave it as well, and that is because they are not willing to put in the effort when it comes to enhancing their lives.

245

They expect just to say a few phrases and the magic happens. This is due in part to how the media portrays magic. Look at the popular television series Charmed. It shows three witches who fight evil, and all they do is use a few simple spells, and that is not reality. The same goes for most literature out there. Wiccans are portrayed as people who get together in the woods, say a few spells, wave a few herb sticks, and boom—magic. It is harder than these portrayals.

Spells take practice and require executing multiple times to master results. There are also several different parts to spells that you must master, once mastered; you get to move on to the next level and practice those spells for hours on end before you get any results. To become a powerful witch, you must put in a lot of time and be dedicated to your craft. The cost of being lazy will have you remain at the same level for ages.

You cannot expect life enhancement to make your life one of leisure. This is yet another reason people leave Wicca. They expect to be able to make their crush fall in love with them and to use magic to become rich, and that just doesn't happen—at least not right away. Those things take hard work and dedication.

People have also joined and fell off the wagon, by becoming black witches. They found out ways to make themselves rich, and force someone to fall in love with them. However, that magic comes at a price, and the price is not cheap.

These people will literally sell their souls to a demon to achieve what they want. You want to stay away from these witches. If one were to die from a black witch, their soul would be tortured for all eternity. You will not be reincarnated; you will be sent straight to purgatory.

Purgatory is where the spirits of people who have done evil things and used black magic go to in the afterlife. It is not where you want to end up. Your spirit will be torn to pieces every day until the end of time, and even though your body will be dead, you will still be alive to feel it because you are your spirit. Let those who join Wicca and turn to black witches' parish on their own accord.

Anyways, how do you enhance your life with magic? You connect with the earth. You connect with other people. You fill your life with things that will enrich you and bring you joy. These things are possible with magic. It may seem that magic can't do anything that you can't do yourself, and maybe there may be some truth to that. However, being in the Wiccan religion, it makes it a lot easier to do these things with magic, rather than without magic.

Here's how magic can help you enhance your life:

Making Friends - Friends are hard to come by, and even if you have a big group of friends, they may not be the best of friends to have. As humans, we are attracted to what is known as shiny people.

These are usually the people that are fun to hang out with. However, these shiny people are generally not the best people to be around, as they seem only to hang around if you can do something for them. Humans are also easily drawn in by dramatic people. These people are the ones that are always loud, and always doing something that they shouldn't be doing. It is exciting, and it is fun. However, if they turn on you, it can be an unpleasant experience. These people can be toxic, and toxicity is the best way to ruin a friendship.

You want to hang onto these people because you think that they bring a lot of joy to your life, but the truth is they are only dragging you down. Usually, people feel obligated at the requests of shiny people—

starting to ring any bells? To spot a toxic friend all you should do is try to do something that you want to do for yourself or ask for a favor, and watch them try to drag you down or not participate.

This is where magic comes in. Magic will draw in the right type of friends so that you can make a lasting bond with them, and not have to worry about them walking out of your life because you reach a milestone in your life, and can't take them to the mall twenty times a week anymore. Instead, these friends will root for you, encourage you to be the best that you can be, and they will not bat an eye when you do something to improve your life.

Magic will help you find the love of your life and someone who will bring you soup when you are sick. You will attract the type of person who doesn't care if you are wearing your pajamas all day or wearing a $300 dress when you see them. These friends are hard to come by, and magic will fill your life with these friends. This way you can ensure that you are making friends with the right kind of people.

Help You Find True Love - True love is the hardest to find. You may fall in love several times in your life, and you may even get married, but chances are it is not everlasting love. Love is everywhere, and at times it can be easy to find.

However, true love hard to find, because they are not looking for the right identifiers. They want excitement and butterflies forever, and while those are all well and good to have with your partner twenty years from now, the butterflies eventually fade, or they will not happen as frequently. When that happens, you want to be still able to wake up and kiss the person beside you good morning and feel good about it. If you don't, how will you ever love them for the rest of your life?

Find someone who even when the butterflies fade, gives you a warm feeling in your heart, and makes you happy. True love is the love where you can argue all day, and then laugh and be happy for months on end. True love is waking up next to the one you love, and seeing them in their most vulnerable state, and loving them even more.

This love is the love that people strive for endlessly, and it is a love that not a lot of people find. Some are tricked into thinking they found it because the butterflies last longer than usual, then they get married, and five years later, they get a divorce. This is because they just found someone that they lusted after longer than usual.

Enter magic. Magic will bring you someone who can make your heart race, and make you feel calm at the same time. It will bring you the person who will hold your hair when you are sick, and rub your feet when they are sore. It will bring you, someone, who will help with the dishes for the rest of your life. Someone who gets up with you at two in the morning to bake cookies when you can't sleep.

You want someone who is encouraging the Wiccan religion so that you can be yourself around them. Once you let go and let fate show you who you should truly be with, these spells will help take your relationships, and make them strong, and at the same time help you form a bond with someone to create an unbreakable relationship.

Letting fate take over is the hardest part. You want to find someone who you like, but most people do not trust fate to make that choice because they already have someone in mind to be their forever love. They do not want to relinquish that control for fear of something going away.

Are you going to fall in love with someone who is truly the one for you, or are you going to spend the rest of your life fighting with the person you married, and using countless spells to try to fix your relationship? The choice is for you alone, but with a little patience, and a little time, you will find the person that you have truly been waiting for.

Courage - If you are a person who is not particularly courageous in any aspect of life, do not fret. You are not alone. The average person has at least one area in their life where they lack in the courage department. This can range from being talking to strangers or trying to make it up in the business ladder. There are many parts of life that require courage; it is impossible to be courageous enough for all of them on your own.

For instance, you may be able to go skydiving, but the thought of talking to that gorgeous person who has caught your eye completely terrifies you. And that is okay because you can't be courageous at everything. Or maybe you are great at talking to people, and doing public speaking, but you are terrified to ride an elevator.

There are different fears out there, and you cannot conquer your fears without courage. A lot of people overlook magic and how it can boost your courage levels up. Courage is important, and spells can make you a little stronger. As a witch, it is one of the most important things you can have because you are going to have to stand up to people.

Whether it be to save an old tree from a company that wants to tear it down, or stopping a black witch from ruining someone's life, lots of acts require courage.

Magic can help, and it can bring you so much more than a little bit of courage. Magic can make you feel like you can take on the world. You will feel like you can do anything, and that is what you want. Just remember that the effects are not permanent, and you may have to reapply the spell a couple of times.

Magic gives you the courage until you find it on your own, after a few times of realizing how great it feels to stand up to something that terrifies you, you will not need the spell anymore because you will be able to be courageous on you own.

Luck - Luck is hard to come by, and lots of people need it. You need luck when you are playing the lottery, and you need luck when you ask the love of your life to marry you, and that is something that not a lot of people think of either. Just like courage, luck is something that you need to get by in life. It is not always hard work that you should rely on because sometimes, hard work can only get you so far. Such as in a big law firm, where you and the partner's pet are vying for a promotion.

You may do the harder jobs, and work the hardest, but they have the advantage of you because they are a favorite. In this case, a little luck may help. Luck can ensure that they are paying attention to your hard work, rather than having a clear winner picked out before the race even begins.

You can use a few simple spells to make talismans and good luck charms, as well as just cover yourself in an aura of good luck with some spells; these spells are generally not difficult. However, the more luck you desire, the stronger the witch you would have to be, because, the stronger the witch, the more powerful the spell. You also have to "reapply" less when you are more powerful. Even more, a reason to practice, right? Everyone wants to be lucky, so make sure to work on becoming the best witch that you can be.

A real-life scenario would be a job interview. You want to use these spells without abandon, because the more luck you have, the better off you will be in an interview, and you will hopefully land the job with ease. Don't get too cocky, even though you may apply and interview, if you are not a good fit, you may not get the job no matter how much magic you use.

Recall there is a major difference between confidence and being cocky. Confidence is knowing you can do the job. Being cocky is thinking that without any training you can do it better than everyone else. Cocky thinks that you are a shoe-in for a job you have never had any experience with. Confidence is knowing that you are a strong and quick learner and will be good at the job without any training. You want to be confident, yet humble. Know that you are not the perfect person for the job, but also know that you are the best candidate.

Clarity of Mind - Have you ever had a question that is burning in your mind or a decision that you had to make that was really hard? Did it take you longer than you care to admit to achieve what you wanted with these scenarios?

That happens to everyone at some point in their life, and it is entirely normal. You want to have a clear mind, and it is harder to achieve than you would think. And, even if you clear your mind, a lot of times it is still hard to find a clear answer. You search and search, but there are pros and cons to everything.

This makes it hard to find yourself the time to do what you want to do when you want to do it because you are still agonizing over making the decision or trying to figure everything out—decisions can be messy.

If you are having trouble figuring out where to go in life, you can use a spell to help you figure things out. There are many spells that help you open your mind to make the right decision, and a lot of it has to do with Divination. Yes, prophesying helps you make the right choices because you will be able to get an idea of what will be the outcome of your choice. There are spells out there to clear your mind, and there are spells to get the answers that you desire.

These spells are the ones that you want to use to find your way in life and really make the right choices. Perhaps you are wondering if your spouse is cheating, and you do not know if you should pursue the matter. Do a spell and get the answers you are looking for. Don't feel guilty if they are not cheating. You are not going through their personal effects, rather doing your research before confronting them and that is what a rational person does.

Banishing Evil - Let's face it, a lot of times, we are surrounded by evil. This world is a demonic playground, no doubt about it. In these times, it becomes harder to find a pure environment, and a lot of times those who are good are under attack from the world.

Have you ever felt like the entire world was against you, and even though the evil people seem to be living good lives, you are miserable?

That is what a lot of people deal with when they try to lead decent lives because it seems that life does not want good in it and rewards evil. There are ways to keep yourself pure and keep your environment pure as well. Have a good place to do your magic. You want your mind to be pure and clean from attacks of other, evil witches as well.

There are several spells out there for purifying not only the area but your mind as well. One of the most common spell types for purification is known as smudging.

If you are regularly practicing, you should probably smudge your area before each spell, but if you are not practicing often, once a week or biweekly should suffice. Just make sure that you purify it before you do a spell. The purer you keep it, the more effect your spells will have on your life and evil forces will not be able to counteract your spells.

There are several other spells that you can use to make sure that you are keeping your mind and environment pure from the evil that lurks around.

Candles are essential to this (white candles especially). They give you pure energy in which to perform your spells. White candles act as a channel directly to the Goddess herself to help you keep other entities from answering your calls. Although most spells do not call for white candles, it is best to light one whenever you do a spell.

Healing - As you a Wicca beginner, you can relieve side effects and many other issues that dwell under and on top of the surface of one's skin. Mental illnesses are something that you can help with. While you cannot cure these diseases, you can help alleviate the symptoms of things such as depression and anxiety.

You can also help someone who has PTSD sleep better at night. Magic when used to help people, including yourself, is wonderful. It also does not take a lot of magical strength to help alleviate the symptoms of illnesses, unlike with pain and suffering from a major physical injury.

Prosperity - Have you ever been unemployed and found yourself searching high and low for any source of income just to keep the lights on? It isn't fun, and nowadays it is getting harder to find jobs that are enough to pay the bills and keep food on the table. That is the downside of the world we live in. Jobs are becoming electronic and outsourced. And unfortunately, unless you live in a commune, you must have money to survive.

There are a lot of spells to help you have the upper hand with prosperity. It is a good idea to find a plethora of them to douse yourself with luck and prosperity if you are ever in need of it. The same goes for healing spells.

Master the Art of Meditation

It is best understood that meditation is a silence through which you can listen to your higher self. With concentration and focusing attention on the higher level of consciousness that exists in each of us, meditation helps. A daily meditation session can clear the cluttering mind and maintain a clear communication channel.

An Introduction to Meditation

It is best to describe meditation as' listening.' It is the art of hearing the Higher Self or the Inner Self. Some describe it as hearing the gods, or the creative force. It could simply be said that the Higher Consciousness is listening, even. All these things can be meditation. Meditation leads to personal advancement when used properly. Meditation is the simplest of all spiritual advancement techniques and can be practiced in a group or even on its own.

Meditation is a practice that calms the conscious mind, the mind that deals with everyday activities and life as you know it, and allows you to channel your higher consciousness, also referred to as subconscious, the part of your mind that is responsible for involuntary bodily functions, reflex actions, and what you might call' Universal Memory.'

The Dynamics of Meditation

To fully understand the dynamics of meditation, first the make-up of the human consciousness needs to be realized, and it needs to be recognized that humans are both physical and spiritual beings. These two facets of human nature are tied together at the vital centres, which are referred to by their Sanskrit descriptions –

Chakras. During the act of meditation, psychic energy travels through these chakras. The *kundalini* force is a potent force known as the 'Serpent Power', and once the *kundalini* flows within you, your chakras begin opening up in succession.

Mastering Meditation

If you approach the art with the wrong technique, or even simply approach the art without any technique at all, you may fail in meditation. Concentrating on your' third eye,' the area one inch above your brow line and one inch inward of your forehead, is believed to concentrate energy in your highest chakra. In the Third Eye meditation technique, the direction in which you focus your eyes also plays an important role. Turning your eyes above the horizon has to do with the energy in your higher consciousness and your spiritual energy. Focusing your eyes straight out is about your conscious mind, while focusing down is about the subconscious mind.

It is best to select a position to meditate in when performing meditation. Meditation is known to be performed in the lotus position conventionally, but this position is not always comfortable, so it is better to be comfortable in another position of your own choice.

You are free to assume any position as long as your spine is straight– either sitting on the floor, on a chair, or lying on your back. The more comfortable you are, the more energy and mind you can concentrate on. When selecting an area to do your meditation, it is important that the chosen space is quiet and, of course, your cleaned and censored circle will be the best choice.

However, if for whatever reason you select another space, it's best to clean up the space and censor it like you did with your Circle. While facing a specific direction in meditation is not necessarily important, facing the east is sometimes suggested.

Your comfort, however, is the most important thing, and so if you have a better view in another direction, do not hesitate to face it! You are also free to select the time of the day you meditate, as is the position you choose and the direction you face and the space you choose. It is best, however, to stick to that particular time of day to meditate every day so that your meditation is consistent. Thus, choosing the most convenient time is best, one that will be quiet and peaceful but still achievable every day.

It needs to be done consistently to remain successful and to be successful in meditation. Some recommend meditation between fifteen and twenty minutes a day, twice a day. You might get by with a single fifteen-minute session per day at the bare minimum. Consistency is key again– so it's important to stick to the number of sessions as well as the times.

How to Do a Wiccan Meditation

Wicca is really a modern religion full of ancient traditions of witchcraft. The practices of drawing from the moon and invocation of the goddess are identical to mediation, but you might deepen the Wicca practice and promote peace with the divine through daily meditation to improve clarity and serenity.

Grant your mind a deep meditation status.

Relaxation instruments like candles, incense, and singing will assist you in a relaxing relaxation state. You can listen to a singing CD or sing the name of your favorite deity or goddess. Keep the lights low or disable them.

Choose a relaxation spot that resonates with you.

You'll also want to practice your counseling outside if you practice Celtic Wicca. Your love for nature's sights smells and sounds your meditation. Most Wiccans prefer to mediate on their altars, especially when the weather is not good. The key is to choose a place to meditate that will naturally make you feel relaxed. Make sure the room is silent and not disturbed as you mediate indoors.

Find a convenient spot.

If you sit down or lie down or walk, as long as you are comfortable and relaxed, it doesn't matter. Your goal is to be alert and receptive, so don't fall asleep so comfortable.

Decide which kind of mediation you are going to do.

Passive meditation is the way to allow images to arise in your mind and to focus on these images or symbols. You should consciously meditate on the image or symbol on which you want to focus, with open or closed eyes. If you allow a symbol to enter you or if you choose the symbol, send the image that you have selected. Subjects to be considered include: Magic / magic God / Goddess Magic(ies) Number(s)Tree(s), Flower(s) or plants Gems (crystalline, amethyst, sapphire,

Close your eyes. Close your eyes. Concentrate for a few minutes on your intake.

Observe breathing for yourself. Bring your sensing to your feet if your breathing is slow and steady and shift your focus all the way up to your body. Remove any tension in your body that you feel. You can also pause and reflect on stress and wonder why there is pressure

Visualize positive energy that fills your life.

Respire in and picture your feet with white light to the top of your head. Exhale the white light and let it loose into your magic space.

If you practice passive meditation, allow thoughts to surface.

If you are fascinated by a thought or image, start focusing on it, then let it go and allow the next thought to surface. When you choose to do active meditation, close your eyes, and focus your attention on the symbol or picture you have selected. (If your thoughts begin to fall, return to the focus of your breathing and start over.) You can keep your eyes open and concentrate on your preferred symbol if you prefer. Give it your full and look at all facets of it.

Maintain a notebook and pen in the area.

Perhaps you want to pick up ideas or draw pictures during your meditation. Go to your meditative state once you have done that. End your session with thanks.

Conclusion

Wicca is a powerful way of life. It is an essential reality that can bring you so much inner harmony, peace, abundance, fertility, and prosperity on all levels of your life. You can give great thanks to the life that you have as we are all here to live and seek our truth with the Great Mother and the Father Sky, held by the universe as we explore our eternal destinies and practice knowing who we are from deep within the blanket of Magickal truth.

I am here to give you all of that faith in yourself and knowledge of the Wiccan path so that you can further your own Magick and self-discovery. I hope that you have found the information that you needed to inspire an even deeper existence within the craft you are creating in your life.

Let these ideas, teachings, guidelines, and tutorials help you gain the confidence you need to support a fully alive and awakened Wiccan practice of your own. You are your true power and to worship the divine in all things is the essence of wholeness within your life and yourself.

As you move forward on your journey, continue to teach yourself new concepts, histories, methodologies, and transformations to help you build your practice into the work of art it is destined to be. Let your intuition be your guide and give you all of the courage you need to fulfill your dreams of Magick.

Anything you do from here forward will be a gift to getting yourself on track with your own spells, rituals, altar space, Book of Shadows and daily practices. There is such abundance in this way of life and so many ways to enjoy it. You can be truly crafty and creative with your work and your inner world to bring more harmony into your life, the second main take away from this book.

The final takeaway is that Wicca brings you into divine connection with all of the energies of the universe. It shows you that we all have a significant part to play in the energy of all creation and that as you practice your rituals and spells, you are declaring that you are present and available to live your life through Magick and awareness of all that is around you.

Take these lessons to heart and do with them what you will. Harm none and remember the Rule of Three. Let the blessings of life unfold through the seasons along with the cycles of the Sun and Moon. Give thanks to the wind, the water, the heat of the fire, and the firm soil underfoot. Breathe Magick into your life every day and ask to know what you must in order to keep growing in your powerful path of Magick.

Introduction

At one point, witchcraft was considered a legend. Not now. Not anymore.

In today's world, witchcraft does not just exist, but it thrives among the masses. Who are the masses that we are referring to? After all, it is not as if we see a lot of witches roaming around the streets of New York, unless they are cosplaying.

Sure, you do not see many witches out in the open, but that does not mean they do not exist. Not all witches wear black clothing with hairstyles that look like they want to defy the laws of gravity and eyeliner so dark that they could absorb all light.

Not that gravity-defying hairstyles and black eyeliner are bad. However, people have this perception that witches are outcasts. Even though most witches choose to keep their practices a secret, they do not consider themselves as outcasts. However, they do not avoid society. They do not shut themselves in a dark room devoid of any light and with enough witch décor that it could become the scene for the next Exorcist movie.

They are among us all.

In fact, many witches are fairly open about their beliefs, preferring to engage with people and connect with like-minded individuals. If you browse through the vast universe of the internet, then you are bound to come across groups of witches who regularly host meetings, events, and activities. People are free to join them and learn more about their world.

Just what are these witches? Are they people who worship dark magic and sinister entities? Do they create potions inside a large cauldron where they mix odd ingredients like elephant toes and a gecko's tail just so they could win the lottery?

Not even close.

The witches you see today are thoughtful, intelligent, compassionate, and community-conscious people. Many of them have regular jobs and take meaningful part in cultural and societal activities. Witchcraft is a not a devolution of the human belief system; one that takes us back to times of superstition. Rather, one could think of it as an evolution of human beliefs; a step-forward if you will.

Witchcraft is far more relevant in today's world than many of the religions practiced around the world. It focuses on social and personal responsibility. It accepts the fact that the universe has mysteries we are not completely aware of and that we should raise our consciousness to higher levels. Some of the concepts that are ingrained in the religion of witchcraft are: respect for nature, equal rights for all, planetary care, brotherly and sisterly love, and family bonds. Yes, witchcraft is a religion and it is not just because people believe it to be so. It is because the U.S. courts had declared it so in 1986.

When reading the above, most people are rather taken aback. They don't expect witchcraft to be that forward-thinking. What they do not realize is that the reality of the situation is that witchcraft is a way of life that expands our horizons about the planet called our home, the people we interact with, and about ourselves.

With this newfound recognition about the ways of witchcraft, numerous people end up becoming "Seekers," or those who are looking to adopt a witch's lifestyle. How can one become part of it? There lies the problem.

If you would like to join the Christian faith, then you know that your first course of action would probably be to approach a church. For Muslims, their building of faith is a mosque and for Hindus, a temple dedicated to a specific god. When it comes to witchcraft, there is not an official establishment that governs the matter of members. If you are looking for information to help you understand more about the religion, then you are going to find it. However, if you are seeking ways to join it, then you might find yourself at an impasse.

Witches congregate together in groups known as covens. Most of these covens are still wary about new members that they do not simply open their doors and roll out the red carpet for anybody. Who can blame them? People still talk about witches as though they are discussing a new species of mole rat.

Here is the thing: witches part of covens are happy to change the misconception people have about them. They are willing to assist in your quest to figure out the religion. Getting into the coven is another matter altogether.

Most would-be witches, out of sheer frustration, simply end up creating their own covens or go solo. When this happens, these witches often end up feeling "out in the woods," in a manner of speaking. In other words, they become lost. They are unsure of what sources they should use as reference for understanding witchcraft, often drawing upon any or all available sources they encounter. This becomes rather dangerous because they might always take information from reliable sources. Moreover, there are also many covens that base their beliefs on strange rituals with sufficient helpings of Satanism and Voodoo. With such odd practices, witchcraft tends to get a bad rep and new witches are often lured into false practices.

Witchcraft is a rather "loose" religion. It does have some foundational tenets and ritual patterns, but it is not like other religions where the rules are specific regarding various facets of life. It is for this reason that witches can expand practices into different areas. Think of witchcraft as a river. There is a path that it takes, from the top of the mountain to the sea that it connects to eventually. Along the way; however, the river can branch out into numerous tributaries. The same rule applies to witchcraft. Each of the tributaries represent the different covens that exist today, moving away from the main "flow" of beliefs, but taking their own journey.

This is why it becomes necessary for people beginning on their journey into the world of witchcraft to have their own guide. Using this guide, they will able to understand witchcraft better and with the right information. This guide can help these individuals — or a new coven — practice their beliefs in a way that holds the values of witchcraft. It also helps individuals become part of covens easily by having knowledge that is as good as — if not better than — any of the members of the coven.

Christianity has a few denominations such as Roman Catholic, Protestant, Methodist, and so on. It is the same with witchcraft. As you navigate the religion, you might discover various denominations. Just like how one form of Christianity is not right for everyone, one section of witchcraft does not work for every person. But that is what makes witchcraft exemplary. We are all different. Each of us are part of different cultures and ethnic backgrounds. We have certain principles and general guidelines that we use to navigate life.

Witchcraft is a journey about you. It is about bringing out the best part of you, all the while teaching you how to respect yourself, others around you, and the world as a whole. It is akin to the journey one

265

takes when they practice yoga in that it is spiritual as much as it is magical.

While this book is mainly prepared to act as a guide, you can also think of it as a witchcraft course, one that will guide you through many aspects of the religion and instill the right information.

With that in mind, there is so much that we are going to understand together. After all, I am going to be guiding you as a friend. Think of the very act of reading this book as joining your first coven.

You are going to be filled with sufficient wisdom to venture forth on your own path and either become a witch all by yourself or discover a real coven that is meant for you.

Welcome to the world of witchcraft.

Bright blessings.

Chapter 1: Being a Wiccan and Being a Witch

This chapter is meant to help to further help you identify which category you are going to fall into should you start practicing witchcraft on a consistent basis. The term witchcraft and Wicca are often used interchangeably, as well as the term of a witch. It can get confusing, so this is meant to make it a little easier to understand the different labels and terminologies, so you can further develop your own sense of what it means to practice witchcraft.

First, as stated witchcraft refers to the worldview and practices associated with rituals that are believed "to harness and focus cosmic psychic energies to bring about some desired change". These actions and practices are also known as magic. Modern witchcraft as it is known today is apparently the largest subset of Neo-paganism, which translates literally to a new-paganism. Within those who practice witchcraft, the largest section of approximately 600,000 people in the United States identify as a Wiccan. This means that they follow Wicca as a religion. Wicca was recognized as officially being a religion in the United States in 1985, and since has branched off into several other subsets.

The differences between the smaller subsections of Wicca are often small. Alexandrian Wicca was founded by Alex Sanders in 1960, and is often confused with the traditional Gardernian Wicca. Their differences lie within the names of their tools use, deity and elemental games differing, as well as small changes within the rules of what is needed to practice certain rituals.

Algard Wicca is a fusion of both Alexandrian and Gardnerian Wicca, founded in 1972.

Dianic Wicca is a strictly feminist tradition, growing out of the United States that focuses solely on the importance of the Goddess rather than constantly pushing the notion of gender polarity of the original Gardnerian tradition. (Traditional Wicca celebrates the union of a male God and a female Goddess.) This form of Wicca focuses on the plight faced by woman, and applies a very female-centered focused approach to all issues as they arise.

Druidic Wicca believes that all nature is God-like and that everything in nature is connected. Little is known about the rituals and magic applied, as Druids have historically been known to maintain their history through oral communication sole. They have more of a metaphysical element within their traditions and beliefs than the original Garderian Wicca does.

Solitary Wicca is the kind of Wicca that most people practice in the modern world, when they are first introduced and drawn into the religion. Clearly, due to the title, this form of Wicca is practiced alone, without the use of a coven; which is a group of witches of whom practice spells and rituals together and meet during certain times of the year that are most important in the Wiccan Calendar. This is more than likely where you are going to begin your journey, should you choose to identify with the core beliefs of what it means to be Wiccan (which will be listed later).

Eclectic Wicca is the practice of one's own Wiccan traditions, or the blending of other traditions into one's own practice. This form of Wicca doesn't strictly follow one set of rules in accordance to practice.

Now that you have learned about the different kinds of Wiccan traditions, it is time talk about the concept of witchcraft and how it is linked, or not linked to being a Wiccan. As this book strives to focus on the spells and magic (spelled with a 'k' in the Wiccan religion), the concept of being a Wiccan is going to sit separate from these actions independently. Witchcraft is precisely that; the actions that attempt to have influence over energy and outcomes in our daily lives with specific tools. Some people who practice magic, belong to covens, or participate in rituals do not call what they are doing witchcraft, as they do not enjoy the negative association with the word 'witch' and its historical connotations. That goes the same for those who do not want to call themselves a witch; the term may be too embedded within pop culture references for a person to feel like they can claim it.

Then there are others who use the term witch as a method of re-claiming a title that one had such a negative association ; they take pride in their title as witches because they are living as modern example as to why the beliefs and assumptions about witches were incorrect.

Therefore, in simplicity, you do not have to be Wiccan to practice witchcraft, nor do you have to practice witchcraft to be Wiccan. Many people who do not practice witchcraft do not call themselves witches for this reason, but still commit themselves to the core beliefs that Wicca promotes. There are many forms of witchcraft that have excited, and still do exist, outside the realm of Wicca and its other subsections. In fact, there are so many other versions of Wicca, non-

Wicca witchcraft, and forms of Paganism that make the forging of one's own spiritual path so intriguing, simply because it does not rely on a rigid list of rules that one must abide by.

Chapter 2: Understanding witchcraft

What makes someone a witch?

There is absolutely no one on this earth that can know if you're a witch other than you. As I mentioned above, witchcraft includes so many different practices and beliefs and if you resonate with *any of them*, then you can call yourself a witch. That being said, I know that it can be really hard to pinpoint if you're actually a witch or just enjoy the culture. As I said, many people don't consider themselves witches, simply Wiccans and you might not know if this is your path or if you are in fact a witch. I am going to outline below the characteristics of a witch as well as the signs that you might be one. You can also look into your past or childhood (I have done this) and you'll probably find an instance or two where you were in touch with your witchy side.

Characteristics of a witch

Witches are very in tune with mother nature. They love being outdoors and are able to feel a spiritual energy when in the presence of nature. They also feel an overwhelmingly spiritual connection to the moon and might even feel themselves being drawn to it on the night of the full moon. Witches love animals and plants which often means they are vegetarian or vegan. Witches who do eat meat or processed foods will often feel sluggish or like their energy is being drained. This is especially true after eating fast food.

Witches are very aware of the energy in a location or with a person. They can feel negative or positive energy very strongly. Witches will often feel an overwhelming sense of energy (either good or bad) when in the presence of a location with long histories, such as an ancient ruin, or an old house. They also feel a very strong energy when in the presence of a cemetery, war zone or another place that has a history of death.

Because witches are so in tune with energy, it means they are very empathetic and even emotional. Witches can strongly feel the energy of a person who is suffering. Hospitals are a very overwhelming experience for a witch. He or she will pick up on the energy of the people in the hospital and could even break out into tears for no reason. Witches can be seen as irrationally emotional. This is simply because they can pick up on the energy of other people and so they might cry or get upset even if they have no reason to feel that way. This makes witches feel a strong need to help and heal others which is a big reason for why they partake in witchcraft. Most of the time it is for the healing and wellbeing of those around them.

Witches are human and they look like everyone else to the naked eye but deep down they know they were put on this earth to do more than the average person. For this reason, witches may always carry a sense of feeling different or like they're not like everyone else. This is often very prominent in the childhood and teenage years. They have interests that differ from their schoolmates and often search for movies, books, music and hobbies that are considered alternative.

If a witch is going through teenage years or early adulthood without knowing he/she is a witch, this will cause a lot of frustration and anger. Teen witches who do not know they are witches will have a lot of teen angst whether they show it outwardly or keep it to themselves. This frustration and inner struggle will subside once the witch starts practicing witchcraft.

Signs that you are a witch

The most common signs that you are a witch.

- You feel an overwhelming tie to nature, this includes animals, the environment, plants and the universe.

272

- You feel the presence of a feminine goddess, especially in the presence of the moon.

- You have premonitions or dreams that come true.

- A deep curiosity or interest in all things occult and magick.

- You have the ability to manifest your desires or have an impact on the universe. For example, if you are thinking about a friend and then they text you. Or you forgot your wallet and a friend offers to pay for dinner without you asking.

- You feel a duty to help and heal others. You want to take away suffering from both humans and animals.

- You don't like the doctor and find yourself rejecting traditional medicine. You even avoid taking things like Advil or cough medicine and would rather use teas, or other natural remedies to heal yourself.

- You're aware of the seasons and know instinctively when the change of season is happening. You can smell the change in the air and feel a difference in temperature much sooner than anyone else.

- You feel crystal energies and are drawn to crystals. You like the way they look and the way they feel.

- You see signs. You pick up on symbols or signs and can interpret the message they are trying to convey. This could be seeing cloud formations, symbols or certain numbers.

- Seeing ghosts or spirits. This can mean physically seeing them or simply feeling their presence.

- You are interested in alternative lifestyles; you don't like things that are considered normal.

There are many more signs that you are a witch but these are the most common ones. You don't need to feel all of these but if you really are a witch, you will likely experience at least a few of the different signs. Remember that the only person who can tell if you're a witch is you!

Practical Magic

Some people think of magic and the occult as being a very mysterious exploration of elaborate and secret rituals that will only be allowed to be seen if you are a member of the coven. Others see witchcraft as an "every once in a while" activity that makes you feel "witchy" and mystical.

On the contrary, practicing witchcraft has its practical uses in our everyday lives and can be of great benefit to anything that we do. Your attention to the way it works and how to use it will help you to understand that when you bring the ritual of magic to all things, not just the great celebrations or the intense and dramatic rituals, you are gaining so much more energetic influence toward what it is you are wanting to accomplish.

There are literally hundreds of thousands of spells for all manner of need and desire. You can cast magic in your craft to enhance your career power or become the boss in your line of work. You can invent spells that are about keeping your house free and clear of negative energies and vibrations. You can create rituals for going to bed and inducing dream states. You can even cast magic that will help your vitality and energy.

Practical magic means that it can be used for everything and anything you need it for, especially the little things in life that need an extra bop on the head from your wand and your broomstick. You can begin to understand this reality the more you practice with the tools that the Craft offers to you. If you have a great idea for something you want to occur in your life, you can make a magical expression of it through your spells and rituals.

However you are wanting to practice, it can be a very reliable source of empowerment and embrace what you need to do to put a little more magical oomph into your life. There are people all over the world who use magic in an everyday way, creating methods to make an offering to whatever it is they value the most or are trying to make manifest into reality. The Craft is like casting a line of connection to the great divine and telling the whole Universe what you want to do, be, receive, let go of, and become.

You can think of it as how you would make a simple soup for dinner, or water your garden. It is akin to cleaning the household or organizing your tools and equipment in your garage. Crafting magic is certainly more fun than the daily life chores we all have, but consider that it has a greater meaning and impact when you bring it into your life in a practical way.

Your Personal Power Empowered

So much of magic is about empowering the self. There are a lot of religions that reflect a lot about the selfishness of empowering the self or choosing to enrich your life through being the divinity of your own world and reality, but the truth is that when we are all in divine connection to ourselves we are empowering all things in a much brighter way.

You can see it as a personal spirituality if you wish and your journey with the Craft will help you discover and uncover your deepest, truest self and purpose as you can continue to practice. So many of the spells and rituals that you perform can be very strongly connected to your own personal gain and that is a good thing. You will work to create connection and gratitude with the energy of all things as you do this to create a balance and it will help your personal empowerment, even more, when you do.

The best ways to help yourself succeed in your own life are to put energy, thought, and devotion to it. Your spiritual work has a great life-force energy to it and no matter what you are working on in your life or bringing practical magic into, you will create a reality of personal success and triumph because of your desire to make it manifest and show the Universe what you want!

It is such a creative and fun way to embrace your wisdom and inner power. There is a reason so many witches of old were persecuted and burned at the stake: they were terrifying to people because of their personal power. At a time when you were meant to be solvent and in devotion to one male god, the majority of women and some men who practiced witchcraft were powerful people who could ruin the practice of other, more "important" beliefs and religious practices.

The truth is that all of us possess a unique inner power and in our current age of technology, social media, and competing to be the "best" at everything, we lose ourselves in a great sea of trying to be someone we are not. When you are practicing the craft, you are focusing on you, or whatever it is that you want to magically work with, and you are listening to your inner path and power.

It is what will align you with your greatest sense of self and deliver you into the life that you actually want, not the one you are pretending to enjoy for the sake of "fitting in."

As you look around at your life, notice what you need to bring into it for yourself. Look for ways to empower your own magic and true purpose and make that the center of your Craft. You can give blessings and gratitude to the great divine for showing you the road to get there, but magic is very personal and will help you find the right way to craft for YOU.

So Mote It Be!

There are a lot of sayings in the Craft that will help a witch put a period on the end of a spell. You can really drive your purpose into creation with a few simple words. Words carry so much meaning and power and as you look at a lot of the different spells in this book, or from other resources, you will find that there is a poetry to casting magic.

You certainly don't have to be a poet, or even good at writing to come up with your preferred words or phrases. You can simply state what is clear, direct, honest and true, in order to get your magical purpose and message across to yourself and the world around you.

One phrase that is so often utilized to cap off your regular incantations is "So mote it be." This phrase will appear regularly in the spells in this book and you are likely to see it in a lot of other witchcraft resources as well. "So mote it be" is a declaration that says "this is what is happening," or "this is my truth and there you have it." A variation of this phrase that you might often see is, "And so it is." This conveys the same idea of creating truth around your magic and declaring that it is already in existence.

The words you choose to use in your magic and crafting are very important and are what carry your message through the energy of all things. The words you use to declare your purpose will work best when they are clear-cut and honest, rather than overly descriptive, convoluted, and uncertain.

When you are not sure about what you want to say, you can simply think about what it is you are trying to manifest. You can picture the outcomes in your mind and see it in your head as if it already exists. Even if the words aren't spoken, the energy of your intentions comes through in the form of thought or vision and can still be carried forward through your magic. And all it needs at the end is a simple phrase to really drive it home: So mote it be!

Doing What Needs to Be Done While Harming None

The greatest challenge for all witches is to be careful not to make magic that would intentionally cause harm or pain to another, even if that other being is a creature, or a plant, or a tree, and so forth. The energy of all things is greatly interwoven and so there are aspects of making magic that is challenging when you are working to avoid harming anything.

The resources for casting magic are often obtained from our physical world. We harvest, wildcraft, or purchase materials and items in order to have the tools we need to cast. Sometimes, cutting down a whole bushel of herbs for your apothecary cabinet can feel like you are harming something; a living plant that has just as much right to be here as you do.

The principles of magic state that as long as you aren't doing anything that will bring harm to anyone, then you should carry on with your magic. I find that the best way to make sure I am not harming anything is to ask. Before I harvest any herbs from my garden or from the wild,

278

I ask the plant if it's okay. I describe my purpose and intentions and I almost always get a clear message from the plant or flower.

The key to understanding magic is to look beyond what the physical world has taught or shown us is real, and behave in accordance with the laws of the spirit in all things, even the rocks, and stones you may collect to put on your altar. You will want to perform magic, and it must be done, and the trick is to do it while harming none. You can see how talking to a rosemary bush might look crazy to a lot of people, but are those people practicing magic regularly?

When it comes to people, you must be truly careful. You certainly wouldn't want to incur a lot of karma you don't need to bring into your life and even if you are feeling bitter and rejected because you got dumped, it's not a good reason to hex someone. The better choice would be to create a ritual of letting go of that person and use the magic of self-empowerment rather than vindictive retribution, in order to help yourself recover.

You don't need to focus on other people when working with your craft, unless you have their permission, of course. You can make magic with good intentions and communicate with the energies in all things to make sure that you are choosing the right path with your craft. Your energy will respond that much better to the magic you create if you are working from this point of view. Talk to the world around you, ask for permission, explain your cause, and focus your magic on your own power and not on disempowering others.

Connecting to the Divine in All Things

Witchcraft is an amazing path to connecting to the divine in all things. Working with practical magic offers you an opportunity to explore another dimension of reality and bring light to these greater forces.

For many Wiccans, the Goddess Moon and the God Sun are simple enough choices, while other Pagans and witches will choose from a much broader pantheon of cosmic deities who have been discovered and named throughout time and each represents a specific reality or life energy. These energetic life forms are what give meaning to our individual crafts and can bring a higher sense of purpose and truth to what we choose for our practical practices.

A general rule of thumb when beginning a ritual or spell, or casting a circle of protection, is to humbly offer your gratitude and thanks to the energies or deities that you are calling upon, thanking them for their arrival into your work and their connection to your magic. Whether you can sense their presence or not, you are invoking a bigger feeling of purpose when you incorporate and invite this intentional energy into your rituals.

Your energy is enhanced when you ask for another source of energy to aid and assist you. It is a part of the way crafting magic works. We are all in this together, and however, you choose to view and incorporate the source energy of something into your life practice, you will have a greater light shining through all of your magic when you connect to the divine.

Understanding witchcraft means you are willing to look at the world with more open eyes and deeper wisdom and intuition. You can find all of these answers when you go within yourself and learn from the ancient, hidden magic concealed there. You were born into the modern age, but your ancestors passed these universal truths down to you and your link to the Craft lurks within you and it always will.

Understanding witchcraft is all about understanding the rhythms of the life you live in accordance with the world around you.

Life after Death and Reincarnation

The cycle of birth–life–death is obvious to all of us, but for many witches the cycle does not stop there. Instead of life ending when the body dies, they believe an individual's soul, spirit, or personal energy travels to a realm beyond the physical one and will eventually be reborn in another body in another time and place. Many of them view earth as a "school" and believe we come here as human beings to learn. This cycle continues until the soul has worked through all the lessons it set out to learn. Having completed the cycle, the soul retires to a place of joy and regeneration.

Of course, this idea isn't unique to witches. Christians, Muslims, and people of many other faiths believe our souls continue on after our bodies die, and Hindus have believed in reincarnation for thousands of years.

Where Do Witches Go When They Die?

Christianity has its heaven. Buddhism has nirvana. Where do witches go when they die? Many Wiccans believe that their souls go to the Summerland, a resting place before reincarnation into new bodies, in an ongoing cycle of birth, life, death, and rebirth.

Living in Harmony with the Earth

Witches realize that we are dependent on the earth and therefore it makes sense to engage in practices that enrich both ourselves and the earth. "It's sacred ground we walk upon with every step we take," some witches sing. They seek to live in harmony with all of nature and to balance energies that have gone askew in our technology-driven society.

We often refer to our planet as Mother Earth, and indeed she is mother to us all. In a sense, that makes everyone and everything on earth part of a huge, extended family. When you know that you are a part of a greater whole it becomes more difficult to act against that whole. To do so would be counterproductive and would harm your kin, your friends, and yourself. Witches try to move gently, to respect all life, and to honor the sacredness in all things and in each other. If we can do this, we can heal the earth and the earth will heal us.

Green witches, in particular, devote themselves to this path. Some witches may work to protect endangered lands and wildlife, feeling that the loss of these would be a crime against Gaia (one name for the earth's spirit; in Greek mythology, goddess of the earth). Others donate money or time to ecological causes, and they often send out positive energy through spells and rituals. Later on, you'll learn more about how to do your part to create greater health, peace, and well-being in your own part of the world and beyond.

Signs and Omens in Nature

A rock, a flower, an herb, a tree, or an animal may hold special meaning for a witch, depending on when and where it appears and what's going on in her life at the time. For example, if a wild rose suddenly blossoms in her yard, she might take it as a positive omen of love growing in the home. A clever witch will take this one step further: She'll thank nature for its gift, dry some of those petals, and turn this little treasure into love-inspiring incense. In this manner, a witch may find herself re-inspired by a childlike wonder toward the planet and the small things that we often overlook in our busy lives.

Natural Magick

If you are serious about being a witch and doing magick, you'll need to get in touch with the natural world around you—it has much to teach you and many gifts to offer you. Today, most of us are more familiar with computers and smartphones, offices and shopping malls sealed against the weather, than we are with the sight of crops growing in the fields, the sound of streams rippling over rocks, or the scent of moist leaves on the forest floor.

Go for a walk outdoors. Reconnect with the feeling of the wind blowing through your hair. Listen to the birds that live in a tree in your yard. Watch the sunset. Take time to smell the flowers that bloom in the park during the summer. The natural world is just as natural as it ever was, except there's less of it than there was twenty-five years ago—and most of us don't make a point of enjoying it often enough.

As you begin to rediscover the natural rhythms around you, you'll also start to notice how they affect the flow of your inner life. When you become accustomed to doing this, you'll find that you feel more in sync with everything around you, and with yourself. You may not be able to align your life with the changing seasons the way our ancestors did—nor is it really necessary. However, expanding your awareness of the cycles of the earth and the cosmos will put you in touch with powerful energies beyond your own immediate skills and enable you to do magick more effectively.

Good witch, bad witch: which is which?

Despite the ugly face that religions have tried to put on witches, historically most have been concerned with helping individuals and communities. As we've already said, fear and misunderstanding underlie the foolish ideas many people hold about witches. Once you get to know them, witches are pretty much like everyone else; they just see the world a little differently.

Ethics

Some witches may not concern themselves with the ethical results of a spell or ritual—what counts is that the spell works. With a spell, you're attempting to stack the odds in your favor—or in another person's favor, if the spell is for someone else. You're attempting to influence something in the future.

Magicians recognize that even though the human mind and spirit have unlimited potential, we can't possibly foresee all the possible outcomes of a spell. Human beings are not omniscient, and sometimes even good intentions lead to terrible results. Just to be on the safe side, you might want to end a spell or ritual with a phrase such as "This is done for the greatest good of all and may it harm none." In essence, this turns over responsibility for the outcome to higher (and wiser) powers who have a better understanding of how to bring about the best possible outcome.

What If Someone Important to You Is Opposed to Witchcraft?

Arguing about it is the worst thing to do. You're not going to change anyone's opinions about spells or anything else. Your best bet is to follow your practice in private. If possible, step back from the situation and try to look at the other person as a teacher. What lesson can you learn from this opposition?

Your Personal Code

As a beginner to the wonderful world of witchcraft, you will learn something new every day and experience new sensations and feelings as you explore your newfound path. Some may surprise you, some will challenge you, and lots will fascinate and excite you. One thing you can be sure of now that you've started down this road: You'll never be quite the same again.

Chapter 3 : Meditation for the Modern Witch

In modern society, meditation is often linked with certain activities, such as yoga. And this makes sense because meditation has long gone hand in hand with yoga and other such practices. But the practice of looking inward and making sure you spend time with your own mind is something that anyone, regardless of their taste for yoga, can do. And if it something that all magic practitioners *should* do.

The Purpose of Meditation

Meditation, also sometimes referred to as mindfulness, is the act of looking within yourself for peace and calm. Many people struggle to find this in today's world, myself included. Indeed, there has never really been a time where the majority of people were good at finding their own peace. And modern life is so fast-paced, it is hard to believe that we can do it. But we can. You can.

The exercises outlined below are a good way to start your meditation practice. You might have to do them several times before they become easy or even productive. It all depends on how hard it has been for you, up until now, to fully look at your energy. Meditation is not easy. It forces you to look at yourself, truly. But it will strengthen your magical practice more than just about anything else.

A Basic Grounding Exercise

Grounding is the first and most important thing a witch must learn to do with their energy. It is through grounding that you will form the foundation for the rest of your magical acts. If grounding your energy sounds like something from an electrician's handbook, you are not far off. When you ground, you will extend part of your energy down into the ground and use this taproot to siphon off the energy you do not want or energy you cannot contain. It will also allow you to more easily wield energy from a higher power because you can channel excess down into the ground.

Of course, your grounding point might not be the actual ground. Depending on your energy source, you might ground to the frame of a building or the bed of the ocean. You might even ground to the vast calm of space if that is where the majority of your energy comes from.

But, to begin, you should practice grounding into the earth beneath your feet. In order to do this, you will first want to sit down on the ground and close your eyes. Find yourself a comfortable position and focus on letting all the tension flow out of your body. You can start with your fingertips or your toes and work out from those points. You will want to keep tension in your core so that you do not harm your back. But make sure you release the tension around your eyes and across your temple as well as in your mouth. Your shoulders will also store stress, so you might have to take a few deep breaths to relax them.

When you have released the tension, it is time to check in on your breathing. Inhale as deeply as you are able without rushing yourself or forcing a deeper breath than normal. Count the number of seconds this takes, then hold your breath for two to three seconds. Slowly exhale while drawing it out until your exhale takes one to three seconds longer than your inhale. Throughout your grounding practice, whenever you get frustrated or lost, come back to your breathing and releasing the tension that will build up.

Focus on your breathing for a dozen breaths or so, then shift your focus to a mental image of yourself. It can be as realistic or as fanciful as you like. Once you have the mental image clear in your mind, imagine a taproot of your energy burrowing down into the ground from the base of your spine. Or imagine a network of roots burrowing down from every point where your body connects with the floor.

If you are sitting on the second floor of a building – or higher – you can either visualize your energy running through the floors beneath you to reach the ground. Or you can keep your focus solely on the mental image of yourself and see yourself sitting directly on the earth to make the grounding easier.

Burrow your root or roots as deeply as is comfortable. Then, when you feel stable and connected, begin to feed all the negative energy you hold down into the ground. This will pass the energy into the earth, which will cleanse it so that it can be returned to the world for new uses. You can take as long as you like to do this, alternating your focus on your breathing, your tension, and the motion of your energy. Although this might not seem like it, this will is the most basic form of energy manipulation, which is a key skill for all witches. And, after you are comfortable with this technique, you can move on to centering.

A Basic Centering Exercise

Grounding and centering are usually discussed as if they are one single action. But they are, in fact, two separate practices with different focuses and outcomes. And, as such, they can be performed separately. You should make sure that you know how to ground, at least at a basic level, you can move on to centering.

If you move directly into centering from grounding, you can use the same mental image you used for your grounding exercise. If you are centering without grounding first, however, you should create a new mental image. In either case, your mental image should include threads of your energy radiating out from you that connect to every place you spend your energy.

Some people see their energy as shining lines in a color that they feel reflects them. Others see their commitment lines as black cords, chains, tethers, or even strands of tinsel or fairy lights. You might even find that different commitments have connections that look unique to each one. There is no one single way to view your connections because, as I said before, magic is incredibly intimate and unique to each person.

Once you have visualized all of your commitments, you need to evaluate them. Go through them one by one and make sure that you approve the connection or that you have to leave it in place. If you do not want the connection to continue, you can unhook your energy from its recipient and rolls the energy back into your core. If the commitment is long-standing, you might have to perform an additional spell to permanently disconnect yourself from the recipient. And many connections require mundane action to fully sever. But centering is a good first step to identify which connections require this sort of attention.

If you choose to leave a connection in place, make sure that it is only getting the energy it needs. There are certain connections that you may want to feed a great deal of energy into. But there are others, such as groups you are part of whether or not you want to be or a job that does not reward employees for going above and beyond, that you do not need to invest a great deal of energy in. If you have these sorts of connections and cannot sever them, you can place a throttle or brake on it so that you do not spend energy in places that it is not needed or will not be appreciated.

One by one, go through each connection. Each one that is disconnected can be rolled back into your core and absorbed back into your pool of usable energy. If you have grounded yourself before you centered, you can cleanse this energy by feeding any unwanted remnants of the recipient – or your feelings about them – by feeding the energy down into the earth.

Centering allows you to make sure you are spending your energy wisely. It is an excellent practice for all magic users. But it also causes you to look at yourself and the way you spend your energy. You might find that you commit your energy to things that you do not really support or realize you spend as much energy on as you do. Looking this closely at yourself can be difficult. But you will find that your magical practice – and your life in general – is elevated by knowing yourself that much more fully.

Meditations for Magic

There are many other meditations you can do to elevate your magical practice in addition to grounding and centering. Many of these meditations are not so much guided by an outside force as guided by the direction your own thoughts take.

A common misconception about meditating is that you have to clear your mind of all thoughts. That you have to think of only white noise in order to effectively meditate. But this is simply not true. Thinking of only white noise does not allow you to be aware of your own thoughts or to control your own energy. And, more than that, our brains are not wired for silence. Even when we are asleep, our minds are talking. Dreams help us process information we picked up throughout the day and work through things we are worried about. Our brains are never silent.

Meditation is no different. You do not have to clear your mind completely. And you may find that you cannot clear your mind the way you think you might have to. Instead, you have to learn to let your thoughts come and go as they choose. You might choose to focus on one thought or follow one particular thought when you are trying to learn something about yourself or a situation. But you must let the rest of your thoughts come and go without trying to hold onto them or dwell on them.

Meditating to discern information is a little bit different, however. If you want to use your meditation as a means by which you learn things – either about yourself about situations, spirits, or people around you – you will want to go into your meditation with a specific thought in mind. The thought should be focus on what you already know. Then, after you have grounded yourself, you can follow this thought and see where it takes you.

The interesting thing about thoughts, when you work with magic, is that they take on lives of their own. Intention fuels a great many spells, and intention is nothing more than highly focused thought. To that end, you will find that your thoughts tend to take on a life of their own when you are working in magical spaces or trying to perform magical acts. This can be both a blessing and a curse.

Active thoughts might distract you from a spell or call your attention away from your meditation. But they can also inspire creativity. Or, in this case, they might help you learn something new. When you turn your thoughts to yourself and the hidden things within your mind, this is referred to as Shadow Work.

Do not let the name fool you. There is nothing dark about shadow work, save that you look at things that do not normally see the light. But this is not a bad thing. Shadow Work should only really be attempted by witches with a fair amount of experience and a good grip on their energy. But, that said, it is an important step in most magical journeys. When you are ready to take on shadow work, you may find that it changes much more than you expected.

Everyone has things about themselves that they are not fully ready to face. Old memories, bad habits, or toxic connections that we are not ready to address. And most people can go their whole lives without facing these issues head-on. But, as a magic worker, you are not like most people. The further you go on your magical path, the most important it is for you to address these traits or these shadows. Going about your magical practice without facing your shadows leaves you open to negative energy. And, more importantly, it can cause energy drains that prevent you from reaching your full magical potential. So start small, with grounding and centering. But do not be afraid to follow your thoughts and plumb your shadows when the time comes.

Protection Spells

Protection spells are a witch's bread and butter, so to speak. They were the spell most commonly requested when magic wielders were more involved in everyday life. And they will likely be the majority of what you spend your energy on. The world is a dangerous place. But when you can control the flow of your own energy, you can take a little bit of uncertainty out of it.

Protecting Yourself

Your magic is an amazing tool. It can do so many things and cause so much change. But, first and foremost, it is an extension of yourself. So it makes sense that you would use it to protect yourself.

Magic is best used as a protection against other energy-based attacks or dangers. Negative spirits, other magic users attacking you through magic, or people who suck away your energy without realizing it can all be stopped in their tracks with the right kind of magic.

If you have other concerns regarding your personal security, you may want to look into additional options. Magic is a tool, not a miracle solution, and should be treated as such. And, when it comes to keeping yourself safe, it is best not to leave things to chance.

While there are many spells you can use to protect yourself, I prefer the mirror spell. It requires nothing but the ability to ground and center as well as a bit a visualization. At most, you will need to find a quiet place where you will not be disturbed while you envision your protective barrier. Once it is in place, however, you can do regular checks to make sure it is still strong without having to spend quite so much time on it all at once.

And while it is important for you to know your way through your grounding and centering exercises, you do not have to be an expert before you give this spell a try. In truth, it is one of the first spells new magic users should learn. Yes, it is only a tool in your kit. But you will encounter a great number of unusual energies and entities on your magical journey. And it is always best to be prepared.

To begin this spell, sit somewhere comfortable. As I said before, you will have to dedicate quite a bit of time to the visualization the first time you form your protective mirror. So it is a good idea to cast this spell while you are in a comfortable position. You might also want to let the people in your household know that you need some time alone. Though they do not have to tell them what specifically you will be doing if you are not open with your practice. Telling them you need some time is just one way to ensure you will not be interrupted until your visualization is firmly in place.

Raise your protective wards or circle as you would for any other spell. Then settle yourself into the most comfortable position you can manage. Close your eyes and go through your grounding and then your centering practice. Go slowly with both steps. This spell is about you and your wellbeing. So being very deliberate and precise with both your grounding and your centering is a good way to keep your mind in the right place.

When you ground, make sure that your energy is firmly rooted. And take the time to ensure that your foundation really fits your energy. The grounding guide in this book is geared for earth witches. But there are many options out there. Anything that gives you a sense of permanence and a sense of security is a good thing to ground into, so long as it is not another person. As I mentioned before, always ground into something greater than yourself so you can trust that it will support you.

Once you are ready to center, spend a little more time than usual on identifying where your energy is going. Take time to deliberate over each connection and make sure it is something you want. If you do not want it, remove the connection. And, if you do want to keep it, ensure that you are only giving it as much energy as is really necessary. For some things, such as family or passionate endeavors, we often want to give it our all. And there is nothing wrong with that. But certain things like work or commitments to groups, require a certain amount from us. When we give more and are already spread thin, we get very little return on the investment, and it can leave us feeling drained.

Draining your energy reserves is one way that you can leave yourself vulnerable. That does not mean that you call negativity into your life or anything like that. But negative energies can detect when our defenses are low, and they choose those times to attack. You will also find yourself vulnerable to more mundane stressors when your energy levels are low. Things that you would normally shrug off become unbearable, and this, in turn, can lead to more problems.

So weigh your connections carefully. And if you find that there are connections you want to fully sever that require mundane action, make a note to handle those as soon as possible.

Once you have completed both your grounding exercise and your centering practice, focus your attention on your mental image of yourself. You used one for your centering practice, and that one can be used for this visualization exercise as well. Starting with your feet, narrow your focus to one part of your body. As you do, imagine a sheet of armor encasing you. This may sound suffocating, but it is your visualization. You can make the armor as lightweight and breathable as you like without risking its durability or efficacy.

Your armor must also be reflective, hence the idea of Mirror Armor. This reflective surface will turn negative energy back on the people who sent it to you. You may feel the touch of their negative energy, as you would feel a blow through armor. But you will not be touched directly by it. And that can make all the difference when you are dealing with an intensely negative situation or person.

This is also why going through the visualization slowly is so important. When I do this spell – and I have done it a few times because it does need to be refreshed whenever the armor wears thin, just like real armor – my mental images resemble something out of an old cartoon. Flashing lights and stirring music as shining armor nearly mythical in appearance outfits me from head to toe. These images take quite a bit of time to complete, as you can imagine. But it is time well spent. When I open my eyes in the end, I am confident and content in the knowledge that I am protected from any negative energy that comes my way.

Your visualization will probably differ from me. And that is a good thing. Everyone has something about them that sets their energy signature apart from the other people around them. That difference is what attunes your spells to you. And, in this instance, it is what will make your armor so effective. No energy can get past your armor unless it is intended as a benefit for your specific energy signature.

Visualizing a coat of armor, starting from your feet and working your way up, will take some time. But as you can see, it is time well spent. Start with your feet and move slowly up, taking time with the joints and places where movement would wear clothing or armor thin. Even psychic armor – and that is another term for what this is – will wear thin through the normal wear and tear of life.

When you reach the top and complete a head-to-toe suit of armor, envision is sinking into your skin. This does not hurt, and it does not cause discomfort. Rather, it should feel a little warm and comforting, like your favorite sweater or that moment right after you slip into a warm bath.

Take a moment to thank the higher power you work with. You put quite a bit of energy into your armor, and so did the energy source. Showing gratitude and giving thanks will go a long way in making sure that your relationship with your chosen energy source stays a positive one.

Open your eyes and take a moment to orient yourself to the physical world. This may take a moment, depending on how long you spent on your visualization. When you are steady, open your circle and rejoin the flow of normal, mundane life. You may find yourself feeling weak, hungry, or dehydrated. This is perfectly normal after controlling and expending so much energy. It is important for your health that you get a snack, some water, and some rest. Do not try to perform any other magical workings on the same day you set your mirror armor, as it will leave you dangerously drained. As a lesser consequence, your secondary spell will be weaker than it would be if you let yourself rest for a day instead.

As I mentioned before, you will have to reapply your armor from time to time. But so long as you check in once a week or so – something you can do with your centering practice – you will be able to catch any weak spots in the armor before they spread. You should also check in if you go through a particularly rough experience or deal with a particularly negative person. When you find a weak spot, put the same energy into mending it as you did into creating your armor in the first place. It may be exhausting, but this level of personal protection is more than worth the effort.

Protecting Your Home

Some of the oldest forms of witchcraft can be traced to spells and enchantments that ward off bad luck. These took the forms of magic talismans, carvings on door frames, and prayers written into the very foundations of a home. Most modern people don't have access to the inner structure of their home quite so easily any more. But there are still many ways you can cast a circle of protection on your home.

Witch jars are adapted from many of these ancient methods. Rather than burying a single enchanted item beside your front door or at your garden gate, you gather a collection of small items and add them to a jar. That jar is then buried in place of the single item.

The following items are things that people often put inside witch jars:

- Nails

- Thumbtacks

- Thorns

- Sewing pins

- Broken glass

- Broken pottery

- Broken CDs

- Old kitchen knives

- Screws

If it is sharp and could hurt someone that wants to cause problems for you, your household, or anyone inside of it, you can put it inside a witch jar. You just have to find a jar large enough to fit the items but small enough that you will be able to dig a hole for it outside your front door or beside your front gate.

Once all the sharp things are in your witch jar, it is time to add the stinging ingredients. These are liquids or spices that would sting terribly if they were to enter a wound. Some common options are:

- Vinegar

- Lemon Juice

- Pepper

- Cinnamon

- Red Pepper flakes

- Ground ginger

- Wasabi

If you do use liquids like vinegar or lemon juice, be aware that they are acidic. They may not react well if you choose to use something like broken CDs. And, over time, any liquid will corrode metals submerged within them. If you find that the protection spell waned over time, your sharper ingredients may have corroded. You will have to dig up the original witch jar and create another one.

Witch jars are very easy to assemble. And, because you are working with the energies of your whole home, you do not need to raise your wards, ground, or center before you create one. As soon as it's done, bury it at a common entrance and exit to your home. If you leave it sitting out, the protective energies may fade and wander outside your property lines, as they are not rooted in the ground on which your home stands.

Some readers might find the idea of a witch jar uncomfortable. After all, it looks like magic intended to cause harm. And though many witches use curses and hexes without hesitation, there are those who might not be comfortable with such magic. If you are one such person, you can rest assured that this spell is not intended to inflict harm on specific people. It is not a curse.

 Rather, a witch jar is a kind of warning system. It will give a small "sting" to anyone who tries to cause harm to those living within your home. It acts much the same as a mirrored protection spell, which reflects a person's energy back to them. But the witch jar has the added layer of the "sting" to ward someone off from trying their actions again.

Chapter 4: Guide of Spells with Candles, Moon, Crystals, and Herbs

Flame magic is probably the least complicated type of spellcasting, and in that capacity, it doesn't require a ton of extravagant ritual or formal instruments. Anybody with a flame can do magic. Recall when you made a wish before you blew out the candles on your birthday cake. A similar thought applies to light magic, just rather than merely seeking after your willingness to work out as expected, you're pronouncing your goal. All things being equal, the birthday light ritual depends on three mysterious critical standards:

- Settle on an objective.

- Imagine the final product.

- Center your aim, or will, to show that outcome.

Picking a Candle

Most experts of mysterious frameworks will disclose to you that the size of your flame truly isn't significant. Huge candles might be counterproductive. For example, a light that takes three days to consume can be profoundly diverting to somebody working a spell that relies upon the flame burning as far as possible.

Commonly, a small decrease in light or a votive flame will work best. Sometimes, a spell may require a particular sort of view, for example, a seven-day spark or a figured flame to speak to a specific individual, a type of thoughtful magic. One of the most famous candles, in all honesty, is the little menorah candles sold by the box in the whole area of the supermarket. They're around four inches in length, white, unscented, and thin. Along these lines, they're ideal for spell work.

You ought to consistently use a fresh out of the plastic new candle for spell work and not candles that you have used at the supper table or in the washroom the day before. As indicated by some mystical conventions, a candle gets vibrations from the things around it once it begins to burn. If waves have corrupted a pre-used candle a few people trust it will prompt a contrary or inadequate supernatural result.

Candle Colors

With regards to hues, you may wish to have an assortment close by for various mysterious purposes. Usually, color messages for flame magic are per the following:

Red: Courage and wellbeing, sexual love, and desire

Pink: Friendship and sweet love

Orange: Attraction and consolation

Gold: Financial increase, business attempts, and sunlight based associations

Yellow: Persuasion and assurance

Green: Financial increase, bounty, and richness

Light Blue: Health, tolerance, and comprehension

Dim Blue: Depression and powerlessness

Purple: Ambition and force

Darker: Earth-related or animal related activities

Dark: Negativity and expulsion

White: Purity and truth*

Silver: Meditation, instinct, and lunar associations

* Note that in numerous Pagan rituals, it is adequate to use a white candle instead of some other color.

Using Your Candle in Ritual

After you've chosen a candle, oil or dress it before use, it is a strategy by which you'll set up a telepathic connection among you and the sun itself. You're charging the flame with your energy and individual vibrations and anticipating your aim into the wax before you use it.

To dress a candle, you'll need some essential oil; numerous experts like to use grapeseed because it has no smell. Another alternative is to use different flame magic oils from one of the mystical supply stores. Start at the highest point of the candle, and rub the oil down to the center. At that point, start at the base of the candle and rub the oil up towards the center, finishing with the last relevant point of interest. In certain rituals, the blessing is done the polar opposite way; start in the center and work your way towards the two ends.

If your work calls for herbs to also be used, roll the oiled candle in the powdered herbs until it is covered all around. It's essential to recollect. Nonetheless, that candle is only an tool. It isn't naturally enchanted; however, it's a way to make magic using the component of fire to set one's goal into movement. Similarly, as different instruments are used dependent on what the otherworldly goal may be, candles ought to be deeply washed down before they are used for a spell.

The most essential type of light magic uses a bit of shaded paper that coordinates the purpose of your flame. Choose what your objective is, and compose it on the bit of paper.

In case you do a cash spell, you would record your goal as: "I will turn out to be monetarily prosperous." In certain conventions, you would write down your objective in an enchanted letter set, for example, Theban or Enochian. Since this is a cash situated spell, we would choose either a gold or green bit of paper or a flame of a similar color. As you record your objective, imagine yourself accomplishing that objective.

Consider the various ways by which your objective may show, for example, getting a raise at work spell. Maybe somebody who owed you cash will show up out of nowhere to reimburse their obligation. On the other hand, possibly you will get a considerable tax refund check!

When you've recorded your objective, overlay the paper, focusing on your expectation the entire time. A few people like to say a little spell as they do this. It doesn't need to be anything extravagant. You can use something as vital as:

Additional cash come to my direction, I could use a little money today.

Additional cash come to me, as I will, so it will be.

305

Put one corner of the folded paper into the candle's fire and permit it to burst into flames. Hold the paper as far as might be feasible (without burning your fingers) and afterwards place it in a fire-safe bowl to burn the remainder of the route all alone. Let the flame go out totally. When the fire has diminished; discard it, as opposed to saving it to use again for another spell. Generally, there's little left except for a stub of wax, and you can either bury it outside or discard it in whatever way you choose.

Candle Magic for Divination

In some mystical rituals, candles are used for divinatory purposes. The two most customarily used techniques for flame divination are reading the wax and the way that the fire burns.

To divine by how the fire burns, you'll need to focus on whether the fire burns low or tall, if it flashes, or if there's more than one fire. Two flares could mean somebody from the spirit world is helping you arrive at your objective. Indeed, even the colors found in the fire may give you a clue about the adequacy of your spell. Be that as it may, there's no agreement about what these signs mean. While a few experts accept a fire that burns tall and reliable signals that one's desire will be satisfied, others bring up that the length and nature of the wick can impact how the fire burns, as can an air vent. Concentrate more on your goal than on how the fire burns.

Then again, if you need to divine by reading the candle wax, you'll have to drop the wax into a bowl of cold water. The wax will solidify very quickly and form shapes. Use these shapes to find the solutions to your inquiries, much as you would if you were reading tea leaves.

Chapter 5: Psychic Abilities, Divination, and Predicting the Future

This chapter is going to focus on extra skills involved within the practice of witchcraft inside the Wiccan religion. Again, they are not necessary when trying to become a witch, but may interest you enough to want to pursue them.

The concept of a witch or even Wicca connotes images often, of psychics that set up tents at carnivals and want to read your future. Although no one is here to debate whether or not any of those are legitimate, set yourself straight in acknowledging that Wiccans are not a part of that misinterpretation. What Wiccans and witches are, are people that are greatly in tuned with their intuition, and they follow that. Learning to sharpen these abilities is not about waking up and suddenly being able to read minds; it is about applying various practices that will enhance an ability all human beings were born with. We all have feelings about things that we cannot explain; we call those hunches, or gut feelings. Wiccans believe that every person is born with some level of psychic ability, and it has be either encouraged or discouraged throughout their lifetime, due to culture or particular upbringing.

The term ESP tries to cover every aspect of psychic abilities, such as clairvoyance, clairaudience, psychometry, telepathy, dowsing, precognition, scrying, and mediumship. These are not skills that you can easily tap into. Depending upon your upbringing, certain skills be better than others are. It is going to take time to summon them to the surface when they have been pushed down for so long.

307

Your first step is for you to accept that you are capable of these things. You can start by reminding yourself everyday with a statement such as: "I am open and ready to receive information." Begin researching, whether it be in other books or on the internet. You also need to know, that like most skills, you are not going to be good at every psychic skill. Try to figure out your strengths, and what you feel you may have an affinity for. Most people are generally only extrasensory in one or two ways, so accept this and move forward, investigating your particular psychic skills.

Learning to Trust Your Intuition

It is recommended by most Wiccans that you try to tune yourself to your abilities by paying attention to your senses, rather than blocking them out. This will bring you further into the moment.

If you are a person who does not trust your intuition, and are confusing your emotions with that sensation, here are a few ways that you can clear out your mind and learn to trust yourself when making decisions, or interpreting events in your life:

1. Start by making a simple decision, such as, should I walk or take the bus to work today?

2. One answer will come into your mind. Make note of it. Don't look for logical reasons as to why, just write it down.

3. Breathe in and out, deeply and quietly. That answer that rose in your mind is your intuition. Trust that thought without scanning your brain for reasons why or why not.

4. Now make that decision, and go with it. The outcomes aren't always the best, but that doesn't mean that your intuition was wrong. We cannot know what didn't happen because of the choices we made.

Another exercise can help you further visualize what it means to follow your intuition. This exercise involves the visualization of a traffic light.

1. Clear your mind and make sometime for yourself where there won't be any interruptions. Sit comfortable, breathing deeply.

2. When you feel ready, write down some questions you feel you need answer to in your life. In this situation, the answers will be yes, no, or maybe.

3. Now breathe deeply, and close your eyes. Imagine a traffic light, with a red light, a yellow light, and a green light. The green light will represent "yes," the red light "no," and the yellow light is "maybe".

4. Begin by asking yourself questions you already know the answer to, to help yourself gage the visualization. Ask yourself if you are sitting (if you are sitting), if it is the year that you recited, if you have a pet bird, etc. Watch the corresponding colors light up in your mind.

5. Now, ask yourself the questions that you wrote down. Try not to think too much, just ask.

309

6.   Whatever color appears in your mind, which is the answer. That is your intuition speaking directly to you.

Listen to Your Body

Your body can give you signals about decisions you've made, because it is connected directly to your intuition. If you are feeling anxious, it could be your intuition trying to warn you. If you are unsure about a decision too, you can also consult the traffic light method.

Try to pay attention to your body, and stay in tuned with how it is feeling. Try perhaps not to interpret too much at first, but rather, just be aware of it and how it is feeling.

Dreams

Dreams are a very useful way of paying attention to your intuition. This is because when you dream, your subconscious mind is running things, rather than your conscious mind, which is constantly cluttered with other issues you have to deal with. Your mind wants to help you solve problems; it wants to help you figure out your future, so try to allow it. Dreams are generally not very straightforward, so it may be hard to interpret them. There are many websites that can help you do just that. On the other hand, you can begin by simply keeping a dream journal. This can help you pick up possible patterns of imagery and occurrences.

Too Much Analyzing

The analytical mind is the enemy of intuition. The Western World thrives upon notions of logic. If you are person who needs to analyze every thought and action, then learning to trust your intuition is going to be difficult. If your gut is telling you not to date someone, although you consciously feel they are very attractive or not your parents will like them, try to trust that feeling and not go into thinking about why you are having that feeling. An intuition is trying to steer you down a path that it already knows exists, and is not making up new directions for you to follow. Start with simple decisions, like going with the gut meal you wanted at a restaurant, where to go for your birthday celebration, what coffee to order at cafe, what pants to wear to work, etc.

Psychometry

This is a form of ESP that some Wiccans use, and is one that many people find interesting. This is the ability to hold an object and get a sense of the individual. It is definitely possible that you have, in some fashion and degree, felt this before. If you have worn something that belonged to your mother or perhaps something from your grandparent who has passed, there is certain energy being passed down through it. If a person passed in the clothing, or is the person who previously owned it, there is a deep sense of peace and serenity.

You can also get feelings about first impressions of people if you touch them, or if you touch an object that belongs to them. Here is an exercise to help you practice this skill:

1. Practice with someone who you know and trust. Ask them not to tell you how there day has been going. Pick up their hand and close your eyes, focusing on their energy.

2. Let your senses really guide you. Observe what your body is feeling, whether it be warmth, cold, ache, peace, etc.

3. Interpret these feelings. The feelings are not always a direct line to what is going on with them, for example, they may be feeling a sense of discomfort, which could be an abundant amount of things.

This skill can help you during personal interactions. Really all you need is the ability to shake the hand of the person you just met, such as neighbor, a date, a new friend, your partners, parents, etc.

Brain Telegrams and Telepathic Messages

Now, it is understood that a joke was made at the beginning of this chapter to remark upon how absurd the concept of mind-reading is. To clarify, the simplified notion expressed in TV, film, and books is what is being referred to..

Everyone has had moments where they say the same thing that their friend is going to say, or they mentally predict what is going to come out of their mouth before it does. This is what people mean when they refer to people being on that same 'wavelength'; it is easier with those who love and care about because we know them. It is hard to send a telepathic message to someone we don't know well, or to see what is going on inside their skulls if our interactions are not always the best. For now, try practicing this exercise to help you become more intend with the brain waves of others:

1. Try to relax. Regular mediation and visualization are key practices that will help you hone in on your telepathic skillset. Your brain needs to be open to the possibilities surrounding you; if they are closed, you will not be able to send or receive messages to other people around you. Before you begin this exercise, give yourself and your friend time to relax for about 10 to 15 minutes.

2. Choose which person will be the sender, and which will be the receiver. For this example, you are going to be the sender.

3. When you are both ready, try to visualize something in your mind. Start with something, like a teapot. Think of the smells, the color, the texture, the act of pouring it out. It is easier to start sending images rather than thoughts, because images are

easier to pick up. Over time though, you will learn how to also pick up these more complex thoughts.

4. Try picturing a tube running between your brain and your friends brain. Now send your image down the tube for them to receive. Maintain though, the image in your mind as you allow them to receive it.

Perfecting this of course is going to take practice. Start with different images and send them to different friends in your life. You and your friend may be similar in mind, but this is a part of your brain that hasn't been consciously exercised for a long time. Be patient, and eventually, you will be able to transmit thoughts over to people to help you benefit your own life! For example, if you really need that raise, try to transmit the thought of "You are going to realize what a great worker I am and give me a raise!" Do not deter from positive thoughts though; negative transmissions or ones that are not genuine can open you up to more energy that is negative.

Exercising your Psychic Energy

Learning to trust your intuition is an important first step in the process of honing your psychic abilities. Doing this allows you to simply trust yourself and your thoughts, without over analyzing and constantly doubting as to whether or not you made the right decision. Trust yourself and the universe—what is meant to be, will come.

We will explore more exercise that will help you become more in tuned with the right side of your brain; the side that is innately more

314

creative, and spiritual. You probably have heard of the two practices here, as they have become popularized by the movement of Mindfulness within the Western World. Mediation, and visualization, are spectacular tools that will literally help you open your mind, in both a calming and observational manner, and a method that stimulates your imagination.

Visualization

Visualization is the direct opposite of meditation. In therapeutic terms, visualization is used to help people with severe anxiety and panic think of a location or environment that helps them calm down. In the terms of exercising your mind for the sake of psychic skills, it means applying your imagination still, but in a particular situation that relates to your life. This will help you explore further possibilities in your life outside what may have been closing you in as being more 'realistic' and 'practical'. Once you are able to do this for yourself, the concept of predicting the future and what occurs in it won't seem so out of reach.

1. Just like meditation, try to find a quiet, comfortable place to sit or lie down.

2. Before choosing to visualize, come to situation with a particular problem in your life, a desire, a goal, etc. Choose one,

3. Since you have chosen one, go through it, and tell yourself a story about it. You are not meant to solve the problem here, should that be what you have chosen. However, you are meant to see all of the possibilities in any given situation.

4. Do this for about 15 minutes. This is your world, your story; there exist no limits.

That is all there is to it. Like meditation, if you take the time to do this every now and then, your brain is going to be strong, and able to accept the energies of the future that are going to come to you.

Scrying

Every psychic will have their strengths and weaknesses; some are very good at seeing and interpreting images through a reflective or mutable surface of some kind. If the image of an old witch reading your future in a crystal ball is conjured, then you are headed in the right direction.

A witch or Wiccan who identifies as a scryer is a person who is more visually inclined with their future predictions. They will sometimes have crystal balls, or use mirrors, a bowl of water, or even see visions in smoke and fire. These images may seem hokey, or immensely stereotyped, and you would be right in assuming so. Scrying is not something that witches wake up one day and are capable of. As everything described, it is a skill that is practiced and hone, with some witches being better at it than others are.

If you don't think you'd be very good at scrying, try to think about this. A study was done in Germany a few years ago that used sensory deprivation to see how the participants would react. They were deprived of sound and light for a certain amount of time. The participants were then asked to report what, if anything, they saw after the deprivation. Many reported images that eventually turned out to be visions of occurrences to come.

The theory then is that when the sense are deprived or limited, it becomes easier for images and vision to enter your right brain. If you want to try this out, try something similar to the meditation exercise, by finding a quiet comfortable spot, blocking out sound and light. Find a blank wall to stare at. You don't have to stare at it too hard; you can even allow your eyes to blur. Your eyes will eventually darken, getting tired of staring. This is the moment to observe yourself and what you see, in your mind's eye.

If you feel so inclined, you can choose to purchase a crystal ball in a New Age shop. Try to do this as opposed to buying online, because you can't feel the weight or texture of the ball if you order it off the internet. Like many witch related items, it is believed that the ball will choose you, as opposed to you choosing the ball. Go with what feels right. Once you have your ball, spend time with it in the privacy of your home. Sit and meditate with it when you first bring it home. Bring yourself into a semi-dreamlike state, and then open your eyes, looking into the ball. Have them unfocused.Try not to worry about what you see, or what you don't see too much. This is just the beginning!

Some crystal ball enthusiasts believe that it is best to only read your ball when it is a full moon. However, there are also many people who apply it anytime they like. Like all practices of Wicca, it will depend on you and how you are feeling, and what best suits you.

There are many other methods that you apply scrying to, should you not want to spend the money on a crystal ball. You can use anything, from your television screen, to your laptop screen, to the blank screen on your iPhone. The entire point of scrying is learning to interpret images, the way you see images of shapes in clouds.

Here is a way to practice by using the blank screen of your TV:

1. For this practice, do not shut off the lights in the room. You are going to need them in order to see the reflection in the screen.

2. All you need in addition to your TV, is a small white candle.

3. Start by reciting this line in front of your TV: "To the technology born, I give it light, to show me the way, my own inner light. So mote it be." You can write this down in your Book of Shadows for later reference.

4. Light the white candle and place it in front of your TV. Be sure that the candle casts a light on the screen.

5. Stare at the blank television and allow yourself to daydream.

6. In your mind, ask the TV questions about anything that may be important to you; whether it relates to your love life, career, family, etc. Within about ten minutes, the answer should be revealed to you.

As to how to interpret your visions, the answer is simple; it all depends on you. There is no definitive answer for what a certain image might mean, as different images conjure different emotions and associations between different people. An image of a guitar might make one person happy, where it may have negatively associated memories for another person. Think about what the image makes you feel, and the associations that come up when you do this. Write them down in your Book of Shadows, and see how the visions change over time.

You can refer should your visions be dominated by certain shade to, some color references. These colors may indicate what is to come:

White: Protection, positive energy.
Red: Danger.
Orange: Anger
Yellow: Troubled, obstacles ahead
Blue: Success
Green: Happiness, health
Black/Grey: Negative energy

If an image is difficult to see, then it may refer to something in the past or something in the distant future. If the image is very clear, it may mean that there is something going to happen sooner rather than later.

Receiving Remote Messages: Clairvoyants and Other Skills

The certain psychic skills that fall under this category have to do with the ability to receive messages from others, whether it by choice and honing in on it, or without the individual's permission. Read through the definitions, and think about what you feel you may relate to most as a development witch or Wiccan:

Clairvoyants: They receive visions, either while meditating, sleeping, or going about their day.

Clairaudients: These individuals hear things that are not audible to others. These may be voices of spirit guides or messages from other spirits who have passed.

Clairalients: Are people who can smell the spirit world. If your grandparents smoked tobacco, this person could get a whiff of smoke if the spirit is nearby.

Clairambients: Are people who can taste what a particular spirit enjoyed during their lifetime.

Clairsentients: Are able to assess and feel the energy fields around people and other peoples, including animals and plants, and are able to shift these energies if they need to.

Claircognizants: These people do not see or hear things from the spirit world, but are somehow able to get information they would not hav known otherwise.

There are ways that you can hone in on this practice, but most people are usually born with this ability from an early age. However, if you feel you can relate to the any of the above methods of receiving information, reading on about how you can develop your Third Eye.

The Third Eye

There do exist seminars that can help you sharpen your skills. However, if you are still unsure about what abilities seem most like you, then it could be a good idea to begin practicing in your own home.

A person who has a well-developed Third Eye is a person who has practiced and cultivated the skills of clairvoyance. The Third Eye is a part of the body's Chakra system, which is a system of areas on the human body that produce a certain kind of energy. The location of the

Third Eye is the sixth chakra, in the middle of the forward, and is related to having a high intuition and understanding of the world.

The first thing you can do to improve your skill of clairvoyance is to make sure your third-eye Chaka is clear. This can be done through meditation, while using a blue crystal or gemstone such as kyanite, azurite, or lapis lazuli.

1. Begin by dimming the lights, light some candles, put on some music. Anything that will make you feel comfortable.

2. Lie down and play the blue crystal or stone on your head.

3. Breathe deeply, through your nose and blow out through the mouth. Try to breathe as deeply as you can. Do this for thirty to sixty-seconds.

4. Start to focus on the area where the crystal is. Image it opening up the space on your forehead. You may feel a warming or tingling sensation.

5. When you feel like the space is wide open, make sure you are still breathing deeply.

6. Un-focus your mind, and see what comes to you. Stay with that vision, without worrying about what it means or why it is coming to you.

7. If you feel so inclined, try to focus on your ears, and see if you can hear anything coming to you from the other side.

It will take time for you to learn how to summon the visions that you are looking for, or to see them when others ask you for them. All you can do once your chakra is clear, is to meditate, and try to focus on receiving messages, and not judging them.

Dreaming and Future Predicting

Everyone dreams, whether they remember it or not. They are wonderful ways to undercover problems that you may be suppressing, or to use your imagination to open up new possibilities. It is also possible, yes, to use your dreams as tools to see into the future. Dreaming is a place where the subconscious runs wild, as opposed to the conscious mind, where everything is orderly and put in its own place. Many Wiccans believe that dreams are where you can move through different dimensions, called time warping. When applying this, you can go into the past, present and future. This all begins with the concept of learning to control your dream.

Dreams are either extremely surreal, or intensely real. If you dream about cheating on your lover, there is probably something behind it. You may have never had the desire in waking life to do this, but there may be something in your relationship that has gone unspoken, causing you to dream up something that you may be afraid of occurring. Perhaps you are losing interest in your partner, or you feel less attracted to them. There is a possibility that this vision could be of the future, so it is best to accept this, and take the necessary steps to explore how you are feeling, whether or not it be with your partner.

The observe are sometimes called precognitions; the dreams we have that may be indicating to us what is to come. Lucid dreaming is the ability to control your dreams, and maybe thus, organize your future by creating positive visions of it.

Lucid dreams will generally start like any dream; it is only when you are already dreaming that you can begin take control of it. Here are some general steps that you can take if you want to start trying to lucid dream:

1. Start by saying certain statements a few days before you attempt lucid dreaming so you can practice becoming aware of yourself. Try stopping and saying to yourself, every now and then "This is what is happening. I am awake."

2. Before going to bed, practice a comforting nighttime routine. Take a hot shower, wear comfortable pajamas, wash your sheets so they are fluffy and warm, etc. , anything that is going to make it easier for you drift off to sleep.

3. As you lie down, focus on being supported by the bed. Try to relax every single part of your body. Breathe slowly, and deeply.

4. Repeat this statement to yourself as you fall asleep: "I can control my dreams. I can control my dreams." If you want to dream about something specific, say to yourself "I am going to dream about _____."

Once you are within your dream, try to say to yourself, that you are there, and that you are now the one who is going to be in control. Some people use their dreams to improve their self-esteem, self-confidence, or encourages successful outcomes in their lives. Dreamlike states like visualization can help with this too, as it helps you accept something as reality, and act like it is a reality, which will help you more likely bring this reality about. For example, if you want to be promoted, then you can visualize being promoted, and then you will thus behave that way.

Dream journals were suggested to you in an earlier chapter. They are great ways to enhance positive feelings from lucid dreaming and visualizations that you can carry forward into waking life. They are useful for keep track of your dreams, reoccurring images and symbols, so everything is laid out in front of you. You may have a few moments of understanding when you are going through your journal, picking up similar occurrences and visions. Try keeping a notebook with a pen or pencil right next to your bed, so you can scribble it down as soon as you wake up. It will be easier to do this in the moment, because you are more than likely not going to remember the details when you wake up later in the morning (should your dreams occur in the middle of the night).

Try to write down the details of the night before you had the dream, the feeling of the dream, the various themes and occurrences. When you wake up, try to stay still, lying there for a few moments before you sit up to write down the details. Try to recall everything about your dream. Stick with a certain piece of information in your unfocused state, so you can recall every little detail. When you can no longer go any deeper, open your eyes and write in your journal. It doesn't have to be coherent at this point, and try not to worry about spelling or grammar.

Here are some dream interpretations of some of the most commonly dreamed dreams:

FLYING: Is a reflection of your capabilities, and may suggest a sense of freedom.

FALLING: Falling with fear means you're feeling out of control or insecure. Falling happily means you can take on new challenges.

TEST-TAKING: This may mean you are struggling with learning something or feel insecure about your knowledge.

NAKEDNESS: Being naked in public in your dream means you're feeling vulnerable.

TEETH: Many people have dreamt about their teeth falling out in their dreams. You may be feeling insecure romantically, worried about your health issues, or it can be an omen of death or illness of someone you know.

STORMY WEATHER: Feeling overwhelmed or angry.

CEMETERIES: Dreaming of walking through a cemetery means that you are sad, or fearful. You can also be on the verge of rebirth.

The next are less common dreams:

RESTROOMS: Dreaming of going to the bathroom means that you feel you need more privacy in your daytime life, or that you actually have to go to the bathroom and your mind is telling you to wake up.

GARDENS: A garden of flowers means love and happiness, while a garden of weeds may mean that you need to clear your head of something spiritual ache.

PARTIES: This may mean that you are achieving your goals.

ABANDONMENT: Dreams of being left behind generally mean you need to let go of old beliefs and habits.

KIDNAPPING: Someone in your waking life is trying to control you, and you don't like it.

ACCIDENT: Dreaming about an accident means you are in a worried state of mind. There is probably something in your life that has been plaguing you with anxiety.

ADULTERY: If you dream you are cheating on your partner, you may be mixed up in something unpleasant in your life, and this doesn't mean its an affair.

DEATH: If you dream of your own death, it means you are going through a life transition.

RUNNING: If you are fleeing from someone in your dream, you're trying to avoid something in your life that you are afraid to face. If you are running towards something, then you are trying to chase a certain goal.

RINGS: A ring in a dream means loyalty and wholeness. A broken ring means that someone may be questioning your dedication to them.

Always Taking Precaution When Delivering News

Through your various abilities to see into the future and/or interpret images of potential events, you possess the serious responsibility as to whether or not you should relay them to others. This of course is considered most when potential harm may come to another. The indication that this might happen isn't going to be as bright as day-you may have a vision of a friend having to get certain medications, or having bad backache. Everything is open to interpretation, and the more you practice, the more you are going to be able to interpret these events.

However, you must be careful when relaying news to other people. For example, you may have a vision of a car accident. You then relay to your friend not to drive their car anywhere that day, they do anyway, and nothing happens. You may have reading your vision wrong, and that is entirely okay. It happens. However, when or how you decide to tell others about visions, especially when it relates to harm being done them, must be done in a sensitive and precautionary manner. If you are unsure as to whether or not to tell a friend about something that you feel may harm them, try to consult another witch, or someone else you are close to.

Chapter 6: Healing spells

In a similar fashion to spells of protection, there are a great number of spells which are focused on the healing and the betterment of the human body. As a powerful conduit for witchcraft and magic, the importance of good health in Wicca is often underestimated, so being able to cleanse and heal oneself is vital. However, as with many medical concerns, witchcraft such as that detailed below is not designed to replace the advice of a doctor, merely to complement it. You should always listen to the advice of medical professionals.

A spell for healing

This is a great spell for those who are trying to encourage a healing process in others. As a witch and a Wicca practitioner, you will often find that many people are interested in the kind of spiritual, energized healing that this kind of witchcraft is able to offer. Thanks to the power of magic, you can use spells such as these to help with the healing process.

As you both begin to relax, you should feel the positive energies and warmth enter into the surrounding space. These might be spirits, goddesses, or whatever the various elements of your own personal brand of Wicca might involve. These are the spirits who will be helping you to heal. Encourage your patient to begin talking, expressing the various parts of their life which are positive. Whether it is relationships, their career, or anything else, encourage them to focus on the best aspects of their life, bringing these energies to the forefront.

Remain in a positive and happy state, eliciting these emotions from the patient. Have them close their eyes, and you do the same. As well as speaking aloud, the positive aspects and energies should begin to fill the room with a warmth and a strong healing aura. Once you are happy that these spirits are present and that they are positive, you should begin to encourage them to help with the healing.

Quietly so that your patient doesn't hear, begin to list the issues which are afflicting the patient and on which you wish the spirits to focus. During this time, the patient should be focusing on the positive aspects of their life and the things which they enjoy doing when they are at their most healthy.

If you have practiced the protective spells from earlier in this book, begin to create the positive shield using an aura of light. Rather than limiting this to protecting yourself, however, imagine that the light is reaching out from beyond you and layering over the patient. This healing energy will be able to not only prevent negative energies from infiltrating your patient, it will also help remove the negative aspects that might be hindering the healing process.

Continue in this fashion. After five minutes, you and your patient should both begin to feel empowered and protected. Thanks to the layer of positivity that has descended over you both and the protective shield that has been created, the spirits that you have invoked should be able to help you with the healing process.

Once this is complete, begin to encourage you both out of the meditative state. Talk softly and guide your patient back into the room now that they have been cleansed and protected. If needed, you can repeat this process once a day in order to bring the best kind of positive energy to your patient's life.

As well as this healing process, the presence of nature in the patient's life is very much encouraged. It is not uncommon to find that many of those whose healing is slower than they might like have very little interaction with nature. This can be as much as adding a houseplant or two to their home or simply walking through a park. Try to suggest that they strengthen their bond with nature in as many ways as possible as this will boost the effectiveness of your own efforts.

A cleansing ritual with the power to heal

Just as a cleansing ritual can be used to protect against negative and untoward spirits, these kinds of rituals can also be used to help remove similar energies from the body and to assist with the healing process. When you are worried about an illness or are not feeling great, then it can often be helpful to ensure that you are correctly cleansed of these kinds of auras. In order to accomplish this, follow these steps. You will need:

- Incense to burn (sage, preferably)

- A single candle (ideally silver or grey-colored)

- A sprinkling of sea salt

- A chalice or cup filled with water (tap water is fine)

Respectively, these items represent the four traditional elements; earth, air, fire, and water. Place the candle in front of you in a quiet room and light the candle and the incense. Begin to settle into a meditative state and remember that the more relaxed you are, the more effective the spell becomes. For those who are feeling ill or under the weather, this can be a difficult step, but being able to temporarily overcome an illness can be rewarding in the long run.

As soon as you are feeling relaxed enough, you can begin.

As the incense begins to smolder and the scent fills the room, cast your hand through the smoke several times. Allow the smoke to pass over your skin and notice the smell as it fills the room. As you are doing so, say the following words:

"With air I cleanse myself."

Next, hold your hand over the burning candle (not close enough to hurt, but close enough to feel the heat on your palm) and say:

"With fire I cleanse myself."

As you say the words, begin to feel the negative energies and the illness burning and smoldering. Next, pick up a pinch of sea salt and rub it between your forefingers and thumb. Then rub the salt over the palm of each hand and say to yourself:

"With earth I cleanse myself."

Finally, dip your hands into the water and wash away the salt and the traces of sage incense. As you clean your hands, repeat these words:

"With water I cleanse myself."

As soon as this is complete, you can extinguish the candles with your still wet fingers and dry your hands. If done correctly, you should begin to feel the illness and the negative spirits departing over the coming days.

A spell for the release of negativity

If you are still encountering negative and harmful energies in your life, this can have an adverse effect on your health. In situations such as these, the most effective solution can sometimes be to simply ask the energies to leave. The power of Wicca is such that not only will it help you identify these energies, but it will also grant you the power to properly dismiss them from your life. If this is the kind of situation in which you find yourself, then read on to discover the best way in which to deal with these issues.

To complete the exercise you will need only a quiet room and a red candle. Turn off all of the lights and place the candle directly in front of you. As it is lit, begin to enter into a meditation. While you might normally close your eyes, you should instead leave them open and focus directly on the flame as it burns. As you consider the lit candle, focus on the power and the strength of fire as a general force. This is the kind of power that will grant you the ability to drive out the negativity.

Once you have become fixed on the idea of the fire, then you will need to say the following words out loud to the room:

"Any energy that no longer serves me,

please leave now.

Thank you for your presence.

Now I am sending you home."

The way in which you say the words will matter. You will need to fill your voice with conviction, concentrating on the power of the fire before you and turning this power into the tone with which you will drive out the negativity.

Repeat the words, driving them out to the room at large. It can help to visualize the negativity being removed from your body, peeling away like a snake shedding its skin. This is the healing process made real, helping you to find the right energy with which to heal yourself and drive out the unwanted energies.

333

As you proceed, you should feel yourself becoming lighter and lighter. Once this feeling begins to arrive, you may extinguish the candle and resume your day-to-day activities as you begin to heal.

A healing spell that uses light

We have already mentioned how powerful light is as a force and how it can be used to remove negative and harmful energies from your life. As the final step for those who are searching for a healing solution, light could well be the missing ingredient that you require in order to get the best results. For those who have conducted the healing steps, repairing the holes in your aura with light is very important, so read on to discover how it can be done.

Again, find a quiet place to sit and be sure that you will not be disturbed. Using the method of aura creation which we covered earlier, we will repair the holes and will begin with the top of your head. This is perhaps one of the most important areas of the body and will thus need to be healed as soon as possible. Visualize the light resting on your head as a crown, a display of strength which is bound on to the top of your head. Continue to hold this imagine and reach up and touch your head with delicate fingers.

In doing this, you will now need to stretch the healing light down over your body. As the powerful aura stretches over your body, it will begin to fill in any gaps and holes which have emerged and which could be causing you issucs. Say the following words as you do so:

"I ask that my energy body is filled

with pure healing light."

Use these words several times until you feel confident that the healing process is correctly handled and that your aura has been repaired. Once complete, thank the spirits, the goddess, and the elements, and resume your day-to-day life. If you have been feeling ill, it can be helpful to repeat this process several times in order to better repair yourself while you are feeling at your worst.

An incantation for self-healing

Just as an awareness of the power of Wicca is important, turning this power on yourself can be a great way in which to heal general malaise and worry from about your person. For this particular incantation, you will be making use of ancient wisdom to make the most of the healing properties inherent in the art of Wicca.

More than others, this powerful spell is largely dependent on the abilities of the witch. Even if you do not consider yourself much more than a beginner, practicing and perfecting this spell can be essential if you wish to use Wicca to self-heal. As well as this, it can be best used in combination with modern medicine, exacerbating the effectiveness of the drugs which your doctor is able to provide.

The first thing that we will need to learn is this mantra. This collection of words has been passed down and has become known among many Wicca users to be one of the best ways in which to heal a body. Consider these words:

By Earth and Water,

Air and By Fire,

May you hear this wish,

Sources of Life and Light

Sources of the day and of the Earth,

I invoke you here,

335

Heal my body and mind.

Learn them by heart, and be sure to use them whenever you are feeling anything other than your best. The words will help to refocus your energies and drive the power of Wicca's energies to help heal the witch's body.

Bringing harmony and peace to an infected space

While it might seem that the body is the element most in need of healing when a person is ill, it can also be useful to heal spaces. By bringing harmony and peace to a room or home, you can accelerate the healing process and ensure that you have the best environment possible to recover.

It can even be used in outside spaces, though the effectiveness might be limited by both the power of the spell caster and the size of the space available. To carry out this incantation, you will require potted plants of the following herbs:

- Rosemary

- Thyme

- Cinnamon

If you cannot get access to these materials, dried herbs and a generic potted plant can be used though they will not be as powerful. The aim is to transfer the power of the spell into the living plants and to allow them to grow and flourish in the space that needs healing.

First, arrange the potted plants in front of you in a line. If you have just one pot, then place that directly in front of you, making sure that the soil is within reach of both hands. Cast your palms over each of the pots in turn (or over the dried herbs) and say the following words:

Balance and harmony,

Peacefulness and ease,

By the Power of Three

All turbulence ceases.

As you are saying the blessing, imagine the energies that you are able to generate as they flow into the plants. The living quality of the soil is becoming imbued with the healing energy that you are providing, which will in turn feed into the roots of the plant. Once complete, you should place the potted plant into the space that you wish to heal.

The spell will continue to work as long as the plant remains healthy and alive and as long as there is one person nearby who is able to occasionally reinforce the positive energies which are present. With these two factors, the plant should continue to provide a lasting healing help.

Distance Healing Spell

Our final healing spell is designed for use over longer distances. As you might imagine, projecting your power over a long distance can be more difficult than close quarter's magic. As well as this, discerning the results can be difficult, so do not be dismayed if you are not able to notice immediate results. Persist with the spell, and refine your abilities.

To complete this spell, you will need:

- Three large candles (white)

- A picture or image of the person who is in need of healing (the more recent, the better)

337

- A single crystal (preferably quartz)

- A selection of incenses of your choosing.

To begin, place the candles in a semi-circle (half-moon) in front of you. The incense should be lit, placed out of sight, and allowed to burn while you conduct the rest of the spell. Take a hold of the image of the patient and gently place it into the center of the semi-circle so that it is still facing toward you. Place the crystal on top of the picture.

Sit down. Place both of your hands flat against your thighs. Feel your weight moving down through your thighs, legs, and into the ground. Center your weight so that there is a sense of oneness with the ground and the rest of the earth. Feel the healing energies of Wicca driving through you as you breathe, pulled up as you breathe in and pushed down as you breathe out. This is the process of becoming connected to the world and allowing your abilities to travel over a greater distance.

Once you can feel the powers flowing through you, it is time to direct your energy. Take your hands from your legs and hold them above the crystal. Continue to breathe deeply, moving the energies that you have just found into the crystal and driving them towards the intended patient. The crystal is able to focus the energy and direct across great distances. On occasion, you may find that the crystal heats up and increases in temperature. Do not worry if this is the case. It can often be taken as a good sign, though it is not essential.

As you continue to direct the energy, discover the light of the candles as it is laid out before you. Notice the protective ring that they are able to form and focus this energy again through the crystal. The light that is created by these candles is a healing one, one that you are stretching across a great distance.

Finally, imagine the patient as you wish them to be. Imagine them healthy and well, emboldened by the power of Wicca which you have sent a great distance. If you know they are using medicine, then imagine that the drugs are even more effective and that the positive energies that are sent are coating them in a warm glow.

Once this is done. Place your hands back on your thighs and resume a regular breathing pattern. With the incense still burning, extinguish the candles and remove all of the items. The energy which you have sent is complete, but allow the positive emotions to mix with the smell of the incense as it heals the patient.

Chapter 7: How to advance your magic

Before we take the plunge, let it be said there is no correct method to produce a magic framework. Your methodology may contrast broadly from my own, and that is alright. It's likewise significant that there's more than one sort of magic framework you can make.

Both hard and delicate magic frameworks exist. Hard magic includes a severe arrangement of rules sketched out in the story that clarifies the parameters of that magic framework.

On the other, the parameters of delicate magic are to clarify in the story rarely; its profundities, impediments, and starting point regularly stay obscure. Magic itself is certifiably not a parallel world-building component, either. Your magic framework may fall somewhere close to hard and delicate magic on the range. In any case, the main thing while creating an magic framework isn't its depiction; it's the way it serves your story.

The utilization of magic in narrating makes issues. If your plot includes characters using magic to take care of those issues, setting up an away from of rules for your magic framework is the surest method to abstain from corrupting the contention in your story with created mystical arrangements.

 Magic serves more to make a fantastical feel than to fathom your story's contention, and there's no compelling reason to spread out all the subtleties of its utilization and creation. The Hobbits didn't cast an extravagant spell to demolish the One Ring, so the specific parameters of magic held little influence. If your story follows a comparative example, a delicate magic framework might be the correct decision for you.

After you have examined, learnt and experienced working with The Craft for quite a while (a more significant number of years than I can tally), you will most likely wind up having suffered a bend. One that began with straightforward operations and advanced to progressively confused regions and afterwards back again to basic. Just this time you can do something amazing with no instruments, spells or bits 'n bounces because the intensity of magic comes easily from inside you.

There is NO alternate route to understanding, and I imagine that is significant in any of the pathways. Black magic is an excursion and one that should be followed at your own pace and not rushed or surged. Jumping on your flying broomstick before you can walk isn't prudent. Information and experience set aside an effort to pick up.

We never quit learning, and I am continually searching out new roads to study and give it a shot. It is a superb aspect concerning the agnostic excursion. There are such a large number of branches and territories to find out.

The stages of magic structure.

In case you're making a hard magic framework for your story world, I've laid out six basic strides to building that framework beneath. Assuming, be that as it may, your reality uses delicate magic, you should not build up every one of these six components. Don't hesitate to take from this guide what best serves your story.

STEP #1: DEFINE ITS USE.

How does magic show itself? What satisfies its use? What does the user call magic, and what abilities does it give the user?

341

STEP #2: IDENTIFY ITS USERS.

What have magic users brought in your story world? Is magic acquired, talented, inherited, or learned? Are there various groups of magic users? Would anyone be able to use magic, or is it selective to a specific few?

STEP #3: OUTLINE ITS LIMITATIONS.

Is magic or the source that energizes it a constrained asset in your story world? Would magic be able to be taken or subdued? What impact does the utilization of magic have on the user? Is there a top on the users' supernatural capacities? How could an magic user be crushed?

STEP #4: ESTABLISH ITS DANGERS.

Would magic be able to be used mistakenly or for egotistical purposes? Would it be able to be used to hurt others or cause humiliation? What perils does magic pose to the user, regardless of whether legitimately or because the utilization of magic is hated or begrudged by society?

STEP #5: EXPLORE ITS ORIGINS.

How is magic made? Where does it obtain its capacity? Are there various kinds of magic, or did magic expand after some time? What significant recorded occasions in your story world were influenced by the utilization or inability to use magic?

STEP #6: CONSIDER ITS CULTURE.

Has magic stayed discreet in your story world? Assuming this is the case, why? Are there supernatural social orders or a chain of importance of magic users? Is an magic user set apart by their dress, appearance, or some other distinctive factor? Do magic users have their language, religion, celebrations, or other social trademarks?

Rules for your magic

1. taking in originates from different sources and occurrences constantly

We live in the period of data, we can discover more than a million spells on the Web, a ton of books on black magic, and in any case, the one factor which we appear to overlook is that everybody is unique. Learning comes/occurs from various perspectives. We can gain from Nature (that is the thing that witches of Old used to do), we can learn from an instructor or somebody who is further developed than us, we can gain from a book, we can gain from a friendly conversation with our coven individuals or companions, we can learn from a conversation with a spirit, and we can gain from a dream.

The minute we acknowledge we experience a daily reality such that we are both the educator and the understudy, we discover that instructing happens continuously. The more our awareness opens, and we are investigating our lives with wide open eyes, the more we see what everything shows us: sympathy, persistence, appreciation, discretion, satisfaction, astuteness, and magic.

343

2. Finding your style

There is a valid justification why we are how we are, and in all actuality, we chose to be what our identity is. The more we find ourselves, the more we figure out how to get things done in our one of a kind way and respect that mysterious individual way.

There is a valid justification why we are acceptable in divination yet not in spellcasting, or significantly more precisely, we are adequate in reading tea leaves; however, not tarot cards. We do what we think we are acceptable at, that fulfils us, causes us to feel achieved, causes us to feel secure and limits our tension and dread of disappointment. All these happen to the more significant part of us to an intuitive level, yet these instruments of our mind are there regularly.

At the point when we challenge ourselves, gaining some new useful knowledge, escaping our usual range of familiarity,

It requires some serious energy and tolerance to have the option to discover some further information and feel great to perform well in it.

3. A feeling of direction

Black magic, as some other craftsmanship or art lined up with what we believe is our feeling of direction, it is another way to communicate what our identity is and what we came here to do. In a free translation, Buddha said that "It takes an entire life to discover your motivation throughout everyday life." The speedier we discover our motivation, the more adjusted we are with our inner world and the more straightforward to find approaches to respect this reason with our activities and with our words.

344

4. Regarding the Self

Our physical structure is the vessel of our mind, and our spirit is the very articulation of the Divine-yet we gain since the beginning that we are unreasonably not the same as others,

we as a whole have similar requirements, we ought to do as X does. You have heard the tales and the talks. They fill their need; however, at the same time, we as a whole need to remind ourselves to set aside some effort to respect yourselves.

Also, when I state to respect, I intend to appreciate yourself for sure. Be upbeat and do whatever you make cheerful and this as confounded as it sounds came in the necessary sentence from my gatekeeper heavenly attendant. You need to do one thing in life is 'Love yourself'. If we can permit that to occur and we do it all the time not just we transmit magic, we are magic as we originate from a similar divine power that made everything that will be, that was and will be. We are love and love is magic.

5. In honesty there is power

Convoluted spells and rituals have unquestionably a few favourable circumstances, however, have you at any point thought why a sincere wish over a flame or a dream might work out as expected? Since magic is dynamic consistently, in any case, fortified by explicit occasions, dates and magic things, magic occurs primarily and regularly subsequently some of the time it goes unnoticed like a breeze, but the most mystical instrument is the Witch's-body, psyche and soul.

At whatever point you feel that a spell is excessively entangled or doesn't sound useful to you there is a valid justification for that. In the first place, we come back to point two this may not be your style and afterwards to look fine, if it doesn't bode well streamline it. A Witch's spells resemble an artist's sonnets, we may appreciate different artisans, yet at the end, it is our mind that we attempt to communicate through our magic and this will end up being our heritage as Witches.

6. Patience is required

I was more youthful as a witch, and my grandma used to state you need to disregard the spell and exercise tolerance. She used to state the accompanying illustration: When you place a blossom bulb under the dirt, you don't burrow into the earth consistently to check whether the plant is developing as this will inevitably devastate the plant. Instead, you deal with it always, and you stand by persistently for it to grow and blossom.

Lately I do magic, and today I need RESULTS. It may occur; however, this isn't usually the situation. Normal magic happens characteristically, and this requires significant investment.

I remember that I do magic to discover my sister's spirit and just worked for the following 2 years. Even though I got an update from the Universe, this was the situation, and it took 2 years. Yet I was requesting a sister spirit, others scan for their entire life and still are not ready to discover their sister spirit. In any case back to the point, if you need to be a savvy Witch that learns and creates you should regard yourself and give yourself and your practices time to develop and grow.

7. Meditation hang tight for who? What?

As we referenced toward the starting, we gain from everything, yet more often than not, we neglect to close our eyes, let the outside world soften and turn our eyes inside our extremely self. The initial step is to

346

figure out how to purge our brains. At that point inside the void, we figure out how to concentrate on various parts of ourselves... sounds recognizable? Without a doubt, it is called meditation, and there is a valid justification why it has created during that time is as yet perfectly healthy. Why? Since it works and it is useful for building up our abilities with one necessary tool, our breath and brain.

All Witches can profit by meditation, and you see a Witch's support is extraordinary or even a floatation tank however for what reason to go that far when you can sit back on a seat and just close your eyes.

Physical hardship can convey brings about learning ourselves, yet it requires persistence (point 6), and the more we comprehend the inside, the better we will begin understanding everything else. Besides, propelled meditation methods can genuinely assist you with doing stunning stuff from astral projection to creating mystic capacities. So give it a go, have a go at studying yourself, and it will show you the way.

Chapter 8: Tips on How to Start the Right Way

1. The goal is Key.

In black magic, the goal is at the center of everything. It is something you genuinely need to comprehend before playing out any sort of magick. Black magic falls under the Law of Attraction.

The conviction that positive beliefs are magnets for positive, beneficial encounters and negative meditations are magnets for negative educational meetings. Because of the law of attraction, if you have a particular want and focus cheerfully on that craving, it will be satisfied.

It is actually how magick and black magic work. In magick, your goal is the change you need to show in the Universe. In any case, deciding this is just the initial segment. At that point, you have to feel your goal, with all the cells of your body. Picture your desire being granted. What does it feel like? How does it taste and smell? At that point, when it is sufficient, compose it on paper. Be cautious with your statement. If you need it to work, your announcement of expectation must be a solitary sentence, using just the current state, at the principal individual.

Additionally, you should just use positive words. Abstain from using «not» or some other adverse action word structures. An example of a decent explanation of aim is: «I am sure and strong.»

At the point when you have made sense of your announcement of expectation, you can play out whatever spell you wish to do. Yet, recall that you genuinely need to accept your whole reality. If you don't, why would you say you are doing it just because? In this way, to outline, I'd state that my expectation is wishing, wording, and unadulterated resolve. A wide range of black magic rests on this standard.

2. Follow Your Intuition Before Anything Else.

I believe it merits discussing it once more. In black magic, expectation and instinct go together. When evaluating another spell, or ritual, ask yourself: «does it feel right»? You need to close your eyes and tune into your internal direction. If it feels right, keep on. If you have a terrible feeling, stop what you're doing promptly. Consider how you could adjust the spell (or ritual) with the goal that it feels directly for you. At that point, proceed if you feel like it. It is significant in such a case that if you don't feel it, your spell won't work.

3. Know about the Three-Fold Law and of the Wiccan Rede.

The Three-Fold Law takes a shot at a similar guideline as to the Law of Attraction that I clarified before. Trash in, trash out. Bliss brings delight, and outrage just brings more annoyance. The thing that matters is that this law is explicit to black magic. Since in magick, we deal with a vigorous level, the impacts of what we convey will, in general, be to increase.

Now, don't take it seriously. It's not scientifically triple; it's progressively similar to a general idea. An illustrated cast of outrage will no doubt create considerably more indignation. So if you choose to play out any sort of hex, be cautious because there will be results. Trust me, and I've been there.

A bit of neighbourly advice: If you're a fledgling in black magic, avoid any type of black magick. Presently, I'm not telling you ALL black magick is malicious. To be completely forthright, I imagine that the polarity among white and black magick is somewhat fake. My point is, if you're an amateur, you should hold up until you're more experienced to perform hexes and curses because from that point you'll realize how to manage the downside. There are different approaches to express your desires. Better to be safe than sorry.

In opposition to the Three-fold law, this standard isn't about the standards of magick. The Wiccan rede is progressively similar to a generally good rule. For sure, it is fundamentally the same as the Golden Rule that can be to found in all religions. It implies that you should treat others like you want to be treated. Regardless of whether black magic isn't a religion, I accept that following a code of morals is significant.

It frequently affects real specialists and the wannabes and imposters. Like I said before. You can cast curses and hexes; yet at the same time, you can't do it ALL the time. Magick is an unbiased tool that should be used with deference. Besides, if, similar to me, you consider black magic as another way towards profound development, you will find that living as indicated by this standard is advantageous.

4. Research a Lot.

Black magic isn't just about performing spells. You have to read a ton about it, to know all the conceivable outcomes that magick offers. Reading something written by others is the ideal approach to realize what's reasonable to do, without facing any challenge. There is a lot of good books out there if you're searching for book suggestions. Even if you plan on finding a coven, it means a lot if you comprehend the basics of black magic. Also, regardless of if you don't distinguish as Wiccan, it's as yet a decent read.

5. Get a Book of Shadows Early on.

On a similar vein, while doing your examination, I exceptionally urge you to get a Book of Shadows when you can. Your first BOS doesn't need to be convoluted or extravagant. A straightforward scratchpad is excellent. If you start your grimoire early, you would already be able to begin reporting your excursions, from the start. At that point, you'll have the option to return, to see what works and what doesn't. It will spare you a great deal of work later if you need to become familiar with the Book of Shadows.

6. Test a great deal.

Black magic isn't something you learn in books. It is an encounter. You can't state that you're a witch if you never perform real spells and rituals. So don't be hesitant to attempt new things. Simply make sure to report them. What's more, before you test an interval that you found on the web, in every case, double-check if it feels right to you. Like I said before, your instinct is your best guide.

7. Gain From More Experienced Witches.

Plus, if you need to attempt black magic, yet stay uncertain about making the dedication, look if there are clear rituals in your general vicinity. They are also frequently comprised of covens, black magic schools or supernatural stores. Go to them and watch. Notice how it feels, note how the consecrated minister or priestess performs.

8. You Don't Need to Own Every Witchcraft Tool.

Witches can be exceptionally materialistic. In any case, you don't have to possess all the tools, and all the intriguing supplies, to begin black magic. The main instrument you need to practice black magic is yourself, and I imagine that, as a novice witch, you'll see that it's simpler to perform spells and rituals with particular essential tools. Instruments help us to center our aim, and they offer material and visual reference in our training.

In a similar vein, be careful with premade black magic units. Rather than purchasing a pack with all the fixings, you ought to get just what you require for your spells and rituals. For instance, if I were going to cast my first consecrated circle, I would just get a book of shadows, an athame, a cup, a red flame, and a little incense burner with a pack of

351

frankincense incense sticks. What's more, that is it. Notice that the entirety of this can be to found in a dollar store for a couple of bucks. It's a decent method to begin black magic without going through a ton of cash.

Premade black magic units can be expensive. Moreover, you don't pick your things independently. Consequently, they won't also function with your energy as though you had selected them by and by. At last, you'll wind up purchasing different tools that you like better, so you'll be to the left with two of everything, which can be very unconventional. In this manner, simply purchase what you require for your spells, and that's it. Along these lines, you'll assemble your particular raised area step by step and will save you a great deal of room and cash.

9. Learn Simple Spells First.

Before you can run, first you have to figure out how to walk! Along these lines, before doing a wide range of conjuring and convoluted spells, you should initially get familiar with the essentials. Here's a non-thorough rundown of what I consider to be the rudiments of black magic.

10. Completely Plan Your Spells and Rituals.

Before playing out any spell (particularly your first one), plan everything. Use a correspondences outline to pick the best time to play out your magick. Use the moon's, the sun's, and the planet's energies to extend your potential benefit. Pick the hues, herbs, precious stones, images, and all the fixings you are going to use as per their imagery. Make everything work in support of you (that is the reason I said you have to do a great deal of research). Luckily, all great black magic books are enhanced with correspondences graphs, and there are a ton of them on the Web as well, so you won't experience any difficulty finding the data you need.

Chapter 9: Practicing witchcraft

So, you've decided you want to start practicing Witchcraft. Witchcraft is a very broad term used, as there are several types of witchcraft spread across the entire world, varying from country to country. However, whilst each type of witchcraft is unique, its important to remember key things before you start practicing witchcraft.

The first step is deciding which type of witchcraft you wish to practice. There are over 60 types of witchcraft that are used all over the world, or you could be interested in the practices of witchcraft that originate in your own country. Start by researching several different types of witchcraft and then deciding which one you want to start practicing. Those interested in botany may be interested in becoming a Floral Witch, but if you are a lover of all parts of nature, you may wish to become an Animist, as they are in tune with all living things on the planet. It is very important that you are careful depending on your location when practicing witchcraft, as some countries still deem it to be unacceptable, and you could face serious consequences if you are caught practicing by someone.

Once you have decided which type of witchcraft you want to practice, be sure you have the right intention of practicing. Deciding is only the first part of practicing witchcraft. It's important for you to intend on casting magic to manifest a change in the universe with all of the cells in your body. Imagine your wish being granted after the spell has been cast. How does it feel? Is it a strong feeling? Only use positive words to describe the intention of the magic, otherwise the energy will diminish and your intention to cast will fail.

Intuition is key when practicing any form of witchcraft. When you are casting a spell or taking part in a ritual you have created, ask yourself a very key question as you are practicing it: does it feel right? Close your eyes as you cast, and dive deep into your own conscience. Is there a good feeling about the spell you are casting? Or is there a pit in your stomach? If the spell you are casting feels right, then keep going. However, if you feel as if something isn't right, stop immediately. It's not to say that the spell would turn out for the worse, it's more to do with the fact the spell itself may not work at all if it doesn't feel right. Go back to your spell, see if you can alter it in any way in order to attune it to your own personal energy to ensure that it succeeds. Remember, if you don't feel as if it will work, then it most definitely won't.

The one thing that anybody who is beginning to practice witchcraft should be aware of is the importance of research. If you fully intend to become a witch, you must be willing to study, and you must study hard. Witchcraft is not just about performing spells, there are so many different parts of it that will enhance your journey as a witch. Reading up on the type of witchcraft you are studying is a great way to seriously connect with the practice. Many witches recommend reading any books written by other witches who practice the same witchcraft as you to see how they got their start, as well as how they developed as a witch. If you don't think you are able to study up on the practice, then perhaps you should consider if witchcraft is really for you.

Experimentation is very key when practicing to become a witch. Whilst it is crucial that you research the craft in great detail, you won't learn everything by simply reading a book. Practicing witchcraft is an experience best perfected when you are practicing your spells or rituals. Never be afraid to try new things that you find, and if they work well, be sure to document them in your notebook that you should keep for any research related to practicing witchcraft. Before experimenting with anything, be sure that the spell or ritual feels right for you. As mentioned before, intuition is key.

You'd be surprised how many people you come across in every day life that turn out to be witches. Whether it be your neighbour or the waitress at a restaurant, everybody is capable of becoming a witch in any form of witchcraft. One of the best ways to learn about witchcraft and how to practice your chosen kind is by communicating with more experienced witches in your area. Try to find out if there are any covens or circles of witches in your area that practice the same type of witchcraft as you. If you are still unsure about committing to the craft, look and see if there are any public gatherings for rituals. Go along and watch, and see how it makes you feel. The best way to see if its right for you is to watch it be performed in front of you, and see how it affects you. Be sure to ask any questions to the high priest or priestess after the ritual if you are unsure about certain parts.

Not everything in witchcraft can be achieved by simply uttering the spell. Tools and materials are key to achieving full potential when casting spells. However, you won't need to purchase every single thing you can find when you're starting out. Start by purchasing only the things you need for your spells, such as a few candles, an incense burner and other materials you may think you need, but be sure not to go all out. Starting with the basics is a great way to get into witchcraft without spending all of your money on tools you may not even use. Another tip from several witches is to avoid buying premade witchcraft kits. They may have lots in them, but you may not use even half of the stuff inside of them.

Performing a ritual or a spell takes a lot of hard work and effort, its not something that you can simply do on a whim. When preparing to perform either of these things, be sure you thoroughly plan it out. Choose the right colours that coordinate with the right symbolism for your spell or ritual. Use the energy from the natural sources such as the sun, the moon or even the earth, use it to your advantage. This is why doing extensive research is important, so you are able to make everything work in your favour when performing a spell or ritual to ensure success. If you are struggling on what to use, many books on witchcraft contain correspondence charts that will aid you in choosing the correct materials and using the correct energies. If you can't find a book, the internet is also filled with several useful websites that contain the same information.

Some forms of witchcraft believe in keeping what is known as a book of shadows to document any and all of their magical activities. Some may consider it to just be a journal dedicated to their works, however some forms of witchcraft believe their book of shadows to be a sacred document in their possession. Common topics for your book of shadows include spells you've learned or created, sacred texts that you've come across, prayers towards your chosen god or goddess and many more. Some forms of witchcraft will write down their recipes for elixirs, oil blends and incense recipes. Kitchen witchcraft witches will use their book of shadows for their cooking recipes whilst also noting down the magical properties of their kitchen ingredients. It's important to remember that you can use quite literally anything as your book of shadows, whether it be documenting your journey in the form of a scrapbook, or using a simple notebook. If you prefer to use a digital method, several witches have been known to use a secret Pinterest board or even just a Microsoft Word document to record what they learn. Remember to keep it well organised, perhaps even keeping separate books for different topics. It's impossible to go over your findings if the work you have written down is in several different places. Make a contents page for your book and write down numbers in the corners of the pages so you know where to find the information you're after.

Finally, in order to get well acquainted with practicing witchcraft, there is simply one piece of advice that applies to every single part: practice makes perfect. You won't know what works and what doesn't if you keep at it and practice to the best of your ability. It's key that you aren't afraid to try whatever you feel like trying when it comes to witchcraft. As long as you stick to your true intentions, nothing bad will happen (unless you are attempting black magic). Always trust your intuition when it comes to practicing witchcraft. If something feels wrong, change it. If it feels right, stick to it.

A guide to spell creation

Spell creation is a very personal experience when it comes to witchcraft. Some witches will use spells they have found on the internet, but many if not all will create their own spells. It may sound strange, but its for a good reason. Spells are personal to each caster, as they use your energies that you create to power them, and they are specifically written to use your own energies. However, there are several steps that you should follow when creating your own spells to cast.

The first step is to prepare yourself for creating the spell. You can't create the spell unless you are in the right mindset and have the right equipment for creating it. The tools needed are incredibly simple; a pen and paper and perhaps some books that you use to study your chosen witchcraft. Other witches may choose to harness the creative forces by using things such as an altar or creating a dish of materials that you consider to have powerful energies to help you. Others use inspiring scents like a burning lilac candle or a cup of chamomile tea to relax and clear their minds to focus on creating a powerful spell.

After you have successfully prepared yourself for creating your own spell, decide which kind of spell you wish to create. You can create spells for a variety of different things, such as success in a certain project in your life or perhaps developing a relationship with someone. Be sure to focus all of your energies onto creating this spell, and use positive words when writing it in order to ensure success of it working. Using negative words during your spell writing can prove to diminish the energy used to make the spell work, so it's important to charge the spell with positive language to make it work.

Once you've decided on what spell you are going to create and have focused your energy into creating it, it's time to start writing it down. Use words that feel right to you when writing it down, as the spell will be more effective for you if the words have a strong connection to your energies. Remember to use positive language to increase its effectiveness. Some may be wondering why it is better to use a pen and paper rather than type your spell up on a laptop. Some witches believe that letting the intentions flow through you onto the paper through the pen strengthens your spell, something that a laptop and a word processor cannot accomplish. Writing a spell can be done in many ways, as the process has developed over the centuries since witchcraft first began to be practiced. If your spell has simple intentions, you may not need to use sophisticated language when writing it up. Once you have the ideas down, then you can start to play with the words. Be sure to use words that are image-rich so you can easily picture the spell in your mind when you cast it. Some witches considering writing the actions of the spell right into it, for example 'light the incense' may be written down and used in the spell itself.

For less formal spell work, once the words are captured on paper, you're ready to assemble your materials and work the spell. For a formal ritual, or a setting involving a significant event or additional persons, you may want to rehearse the steps once or twice. Consider memorizing the words, too. Memorization is never required, however, when you memorize words, you internalize them, allowing them to enter your unconscious and take on extra power. In addition, not having to read from a piece of paper frees you to watch and be part of the entire process, adding to your own enjoyment.

After casting the spell comes a very important step: the evaluation process. Sit down as soon as you can and take notes about how well the process worked. Did everything go as planned? If you repeated the spell, would you change anything about it to make it more effective for yourself? After finishing your notes, file them away for future use. Some witches warn against talking about newly created spells until a specific period of time has passed, feeling that to speak of it is to release some of its contained power, therefore weakening its strength. Observe these traditions as required by your own practices, but be sure to do your own written evaluation. Come back to it again after time has passed, adding a note about how well the spell worked over weeks or months.

As with any spells or rituals, remove all traces of the process when your cast is complete. Dispose of materials using the appropriate means. This could be by burning them, burying them in the earth, dissolving them in water, etc. Clean and store your magic and writing tools, replacing any used items with new ones for the next cast. Some have considered cleansing their writing equipment with water, others choose to pass them above a candles flame or rub them with a stone in order to imbue them with the elemental powers given to them by the earth.

Some witches believe that creating a writer's talisman before creating a new spell will help to empower you during the process. They will use materials and fabrics that represent strong creative and grounding powers, such as citrine or hematite. Once it is secure, they will then hold the talisman in their hands and visualize the energy created by the talisman pouring into themselves, therefore inspiring them to write their spells with ease.

You have now successfully written your own spell, and you will most likely feel quite proud of yourself because of it. Writing a spell is no easy feat, and each spell is personal to its caster. The more writing you do, the easier it will become for you. Many suggest using several sources of inspiration to help you write, such as listening to evocative music, writing at dawn or dusk, working by a candle or a log fire or surrounding yourself with a comforting scent. Whatever works best for you, put it into practice and you can never falter when writing your new spells.

Conclusion

The journey to becoming a Witch is a long one. There are so many things that you are going to discover. However, one of the most important points to remember is: don't listen to the stereotypes, especially if those stereotypes have been painting Witches in a poor light. Witches have always been a peaceful group of people. They have always cared about the community that they have lived in and the people around them.

Remember that ritual that you read about in an earlier chapter where they walk around a field with broomsticks and pitchforks? That ritual is done not only to improve their own crops, but the crops of others as well.

In many cases, Witches have gone out of their way to learn medicine in order to cure a malady or illness in their community, village or town. The churches often relied on superstition to drive away any problem. When the problem failed to leave, they would blame the person and his or her lack of faith.

Witches would focus on curing people with remedies that they either discovered or learned from others. However, the church had realized that if they allow Witches to continue healing people, then the masses would lose faith in the church.

You are probably aware of what happened next and how many Witches were persecuted eventually.

But the lesson to be learned here is that Witchcraft is a religion of love, compassion, peace, and joy. Even though it does have its dark side, they are mainly used in defense. Know that the journey of the Witch is a fulfilling one. I for one hope that you find much support on your journey. Regardless of what you face, I can wish this for you: blessed be.

Introduction

Witchcraft is quite a broad word with a deep meaning. Basically, witchcraft is a craft practiced by witches. It is referred to as witchcraft and not wizard craft since, in ancient times, witchcraft was mostly practiced by women.

The meaning of witchcraft varies between different cultures and societies. Therefore, it might be hard to have a precise definition. It is better to apply the significance or meaning of witchcraft with caution due to different cross-cultural assumptions. In most traditional cultures worldwide such as Africa and traditional Native American communities, the term witchcraft is normally associated with people who are known to use metaphysical means to cause harm to other people. In other places, witchcraft was an art practiced by people who lived close to nature and understood the herbs that could cure people of different diseases. This was a unique service that not everybody could understand. Witches were able to learn the different properties of many herbs and plants since they stayed close to nature.

However, when it comes to the modern world, especially among the young generation and white people in America and Europe, the meaning is different. In most cases, the world may often mean benign or positive practices of modern paganism. It may also refer to a divinatory or healing role. Societies and groups which believe in witchcraft normally come from backgrounds of people who see the world in a magical view.

Furthermore, witchcraft cannot be limited to a specific definition. To some people, it can be a whole religion such as Wicca or just a part of it. It can also be the standardized version of what our ancestors passed down to us with a good example being the British Traditional Witchcraft. Whatever form witchcraft might take from the magic of common people to the forgotten people, at the end of the day, witchcraft has everything to do with the involvement of some objects beyond the magic creator.

You can practice witchcraft alone or in groups called covens. Both situations are fine, but the main benefit of working alone is the freedom to initiate yourself into witchcraft and begin practicing right away. If you are to work in a coven, then you have to wait for them to initiate you. There is a benefit of working in a coven though. When you are working in a group, you will have a great chance to learn a lot from experienced members. Further, collective worship has the ability to evoke more powerful magic as compared to individual worship.

Witches believe in the power of worship, rituals, and even prayers. In fact, they mostly use them to solve most problems afflicting innocent people. They also understand the power of positive affirmations and the best way to use them in prayers. The affirmations have the power to acquire magic if used with focus and concentration. You will also need to create a special kind of environment conducive enough for worship performance. This is the main reason you will find witches burning fragrant candles and incense. They also have a tendency of uttering chants as they perform their rituals.

Chapter 1: Witchcraft for Beginners

Witchcraft (or witchery) is the act of mystical aptitudes and capacities. Witchcraft is a broad term that fluctuates socially and culturally and in this manner can be hard to characterize with exactness; hence, diverse suppositions about the importance or essentialness of the time ought to be applied with caution. Verifiably, and at present in most conventional societies around the world

- Outstandingly in Asia, South America, Africa, the African diaspora, and Indigenous people group -

The term generally connected with the individuals who use the supernatural intends to hurt the guiltless. In the modern period, principally in western mainstream society, the word may all the more normally allude to benevolent, constructive, or nonpartisan acts of current agnosticism, for example, divination or spell craft. Belief in witchcraft is regularly present inside social orders and gatherings whose social structure incorporates an otherworldly world view.

Witchcraft alludes to the blend of information and abilities, that is, the art that permits one to control reality in constructive or pessimistic manners using individual energy as an engaged idea or feeling, the throwing of spells and the formation of supernatural things using common materials.

Witchcraft is an otherworldly structure that cultivates the free ideas and will of the individual, energizes learning and comprehension of the Earth and nature in this manner certifying the heavenliness in every single living thing. Above all, be that as it may, it instructs obligation. We acknowledge duty regarding our activities and deeds as unmistakably a consequence of the decisions we make. We don't accuse an outside element or being for our deficiencies, shortcomings or slip-ups. If we mess up or accomplish something that causes Harm to another, we have nobody but ourselves to blame, and we should confront the outcomes that happen because of those activities. Pure and simple and no crying...

We recognize the patterns of nature, the lunar stages and the seasons to commend our otherworldliness and to worship the perfect. It is a conviction structure that permits the Witch to work with, not in supplication to divinities with the plan of living in amicability and accomplishing balance with all things.

The spells we do include healing, love, concordance, shrewdness and innovativeness. The potions we mix may be a cerebral pain cure, a refreshing tonic, or a homegrown insect shower for our pets. We try to pick up information on and use the appropriate remedies set on this planet by the heavens for our advantage as opposed to using manufactured medications except if completely important.

Wiccans accept that the soul of the One, Goddess and God exist regardless. In the rainstorm, the trees, blossoms, the ocean, are all in harmony with one another and all of nature's animals. It implies we should treat "all things" of the Earth as parts of the divine. We endeavour to respect and regard life in the entirety of its numerous signs both seen and unseen.

Wiccans gain from and revere the endowment of nature from divine creation by praising the patterns of the sun, moon and seasons. We look inside ourselves for the cycles that compare to those of the ordinary world and attempt to live in agreement with the development of this general energy. Our instructors are the trees, waterways, lakes, meadows, mountains and creatures just as other people who have walked this way before us. This conviction brings a devotion and regard for the Earth and all life upon the Earth.

We likewise worship the spirits of the components of Earth, Air, Fire and Water, which join to reflect all creation. From these four components, we acquire knowledge into the rhythms of nature and realize they are also the rhythms of our own lives.

Since Witches have been mistreated for such a significant number of hundreds of years, we have faith in a strict opportunity first! We don't see our way as the best way to accomplish otherworldliness, but as one way among numerous to a similar end. We are not a missionary religion out to convert individuals to do the same things as we do.

We are happy to impart our experience and information to the individuals who look for our insight and point of view, be that as it may. We accept that any individual who was intended for this way will discover it through their hunt as the Goddess addresses every one of us in her time and way. Wiccans practice resilience and acknowledgement toward all different religions as long as those beliefs don't abuse others or disregard the occupant of "Harm None."

What Witchcraft Isn't

Here are the primary concerns.

Black magic or Wicca isn't a faction. We don't announce ourselves as spokespersons for the divine or attempt to get others to follow us as their saviors.

We don't love Satan or associate with Demons. Satan is a Christian creation, and they can keep him. We needn't bother with a frightened formation of incomparable distasteful and everlasting punishment to terrify us into making the best decision and helping other people. We decide to make the best choice and love our siblings and sisters since it IS the right thing, and it feels great to do it. I guess it is a development thing.

We don't sacrifice animals or people since that would disregard our essential occupant of "Harm None." Anyone who does and claims to be a Wiccan or a Witch is lying.

We have no compelling reason to take or control the existing power of another to accomplish magical or otherworldly powers. We draw our energy from inside, our relationship with the divine and nature.

We don't use the powers of nature or the universe to hex or cast spells on others. Once more, "Harm None" is the whole of the law.

Witches have strict confidence in the Law of Three, which expresses that whatever we convey into our reality will come back to us threefold, either wonderful or horrible. Because of this, a "Genuine Witch" would hesitate in doing magick to hurt or control another because that boomerang we toss will at the end return to us a lot bigger and harder than when we threw it.

It is not necessarily the case that Witches are great; we are human too merely like every other person and commit errors and blunders in judgment. Similarly, as there are guardians who love and support their kids, there are guardians who misuse their youngsters. As there are numerous who dedicate their lives to giving and helping humanity, moreover there are the individuals who give their lives to exploiting and using individuals for their benefit. Shockingly, similar blemishes in human instinct apply to witches as well.

The majority of us ceaselessly endeavour to consider every possible result of our musings and activities while stopping to genuinely think about the outcomes before supporting a ritual, spell or ritual that could stray. It is the point where we follow the way with the love for the Goddess in our souls and stick to the essential inhabitant of the Reed that our works are useful and we accomplish congruity and balance with all things.

The core of Wicca isn't something summarized into a couple of short words and can frequently take on a different importance to each since the Lord and Lady contact us in various manners. To increase your full comprehension of the Craft, I encourage you to visit different pages on this site and to follow the links to a select gathering of different Wiccan and Witchcraft sites. Through the knowledge and words set down through the ages, you will find you can comprehend the premise of our beliefs and how they may concern you.

Your internal voice will likewise immediately inform you as to whether the aim of what you are reading is for shallow purposes to profit self as opposed to attempting to profit all. Make sure to read with your heart, for the point where you see life and the world with your heart and soul is when you genuinely increase your comprehension of what Wicca is.

The Witches are about, well, witches. Witches detest youngsters. Furthermore, honestly, we realize that "detest" is a trustworthy word.

The religion Wicca is a black magic based religion. Once in a while, the words Wicca and Witchcraft are used reciprocally, yet they are not equivalent words. While every single dynamic Wiccan practices

Witchcraft as a significant aspect of their strict recognition, not all specialists of Witchcraft are Wiccan.

Witchcraft is an otherworldly practice that might be seen in regards to a religion. However, it's anything but a strict act of itself. Some may have a place with one of the numerous advanced Pagan religions, or they may have a home with one of the Abrahamic faiths.

What Do Witches Do?

Indeed, witches have consistently been human magic producers - individuals who use old stories, nature, and old, profoundly felt superstitions and practices to change or impact events. At the point when Christianity turned into the overall religion in Europe, a significant number of the antiquated "agnostic" beliefs in spite of everything that had endured, and these included magic making practices. The Christian church persuaded people that these beliefs were related to Satan and it assaulted the negligible doubt of them with extraordinary ruthlessness. For the following 300 years, a considerable number of individuals were tortured and executed. As is confirmed by the Salem witch trials in seventeenth-century Massachusetts, the charges were generally bogus, and the proven false.

The objectives of these assaults were regularly elderly ladies who were unmarried or bereaved and lived alone with small animals like cats for pets. Some of the time, they were criticized because they possessed land others needed, or because they used plants and legends rituals for healing cures, or because they were poor and made noticeable objectives.

Today's Witchcraft

Today's witches of the Western World despite everything battle to shake their recorded generalization. They practice Wicca, an official religion in the United States and Canada.

Wiccans maintain a strategic distance from evil and the presence of underhandedness no matter what. Their saying is to "harm none," and they endeavour to live a tranquil, tolerant and healthy lifestyle in balance with nature and humankind.

Numerous modern witches despite everything perform black magic. However, there's rarely anything evil about it. Their spells and chants regularly come from their Book of Shadows, a twentieth-century assortment of wisdom and black magic. They can contrast with the demonstration of the petition in different religions. An advanced black magic potion is more likely to be a homegrown solution for influenza rather than a hex to hurt somebody.

The present black magic spells are typically used to prevent somebody from doing something underhanded or hurting themselves. Amusingly, while it's likely some verifiable witches used black magic for malicious purposes, many may have grasped it for healing or assurance against the indecency they were accused of.

In any case, witches—regardless of whether real or accused—despite everything face oppression and death. A few people associated with using black magic have been beaten and executed in Papua New Guinea since 2010, including a youthful mother who was singed alive. Comparative scenes of savagery against individuals accused of being witches have happened in Africa, South America, the Middle East and in foreigner networks in Europe and the United States.

The scourge on spell casting circumvent India, Brazil, Thailand, Tibet, and other nations where it as yet is practiced and well-regarded. Africa has numerous kinds of witch specialists who cast spells, read the future, heal the injured and look for signs for direction. A Tibetan Buddhist priest will fill the role of a detestable soul from pre-Buddhist beliefs in a ritual move to drive out evil. A Sri Lankan shaman treats sicknesses by attempting to reestablish the body's inward energy balance. The Chinese built up the antiquated mystical specialist of feng-shui, which is presently well known in America.

Wicca is the most broadly refined type of black magic in America. However, different kinds of enchanted beliefs are mainstream -, for example, crystal gazing, New Ageism, and the rediscovery of herbalism and alternative medication.

Present-day witchcraft comes in a wide range of flavors. However, there are a few similarities across conventions. Be that as it may, nothing absolute can be said about Witchcraft.

Witchcraft is frequently used in the modern setting as a catch-all term. Many Witches practice the more common types of witchcraft, yet mix them with mystical and profound practices additionally found in present-day divination, shamanism and speculative chemistry.

Most professionals of witchcraft will contend that witchcraft isn't heavenly; however, one of the numerous ways we people outfit nature is basically. The energy used in witchcraft can be compared to power being directed into a wire to light our homes or gas in an ignition motor to control a vehicle. Black magic works with the forces of nature to achieve the ideal outcome. Witchcraft can't make anything happen that couldn't have happened in any case if the circumstance was perfect.

While a few Witches accept that the capacity to practice black magic is an innate characteristic, most Witches concur that anybody can do witchcraft if they are happy to set aside the effort to learn and practice the aptitudes required to do it. While a few Witches learn the Craft from guardians or grandparents, many learn it all alone or from other, separate Witches. Most covens and individual Witches won't acknowledge understudies who are not identified with them until they are 18 or even 21 years of age.

Many Witches practice in covens of different sizes or progressively easygoing meetings. Many practice alone or with only close relatives. Most who practice witchcraft in groups practice alone also.

Various Witchcraft conventions and covens have different standards for administering the training and lone witches additionally set principles for themselves to follow. These principles can change significantly between rituals. Some restrict the utilization of witchcraft for own advantage while others demand that if you can't use witchcraft to support yourself, you can't help any other individual.

Some preclude the utilization of witchcraft to meddle with free choice of someone else or to hurt anybody. Others state that releasing a wrong unhindered or unpunished is wrongdoing in itself. The expression "If you can't hex, you can't mend" or "if you can't revile, you can't fix" has been heard in many Circles.

Most accept that whatever energy you convey, positive or negative, will come back to you somehow or another through the subtleties can differ broadly. Some agree that these reasonable laws of return can be dodged by specific activities or rituals, while others accept that they are unpreventable. The main constant is by all accounts that each Witch's involvement in and meaning of witchcraft and the principles related to it is impressive.

375

Chapter 2: History

It is important to understand the term witchcraft and its background in society. Anthropology has almost always defined the term in a negative way. This is where the evil witch stigma and myth comes from. Anthropologists have commonly defined witchcraft as the "conscious intent of causing harm." They say that witches would use rituals, magic, spells and manipulate substances such as herbs in order to assassinate political powers, harm innocent civilians and hurt their enemies.

What needs to be understood here is that there is a major difference between what people have said witches were doing and what they were actually practicing.

You see, we get our historical evidence mostly from Christian sources. This is because Christians were the most highly educated groups of people and pagans, heathens or other people living on the fringes were not usually the ones writing books. Therefore, we must take any accounts of witches or witchcraft written by those historians with a grain of salt.

We know that during the witch trials, Christians burned witches at the stake and justified these actions by saying they were evil Satan worshippers who sacrificed babies and poisoned the town's water supply. It wouldn't look very good on Christianity if they were burning people simply because they were pagans and lived an alternative lifestyle, although that is probably exactly what happened.

Living a life that was not Christian meant that these pagans were not falling under Christian power and that didn't sit well with them. Christians have historically done this to many groups of people who have not abided by their religion. They have also persecuted Jews, Muslims and lepers and simply used them as a scapegoat. Although it will likely never be historically proven, the chances of witches being used as a scapegoat by Christians rather than practicing evil are very high - in my opinion.

As we know from earlier in this book, Margaret Murray was the first prominent historian to write about how the witches burned at the stake were not evil Satan worshippers but were practicing a pre Christian religion, called witchcraft.

Before we go further, I feel it is my duty to remind you that many historians have discredited and disagreed with Murray and her theories on witches, meaning that we probably will never know the truth about pre-Christian pagan rituals and practitioners of witchcraft. That being said, we *do* know what Gerald Gardner had in mind when he was establishing the modern practices, we observe in Wicca today.

Chapter 3: Some Different Types of Witchcraft

The word witchcraft evokes different reactions, especially in the modern world. Witches are people who strain to have a relationship with their natural environment. They wish to recognize the sacredness of nature. Up to date, the practice of witchcraft rituals and practices that are believed to focus and harness energies still exist.

The major differences between modern and traditional witchcraft

Modern witchcraft is still going strong despite all the controversies surrounding it. There are notable differences, but that could be due to the fact that times have also changed. Below are some ideas on what the modern witchcraft looks like and what could have changed from the past.

a) Witchcraft as a religion

In most of our traditions, witchcraft is treated or believed to be a form of religion. Even up to now, it can still be a religion. Basically, witchcraft is a spiritual discipline. Nothing much has changed though, witches still use witchcraft to describe their religion and beliefs. They still cast spells and warship, various goddesses and gods, if not deities.

b) Different types of witches

The modern-day witch is not a common witch throughout the world, and they have their differences as they all believe in something else. There are some others who work in a coven while others still practice alone. There are others who follow a religion like the Wiccan religion. There are even Christians who describe themselves as witches simply because they do their magic by worshipping their God. Other witches describe themselves as pagans but of course, not every pagan who is a witch.

c) Use of magic

The traditional is best known to perform magic. However, even the current witch still uses magic to cast her spell and worship her deities. Even now, witches still pose tools such as candles, herbs, books, and all the necessary tools a witch should wish to keep. Although in the current society, the word magic is a bit scary, unlike in the past. All in all, there are witches who still perform rituals for different reasons.

d) The seriousness involved

Witches who still practice witchcraft in the current world do so because they are serious with the practice they believe in. With so much to do in this busy and they still find time to connect with nature, worship their deities and cast spells. This is a clear sign that they have taken the practice with the seriousness it deserves. This is truly their way of life since most of them practice it until they die.

e) Freedom of worship

The modern-day witch is satisfied with her job, and some have even gone ahead to make it a professional. They are not afraid to say what they do and believe it. Some even have functioning websites, and they proudly refer themselves as witches. In the past, when witchcraft was being treated as a form of devil-worshipping, so many innocent lives were lost. This explains why most witches in the past have done their business in private. Because of the freedom of worship these days, most witches are doing their rituals and practices in the limelight. For instance, the Wiccan religion practices their ceremonies, such as handfasting in broad daylight without fear of discrimination.

f) Wrong perception

The biggest challenge a modern witch has to deal with is the perception some people have concerning witchcraft. Some think witches are Anti-Christian. Witches are not Christians, but they do not disrespect Christians. They just have their different way of worship, and that is all. The only things witches don't approve is bad behavior, racism, and any wrongdoing. As they do so, they do not do it targeting a specific group. Just like the way they respect other people's beliefs, it would not be too much for them to request the same.

Another very wrong perception people have of the modern witch is the idea that she could be a devil worshipper. People of other faiths, especially the Christian view witchcraft as a form of devil-worshipping and this is far from the truth. It is unfair to look at a witch's tools and sees your description of Satan in them. Before you judge someone, do thorough research and have a clear understanding of witchcraft.

g) Not every witch who owns a cat

Cats were associated with witches in the past. Most witches loved cats, though. If you are expecting to identify a modern witch because of a cat, it will be almost impossible for you to recognize one. Most of them do not own cats. More so, there are people of other religions, but their favorite pet is a cat. Do not go calling them witches because they are not. Not unless someone shares their religion with you, it is very hard to know if your colleague or neighbor is a witch or not.

There are numerous sorts of black magic, a large number of which cover and which can all be characterized in various manners by various individuals, different kinds of witches one can become and a portion of the realities behind what separates each in the realm of black magic. Yet here are some unpleasant rules for their assignments:

Witchcrafts of African

There are numerous kinds of black magic in Africa. The Azande of focal Africa accepts that black magic causes a wide range of obstruction. The "blessing" of black magic, known as mangu, is passed from parent to kid. Those having mangu aren't even mindful of it and perform magick unwittingly while they rest.

Appalachian society magic

The individuals who practice black magic in the Appalachian Mountains consider great to be malicious as two extraordinary powers that are driven by the Christian God and Devil, separately. They accept there are certain conditions that their magic can't fix. They additionally believe witches are honored with paranormal powers and can perform

380

ground-breaking magic that can be used for good or evil purposes. They seek nature for signs and omens of things to come.

Witchcrafts of Green

A Green witch is fundamentally the same as a Kitchen/Cottage witch (see beneath) with the particular case that the Green witch practices in the fields and woods to be nearer to the Divine soul. The Green witch makes their own tools from free materials from outside.

Fence witchcraft

A Hedgewitch isn't part of a gathering or coven. This witch practices magic alone and works more with the green expressions, homegrown fixes and spells. In the good 'old days, Hedge witches were nearby wise men or ladies who healed sicknesses and offered guidance. They can be of any religion and are viewed as customary witches (see underneath).

Genetic witchcraft

Genetic witches have faith in "endowments" of the art that are with a witch from birth, having been passed down from ages previously.

Witchcraft of Kitchen/Cottage

A Kitchen witch, or Cottage witch, practices magic around the hearth and home. The house is a consecrated spot, and the utilization of herbs is frequently used to bring assurance, success and healing. Kitchen witches regularly follow more than one way of black magic.

Pennsylvania Dutch hex art or "Pow-wowing"

At the point when the Germans initially showed up in Pennsylvania, Native Americans were there, so the expression "pow-wowing" to portray this training may originate from perceptions of Indian social affairs. Pow-wowing incorporates charms and mantras going back to the Middle Ages, just as components obtained from the Jewish Kabbalah and Christian Bible. Pow-wowing centers around healing sickness, safeguarding animals, finding love or throwing or getting rid of hexes. Pow-wows believe themselves to be Christians invested with heavenly powers.

Customary Witchcraft

Customary witchcraft regularly follows science, history and expressions of the human experience as its establishment. While having similar regard for nature as the Wiccan witch (see beneath), conventional witches don't revere the god or goddess nature nor of Wicca. They will contact the spirits that are a part of a hidden soul world during ceremonies. Magic is more functional than formal and focuses enormously on herbs and concoctions. This faction of black magic additionally has no law of hurting none yet believes in duty and respect. Hexes and reviles, like this, can be used in self-preservation or for different kinds of insurance.

Wicca

Wicca is one of the modern Pagan religions that worships the Earth and nature, and it is just around 60 years of age. It was created during the 1940s and 50s by Gerald Gardner. Gardner characterized black magic as a positive and stimulating religion that incorporates divination, herblore, magic and mystic capacities. Wiccans make a vow to make cause no Harm with their magic.

Humanities Witchcraft

Anything an anthropologist calls "black magic," for the most part alluding to either or both of the accompanying implications:

1. The acts of autonomous (genuine or assumed) magic users who are associated with any event in some cases use their magic outside of the general public's acknowledged social standards

2. An apparent state, frequently automatic, of being a beast who can revile individuals with the "stink eye."

Christian Witchcraft, Christo-Wicca

The beliefs and practices of the individuals who blend Neoclassic Witchcraft (see underneath) as well as Neopagan Witchcraft (Wicca) with a liberal type of Christianity, in this way making new Mesopagan forms of Wicca. The individuals who do the last are taken a gander at askance by most Wiccans, who are slanted to consider them "apostates."

Usually, everything except the most liberal of Christians considers individuals doing any flavor at all of the black magic to be blasphemers, since Christian clerics, evangelists, and priests should have a total imposing business model on all exhibitions of magic.

High Witchcraft, Cunning Craft

The acts of the individuals that numerous modern witches believe we're the first witches, however, who are all the more appropriately known as the wise people. These people were only from time to time called "witches" (at any rate to their countenances) and could have any or all the accompanying in their bag of stunts: birthing assistance; healing with magic, herbs, and other society cures; causing premature births, mixing love elixirs, and toxic substances; divination; and throwing of hexes and favours. Exemplary Witches have kept on existing right up 'til the present time, in ever-diminishing numbers, for the most part in the remotest towns and among the Romany or other nomadic groups.

Criminal Witchcraft

Black magic is an initiative brought about by the individuals who used the term first: the associated or genuine use of magic for harmful purposes - at the end of the day, supernatural misbehaviour. It is most likely what "Wicca" initially alluded to, irritating as that might be to present-day Wiccans, and is fundamentally the same as how anthropologists characterize black magic.

Devious Witchcraft

A nonexistent faction of Devil admirers developed by the medieval Church, used as the reason for assaulting, torturing, and slaughtering scores of thousands of ladies, kids, and men. The clique was said to comprise of individuals who revered the Christian Devil in return for supernatural forces they used to profit themselves and harm others. They used to call this "Gothic Witchcraft."

Dianic Witchcraft

1. A proposed medieval religion of Diana or potentially Dianus admirers (Margaret Murray's thought).

2. The term used by some henotheistic Neopagan Witches to allude to their focus on the goddess as more significant than the god.

3. The term used by some Feminist Witches, particularly the individuals who are dissident, to depict their practices and beliefs.

Varied Witchcraft

A varied witch doesn't have one set of religion, practice, convention, or culture that they pull from. Their training gets from numerous sources and, eventually, turns into the witch's own. They may worship a higher being, or their practice might be principally common, or it may be its sort of otherworldly. A mixed witch, at last, makes their own "rules" with their training—it is extraordinary dependent on the individual witch.

The beliefs and practices of those on the liberal/heterodox finish of the Wiccan range. See "Conventional Witchcraft."

Ethnic Witchcraft

The acts of different non-English-talking individuals who use magic, religion, and elective healing techniques in their networks and who are designated "witches" by English speakers who don't have the foggiest idea about any better.

Family Tradition or "Fam-Trad" Witchcraft

The practices and beliefs of the individuals who guarantee to have a place with (or to have been instructed by individuals from) families that were "underground" Paleo-or Mesopagans for a few centuries in Europe or potentially the Americas, using their riches and influence to remain alive and secret. The lion's share of the individuals you will ever meet who guarantee to be Fam-Trad Witches are mostly lying, or have been the deceived by their educators. Family Tradition Witchcraft is likewise at times called "Innate Witchcraft" or even "Hereditary Witchcraft." These last terms are used by those individuals who figure they should guarantee a witch as a predecessor to be a witch today or who believe that such lineage "demonstrates" them to be preferable witches over those without such heritage.

Women's activist Witchcraft

A few new monotheistic or henotheistic religions begun since the mid-1970s by ladies in the women's activist network who had a place with the ladies' otherworldliness development, as well as who had contact with Neopagan Witches. It is somewhat an outgrowth of Neopagan Witchcraft, with male divinities booted unceremoniously out of the

386

religion totally, and halfway an aggregation of free and diverse do-it-without anyone's help covens of profoundly slanted women's activists. The beliefs, as a rule, include venerating just the syncretic goddess (who are all goddesses) and using her as a wellspring of motivation, enchanted force, and mental development. Their grant is regularly horrifying, and men are typically not permitted to join or take an interest.

Note, numerous different assortments of Witches likewise view themselves as women's activists or act like ones whether they use the term or not.

Goth Witchcraft

Individuals in the "Goth" subculture who practice at least one assortments of Neoclassic, Neopagan, or at times Neodiabolic Witchcraft. Goth Wiccans will participate in the global spotlight on "dark" divine beings and goddesses (which means ones that model such issues as death and the black market) and attempt to look frightening.

Grandmotherly Witchcraft

Alludes to the propensity underlying among current Witches of professing to have been started at an early age by a mother or grandma who had a place with a Fam-Trad. However who is presently advantageously dead, doesn't communicate in English, as well as is in any case inaccessible for addressing.

Neoclassic Witchcraft

The present acts of the individuals who are intentionally or unwittingly copying a few or a significant number of the (genuine or expected) exercises of the Witches Classic/Folk Cunning and who themselves (or are called by others) "witches."

Enormous Witch

Enormous witches are contemporary witches who look to the universe, crystal gazing, and space science and work those components and divine energy into their training. Additionally called "Star Witches," these witches frequently follow the planets and the arrangement of the stars and base their spells and rituals on the various situations.

Single Witch

A single witch can be any kind of witch, yet they decide to practice alone as opposed to with a coven. It could be by decision or because they haven't found a gathering to work with yet. There are likewise legends that lone witches are resurrections of witches who have been practicing for ages and at pubescence, their insight stirred. Since they as of now recollect and comprehend the specialty, their requirement for a coven is not precisely a more up to date witch.

Mainstream Witch

Mainstream witches despite everything cast spells, use precious stones, herbs, oils, and candles, however, they don't add otherworldliness to their training. Mainstream witches don't worship a god or higher being—their training is entirely non-strict. They don't trust in the force behind energy or that there is energy in their work. It is not necessarily the case that a mainstream witch CAN'T be profound; their work mustn't be. The two are entirely independent.

Chapter 4: The Magic and Spells of Witchcraft

Casting witchcraft magic spells is an art that can only be performed by a witch. If you happen to work with a group of witches, also known as a coven, you will have more energy and strength to cast a spell. The issue is, you need to cast more energy in a spell to have better results.

The power of witchcraft magic spells cannot be underestimated, and it should be handled with a lot of care. Looking for a spell and you have not yet studied witchcraft in details may not be very useful to you. You need to understand witchcraft to know how certain things work. If you just receive spells from someone who has not yet studied the craft, high chances are you will not receive the results you had expected.

How to become a witch

The problem of making witchcraft your profession is the misconceptions surrounding it. Just forget about the corny incantations, broomsticks and all those fearful information about witchcraft. Witchcraft is a personal practice, and it is a method of folk magic. It involves an in-depth knowledge of the spiritual world, the natural world, and oneself.

Do you feel like you have a connection with such worlds and are not content with the traditional beliefs? Well, witchcraft might be the right profession for you. This will give you the best opportunity to learn more about this spiritual world. Remember to be prepared as this is a lifetime journey and practice. The impressive thing about it is that it is a fulfilling occupation if you do in the right way and in the right place.

If you want to become a witch, there are certain basics you should put in place. For example, start by reading articles that share about witchcraft and the like. Make sure you read your notes and understand them. You also need to do more research on the topic. After that, start a regular meditation regime, experiment with the energy, and start to practice the spells. In everything you do, make sure you find your strength and choose your witchcraft niche from there. From there, learn to adept spells, write your own and continue reading. This is a journey with no end. In addition to that, below are ways that can help you fulfill your desires of becoming a witch.

Learn more about witchcraft

Unfortunately, you will not come across a central school which teaches witchcraft or spell casting. There are things you will learn from different sources. Even the novices and non-practitioners do not have enough facts to figure out what is real and what is not. In fact, becoming a witch will need you to be more committed to this life long journey. A lot of research, patience, and study is needed if you are to meet your expectations. Different schools of thought and traditions will be more appropriate depending on your personal interests and what you intend to achieve.

Some of the common styles of witchcraft are;

a) Neo-paganism and Druidism

These styles of witchcraft and other ancestral witches might be ideal for you if you are interested in history and tradition. They are more specific with the seasons and rituals.

b) Wicca witchcraft

It is more recognized in the United States. It often revolves around Gaia-study, meditation, and nature-based spells. If your interest is in the use of herbs, crystals, rituals, and essential oils, this option might go well with you.

c) Regional and esoteric witchcraft

You need to have a strong connection to the place you live in if this is going to work. You can begin by researching the local practices. Some common witchcrafts include Santeria, Stregheria, Fari, and Pharmakos, among other cultural witchcrafts.

Witchcraft is not for specific people only. It can be practiced by everybody so long as they are comfortable with it. Further, secular witchcraft is not associated with any religion, belief system philosophy, and the like. In other words, anybody from any religion is free to practice secular witchcraft.

Another important thing to note there are some practices which are closed. In a closed culture or religion, you can only join the group if you are formally initiated into it. That is when you can now be considered as a member of that particular faith or community. After the initiation, you will also be allowed to take part in most of their spiritual practices. If you are not sure if a certain culture is closed, the best way is to enquire from a member of the group.

Research more on the topic

You need to learn in details about the different histories and traditions. You can get this information from a wide variety of sources. Do not limit yourself from one source. Make it your business to source information from any source that seems educative. You will never come across one specific book with all the details you need to practice witchcraft. There are no specific rules and principles for all witches in the world. If you have come across anything claiming that to be possible, then that is a lie.

391

Your practices as a witch, are not the same with another witch. They are specifically yours and nothing more. Henceforth, it is better to do your research and stand strong in what you believe in. It is perfectly okay to read some classics, but at the end of the day, everything should go towards your own practice and your personal understanding of witchcraft. Another thing to note while reading those awesome classics is the fact that although some authors wrote amazing books with credibly useful information, they have been dead for quite a long time and so the information in that book is a bit outdated. Although it can help you in a way, you need to read more recent information to stay updated in your profession.

Be specific with what you intend to achieve

You need to know your destiny for you to succeed in this profession. Begin by developing personal goals. They will greatly help you to know what you want to become now and for the rest of your life. As mentioned earlier, becoming witchcraft is a personal journey, and you are the only one who can shape it. For that reason, commit yourself from learning can, writing your personal goals and most importantly, practicing what you can. You can even keep a record of what you intend to explore now and in the future and what you want to discover. To be more precise, you need to know what you expect to achieve from witchcraft, the types of spells and incantations you intend to perform, what you want to learn from this profession and most crucial, what you expect to gain from practicing witchcraft.

Casting and use of spells

To have a clear understanding of witchcraft, you need to understand the meaning of spells and how to cast them. To put it in the simplest form possible, spells can be termed as procedures. Using a spell helps you to do two things. One, you will be able to prepare to go for your intent and secondly, it will direct the energy needed to draw your intent to you or create a path for you to reach it. You need to know what is required for the rituals you intend to perform. There are different objects and methods which are used for casting depending on different traditions.

Although the underlying principles of casting a spell are more or less the same, you can design and execute a spell in different ways. Just like the way you see different buildings with different designs but all of them were built with specific basic engineering principles, the same case applies to witchcraft. There is a common foundation that every witch must observe if things are to turn up as they should. How a witch will cast her spells will depend on different factors such as religion, philosophies, the witches' methods, preferred tools, and so on.

Five essential parts to cast a spell

Preparation

You need to do some preparations for you to cast a spell. This is the stage where most of the preparations are done. At this stage, you begin by defining your intent. You will identify what you need and determine what you intend to achieve with this spell. You have to be very specific and precise. This is not the time to be uncertain with what you want.

Be focused enough to be able to say what you want in just a few words. Remember to be positive and strive to have positive goals. For instance, instead of casting for a spell not to be single anymore, cast a spell to find your soul mate. If your overall goal is quite complex, then consider breaking it down into small specific goals. Do a specific spell on each of the steps or changes you think it will take to achieve your intent. Results of specific spells are more logic that is excepting to change everything with just one spell.

If you find it difficult to remember everything which is normally the case, then consider writing the spell. Familiarize yourself with it. If you want, you can memorize it, but that is not a requirement. The most important thing is to be well familiar with all the necessary steps and what you are supposed to say. Everything must flow out naturally without being forced. You can use notes if you must but let everything flow well. Avoid stumbling over the notes. If you are familiar with the notes, then a mere glance of them will help you to cast the spell perfectly.

If you wish to work with magical timings, then it is important you determine the timing. Next, gather all the materials and supplies you will need to cast the spell. You can make a list of those requirements and recheck that list just to make sure everything is there. You cannot start the procedure and then all over sudden remember there is an item you forgot to bring along. That is not how things work.

The place you are working on needs to be very neat and in the right shape. If you feel the need to cleanse and purify it, please go ahead and do so. If you feel the kids might disrupt you, you can send them to the granny and put a "do not disturb" sign on the door. Your peace of mind is crucial here. The last thing on the preparation part is to prepare yourself. After all, you are the main person here. Some of the preparations you can do are to have a light meal or even fast if you can. You can also take a cleansing bath or just look for ways to purify yourself. Take time to meditate and center yourself. If you observe that, you will be good to go.

State of mind

Your state of mind is of great essence here. It needs to be conducive to your goals right from the beginning. In fact, it is important that the state of your mind be prepared from the beginning until when your intent is manifested. Your state of mind has everything to do with the outcome of the spell. Therefore, it is important you maintain mental discipline all the time. One of the best ways to do it is by regular meditation.

Try as much as you can to maintain positive thoughts, especially in the days or weeks leading up to the casting of the spell. Never entertain any doubts. The worst thing you can do as a witch is to doubt if it will work or you might mess things up. Refrain from such thoughts completely and learn to believe in yourself.

During the spell, you surely want to wants to achieve the most conduce environment for magic and energy work. This state is referred to as Alpha. It is a meditative state where your mind is relaxed and aware of its surroundings. It enables you to maintain consciousness and at the same time, open your subconscious. This is a time when you are just focused on the present. You are not worried about the things you need to do in the future or the wrong you did in the past and what you ought to have done. You are so carried away that you do not even notice how time has passed. You are so absorbed in the activity that you cannot even remember whether you are hungry or not. You have just dedicated all your mind there.

After casting the spell, you need to ensure your mind and thoughts stays positive. Do not entertain anything to ruin that current special state of your mind. When you entertain negative thoughts, you end up sabotaging the outcome of the ritual you have just performed. The best way is to just forget about it, but if you want to think about it, then make sure your thoughts are positive. Do not put on doubts and worries. Be optimistic and know that whatever comes may you will achieve your goals.

Link to your intent

When you are in the state of Alpha during the spell, make sure you establish a psychological and metaphysical link between your intent and you. There are different ways to achieve this. You can even throw in several of them to achieve it.

Make the state of your intent saying and listening to it. Continue to make it a reality and start to forge a connection between your intent and yourself. Another option is sensory stimulation, whereby you pick some images, sounds, tastes, scents, and objects that easily reminds you of your objective. The more you can have creative visualization of your intent, the better.

Symbols and images are known to have a strong effect on the subconscious. Make sure you only use the ones that make sense to you. Do not use what another person used even if she is a witch like you. Use what works for you.

Raise and direct energy

Do not begin to raise energy before you are fully focused on your intent and have connected yourself with it. There is a part of your energy which will come from your internal sources such as your thoughts, desires, and emotional state. Therefore, you must ensure that your mind is fully focused on the intent. The rest of your energy will come from external sources. Examples of this energy include the deities you might invoke, the tools you are using, correspondences, the elements, components, the earth, moon, sun, other planets, and other participants if you are working in a group.

Depending on your chosen method of raising it, the energy should come slowly and increase as time goes by. Do not stop halfway; work on raising the energy until you feel it has reached to the climax. In regards to the duration, this will depend on you as an individual. There are some who can do it, and within 5 to 10 minutes, they will have reached the climax. Others will spend hours to achieve the same results. It will take you sometimes to know the duration that works for you. The secret here is to be patients as you do more research and find out what works for you.

The next thing you do is to direct and release the energy. You are able to do so by keeping your focus on the intent. You can release the energy in a number of ways. There are some who will stomp and shout while others will burn or break something. If you are using a potion or an infusion, you can drink it. This is a great way to seal the spell with a final gesture or thought. It will also signify that whatever you were doing is done. Once you are done, remember to ground. This is the final step of working with energy.

Creating channels

To begin with, you need to understand what a channel is. The casting of spells is the process of raising energy and being able to direct it to your intent. The path your energy chooses to follow can also be referred to as a channel. Creating a channel basically means creating ways for the energy to flow in freely between you and your intent. You need to put yourself in a position where the energy will find room to manifest your desires.

Most of the spells that become effective have a channel they use to travel. You should create a very strong conduit for your energy to remain focused and strong. For example, if you apply a spell for good health, do not just sit there and expect things just to happen. Look for possible channels like visiting a doctor for treatment, following your treatment plans, pay attention to your diet, use alternative healers, and take care of yourself. This way, your energy will have a clear path to follow.

Tools of witchcraft

To begin with, it is important to note that it is not a must you use a tool to perform witchcraft. It is perfectly possible to perform potent spells without using any equipment. However, you cannot underestimate the power of tools since you are dealing with mystic forces that are not visible to the eye. Tools are essential as they will enable you to focus better on your intentions and concentrate enough to raise the energy. This way, your spells are in better condition to manifest easily.

Tools are your greatest allies as a witch, especially if you are a beginner. They help you to direct your energy in the right direction. In addition to that, tools add visual impact and decorum to witchcraft. They also help you to get yourself into an altered state of consciousness. They are an essential part of any spiritual work.

Over the same, do not think that you are supposed to own every tool listed below. There are tools which possess similar functions. So, if you end up owning everything, some will be useless. When choosing your tools, only take the ones that appeal most to you. You do not necessarily have to spend all your money on an expensive metaphysical store. In fact, some of the best tools you can ever have are the one you have made for yourself or the ones you just find by luck. That being said, below are some tools of witchcraft you should consider owning.

The altar

Any witch, pagan or Wiccan must own an altar. This place should be sacred since it is the place you will be interacting with your guides as you perform your spells. A witch without an altar is like a human being without a home. Your altar does not have to be expensive, beautiful, or complicated for it to be effective. Just have what you can, what makes you more comfortable and focused. Ensure you maintain cleanliness in that place all the time.

You should also have an altar cloth. The cloth provides a simple and easy way to decorate your altar. Choose the material and color of your cloth depending on what you like, and according to the purpose of your ritual. You can even use scarves as alter cloth. Do not be afraid to think outside the box. Be ready to explore the world.

Boline

Boline is a half-moon shaped small sickle. It has a white handle. Traditionally, this extraordinary blade was used to harvest branches, flowers, and herbs. Witches of these days are using mundane knives or letter openers instead of boline.

Altar tile

You can make an altar tile from various natural materials such as stones, ceramic, wood, and metal. They are normally round or square in shape. An altar tile is engraved with power symbols like the wheel of the year or the pentagram. Due to the grounding power it holds, it is able to assist the energy to stay focused during casting of the spells.

The blades

You need to own a blade of you are going to practice witchcraft. It represents the movement, masculine energy, and the act of cutting something. Blades are also associated with the element of air just like the Swords tarot suit.

Athame

Many witches possess one or more ritual knives. The athame is a double-edged knife, and it is normally used to cast magic in the circle. The traditional Athame had a black handle. You are not required to sharpen your Athame since you will not be using it to cut physical things. You can just use yours to curve sigils and runes on candles.

The broom

The broom, also known as the besom, is used to symbolize the union of God and the goddess. It has a phallic shape which is associated with masculinity. The other three-part design is used to symbolize the three cycles of feminism. The broom is associated with elements of water, and that is why it is used to cleanse your space before performing a ritual or casting spells. Hence, cleanse your space by simply swiping your broom around the room in a clockwise direction. After that, open the door close to you and sweep everything outside. This is very crucial as it will ensure the negativity does not return.

Remember to consecrate your broom before you begin using it and make sure that it was not used for the mundane cleansing. Keep it on top of your front door to act as a guardian against anything evil that may befall you. In pagan weddings and handfasting ceremonies, a broom plays a very important role to the newlyweds. The newlyweds' couple is supposed to jump on top of the besom to welcome fertility, harmony, and prosperity in their new home. If you want, you can craft your own broom the way you want it to be.

Sword

A sword is more similar to Athame, but it is a bit larger. In most cases, it is used to make the limits of the sacred circle in large, public outdoor rituals. The major different of the sword and the Athame is that the sword can only be possessed by the High Priest or High Priestesses of a particular coven.

A book of shadows

The book of shadows was a traditional document which contained some rituals, religious texts, and spells from specific Wiccan. These days, there are so many witches who are using this book as a journal of their ritual practices and magical work. With just a pen, a paper and your book of shadows, you would be amazed by the number of magical works you can do. Get impressive results by adding a sigil or a rune. You will surely love the results.

Candles and candle holders

Candles and candle holders are tools that every witch should possess. In fact, they are the easiest and cheap tools every witch can afford. There are so many different ways to use candles as a witch. You can use a candle to summon deities, guardians, and various entities. You can also use a candle to manifest a goal, to light your way in an astral projection and symbolize the element of fire, among other things. Further, the use of candles is a nice way to set your mood to perform a spell.

There are witches who believe that if you just blow away your candle anyhow, you will be disrespecting the fire spirit. For that reason, it is better to use a candle snuffer instead. There are others who believe that

401

before you blow away the candle. You should thank the fire spirit. What you believe in is what will work for you better.

The Cauldron

The cauldron is used to symbolize the sacred womb of the goddess. In most of the Celtic traditions, the cauldron is used to represent the goddess Cerridwen. She is known to stir endlessly and elixir knowledge and inspiration from her giant pot. The traditional cauldron has three legs, and it is made of cast iron. You can associate it with different elements depending on its use. If yours is made with cast iron, then you can use it burn herbs, incense, offerings, sigils, wishes or even perform pyromancy divination done by reading the flames. You can still use a cauldron for cooking ritual meals or brew potions and remedies. However, if you choose to do so, then make sure you have a separate cauldron for the preparation of food. This is important because ritual use will make your cauldron unsuitable for cooking your meals.

Herbs and essential oils

Herbs and essential oils have their own magical associations. Herbal magical is a branch of its own when it comes to witchcraft. You can include herbs and oils in your spells in so many different ways. Herbs are commonly used in the dried state while the essential oils are diluted with vegetable oil. There are so many ways to use herbs and oils such as baths, kitchen witchcraft, magical teas, talismans, incense, and the like.

Dolls

Dolls are very useful when it comes to witchcraft. Interestingly, dolls are 3D images in witchcraft. They help you to focus on your intentions. Dolls represent different entities right from human to spiritual. You can use s doll to represent a person as the target for your spell. Just remember to seek their permission first. It is also possible to use a doll to represent yourself. Use different colors and physical parts association to manifest certain things to your target. You can also incorporate dolls in your alter to represent deities.

Crystals

Crystals are a fundamental aspect to many witches out there. There are not just mere rocks, and there is more to that. For instance, if you take your quality time to know your crystals, you will be surprised to discover a good friend. Each of these unique stones possesses a unique frequency, and you should form a habit of meditating with your crystals. You can experience healing on a deep level in aligning with your crystals. They are like batteries charged with the power of the earth or nature. Use them on a regular basis to cleanse your aura, manifest your intentions and meditate. Do you already own crystals? If yes, use them wisely and remember to cleanse them often.

Ritual clothing

There are certain pieces of clothes that are worn to perform specific rituals. Such a cloth item is referred to as ritual clothing. It can be a hat, robe, mask, or a cloak. You can also have pieces of jewelry like crystals or occult symbols. There are witches who prefer to perform their rituals in skyclad or ritual nudity. Their aim is to appear in humility before their deities.

Although you can still perform your rituals in your normal clothing, putting on ritual clothing assists you to attain the needed mindset to cast a spell. Plus, there is power in the color of your clothing, and it can affect the way the energy behaves in the sacred circle. The norm of public ritual is to wear black clothes. This is crucial because black clothes absorb light hence keeping away the practitioners from any distractions whatsoever.

Containers

You surely need containers as a practitioner of the Arts. Otherwise, where will you store your harvested ingredients? Bottles, jars, boxes, chests, and pouches are essential tools in witchcraft. They can also become active tools for your spells. Most of the performances will require the use of containers such as witches bottles, honey jars, reiki boxes, manifestation boxes, spiritual baths, and witchy brews.

Mortar and pestle

You will need a mortar and pestle to crush the herbs and resins to make herbal powders. It can also be used to fabricate incense, potions and various brews. Remember to be mindful of the intent you are putting your herbal powders as you crush your herbs. Note that the act of crushing your herbs has the power to reinforce your spell. Also, make sure you use a different mortar and pestle when cooking ritual foods. That's because there are certain plants and resins which are used in herbal magic, but they can be toxic if consumed.

Offering bowl

Any devotional shrine must have an offering bowl. It is just a simple container where you will be placing your offerings. You can either use one bowl for all your deities or have different bowls for each entity you work with. You should not restrict yourself to a bowl only. You can use any form of a container including a flat rock, a trunk, or even a dish. Simply choose something that works for you, and all will be well.

Rope

Just like other tolls, ropes are essential in witchcraft. They can be used to tie herbal pouches, talismans, or even perform spells. You can also use the rope to make a witches' ladder and knot magic. The multiple knots tied on a rope when casting a spell are the ones known as magic knots. They originated from sailor's superstitions, and these days it has become the norm in sea witchcraft. Two major rituals which involve rituals are the Beltane Maypole and handfasting ceremonies. The hands of the bride and groom as tied together using one of the many ropes during a handfasting ceremony. The knots symbolize the unity the couple should have, and the robe binds them together forever.

Statues and visual representation

If you are looking for something special to add to the altar, then go for statues and visual representations. Even though they are not normally used as active witchcraft tools, they can still play a major part by helping you visualize the entities you want to work with. You do not have to strain your finances to own a statue, you can just craft your own, and it will still serve the same purpose. Alternatively, you can use a tarot or oracle card and draw the entity the same way it appears to you in your mind. Apart from statues and visual representation, be kind in your offerings.

Music and instruments

Music in any form is of great importance to the spiritual world. You can have recorded music, drums, bells, singing bowls or even your own voice. Any of them holds the magic that cannot be assumed. Music is actually a special kind of intention expressed using musical sounds. Alter bell is made of metal, and that is why it is associated with elements of water. You can either use it to summon or to banish the spirits. For instance, after calling the elemental guardians, Wiccans ring the bell. You can also ring the bell to differentiate the different parts of a ritual. You can ring a bell, emit a loud sound, clap your hands, or beat a drum to banish negative spirits from a particular space.

How to set up an altar

You do know that you cannot practice witchcraft without an altar, right? You definitely need an altar. You will use it every time you perform a ritual. In fact, just the same way you spend quality time with your book of shadows is the same way you will spend your quality time at the altar. The beauty of a well-appointed alter is that it will keep you grounded and give you an opportunity to explore your new practice. The good thing is that it is very much possible to make your own alter from scratch without incurring excess costs.

If you are finding it difficult to find an altar and there nothing in your house that can function as an altar, simply choose a sacred place within your home or outside if you like and make it your altar. The place should be quiet and free from noise. Do not choose a place that people in your house like to hang around. Let that place be isolated from the usual daily activities. If possible, choose a place with a window so that you can have a view of nature as you meditate or cast your spells.

Most of the necessary components of an altar are things you already own. An altar should be a raised surface like a table, a desk, a stump or a table and they are used to as loci in spell-casting, ceremony, invocation, worship, prayers and chanting among other practices. Apart from the chosen surface, you will need a covering cloth though not a must. Other tools include broom, Athame, candle, chalice, cauldron, incense, pentacle, and wand.

However, every altar is unique, and you should set up yours to reflect your personality, aesthetic, interests, and the goals you hope to achieve. These items are mentioned here because they are commonly used, but it is not a must you have them in your alter. Feel free to customize, modify, and change it according to your needs and preference. It should be a place that makes you feel relaxed and invigorated at any time you go there.

Apart from the traditional components of setting up an altar, these days, there are so many other materials that are being used to assemble an altar. They are unique, and they depend on individual taste. They can also be changed from time to time depending on the seasons, the deities one is working with and other issues. Some of the commonly used options include live plants, animal remains, jewelry, minerals, rocks, crystals, dried herbs, flowers, drawings, crafts and anything else you might find useful in this journey of witchcraft.

Now that you know what is expected of your altar, below are simple steps to guide you. They will help you come up with your own altar without necessarily spending a fortune. If you want an expensive altar, you are not prohibited, though, and you can go ahead and make it super expensive. This guide is meant to assist any witch out there who would want to have an altar with or without money.

Select the surface of your altar

The first thing you do when setting an altar is choosing the place that will serve as the altar. Remember that that place should be raised. A table is the most ideal, but if you have anything raised and can harbor all your tools of the trade, then you can use it as well. Size does not matter so much as long as the surface is spacious enough to accommodate the items you wish to put on your altar. Some low-cost or even free altar choices include;

Tables

If you have access to a number of tables in your home, you can convert one into an altar table. If you don't have, you can buy an already used table at a cheaper cost compared to a new one. In fact, the old and weathered tables tend to have more charms and character than a used one, but if you want to buy a new, the choice is yours. The important aspect here is the height. Choose the one that is appropriate with the manner you prefer to practice be it kneeling, sitting, or standing.

Stumps

If you have access to a flat stump, then it can form as a surface to your altar. The good thing with a stump is that it gives your altar a more natural look. Being connected to nature is something important to witchcraft. This form of a surface is free from the hard lines that come with manufactured furniture. More so, stumps are cheap, and if you know where to get one, you can do so at no cost. You can even create your own stump if there is a felled tree trunk near you.

Milk crates

It is often hard to lack something in your home to use as a surface to your altar. For example, you can use a discarded milk crate, mail bin, dresser drawer, or anything like that and transform it into your altar surface. If one crate does not provide the space you need, you can consider placing four of them, then cover them with a cloth. They should be able to provide you with enough space to put all your necessary tools of witchcraft. If you want a flatter surface, you can use a piece of card stock and place it on top of the inverted crate.

Choose the location to set up your altar

The two important factors that should be able to guide you on the most appropriate space to set up your altar are your choice and convenience. Different witches will choose to have their altars in different locations. It is a matter of preference. As you choose the place to set up your altar, below are factors to guide you.

Indoor or outdoor

Individuals who frequently commute with nature and natural elements as part of their practice are fond of outdoor altars. It is important to note that if you opt to place your altar outside, you should be prepared to transport your items from the house to the altar and back. This means that you will have to assemble and disassemble because if you leave your tools outside unattended for a long time, you may end losing your valuable tools. They can also be damaged, stolen, and many other eventualities. If you are not comfortable with outside hustles and you want to set up your altar in a more permanent location, an indoor location is a good option. You can even select a location in your home and keep a permanent altar. In case you want to cast your spells from outside once in a while, you can keep a portable altar kit for outdoor practice.

Directional orientation

Many witches opt to orient their altars in a particular cardinal direction. However, most rituals require the practitioner to perform them facing the north, and that is why this direction has become quite popular when it comes to altar orientation. There are also other individuals who choose to have their altars facing east or west. They do so with the aim of embracing and honoring the rising and setting of the sun. It is your choice to place your altar facing any of the four traditional elements depending on the one you resonate with. Before you do so, learn what they all stand for and made a wise decision. East is associated with air, west with earth, north with water and south with fire. Do enough research and choose the most suitable option.

Classic altar tools

Choose your tools wisely. You need tools to honor higher beings, offer thanksgiving rituals, and perform many other spells. All these would be hard if you do not have the necessary tools. Although you can still cast spells without any tools, they are still important as they are the backbone of any religious rituals. You need the proper tools to achieve the desired results.

Basically, simple and freely created altars can still be functional and magical just like those which cost a fortune. The good thing with a budget altar is that it will also require a small area to set it up. Hopefully, this guide will help you to create your altar in a special place regardless of your financial position.

Chapter 5: The Magic of Crystals

The practice of magic actually doesn't require any supplies or tools at all. When we are in alignment with our truth and our purpose, we can instigate the energy of transformation and change with our very own energy, thoughts, beliefs, and wisdom. There are so many people alive today who are manifesting their goals and dreams without magical tools and supplies, and they are not Wiccans and witches, looking for magic spells to cast and rituals to call upon their purpose.

Without tools and supplies, it is certainly possible to make an effort to positively manifest what you want in your life; however, with the use of certain elements and ingredients, you can amplify your mission and enhance its potential to succeed. The basic rule of thumb with all things is that we are all energy. Everything is energy, even the chair you are sitting on right now. With all of the ways that energy works, it makes sense that using certain available energy to accomplish your goals will help you make a bigger shift and transition into your plans and intentions.

The items you use will all have a very different but equally beneficial attitude toward your spells and craftwork, so anything that you use will be determined by the quality of your spells and what you are trying to accomplish with them. Many of them will revolve around a specific goal, while others will have a more general application. The supplies needed for each endeavor will allow you to demonstrate your intentions as a practice and not just an idea or a dream; they will be conjured into existence with the clarification created with these items.

The first magical item that you will need to learn about is the crystal. Crystals are oddly described as being inorganic when nothing could be further from the truth. As an element of the Earth, created by her very

411

pulse and elemental push and pull, crystals and gemstones are formed over a long period of time under certain conditions. They are grown, like plants growing in soil, and to any Wiccan or witch, they are very much alive.

Crystals and gemstones are sought all over the world and are prized and valued for their looks, as much as they are appreciated for their very nature. In the Wiccan community and those who study the qualities of these magical items, there are certain magical properties connected to the energy of each stone that will provide a specific result when applied to your rituals and spells.

You can find hundreds upon hundreds of different crystals and stones and discover the secrets of what energy they possess and help to amplify and manifest in your own spiritual work. When you connect the identity of each stone to yourself or the spells you are practicing, you are calling upon that energy to create a shift or transformation in the energy of all life. You can view it as a way to add some gasoline to your fire.

Common Crystals and Gemstones

Amethyst — It is a purple-colored crystal that helps with addictions, breaking habits, sobriety, as well as, clearing channels for open communication with spirit, psychic visions and dreams, inner-strength, discipline, and quelling or calming fears and worries.

Carnelian — a brightly hued orange stone that elicits energy of courage, motivation, passion, and determination, as well as directness, action, individual success, manifesting goals and dreams, and illuminating purpose.

Citrine — It is a yellow-hued crystal in various tones and shades that enhances the energy of personal power, joy, warmth, friendship and camaraderie, manifestation, and producing powerful results.

Hematite — This stone has a powerful magnetism and is used for drawing things toward you in any kind of "attraction magic" you are working on. It is also a grounding and protecting stone that creates helpful stability and honest perspective.

Kyanite — This stone can come in more than one shade, and all have a somewhat different energy. Blue kyanite is another stone that will cleanse energy, including that of the auras and chakras, and it is one of a very few stones that does not require periodic cleansing after rituals and spells. It is a stone of personal truth.

Moonstone — The color of the moon, milky white with grey, it can also appear with rainbow iridescence and illumination within it. It is a powerful stone of Goddess energy, intuition, clairvoyance, empathy, kindness, matters of the heart, and all matters of the moon. It will also help with cycles of death and rebirth.

Onyx — It is a hard, dark, or black stone that aids in banishing and releasing. It repels negativity and matters of conflict; it is also known to boost inner strength and confidence while grounding and protecting the holder.

Obsidian — Another dark-colored stone known for its grounding and protective qualities, obsidian has an ability to shield the wearer and dispel negative stress and tension. It is also said to help enhance truth, as well as help your mind travel to unknown realms of possibility with clear sight and acceptance.

Quartz — This crystal is clear and appears as if it were a shard of glass. Quartz can come in a variety of shades, including rose quartz, smoky, quartz, and yellow quartz, etc. Each hue has a different energy to consider for whatever spell you are casting. Clear quartz is an all-purpose stone that enhances the energy of spiritual growth and awakening, helps to amplify your purpose and intentions, and clears energy as it balances energy.

Tiger's Eye — This stone has a golden-brown warmth and a shimmering set of subtle stripes within it. It will offer the energy of perception, courage, truth, and honesty, cutting through illusions and bringing to light any malicious or manipulative intentions.

Tourmaline — The black-hued tourmaline will repel negative energy and forces and prevent the holder from psychic interference from the spiritual plane that might feel unwanted or negative; it is a grounding and shielding stone that protects, cleanses the auras, and breaks obsessions.

Each of these stones will offer you the magical properties listed, and when you combine some of them together, they will work cooperatively to support your spells and craftwork. The action and qualities inherent in these stones are noticeable, even when you hold them in the palm of your hand. You may have to work up to this skill over time and through your personal practice, but it is something that anyone can do. When you hold a stone in the palm of your hand, feel its vibration and frequency. You will notice a form of energy or a feeling, a sensation of its connection to your energy and frequency.

Choosing the Best Crystals for Your Practice

The best crystals for your practice are the ones that call out to you and present themselves. You can, of course, go through your shopping list of what stones to buy to have the perfect altar set up, and you wouldn't be wrong to do it that way. Part of the fun of magic and working with the divine energy in nature in your practice is to let it communicate with you and listen to what it is saying.

When you go to a local shop in your area, you are able to handle each stone and find the energetic "pull" of each one. Some may feel stronger than others in connection to your energy, and these will be very useful to help you align your own energy, specific to what that stone is offering to help you shift, reorganize, and change.

Other crystals and stones are less about the energy of the self and more about the energy of your magic work and practice of Wicca. You can handle these stones and not feel strong energy from them as they are not working directly with your own energetic vibration at the time of first handling them, but they will resonate with whatever particular form of magic you are hoping to manifest. As your own energy shifts and transforms, so will the pull to the certain crystal's energy. In accordance with the energy of all life and all matter, we are in a constant rebalancing of our inner energy with our outer world of energy.

The plans you set in motion with the use of specific crystals and stones will help you to better align with the magic of what each will offer to your powerful practice. You can buy stones on the internet, and if you are already sure that it is the right stone for you, there is nothing much wrong with this. One thing to consider, however, is to make sure you are purchasing these magical items from places that are sustainable and have their collection of stones sourced in reasonable ways that are as healthy to the environment as possible. Crystals and stones come from all over the world, and there are many mining practices that are harmful to the Earth. See if you can find online resources and local shops that source their magical items in an environmentally friendly way.

Caring for Your Crystals

Crystals are easy to care for. They only need a little bit of cleansing and recharging, and here is why: crystals take on the energy of their surroundings. You can hold a crystal in your hand for hours to help you relieve stress and anxiety, and the crystal will help pull that energy out of you while it rebalances or calms the energy you were experiencing.

Likewise, within a spell, if you are casting a specific purpose and you are using a crystal to imbue your spell with certain energies, you are aligning that crystal with that spell so that it has that energy also. When you want to use that same crystal for another spell or ritual, you will want to clear the energy of the old spell so that the energies aren't confused.

Clearing the energy of your crystals is as easy as 1-2-3. Charging them is a little bit more intricate, depending on what they are being charged for, and as you will see, both are equally helpful and useful.

Clearing Crystal Energy

To clear a crystal, you can use one of the following methods:

Sea salt – Immerse the crystals into a dish of sea salt. Salt is very cleansing and grounding to all energies.

Sea salt in warm water – Make a saltwater bath for your crystals, and let them sit in the water for approximately 10 minutes. Afterward, rinse and dust the salt off and let them air dry or sundry.

Sun Bath – Set your crystals out in the sunshine to clear the energy stored within. You can also use the rays of the sun to charge your crystal with the sun's power.

Bury in Soil – Submerge your crystals into the earth, in your garden, or a potted indoor plant. Soil grounds and clears energy and will have the same impact on your stones. Leave underground overnight and rinse off in the morning.

Smudging – You can use purifying smoke from a sage bundle or other incense to help clear the energies. This can be effective when you need to do it in a hurry and don't have time to wait for hours of sunshine or minutes in a salt bath.

Use other crystals – As you read earlier, Blue Kyanite is a stone that will never need clearing because of how its energy works. You can use a stone like this to help clear and balance your other stones. Set the stones that need clearing next to, or on top of, the kyanite for around 45 minutes to an hour.

Clearing the energy of your crystals and stones is something that can occur as often or as infrequently as you determine. If you are not using your stones all of the time or regularly in spells and rituals, then you will likely not have to clear them as often; however, if you are regularly using them, you will find it very beneficial to clear that energy out more often to help all of your rituals and spells work more smoothly.

Charging Crystal Energy

Charging crystals can be as simple as setting them out in the sun or as complex as inventing an entire ritual around charging and consecrating your crystals. There are reasons for either approach. Here are some of the ways to charge your crystals.

With Sunlight and Moonlight – All you need is a little time in the sun or the moon to help charge your crystals of the power each one possesses. The moon will offer different energy to that of the sun, so you can decide, according to the type of spell you are performing, which energy will be best. You can also use a 24-hour cycle to charge your stones with both masculine and feminine energy and sun and moonlight.

With a Circle Casting – Casting a circle of magic is creating a sacred space for your rituals and spells. You can use a magic circle for the specific purpose of charging your crystals by setting them where you want them to receive a certain kind of elemental/directional energy. If you are casting a circle, and you need a certain crystal to have the energy of the north, you can place that crystal in that specific location in your circle casting to call upon that energy to charge it with. This is the same l for the other directions. You can also simply place the crystals in the middle of your circle and envision them being transformed by light, while they sit with the power of the elements.

With a Ritual or a Spell – There are many different spells and rituals you can use to transfer energy into your crystals to charge them. A significant number of spells and rituals may call for an already charged gem or stone and so having a separate ritual to charge the crystals can be helpful, or you can just incorporate that step into whatever your overall purpose is and spell casting outcome.

In Front of the Fire – Fire is a great tool for charging. If you have a fireplace at home, you can have yourself a special fireside ritual to charge your crystals by setting them on the tiles in front of the fire and letting the light reflect into the energy of the stones. If you don't have a fireplace, you can just use candles (see next option).

With Other Magical Items – You can use the other tools and supplies available to you if you are interested in making more magic of that kind. Setting your crystal in a bowl of fresh or dried herbs that have a specific form of energy will do the trick, or surrounding your crystals with candles and firelight will work well.

When you are ready to charge your crystals, you are probably ready to use them for some important magical purpose. When you do not need your stones and crystals for anything specific, you can leave them as they are on your altar space, or you can carry one or two with you around when performing your daily life's tasks and let them provide you with helpful energy and motivation, whatever the stone is offering to you.

Collecting crystals is a really fun thing to do, and if you are anything like me, you'll have a significant amount for each kind of opportunity to assign such powerful creative energy to a variety of useful spells and rituals.

The next few pieces of information are opportunities for you to practice using your crystals and gemstones in your rituals. A spell for cleansing, a ritual for charging, and a spell for deepening your connection to the Divine and your psychic abilities will get you started on your journey.

Crystal Spells and Rituals

Crystal Cleansing Spell

This is an example of using a spell to help cleanse and purify your crystals and stones before you use them again for other purposes. It will combine a few of the options from the list above to show you how you can purge the unwanted, stagnant energies.

You will need the following items:

Seasalt

Water

2 bowls (preferably glass, wood, or ceramic—nothing plastic)

A ritual cloth

White sage bundle for smudging

Lighter or matches

White candle

Steps for the Crystal Cleansing Spell:

Lay your ritual cloth, either on your altar or in your circle if you are casting one for this purpose.

Put the sea salt in the bowl and add warm or tepid water. Work the salt into the water, stirring clockwise to dissolve it.

Light your white candle with a purification blessing, something along the lines of:

"Sacred candle, burning bright, let magic fire cleanse by rite. Crystal stones of beauty shine, burning candle, cleanse with your light."

Set the stones and crystals you are clearing into the saltwater. Allow them to sit in the bowl for 10 minutes. While they are in the bowl, you can picture a beam of white or silver light, coming down from the sky and through the water into the stones. Imagine the light clearing all the stored energy. (optional step)

After ten minutes, remove the stones from the saltwater and rinse them, and put them in the other bowl, pouring fresh, clear water over them. Rinse them and then lay them on the ritual cloth near the candle.

Light the sage bundle and get it smoking. Cover the stones in the smoke for as long as it feels right. Put out the smudge stick when you are done.

Blow out the candle, and say something along the following lines:

"Magic stones of crystalline light, may you be cleansed by salt, water, smoke, and candlelight."

Finish the spell by arranging your stones where they like to live and cleaning up the ingredients. Close your circle if you cast one.

Use this spell, or modify it to use some of the other cleansing and clearing methods. Make sure you are getting the most out of your crystal energy work by keeping them free and clear with regular cleansings and purification.

Crystal Charging Ritual

This ritual will be a way for you to honor the power of your stones and giving them a magical ritual to become more empowered to your needs and practices. The ritual is simple and will incorporate a few of the options from the list above.

You will need the following items:

A ritual cloth for setting the stones in the Sunshine

A large piece of blue kyanite

A large piece of clear quartz

Any stones you want to charge

A bowl of soil

A bowl of water

One purple candle

Lighter or matches

Steps for the Crystal Charging Ritual:

On your altar or another workspace, connect to your stones by burying them in a bowl of soil. Make sure the stones and crystals you want to charge are fully covered with earth.

Place the blue kyanite and the clear quartz on top of the soil and leave this arrangement overnight. (You can set this up right before bed).

In the morning, remove the kyanite and the quartz from the soil and rinse the stones in the bowl of water so that they are free of dirt. Set them back on the altar and light the purple candle, saying something like this:

"Sacred flame of spirit known, bring balance and vision to these crystal stones. Open their worlds to my sacred desires, to bring forth more energy of the divine inspired."

Play around with the words, depending on how you want to charge the energy. You can make up any words that will fit into your practice and purpose.

Let your crystals sit with the purple candle for a while in the early morning hours and then either snuff out the candle, or allow it to burn all the way down (the timing of burning depends on the size of the candle.

Bring your crystals and your ritual cloth outside and find the "right" place for them to bathe in the sunshine. You may need to look for a place that is in a wide-open area and which will not get a lot of shade over the course of the day. You may have to monitor them and move them around so that they are always in a patch of sunlight.

Lay the cloth and the stones on your altar space. You can arrange them however you like. Include the Kyanite and Quartz that you used so that they can be charged in sunlight as well.

Allow the crystals to sunbathe until the evening or Sunset. If your crystals are in shadow, it is time to bring them inside.

Once you are done charging them in the sun, you can align them on your altar space and use them for any other spells or rituals you have charged them for.

You can make modifications to this ritual and add some other supplies, like herbs and flowers, or some incense. It is really up to you how you choose to make the ritual more impactful to your personal practice.

Crystal Spell for Connection to Psychic Ability and the Divine

This spell will use a combination of crystals and stones, as well as a combination of charging methods and then using the charged stones to enhance the spell so that you can see how it all looks together.

You will need the following:

A sage smudge stick

A lighter or matches

A piece of Amethyst

A piece of Clear Quartz

A piece of Citrine

A piece of Moonstone

Two silver-colored candles

One purple candle

Steps for the Crystal Spell for Connection to Psychic Ability and the Divine:

Cast whatever protective circle you like for this ritual, calling in the four elements at the four directions.

At your altar or workspace, set the candles in a triangle formation so that the two silver candles will be at the base of the triangle, and the purple candle will be on the top point.

Light the sage and smoke the altar and the candles so that they are cleansed and purified. Cover your own body in the smoke, or waft it toward you to help cleanse your energy as well.

Set the stones together in the center of the candle triangle, and let them sit without touching them again.

Light the candles, one by one, and invoke the energy of spirit you want to ask to come through your connection to these stones. Add the lessons you learned from the charging ritual above, and see the energy of light coming into them and charging them with your purpose. Use your thoughts and intentions to invoke the visions of what you want the stones to carry.

Spend several minutes in meditation with your crystals and communicate through the stones and fire energy with the spirit that you are welcoming psychic visions, dreams, and interpretations from the beyond.

Once you have allowed the crystals to become enhanced with your purpose, remove them from the center of the triangle, and allow the candles to continue burning as you lie down on the floor or on a mat (you can lay down on a sofa or bed as long as it has been cleared and purified before sacred magical use).

Make sure you are in a comfortable position and then lay the stones on your forehead. If they do not all fit on your forehead, lay one above your crown on the floor and the others to the sides of your ears. It doesn't matter which.

Lie in meditation in your sacred circle or space, and allow visions and information to come to you through the stones. Be patient and let the timing naturally unfold. Receive information from the spirit through your psychic link and wait for everything to fall into you as you relax in this position.

When you feel like the meditation has come to an end, you can rise back up and place the stones back on the altar. Sit in quiet reflection in front of the candles and allow them to burn while you interpret the message.

Place the stones under your pillow while you sleep to enhance psychic dreams (optional).

Our connection to all life can be enhanced with these simple, magical items. You don't have to use crystals in your work, and they will always offer as much as you are willing to allow. They are powerful energy and are able to magnify and amplify any magical practice you have. These spells and rituals are just the beginning. There are so many uses and applications for crystals, and you can explore and find new ways to use them all the time.

Why is Moon Cycles Important when Casting Spells?

The Moon is Earth's only natural satellite. She goes with and impacts us from numerous points of view, regardless of whether we can't generally see it. Most Witches are amazingly sensitive to the lunar cycles and can detect the impact the Moon and its phases are having on them. It can be used to settle on better choices and anticipate better outcomes, thus.

It has demonstrated that the cycles of the Moon have various impacts and effects on the Earth and every living being. The lunar phases can modify the sea tides, the climate, our sleep patterns, our states of mind and numerous other things including paces of richness, brought about by the additional light the full Moon provides. Throughout history, Witches were very much aware of the influence of the Moon and her evolving stages. They created spells and ceremonies that conform to exploit this energy as would be prudent.

Best Spells to Cast on Each Moon

There are 8 cycles of the Moon, and we can assemble them into four essential phases:. We should recognize what the rest are and how they can influence your Magic by what spells to cast during each lunar stage.

Living By The Moon

Living by the Moon can necessarily assist your life with running all the more quickly. If you are a magick expert, timing your spells or rituals with the moon phases can be contrasted with swimming with the current. Spells cast at the proper time will acquire added oomph, as it is simpler to accept the way things are than against it.

Living by the Moon's cycles can assist us with feeling more advantageous and lively as well as support in helping us in the arrival of old propensities that never again serve our most elevated high. The key is to work consistently with nature, never against it, that is except if you're up for a battle that you without a doubt can't win.

WAXING MOON

The Waxing Moon is from the minute after it is New until the minute is Full. It is the time to do spells for growth, starting new ventures, commencement and improvement. "Increase" is the employable word, similarly as the Moon is expanding.

Waning moon

During the Waning Moon (from the minute after it is Full to the minute it is New), do spells to oust underhanded impacts, diminish or expel snags and disease, kill foes, and to get rid of hurt. Here, "decline" is the employable word, as the Moon's light is diminishing.

The three days after the New Moon are the essential occasions to work spells for development and beginnings which should show at the Full Moon.

The days not long before the Full Moon are the most remarkable occasions for realization and consummation.

The Black or Dark Moon is the most favourable time for banishing and killing spells.

New moon

Characteristics: Beginning new pursuits, fresh starts. Additionally love and sentiment, wellbeing or job hunting.

Waxing moon

(The New Moon is waxing until it arrives at the Full stage)

Qualities: Invoking beginnings, new tasks, ideas, inspiration, energy, essentialness, and opportunity. Additionally, useful magic, for example, love, riches, achievement, courage, friendship, karma or wellbeing.

Full moon

Qualities: Fruition manifesting objectives, supporting, energy, healing, class, and power. Likewise, love, information, lawful endeavours, cash and dreams.

Prime time for rituals for prediction, insurance, and divination. Any spell that needs additional force, for example, help getting another line of work or recuperating from certain conditions, should be possible at this point.

Melting away moon

Characteristics: Knowledge, mystic capacity, scrying, switching conditions. Banishing, releasing the old, expelling unwanted negative energies, enslavement, ailment, or antagonism.

Dark MOON

(At the point when the Moon isn't apparent in the sky, not long before the start of the following lunar cycle, otherwise called the Balsamic stage.) The dark Moon is a period for managing aggressors for investigating our darkest breaks and understanding our angers and interests and additionally bringing equity to hold up under. Extremely intense for prediction work.

New Moon

It is the main period of the lunar cycle. It begins when the Moon is hidden (this state goes on for one day and is otherwise called a Dark Moon) since it rests between the Sun and the Earth. On the next few days, the Moon gradually starts to show up in the sky. The energy of the New Moon is related to meditation, self-investigation and meditation on ourselves. An open door for a new beginning and a New You.

New Moon Spells

The energies of this Moon phase aren't generally going to build your forces of manifestation. Rather than doing magic during the New Moon use this opportunity to build up a general goal for the lunar cycle that starts today. Work on your own space: clean your ritual area, begin or enliven your Book of Shadows, look into spells on the Web, or wash up. Ruminate over your wishes and wants, yet also on your questions and fears. Plan and consider all you need to imagine and accomplish during the following 28 days!

Waxing Crescent

This period of the Moon begins three days after the New Moon when you can start to see a little segment of the Moon in obscurity in the sky. The sickle Moon is the image and portrayal of the Wiccan Goddess, epitomizing Manifestation and Abundance.

Waxing-Crescent-Moon-Spells

Do magic that will assist you in developing your business or your profession. It is a decent time for the long haul or material-gain spells, for example, a cash drawing spell or a ritual for getting another line of work. Concentrate on your work and your instruction. Abstain from thinking about your objectives as something that is later on, yet instead as something that is as of now beginning to occur. Additionally, charge your Moon Water on the Waxing Crescent Moon.

Harness the intensity of this lunar stage by working with this kind of spells:

First Quarter

This stage starts around seven days after the new Moon. It is an astounding time to make a move concerning your most profound wishes and to address your biggest blockages. It is an incredible time for development and self-healing. As a continuation of the last stage, the energies present right now can assist you with feeling progressively clear and mindful of how your instinct and second natures are created.

First Quarter Moon Rituals

Use the energies of this stage to improve on both otherworldly and enthusiastic levels. As the Moon is developing fit as a fiddle, you can concentrate on self-development. It's a period of abundance so use it inventively, allow the right things and individuals to come to you and pull in the essential things you wish to see a higher amount of. Do wellbeing and magnificence medicines, center around self-improvement, for example, expanding confidence and self-esteem, family and fruitfulness, and work on building up your Powers of Manifestation.

Since this is a thoughtful and profoundly charged moon stage, you will need to take a shot at reinforcing your Witch Powers. If you are a Beginner Witch, feel free to cast your first simple spell during this time:

Waxing Gibbous

It is the fourth moon stage. It begins the tenth day after the New Moon and goes on until the thirteenth day after it. It is an opportunity to show restraint. Perceive the intensity of the Universe and let it take control. Delay your activities and instead watch the state wherein your undertakings are. Unwind, examine, and plan your best course of action.

Waxing-Gibbous-Moon-Rituals

Pause and create tolerance. If you have begun enchanting during the past moon stages, this is an ideal opportunity to carry on and let the Universe carry out its responsibility. It is a development period where we don't generally need to do anything correctly. Use this opportunity to prepare for the following stage: The Full Moon. Sort out your tools, assemble your materials and add new spells to your Book of Shadows.

Fading Gibbous

It begins the third day after the Full Moon until the seventh day a short time later. It carries a chance to expel and take out negative energies. Use this moon phase to liberate yourself from troubles that are keeping you down.

The Waning Gibbous Moon

Winding down Gibbous-Moon-Spells-Rituals

Banishing ceremonies and any spells to dispose of negative things, and this moon phase supports circumstances. For instance, those identified with separate, partition, expulsion of issues, addictions, stress and other negative emotions.

Last Quarter

This stage begins the seventh day after the Full Moon and goes on until the tenth day a while later. Let the energy of this Moon discreetly finish your expulsion forms and purges. Close any pending issues and discreetly recharge your inward energies.

The Last Quarter Moon

Last-Quarter-Moon-Phase-Spells

The time has come to be mindful and use this lunar phase to rest. You can likewise use this chance to expel yourself from ruinous connections, harmful personal conduct standards or anything hurtful in your life—defeat despair and gloom. A few Witches use this moon phase to cast spells for equity or against foes (for example Dark Magic).

Disappearing Crescent

It is the last period of the Moon cycle. It ranges from the tenth day after the Full Moon until the night before the New Moon. It's a snapshot of conclusion and meditation, don't use it to settle on any meaningful choices or start another task.

The Waning Crescent Moon

Fading Crescent-Moon-Phase-Rituals

If you feel a different association with the Moon, at that point by following the moon phases and acting in kind, it will be simpler for you to interface with the rhythms of Nature, until it turns out to be a part of the cadence of your own life, intermingling with your condition. Much the same as the Moon has a tremendous settling impact on Earth's tilt, the key here is consistently to keep a sound parity, realizing when to clutch your Powers and when to discharge them to the Universe.

Chapter 6: Tarot Cards

Decks of tarot cards have a connection to the occult and witchcraft traditions, including Wicca. Tarot cards are useful magical tools that allow you to read the future or ask questions of the universe. The answers are sometimes vague, but tarot cards can discern the future. This chapter will give you everything you need to get started with tarot cards. This chapter will cover spreads and cards. After reading this chapter, you should be prepared to perform tarot card readings.

Tarot Cards

The tarot deck is a deck of 78 cards. It is divided into 22 Major Arcana cards and 56 Minor Arcana cards. The difference between the two is that the Major Arcana are more powerful. Each Major Arcana represents a stronger idea than the Minor Arcana. The 56 cards of the Minor Arcana are divided into four suits. The suits include Cups, Pentacles, Swords, and Wands. These minor cards are still powerful, and learning each is important. The Major Arcana, on the other hand, do not have a suit, instead it is made up entirely of face cards. Typically, readings only have one or two Major Arcana, but when you do a reading for an advanced witch, many Major Arcana might appear.

When you are giving a reading the first thing you should do is shuffle the cards. It is best to do this in the presence of the person asking the question so that the person's energy will combine with your own during the shuffling process. Next, spread the cards out in front of the person asking the question. Allow her and him to pick the number of cards in the spread. Keep the cards in the order they were drawn in since that determines the card's location in the spread.

Spreads

Spreads are how you arrange the cards on the table when you are giving a reading. Cards have different meanings based on where they appear in the spread. Each position in a spread is associated with something. For example, a card like might represent the future based on where it appears in a spread.

Tarot cards essentially have three meanings. The first is the upright meaning, which is when the card is face-up; reversed, which is when the card is face down; and the last meaning is derived from the position of the card in the spread. Because of the number of meanings, some tarot readings are vague. In this case, the witch should rely on her or his intuition to discern the truth.

There are many different spreads that you can use. These include the following spreads.

· Three Card Spread

· True Love Spread

· Celtic Cross

· Success Spread

· Career Path Spread

· Spiritual Guidance Spread

Three Card Spread

The Three Card spread is one of the easier spreads to do. The Three Card Spread uses three tarot cards to answer the question. As you read each card, you will flip it face up. Continue this process until all three cards are on the table. The cards are laid out from left to right. The cards should be laid out face down.

But what does each position mean? The Three Card Spread is a very versatile spread because the three spots are not strictly fixed. For example, you might have the three cards represent the past, present, or future. Other variations of the Three Card Spread include the following.

· Strengths, Weakness, and Advice

· Opportunities, Challenges, and Outcome

· Option 1, Option 2, and Option 3

· Option 1, Option 2, and What you need to know to decide

· The solution, Another solution, How to choose which solution

Celtic Cross Spread

The most popular spread is the Celtic Cross spread. The Celtic Cross uses 10 cards, and, unlike the Three Card spread, each position in the spread has a specific meaning. Hence, the fourth card always represents the recent past, no matter what the question is. The cards are laid out in a cross-like shape.

1. The first card, called the Signifier, is laid out on in the middle of the table. This card represents the person getting the reading. It represents that person's energy and their state of mind.

2. The second card, called the Crossing, is placed horizontally across the first card. This card is always considered face-up and is never reversed. This position represents what influences or opposes the person getting the reading.

3. The third card, called the Foundation, is laid on top of the first card. This card represents the origin of the question.

4. The fourth card, called the Recent Past, is placed below the first card. This card represents past concerns or events.

5. The fifth card, the Crown card, is placed to the right of the first card. This card represents the present and current obstacles. Beware, however, since not every event this card predicts will happen.

6. The sixth card is the Future. This card is placed to the left of the first card. The future represents what the future holds to the question.

7. The seventh card is called the Emotions card. This card starts a new column, place it to the bottom left of the cross. This card represents the asker's emotions related to the question.

8. The eighth card is called the External Forces. This card is placed above the seventh card. This card represents the influence others have on you as well as trends in your relationships.

9. The ninth card is called Hopes and Desires. This card is placed above the eighth card. It represents the person asking the question's hopes and desires about the question.

10. The tenth and final card is the Outcome. The Outcome is found above the ninth card. It represents the outcome relating to the question.

The Major Arcana

The Major Arcana are all trump cards. Each one is very powerful and you should always pay attention when one appears in your readings. Each of the Major Arcana cards will have a strong impact on your reading. The Major Arcana and their meanings are found in the chart below. Remember that upright cards are cards have the upright meaning, while reversed cards are upside down cards and they have a meaning based on being reversed.

Card	Upright	Reversed
Death	Change, beginnings, metamorphosis, or end of a cycle.	Fear of change, decay, stagnation, or holding on.
Judgment	Awakening, reflection, or a reckoning.	Self-loathing, Doubt, or lack of self-awareness.

The Sun	Joy, positivity, success, or celebration.	Depression, sadness, or negativity.
The Moon	Illusions, intuition, or unconsciousness.	Misinterpretation, fear, or confusion.
The Star	Rejuvenation, faith, or hope.	Discouragement, faithlessness, or insecurity.
The Tower	Upheaval, disaster, or broken pride.	Delayed disaster, disaster avoided, or fear of suffering.
The Devil	Materialism, playfulness, or addiction.	Release, freedom, or restoring control.
Temperance	Finding meaning, Middle path, or patience.	Excess, lack of balance, or extremes.
The Hanged Man	Martyrdom, release, or sacrifice.	Fear of sacrifice, needless sacrifice, or stalling.
Justice	Truth, clarity, or cause and effect.	Unaccountability, dishonesty, or unfairness.
Wheel of Fortune	Cycles, fate, or change.	Bad luck, lack of control, or clinging to control.
Hermit	Inner guidance, contemplation, or the search for the truth.	Isolation, loneliness, or losing your way.
Strength	Bravery, compassion, inner strength, or focus.	Weakness, insecurity, or self-doubt.

The Chariot	Willpower, control, or direction.	Lack of direction, aggression, or lack of control.
The Lovers	Duality, partnerships, or union.	Disharmony, one-sidedness, or loss of balance.
The Hierophant	Morality, ethics, tradition, or conformity.	New approaches, subversiveness, or rebellion.
The Emperor	Structure, fatherhood, control, or authority.	Coldness, rigidity, or tyranny.
The Empress	Fertility, motherhood, or nature.	Nosiness, emptiness, smothering, or dependance.
The High Priestess	Unconsciousness, inner voice, or intuition.	Repressed feelings, lost inner voice, or lack of center.
The Magician	Creation, intellect, manifestation, desire, or willpower.	Illusions, trickery, or out of touch.
The Fool	New beginnings, innocence, or free spirit.	Being taken advantage of, recklessness, or inconsideration.
The World	Contemplation, harmony, or fulfillment.	Lack of closure, or incompletion.

The Minor Arcana

The Minor Arcana represents the majority of cards in the tarot deck. The Minor Arcana are divided into four suits. They are Cups, Pentacles, Swords, and Wands. Each suit is related to one of the four elements, and each suit has a basic meaning.

Cups

The first of the four suits in the Minor Arcana is Cups. Cups are associated with the element of water. Cups generally have the meanings of intelligence, creativity, and intuition. See the chart below for information on what each specific card means.

Card	Upright	Reversed
Ace of Cups	Spirituality, new feelings, or intuition.	Blocked creativity, emptiness, or emotional loss.
Two of Cups	Connection, unity, or partnership.	Tension, imbalance, or broken communication.
Three of Cups	Happiness, community, and friendship.	Gossip, overindulgence, or isolation.
Four of Cups	Contemplation, apathy, or disconnectedness.	Sudden awareness, acceptance, or choosing happiness.
Five of Cups	Grief, loss, or self-pity.	Finding peace, moving on, or acceptance.

Six of Cups	Happy memories, familiarity, or healing.	Independence, leaving home, or moving forward.
Seven of Cups	Daydreaming, choices, or searching for purpose.	Confusion diversion, or lack of purpose.
Eight of Cups	Disillusionment, walking away, or leaving something behind.	Fear of change, avoidance, or fear of loss.
Nine of Cups	Emotional stability, satisfaction, or luxury.	Smugness, dissatisfaction, or lack of inner joy.
Ten of Cups	Fulfillment, inner happiness, or dreams coming true.	Broken family, shattered dreams, or domestic disharmony.
Page of Cups	Sensitivity, happy surprises, or dreaming.	Emotional immaturity, disappointment, or insecurity.
Knight of Cups	Idealism, romance, or following the heart.	Disappointment or moodiness.
Queen of Cups	Comfort, calm, or compassion.	Dependance, insecurity, or martyrdom.
King of Cups	Control, compassion, and balance.	Bad advice, moodiness, or coldness.

Pentacles

The second suit is Pentacles. Pentacles are associated with the element of earth. This suit is associated with peace and protection. See the chart below for the meaning of each card in the suit.

Card	Upright	Reversed
Ace of Pentacles	Prosperity, opportunity, or a new venture.	Missed chances, lost opportunities, or bad investment.
Two of Pentacles	Adapting to change, balancing decisions, or priorities.	Overwhelmed, loss of balance, or disorganized.
Three of Pentacles	Building, teamwork, or collaboration.	Disorganized, lack of teamwork, or group conflict.
Four of Pentacles	Frugality, conservation, or security.	Possessiveness, stinginess, or greediness.
Five of Pentacles	Insecurity, poverty, or need.	Improvement, charity, or recovery.
Six of Pentacles	Sharing, charity, or generosity.	Stinginess, power, domination, or strings attached.
Seven of Pentacles	Diligence, hard work, or perseverance.	Distractions, work without results, or lack of rewards.

Eight of Pentacles	Passion, apprenticeship, or high standards.	Lack of passion, no motivation, or being uninspired.
Nine of Pentacles	Rewards, fruits of labor, or luxury.	False success, reckless spending, or living beyond one's needs.
Ten of Pentacles	Culmination, legacy, or inheritance.	Lack of stability, fleeting success, or lack of resources.
Page of Pentacles	Desire, ambition, or diligence.	Laziness, lack of commitment, or greediness.
Knight of Pentacles	Hard work, efficiency, or responsibility.	Work without reward, obsessiveness, or laziness.
Queen of Pentacles	Perceptiveness, complexity, or clear-mindedness.	Cruel, cold-hearted, or bitterness.
King of Pentacles	Security, prosperity, or abundance.	Indulgence, greed, or sensuality.

Swords

The third suit is Swords. Swords are associated with the element of fire. Swords have the basic meaning of passion and lust. See the chart below for the meaning of each card in the suit.

Card	Upright	Reversed

Ace of Swords	Clarity, breakthrough, or sharp mind.	Brutality, confusion, or chaos.
Two of Swords	Stalemate, indecision, or difficult choices.	No right choice, lesser of two evils, or confusion.
Three of Swords	Suffering, heartbreak, or grief.	Forgiveness, recovery, or moving on.
Four of Swords	Contemplation, rest, or restoration.	Burnout, restlessness, or stress.
Five of Swords	Sneakiness, win at all costs, or unbridled ambition.	Desire to reconcile, lingering resentment, or forgiveness.
Six of Swords	Leaving behind, transition, or moving on.	Desire to reconcile, lingering resentment, or forgiveness.
Seven of Swords	Tactics and strategy, trickery, or deception.	Rethinking approach, coming clean, or deception.
Eight of Swords	Entrapment, imprisonment, or self-victimization.	New perspective, acceptance, or freedom.
Nine of Swords	Hopelessness, anxiety or trauma.	Despair, hope, or reaching out.
Ten of Swords	Collapse, failure, or defeat.	Only upwards, things can't get worse, or inevitable end.
Page of Swords	Mental energy, restlessness, or curiosity.	Manipulation, deception, or all talk.

Knight of Swords	Defending beliefs, impulsiveness, or action.	Disregard for consequences, no direction, or unpredictability.
Queen of Swords	Perceptiveness, complexity, or clear-mindedness.	Cruel, cold-hearted, or bitterness.
King of Swords	Truth, head over heart, or discipline.	Cruelty, manipulative, or weakness.

Wands

The final suit is Wands. Wands are associated with the element of air. The suit is associated with spontaneity and change. See the chart below for the meaning of each card in the suit.

Card	Upright	Reversed
Ace of Wands	Creating, willpower, inspiration, or desire.	Lack of passion, lack of energy, or boredom.
Two of Wands	Making decisions, planning, or leaving home.	Playing Safe, fear of change, or bad planning.
Three of Wands	Expansion, looking ahead, or rapid growth.	Delays, obstacles, or frustration.
Four of Wands	Celebration, community, or home.	Transience, lack of support, or home conflicts.
Five of Wands	Rivalry, competition, or rivalry.	Respecting differences or avoiding conflict.

Six of Wands	Public reward, success, or victory.	Excess pride, punishment, or lack of recognition.
Seven of Wands	Defensive, preservation, or maintaining control.	Destroyed confidence, giving up, or being overwhelmed.
Eight of Wands	Movement, rapid action, or quick decisions.	Waiting, panic, or slowdown.
Nine of Wands	Last stand, grit, or resilience.	Exhaustion, fatigue, or questioning motivations.
Ten of Wands	Burden, responsibility, or accomplishment.	Overstressed, inability to delegate, or being burnt out.
Page of Wands	Excitement, exploration, or freedom.	Procrastination, lack of direction, or creating conflict.
Knight of Wands	Adventure, action, and fearlessness.	Impulsiveness, anger, or recklessness.
Queen of Wands	Courage, joy, or determination.	Jealousy, selfishness, or insecurity.
King of Wands	Leader, the big picture, or overcoming challenges.	Overbearing, impulsive, or unachievable expectations.

Chapter 7: Tools by Spell Type

Generally speaking, magical tools are wildly versatile. They can be used to represent intangible concepts or deities, to direct our energy, and to perform somewhat mundane tasks like cutting herbs or producing ash. In some spells, however, tools have very specific uses. And these uses vary from spell to spell.

There are also tools that appear most often with certain types of spells. These tools are usually limited to stones or herbs, but they can also be certain types of ritual clothing or items as well as items that only fit the theme of a certain spell. In this chapter, I will go over the way certain tools perform special functions depending on the spell you cast, as well as touch on a few tools that only appear for certain types of spells.

Love Spells

Love spells are rather controversial in the magical community. If done incorrectly, they are considered a sort of magical Roofie. They take away someone's free will and cause them to act in a way they do not want to act. Even when done right – when the spell only calls for a certain kind of energy to enter your life in a romantic capacity – some magic users still find them distasteful. Before learning how certain tools are used in love spells, you should consider your stance on the spells themselves.

For those who approve of love spells, I feel I must clarify that I do not condone love spells cast on specific people. Instead, these tools should be used to call a certain kind of energy into your life so that it can connect with you on a romantic or sexual level. At no point should you use this information to get a specific person to see you in a romantic or sexual fashion.

With that rule firmly in place, we can move on to the tools themselves. When you are casting a love spell, the tools take on some very unique purposes. If your magic is influenced by Wiccan practices, you can use your wand or ceremonial knife to represent a male partner while your chalice can represent a female partner. Using any combination of these two items can symbolize you and your partner joining together in a relationship. And, if you are polyamorous, you can use more than two.

Certain stones and flowers also make appearances in love spells, though they are rarely seen in other magical workings. Rose quartz is a very popular stone in love spells, as its pink hue speaks the current modern association between the color pink and romantic love. And quartz itself is an incredibly versatile and useful stone that takes energy very well while being easy to find.

Roses are also very common in love spells. Many spell sachets geared toward finding love will combine rose petals and rose quartz with sweet-smelling herbs and a few other trinkets. These are then placed under the hopeful lover's bed or carried in their pocket until they find the love they are looking for. As with the color pink, red roses are seen as a sign of romantic love in many countries, which is why they are used in spells like these.

Indeed, most spell bags for love spells are red or pink. The color also makes an appearance as the thread color in spell braids or the thread that bundles together herbs that may be hung around a hopeful lover's door. Some people may also incorporate lace or silk, as these are very tactile fabrics often found in lingerie and other clothing designed with romance in mind.

Moon Spells

Any spell that relies on the timing and energy of the moon is a moon spell. Given that the spells rely so heavily on our nearest celestial neighbor, it makes sense that most of the tools and items used in these spells would either display or represent the moon. That is to say, witches who predominantly practice moon magic will usually have ritual knives, chalices, and other tools that all bear the image of the moon. They may even go so far as to get a tattoo of the moon, so as to tie themselves more closely to it.

As with love spells, there are certain stones that appear more often in moon spells than they do anywhere else. Moonstone – also known as hecatolite – and opals are found in many moon spells. Both of them are usually predominantly white, as the moon appears in the sky, but bear a rainbow-like sheen when looked at from certain angles. This sheen is said to represent the energy of the moon.

Many witches, particularly those influenced by Wicca, see the moon as a source of female energy. And, for this reason, statues of goddesses are also more common in moon spells. It should be noted, however, than in some cultures the moon explicitly represents a male deity. So the connection of the moon to female energy is not set in stone. As was true with correspondence charts, you should always go with what feels right to you when it comes to the moon's energy.

Common colors in moon spells include very, very light blues – which also relate to the color of the moon or its aura – and very dark blue. Very dark blues are more representative of the night sky, but they are an excellent backdrop for the brilliant stones mentioned above.

Many moon spells also focus on the use of moon water. Moon water is any water that has been charged with the energy of the moon. This is usually done by putting the water in a clear glass container and then leaving this container in direct moonlight for a given length of time. The exact length of time varies based on the witch as well as the purpose of the moon water. Moon water can charge in moonlight for as little one night or as long as one entire lunar cycle, which is nearly a full month.

Some moon water is charged during very specific phases of the moon. Full Moon Water is usually used for protective spells, fertility spells, and spells to ease menstrual pain. Water from the New Moon is used for banishing spells, cleansing spells, and more aggressive protection spells than full moon water can produce. Witches who rely on moon magic will often charge a great deal of moon water all at once and then save it for use throughout the rest of the lunar cycle.

It is important to note that any water left out under the moon will not become moon water. For water to become Moon Water, it must be placed in a vessel with intention. That intention must then carry through when the vessel is placed in moonlight. Without this intention to mark the jar of water as important, the energy of the moon will simply pass it by.

This intention is what makes most tools effective for magic working. Without the guidance of your energy, the energy of spell will not know where to go or why it should be following the direction of your tools. If a spell is a car, then the energy you raise is the gas you put into it and your intention is the steering wheel. It is your best – and, really, your only – option when you want to steer the energy around you or the spell it is powering. This is just as true when charging Moon Water as it is with any other spell.

Nature Spells

For some witches, all spells are nature spells. Their energy is rooted in nature and the majority of their magical practice is rooted in a religion that honors the earth as a deity in and of itself. When you are this heavily immersed in nature, all of your tools bear nature energy and are for nature spells.

If nature is only *part* of your practice, however, there are a few things you can do to more closely align yourself with natural energies. This will be particularly helpful if you are trying to get your garden to grow better, learn something about the land on which your home is situated, or if you want to try and influence the weather in any way. Nature magic is also good for bringing out the nutrients in food and protecting your pets, as well as working larger spells with other witches to protect the wider natural world.

To more fully tap into natural energies, you should use tools made from natural materials. Yes, metal is technically a natural material. But it is harder to extract from the earth and takes a great deal more processing. Natural magic responds best to items made of natural clay or of wood. You can gather both of these straight from the earth without too much effort, depending on where you live of course. And, with a little practice, you can shape them into just about anything as well. This, of course, brings you right back to the benefits of DIY magical tools.

Choosing items made of wood or natural clay might not be enough, of course. If you choose a wand or cup made from a rare or frequently exploited wood, such as mahogany, you are not going to get a positive reaction from the natural energy you are trying to work with. You would have better luck using a stick from your backyard as a wand. Quite literally, actually, as it would have a stronger connection to you and could be gathered without harming the trees in any way.

You can just as easily connect the rest of your tools to the natural world as well. Stones and herbs are already closely connected to the natural world, of course. But if you get your stones from a quarry that is open to the public, you will have a much more intense connection to them. The same thing will happen if you have something of a green thumb and can grow your own herbs. They will grow in soil that is protected by your magic and can then be harvested with a dedicated harvesting knife (in some practices, these are referred to as bolines). All of this creates a connection between you and the herbs so that they are even more effective when used in your spells.

Kitchen witches – witches who infuse their food and drinks with magic – will find this particularly useful. Handling their herbs from seed or cutting all the way to the cooking pot allows them to connect with the plant's magic from the very beginning. So when they go to add the plants to their cooking, the magical addition is even stronger.

If you are able to grow your own herbs, make sure you charge all of the gardening tools you use. Everything from your gloves to your watering can to the hose you use, can be charged with the intention of infusing magic into the green growing things around you. You can also infuse fresh energy into the plants every time you settle in to tend them.

City Spells

You might not be familiar with the idea of city spells. But as more and more witches are bringing their practice into the modern world, spells focused on life in cities are becoming more common. These spells are usually designed to deal with traffic, rude people on public transport, or even to keep pests at bay in uniquely modern situations.

City spells also usually rely on the energy of a city. The thrum of all the vehicles, the hum of countless human voices, the heat that only rises above a large city. All of these things – and so much more – are part of what set the energy of city magic apart from other forms of magic. There are natural witches that practice within the label of modern witches, of course. And many of them practice in cities. But city magic usually refers to using the energy and materials found in a more manmade world.

This does not mean that you should run out and buy tools that are all brand new, however. Instead, it means trying to fit your practice as organically into your daily life as possible. This touches on another interesting argument in the magical community, however. Many witches feel that modern life is too plastic. And since plastic is causing so many problems for both humans and the animals we share the world with, it seems counterintuitive to use plastic in your magical practice, which is supposed to support a healthy life so that your magic remains healthy as well. You will have to wrestle with this issue yourself and see where your feelings lie.

One way to work city magic into your practice is by buying your tools from a thrift store. You will have to cleanse everything you buy before you use it for magic, of course. But there is something very satisfying about finding a gorgeous wine glass at the thrift store and taking it home to function as your chalice. Or in finding a beautiful ornamental knife and cleaning it up to serve as a ritual knife. It will never cut anything, not while it serves as your ritual knife. But it looks amazing as it directs your energy in your rituals.

You can also find ritual clothing, scrap material, and candles at the thrift store. If you go often enough, you can find everything you need for either magical or mundane purposes. And the truly amazing thing about this is that thrift stores are unique to city life. In smaller towns, there might be a single thrift store that is part of a larger chain. But, for the most part, people just have a yard sale or give to the church rummage sale.

Experienced witches can take this a step farther and may actually seek out items at the thrift store that have a unique energy to them. This then becomes an energy source for them or a focal point for their next spell. Novice witches should never attempt this, of course. There is a very high risk of picking something up with a toxic energy that is masked by an attractive exterior.

But shopping at thrift stores is only one way to tap into the energy of a city. If you live in a city with a lot of local pride, particularly if it is a big city, you can find lots of items printed with the city's name or iconic images of local landmarks. These can be very effective magical tools if you personally have a lot of pride in the city where you live.

You can also tap into the energy of a city using tools very specific to a large cities. These include bus tickets to show that you have traveled the city's roads, which can help you tape into the energy that builds up on streets and thoroughfares when they are traveled regularly. You can also use subway maps as magical tools by tracing the lines of the most populous routes to tap into the energy they generate.

If you do not live in a big city, you can do much the same thing with a layout of the electrical lines in your home. You can trace your finger over the blueprint lines and tap into the energy that runs through your walls.

Herbal Power

When you're talking about magical symbolism, herbs and plants hold the power of the four elements in one single plant. Plants start out as seeds in the Earth. This is where they receive minerals in order to sustain life. Then the Sun, which is Fire, helps them to convert carbon dioxide into oxygen. Then Air, in the form of wind, helps to foster plant life, which stimulates the growth of leaves and stems and will also scatter the seeds around so more plants can grow. Lastly, they also need Water in order to live. But plants also play a part in the regulation of Earth's water cycle by purifying the water, and helping it move from the soil into the atmosphere. This is one of the best places to see all four elements at work together.

But this is not the only way that herbs are powerful. When they are used as medicines, they don't have all of the side effects that modern medicines have, and they help to keep your body balanced.

Every spice or herb that is used in cooking comes from a plant. They are formed from the roots, leaves, bark, seeds, fruits, or flowers. They are not only able to make your food taste great, but they are also used to preserve them. Spices and herbs can also be antiviral and antibacterial properties, and they also have lots of trace minerals and B-vitamins. They also have lots of disease-fighting antioxidants.

Herbs are also able to help people improve their spirituality. Herbs have their own consciousness. This consciousness is an extension of Earth consciousness, and plants want to protect, heal, and support us.

The power of herbs is able to weave its way through our body, and works within our cells. They are able to help us rationally understand

459

things so that we don't make decisions based solely on our ego mind and allows our intuition to guide us.

Herbs give us the power to connect with Earth energies. When it comes to magical uses, herbs are also very versatile. Herbs can be burned in order to purify the Air, and they can be used to make incense and oils. Herbal magic is practical, and there is a good chance that you have most of the stuff you need in your kitchen cabinets.

Green Witchcraft

When you are talking about herbal magic, you may come across the terms green witchcraft or hedge witch. These are not the paths within Wicca, or any other Neo-Pagan religion. While there are quite a few similarities between the two, the main one being the use of herbs, their core is very different. The Hedge Witch will focus on receiving information from the spirits, while the Green Witch will focus on the physical realm and the Earth.

Many people who fall in love with herbal magic will end up taking the Green Witch path. The path of the Green Witch is a path of Nature and growing things. Green Witches have an amazing understanding of herbalism and plant life, and they are sure to have lots of information and experiences when it comes to growing plants and using them effectively after they have been harvested. The majority of Green Witches hate buying plants after they have been harvested because they believe strongly in the relationship between the plant and grower and the role that it plays in achieving the best result. Green Witches will always have a garden.

The Green Witch has developed a strong relationship with the Earth that goes much deeper than what they do with plants. Green Witches also like to work with other types of natural objects. Fossils, animal parts, crystals, and rocks are all commonly used in their magic. They will also pay attention to the weather. They will often work with the elements or invoke the spirits of the elements when they perform rituals. Some Green Witches choose to honor Pan or Gaia.

It wouldn't be right if I said that all Green Witches work with the fey, but many of them will. Fairies are viewed as land spirits, and offerings are made to them in order to help look after their Earth. A Green Witch creates a relationship with these spirits where they live or work and might leave them gifts of bright ribbon or honey to keep their goodwill.

The environment is also another important thing for Green Witches. This is true on a personal level as well as a larger scale. They like to live where they have a lot of plants. If at all possible, Green Witches prefer natural materials over those that are manmade. They will also do their best to limit their carbon footprint. This makes them a lot like tradition Witches of old who grew their own produce and livestock.

Procedures and Spells

Whenever you perform a spell, you are basically spelling out the things that you need or want. A spell will bring your more magical vibrations to your endeavors, or it can be used when you have used all of your other possibilities. Each spell performed is made up of four parts: conceive, craft, communicate, and release. The last step simply means that you know it's possible so that you open to receiving it.

All spells are focused, and most are performed in a ritual setting. You are stating your power as the co-creative artist in your life. It gives you a way to consciously work with the Universe.

Spells are most effective when you perform them with gratitude for receiving. Always give thanks for the things that you have and receive.

461

Spells have a lot more to do with trust than control. It's all about honey, your mind and opening up your heart.

Adapting Tools for Your Spell

The tools and their uses outlined in this chapter are only a small sample of the way tools change depending on the spell you want to cast. But there are many, many more kinds of spells out there. And there is a good chance that you will come across spells where you want to use the tool you already have, but you want to have them align more fully with the energy of the spell you want to cast.

There are, thankfully, many ways that you can adapt your current tools to fit the energy source you want to use or the spell you are casting. Some tools, like candles, can be easily replaced. Because of this, you can etch shapes and words into them to merge them more fully with the intention of your spell. You can also fill the candle holder with objects that suit the spell. Seashells for a spell powered by the ocean is an excellent example. You just have to be sure that you don't mind getting wax on whatever is placed in the candle holder.

Other items, like your wand, can be wrapped in wire or thread that has been threaded with beads that match the intention of your spell. The colors would work best if they were taken from your own personalized correspondence chart. But some general suggestions are green and gold beads for money spells, yellow for spells to call in happiness, and black or grey beads for spells that encourage self-reflection.

Changing the color of your tools – even if it's just by wrapping them in different colors of ribbon – is a good way to adapt your tools to fit your spell. You can also turn everyday objects from around your home into magical tools by cleansing and then charging them. This allows you to substitute different items into your practice as needed without buying a whole new set of tools each time you try a new type of spell.

And, of course, you may find that you feel most comfortable using the same general tools for every spell. There is absolutely nothing wrong with this. If you do this, however, I do suggest you try adapting your tools to the spell at hand and see if that increases the efficacy of your magical workings.

Chapter 8: Life-Changing Moon Manifesting Visualization Strategy

After you have a clear intention set and you've got your mind, body, soul and environment on board, you will used advanced, but easy visualizations to enhance the energy of the goal.

Using visualization techniques and repeating powerful affirmations, along with the energy of the moon- we supercharge our dreams and wishes at an even more accelerated rate!

If you can see it in your mind, you can hold it in your hand. Visualization is comparable to a super power! When using the moon to crush your goals, we will use science based, strategic visualizations to trick your brain and bring these goals into fruition quickly!

When it comes to our visualizations two things are important- First, we must fast forward in our mind, and imagine ourselves living in the moment as if the goal were already true. We want to visualize how the situation looks once we have attained the goal!

So, if your goal is to have more self-worth, you will imagine and visualize yourself going to the gym every day, raising your hand in a meeting with confidence, or seeing yourself eating healthy and taking care of yourself.

If you want to manifest a promotion- you will visualize yourself having a meeting with your boss, hearing the great news, moving into your new office, and imagine your pay increase by visualizing massive deposits coming to your bank account!

Do you get it? Your goal is to make your intention as real as possible in your mind. The more detail you can picture the better! You can even write this visualization down and hang it, or place it next to your intention paper.

The second most important part of visualization is feeling the feelings and emotions your intention will bring you. How will it feel when you're self-worth is back? How will it feel when you've finally gotten the promotion you've been working so hard for? It's going to feel damn good! So, the last part of our visualization we FEEL!

You will picture yourself feeling proud that with your promotion you can finally afford to take your family on vacation. You will feel happy that financial stress has been removed from your life. You will feel your confidence build and feel feelings of joy that your self-worth is back!

It doesn't matter what your goal may be- you really want to get deep into the feelings and emotions that will come with this newly attained goal.

So now that you've set your intention, have a good visualization of that intention, and have brainstormed on all the feelings that intention will bring with it- you're ready to put everything together and complete your Moon Manifesting Visualization exercise.

90 second Moon Manifesting Visualization

Sit or lay down in a quiet space.

Close your eyes.

Take a few deep breaths and release any tension in the body.

Picture a funnel at the top of your head and imagine a white light pouring through it, and into your body.

Imagine this light filling your entire body from head to toe, covering every part of your body until every cell is illuminated. Image this light is swirling within you and around you, as if you're floating in a white bubble of powerful energy.

Picture yourself walking down an illuminated path that is leading you to your intention or goal

Arrive at a real-life scenario where you've obtained the goal.

How does this goal look? What are you doing? Who are you with? What can you see, taste, smell and touch? Make this goal as real as possible in your mind- visualizing as many aspects as you can.

Visualize the moment you receive your intention.

How does this intention FEEL? How does it feel to have it? Run through at least 3 feelings and emotions. Smile and make it as real as possible!

Show gratitude and appreciation for this vision and affirm that you know it will be true for you at the perfect time.

Float back to earth enriched by your vision.

Lock in the feeling of power, and know that you are in control of your life, and you have the power to make this happen!

You are going to do this exercise for 90 seconds every morning, and 90 seconds every night before going to bed. The most effective time to visualize is first thing in the morning and right before bed, so of course, you are going to do just that!

You dream deserve 180 seconds per day! This exercise will not only help you attain your goal- it will uplift your spirit, set a positive tone for your day and help you sleep better at night!

Crafting Your Master Plan

Next, we must make a strategic plan that will lead us closer to our intention.

What can we bring in, or let go of in order to be totally ready to receive this intention? How serious are you about this goal? For goals to bloom they must first start with intention, and planning is the next extremely important factor.

What steps can you take to set up your environment? What small actions can you take immediately, and what big actions can you already sense will be necessary? Think about all of the things you may have to do now, and start immediately.

Create your plan the last night of the new moon or the first night of the waxing moon. Remember, each phase has 3 days.

In this phase, we don't have to exactly know how we are going to get there- but we have to plan out some milestones in order for the goal to be fully attained. Don't worry about every step, you will be guided once you start taking action.

For example, if your dream is to get a promotion, and you have only thought and visualized about it, but haven't planned or set yourself up for success- the goal will not align.

You are a magnet, you are constantly attracting and bringing different situations into your life. If you want a promotion, you've got to set the intention, visualize on it and then you must make a plan to speak with your supervisor about it. Set a date, decide what you will say to your boss and plant the seed in your bosses' mind that you're interested.

A second part of your plan could look like gathering all your latest work to show your boss at that meeting, and then schedule a follow-up to seal the deal a few weeks down the road.

An important note to remember, your plan needs to align with the energy of the moon and her phases. Your worst-case scenario would be setting a date to meet with your Supervisor to show you are the candidate for that new high paying position on the Balsamic Moon when energy is null.

Set the date during the New or Waxing phase, and catch your boss when the energy is momentous. When you start planning and scheduling important dates with the moon- your life will transform in ways you did not think were possible.

All of the fine details will work themselves out, doors will start opening and leading you to your goal, but you have got to plan the essential stepping stones you know need to happen to make this baby work!

Planning is essential for any goal to manifest. Plan out a few steps you can take right now and get started right away!

Pro tip: When it comes to manifesting- don't worry about the little details, just focus on the end goal working out perfectly and the steps you need to take to get there. When you take action on your plan, time it with the moon and trust that the energy from the universe is helping you- nothing can stop it from manifesting!

Waxing Moon: Taking Action

Next, we must act on our plans. We must start showing the moon and the universe that we mean business! The energy during the waxing moon is momentous, forward moving and energetic.

These two weeks are a busy time, and really the only two weeks of the month you have to take strategic action.

After setting the intention, visualizing the shit out of it, and crafting your plan- you have to take massive action.

I wish it was so easy, we could set our intention, say a few affirmations, and wallah- it's here! But, unfortunately, this is not how the universe works people. We have to act in order to receive.

We have to show intent and act upon that intent for this system to truly work. Start taking small steps and use this phase to your advantage. The sooner you act, the sooner you shall receive.

Remember to continue practicing your moon manifesting visualization every morning, and every night. The universe works in laws and by visualizing every day, you are using the law of attraction to attract your goal to you rapidly.

Full Moon: Gratitude & Release

The full moon is where we pause, reflect and have a moment of gratitude for how far we've come. WOW, We're doing it. We're making changes, doing the work and each day we are getting closer!

For some of you, you may have never dug this deep into a goal. So, it's time to be thankful and pat yourself on the back.

During the full moon everything is illuminated the good, the bad, the bittersweet, and the ugly. The energy during the full moon asks us not only to be grateful, but to become aware of what isn't working, and release it from lives for good.

It may be part of the plan that needs to go, or it may be a toxic person holding you back, or even an old belief that keeps you stuck. Whatever it is- thank it for what it was worth and let that shit go!

If you are serious about your moon manifesting mission- you must let go and create space for your new manifestation. If toxic people or toxic thoughts are holding you back, the universe will not deliver.

Let go. Release it forever. Say good-bye. You are blooming into the person you want to become and you have no time for heavy energy holding you down.

I recommend performing a Full Moon ritual, taking a bath and sitting outside under the full moon and releasing what needs to go under this energy.

Waning Moon: Reflect & Revamp the Plan

The two weeks of the waning moon, energy is decreasing, slow moving and can almost feel overwhelming, chaotic and confusing. Remember, this is not the time we are beginning ANYTHING new.

These are two weeks we are analyzing the plan- tweaking and changing what we can to do more, to do better on the next moon cycle. In this phase we are looking deep into ourselves, tuning in, and allowing the universe to guide us. Our goal is to stay in tune with the flow and energy of the moon and universe.

You need to really become aware during this phase. Become aware of your thoughts, your feelings and make sure your goal still aligns with your vibe and purpose.

You need to become aware of what's working and what isn't. So many times, we hold onto things in our lives that weren't meant for us. If your plan feels hard or uninteresting, maybe it isn't for you!

More often than not, people find that what they thought they wanted, wasn't for them, and things change. If this is the case for you- that is okay! Move on and start anew, with a new goal, on the next new moon.

On the other side- You may be feeling more passionate about your goal then ever! Signs and synchronities may have already started appearing in your life, or some of you may already be living your dream.

Wherever you are is perfect. You just need to reflect, weed out the weeds and water the flowers now during the waning moon.

Balsamic Moon: Treat Your Self

Balsamic actually comes from the word "balsam" which means to soothe or relax, and this is exactly what this phase is all about. The balsamic, or dark moon phase is the last phase of the cycle and the energy is asking us to let go of all worry, and pause our actions, and to just melt into total relaxation.

These three days where we are in total chill, no f*cks, no stress type of mood! These are three days of the month where total self-love and self-care is first priority!

Some people may find these three days very tough, as most of us do not put ourselves first or set time aside for self-love each month. Others may wish this phase was longer. However, you feel- you should schedule a solo soothing activity or plan to veg out at home.

471

Take a bubble bath, infuse it with essential oils and crystals, light some candles and let your body, mind and soul totally let go. Get a massage, acupuncture, go on a meditation retreat, or take a walk in nature. Allow yourself to be free from your phone and "reality" as much as you can during this phase.

When we give ourselves space from our goal and slow down for a moment, we allow a re-set to happen on a subconscious level. When we begin again on the new moon, we will feel energized, recharged and motivated to keep going.

Life is all about balance, and if you really want to achieve your goals, you have to relax. If you keep going and going, you will get totally burnt out! This is why we must take a break, each cycle, each moon, each month.

Rinse & Repeat

You made it through your first moon cycle and first intention cycle!!! Pat yourself on the back and be proud- you are aligning and becoming one with the abundance of the universe. You may have already attained your goal in just one cycle, but for most of us this won't be the case.

Chapter 9: The Do's and Don't of Witchcraft

While there are no rules to witchcraft and Wicca, there are some general guidelines that you can follow that will make your practice flow more smoothly. Remember, practicing witchcraft is all about freedom, and doing what is best for you.

DON'T think that you have to be a witch to practice witchcraft. As was reiterated several times throughout this book, learning witchcraft does not mean you have to identify as a witch, or belong to the Wiccan religion. Practicing witchcraft means just that; you are a person who practices witchcraft. If you enjoy the name, feel free to use it. You don't have to belong to a coven in order to call yourself a witch, nor do you have to belong to one in order to be a part of the Wiccan religion.

DO research, research, research before you decide to start practicing witchcraft. There is no point in buying a wand, crystal ball, alter, various incense if you do not quite understand what it is you are going to be doing. There is a vast array of information on the internet and in New Age book stores that are going to help you learn about Wicca, witches, and other occult and Pagan practices. When the feeling is right, perhaps, then you can begin creating your ritual space and gathering tools.

DON'T spend too much money on your ritual tools at first. You are just starting off practicing something that may be a brief hobby, or something that briefly sparks your interest. Although this is not our hope, buying a lot of items you're not entirely sure you are going to connect with will waste your time, along with the time you spent looking for these items.

DO choose your ritual items carefully. Once you have decided what you want to actually purchase, or what you want to forge from the earth, take your time finding and purchasing them. Make sure you are holding them, sensing its energy, and sensing your own energy. Try to follow your intuition and choose what feels most right.

DON'T set our to cast hexes on others. Hexes, or curses, do exist within the magical world, but it is highly recommended that you not follow that path, due to the negative influence the energy will have on your life. Negatively cast spells fall under the category of black magic; this is not what Wicca, or the original concept of being a witch is truly existing for.

DO commit to doing no harm to others. There will always be times when we wish the harm of those who hurt us, but allow those to pass through you, rather than to use them as negative energy to put into another hex. Remember the first core belief of Wicca; do no harm.

DON'T let other people bring you down during the beginner phase of your witch-hood. It is personal to you, and important, so anyone who truly cares for you will not make fun of the way that you are trying to live. This is going to be an all around positive experience for you, so try not to let another person's negative opinion influence the important path you are choosing to walk on.

DO make an effort to locate or purchase a Book of Shadows. This is one of the most important tools in your ritual toolkit, and can be used for many reasons, including writing down spells, ingredients, and recalling your dreams.

DON'T wish for too much money. Casting a spell where you get more money for no particular reason sounds very tempting for most witches. It will be easy to start giving yourself money for the sake of it and for you to become greedy. Only ask for money in the more of spells when you truly need it, and keep the universe energies balanced by also donating some of your cash.

DO stay positive about your spell casting. Its going to take more than one try to get things right, or for the spell to render successful. There are many portions of the spell that could have made it go slightly wrong, like setting your intention, or not being able to focus enough on the task at hand. Whatever it may be, don't beat yourself up about it. Its called a practice for a reason! Trust yourself, you are going to get there.

DON'T everything to turn out well instantly. As previously mentioned, this is a practice, not a sport or learning to play an instrument. There is not a single right way to do spellwork, or to practice a ritual. There is no mathematical equation out there that will make a love spell work just as you planned it out. This is why your Book of Shadows will come in handy; you can write out the spells that worked for you, as well as the ones that did not. Use it as a reference to go back and check what may have went wrong, so you can change it up for the next time.

DO try to educate others on what witchcraft actually is. A lot of people will hear about the concept of being a witch, or perhaps that you are practicing to become one. There quick to reject the notion of a modern witch, and instead would rather go with the image of a Halloween-like, cackling old woman on a broomstick. If the person is open-minded enough, you can inform them what actually witchcraft really is; the harnessing energy from the spiritual universe into the physical universe. Even if this sounds too New Age for them, you can tell that its very similarly to positive thinking notions into psychology; the more likely you are to believe you can do something, the more likely you actually will.

DON'T reject the importance of meditation while trying to do witchcraft. There are very few people out there who are able to participate and witchcraft without meditating on a consistent basis. These people are naturally more in tune with themselves and the world around them already. But if you are not, it would be smart to blend in a few bouts of meditation into your week. It doesn't need to be very long, merely 15 minutes at the end or the beginning of your day. Start off three times a week, and watch how it effects the success of your spellwork.

DO what feels best for you. Even through what it says in this book about certain spells, set ups of altars, there is literally nothing set in stone when it comes to practicing witchcraft. Doing what works for you will actually make your shellwork and rituals work better for you, because you are following what energy that is driving you forward.

DON'T worry about making mistakes. This is life, and through every art and practice, you are going to make mistakes. This can happen within your spellwork, or through the application of psychic abilities. You can only learn by making these mistakes, so embrace them!

DO trust yourself while walking along with path. You have decided to participate in something that exists solely to create joy, peace, comfort, and happiness in your life and in the life of others. There are so many other ways that you could be spending your time, ways that could only hurt you in the end. Learning witchcraft is like consciously deciding that you want to better your life, and by learning spellwork, rituals, enhancing your psychic abilities, you are doing just that.

Conclusion

You are on this path for a very important reason. Something sent you in the direction of witchcraft, and whether or not you know a lot about it, or used to think that witches were the stuff of movies and the past, it doesn't matter. Anyone who is willing to dedicate themselves to learning new skills has already projected something positive into the universe. You reading this book is doing that.

You may feel self-conscious initially once you begin further researching which tradition you want to follow, ways that you want to set up your altar, which tools you want to locate and purchase for it, etc. You may worry about other people's judgments about what you are trying to do for your life.

If you live, alone it may be easier to set up your altar, along with your ritual tools. If you do not, it may be harder. You can start off keeping them in a private place, a place that allows you to be yourself and not feel criticized. However, eventually, try to feel strong about who you are and what you are doing to make yourself do better, and feel better. You are not worshipping Satan or joining a cult, nor are you suddenly starting to believe that you can fly through the sky on a broom. What you are doing does contain rationality to it; it is a form of self-care, self-love, and appreciate for everything around you.

Finally, it is time for you to put your words into action. Think of magic that way; the transferring of intention to behavior that is tangible. Everyone has corners of their existence that are not exactly up to par with what they are envisioning. Now, you can manifest though imaginings. Don't just leave your imaginings to your mind; know that they are all possible, and you hold the keys in your hand. The world of Wicca and other witches guarantee that only joy, thriving, happiness and constant growth are in store for you as an individual practicing witchcraft.

Introduction

Have you ever wanted to know what Tarot is all about? Maybe there are people in your life that practice Tarot and you want to learn more about it before diving in yourself. Many people are drawn to Tarot because of the air of mystery that surrounds it. Associated with fortune telling and the occult, Tarot comes with certain negative connotations. You might have heard that you should only have a Tarot deck in your possession if it was gifted to you, or that what you see in the cards will physically manifest in your life. We can thank pop culture and religion for warping the Tarot's intentions. Forget everything that you think you know about Tarot.

What started as a hand painted card game in Italy has evolved into a massive market catering to those seeking entertainment and tools for creating a deeper connection to our inner selves. Anyone can use Tarot cards, and with some practice, you can learn to understand each card on its own and in relation to the other cards. In a nutshell, all Tarot decks have 78 cards that are comprised of 22 Major Arcana cards and 56 Minor Arcana cards. Arcana can be translated as mystery, hidden, or secrets. In this book, we will delve into each card of the Major Arcana which are emblematic and represent life lessons and karmic influences in our lives. We will also explore the Minor Arcana and the way they relate to what's happening in our daily lives.

Because Tarot allows us to tap into our psyche's the cards can act as a sort of spiritual guide for us to develop further understanding and connection in our lives. Developing a sense of connection with your Tarot cards is a crucial step in the intuition and understanding that you'll develop when using them. We will explore ways to develop personal connections to each card and techniques for practicing how to perform readings for ourselves and others. Each of the Major Arcana descriptions contain potential references to questions that are being asked of the cards. This can help you learn to associate the type of question being asked to the representation given in the cards. As with anything that we want to be successful with, Tarot requires patience and practice.

When first learning how to read Tarot cards, it's important that you keep an objective point of view and understand that it's okay to play with them if it's done respectfully. Once you've got a basic understanding of each card or Suit, start practicing reading them in the Reversed, or Upside-down positions. No matter how long you may have been using Tarot, you will always find new ways of interpreting cards and achieve insights that are only possible through time and experience. Remember to keep things positive even when pulling cards that offer troubling contemplation as we are the masters of our own lives and we create our own paths based on the choices we make.

Chapter 1: What is Tarot?

Tarot is a symbolic map of consciousness. This map contains our journey through life in all ways be it practical or spiritual. Reading Tarot cards is a way of divining guidance and wisdom through the way that we lay or spread them out. Their placement and the way they relate to the other cards near them are how we interpret the messages they contain.

It's wise to remember that the cards themselves are not oracles. They do not reveal a future that is lying in wait for us but rather we can use them to create the future we want. It's that revelation that the cards can hold that draws us to the Tarot. The mystery and lore surrounding the cards keep some people away, for fear of negative consequence but others seek to understand them on a deeper level.

While most Tarot readers understand that instructional books on the subject serve as guidelines and give us basic definitions, it's the personal practice by each of us that allows us to develop a style, a technique, and deeper knowledge.

The Tarot is an archetypal map of human consciousness that goes beyond our journey through life both in the practical and the spiritual realms. Reading the Tarot cards is the practice of divination through a particular layout or spread of cards. But contrary to common belief, Tarot reading is not all about fortune telling, and you don't need to possess psychic powers before you can read the cards.
The Tarot cards are used to provide insight into the deepest knowledge of our higher consciousness. They provide an evolved awareness of what we already know deep within.

The Typical Tarot Deck

Tarot cards are divided into two major sections, the Major Arcana which reveals major mysteries, and the Minor Arcana which functions in the revelation of minor mysteries. There are seventy-eight cards in all. 22 cards make up the Major Arcana, and they are numbered from 0 to XXI. Each of the cards of the Major Arcana has a specific name, unlike the cards of the minor Arcana which are usually described by their position in the suit and the suit they are found in. The first card of the Major Arcana is The Fool, numbered 0, and the final card numbered XXI is named World.

The difference between the cards of the Major and Minor Arcana is the Major Arcana helps to reveal the coming of hugely significant life-changing events, while the cards of the Minor Arcana simply help to reveal minor mysteries like everyday occurrences.

More often than not, the cards of the Major Arcana reveal mysteries beyond our control; events that are likely to serve as important milestones in our journey through the Earth. Hence, Major Arcana cards may not be drawn so often but when they are drawn, it means something big is coming. if a divination is made, and a Major Arcana card shows up, it is unlikely your actions will lessen the possibility of that event happening. However, knowing about the possibility of that event occurring in a particular sphere of your life (depending on the question you asked) will put you in a position to be able to handle the coming events with adequate preparedness.

The remaining 56 cards of the typical Tarot deck constitute the Minor Arcana. The suit representing the element fire is known as Wands, the one representing water is known as Cups, the one representing Air is known as Swords, and the one representing Earth is known as Pentacles. Depending on the tarot deck being used, alternative names may be used in the nomenclature of the suits of the Minor Arcana. The Wands suit may be known alternatively as Rods, the Cups suit as Chalices, the Swords suit as Spears and the Pentacles suit as coins. It is not the name that a particular suit is called in a deck that matters, what matters is what element of the universe the suit represents.

Tarot as a Part of Life

Tarot cards are quite popular, and most all of us are familiar with them, even if only to a small degree. We see them featured frequently in entertainment media, used by fortune tellers, witches and magicians as part of a supernatural practice, either to see into the future, form a magical barrier for protection, or to summon spirits and entities from other dimensions. In truth, the way Tarot is stereotypically portrayed in popular media is inaccurate, or at the very least, highly exaggerated. We often see protagonists of films visiting a clairvoyant or cliché gypsy character to discern the next steps of their journey or uncover an important secret; the cartomancer will usually pull an easily recognizable trump card of the Major Arcana from the deck (the Lovers, Death, and the Devil seem to be the most commonly used cards in popular media) and jump to dire conclusions immediately upon seeing it. Usually, the interpretation of these cards is quite literal: The Lovers signify the beginning of a new romantic affair; Death implies a loss of life looming just around the corner, and the Devil is a sign that something wicked is at work in the protagonist's world.

If you're just getting started, dipping your toes into the world of Tarot and metaphysical spirituality, you'd be wise to let go of the expectation of a similar experience; otherwise, you'll be setting yourself up for disappointment. Tarot can indeed be an immensely powerful, life-changing tool but any experienced reader knows that it's rare to encounter a single card that can accurately predict a romantic development, death, or any other specific future event. Every single card in the deck has multiple potential interpretations--for example, the Death card is much more likely to reference change or figurative rebirth than it is to refer to a literal death, and depending on the context provided by surrounding cards, it can often deliver a message of positivity and optimism for the quitrent's future. This being the case, it's important for any Tarot enthusiast to remain open-minded and ready to embrace complexity. In the world of divination through Tarot, there is very little black and white; most of the practice resides in a grey area, and no matter how experienced a reader may be, the deck will always have something new to teach them.

Tarot is for everyone. While it has been historically influenced by philosophical and spiritual trends, Tarot itself isn't connected to any single religion or dogma. Though occult-oriented decks have existed for hundreds of years, the original Tarot decks held no more mystery or darkness than a standard fifty-two card deck of playing cards, and there are plenty of modern decks designed with decidedly light-hearted illustrations. While many turn to Tarot with an interest in seeing into the future, there are those who do not believe the cards harness any type of clairvoyant power; instead, they may use the cards as a means of introspection and self-understanding, much like a psychologist using a Rorschach test to gain insight into a patient's psyche. At the end of the day, Tarot is what you make of it, and the cards can only be as powerful as your belief in them.

Tarot for Today's World

You may have noticed an increase in interest surrounding Tarot. It seems as if we are currently experiencing a sort of Tarot revival where Tarot readings are being performed via live video feeds online, Tarot Clubs are meeting up in public spaces to hold readings and fellowship with like-minded people. What started out as a more mystical practice that helped form the works of many artists and philosophers before us, is now more of an insight into our current lives. Card interpretations can be given without the air of mystery or perceived implications. By removing the smoke and mirrors that have disguised Tarot for too long it is being opened to new audiences that can express it as more of a creative act rather than a metaphysical one. This ability to creatively read a story that the cards present and apply it to certain aspects of our lives is quite attractive. This pull is partly because it's all about us. No one else can truly understand what the cards mean to you on a personal level.

If you've never had your Tarot cards read, start there. You should be able to achieve this quite easily if you are willing to have a reading performed online or if you know of someone in your circle that has a Tarot deck. You can just pull one card, or find out your Birth Cards, or pose a question that you need insight on. Keep in mind that there is still a certain stigma that comes with the Tarot. Many followers of religion still warn against the idea of being able to control our own fates and rejecting God's creation and care over all life. Some leaders in religion are still creating fear around the Tarot by saying its use will attract demons and evil spirits. Even with the negativity that still surrounds the Tarot, many young people are drawn to embrace the mystic. As older generations sought consolation and order to their lives through religion, many people now are finding a sense of control through Tarot.

For many, the meditative practice of reading Tarot cards is in and of itself a reason to continue doing it. Handing over major life dilemmas and decisions to the ancient illustrations found in the Tarot can be both comforting and insightful during times where guidance is needed.

Popular Tarot decks

Decks for novices

Rider-Waite

The Rider-Waite deck makes an excellent first deck for beginners. Originally published in 1909, the deck was named for publisher William Rider, and A.E. Waite, a prominent public figure in the mystic community at the time. The deck was masterfully illustrated by Pamela Colman Smith, using a combination of traditional Christian imagery, Jewish and Kabbalist symbolism, ancient Egyptian references, and modern feminist slant (or, at least what would have passed for "modern feminism" during this era). The deck set itself apart by including an explanatory booklet with a guide to divination, and by illustrating the numbered suit cards with unique narrative details to aid in memorization.

There are several versions of this deck in publication, some with more radiant or muted color schemes, some in larger or smaller card sizes, and many special editions. There's even a set that glows in the dark!

Thoth Tarot, or Book of Thoth

This is a great deck for beginners who want a bit more esoteric energy in their Tarot practice. Produced by English occultist and magician Aleister Crowley, and painted by Lady Freida Harris under his instruction, this beautiful deck was published alongside a book of the same name, including detailed instructions for divination. This can be a great deck for novices, so long as they know how to translate the updated names of some Major Arcana cards. In the Thoth deck, the Magician is renamed the Magus; the High Priestess is simply the Priestess; Strength is retitled as Lust; the Wheel of Fortune is just Fortune; Justice is renamed Adjustment; Judgment is recast as the Aeon; and finally, the World becomes the Universe.

The Gilded Tarot

Inspired by the classic Rider-Waite imagery with renaissance era characters but set in the cosmos with a psychedelic, new age twist. It's particularly useful for beginners because the suit cards are color-coded; this helps to get into the practice of associating the corresponding elements to each of the suit cards as you read spreads.

Sun and Moon Tarot

Painted in soft pastels and a folk-art style, this deck is fantastic for those who are new to Tarot, specifically because the numbered suit cards are labeled with clue words--an excellent tool for memorization. It's lovely to look at and features a more racially diverse cast of characters, and some that shake up gender norms of traditional tarot decks.

The Golden Tarot

Designed from medieval and renaissance era artworks, this historic style deck is great for beginners because the images hold so many detailed clues to the cards' meanings. It's a perfect deck for art history lovers, beautifully designed and full of biblical symbolism; for example, the Empress card uses a painting of the Virgin Mary. This deck uses the suit of Coins in place of Pentacles.

New Mythic Tarot

Originally published in 1986, this deck draws heavily on the illustrations of the Rider-Waite deck but has some minor illustrative departures. The deck is re-imagined to feature a cast of characters from ancient Greek myths, adding an extra layer of narrative content to the card meanings. For example, the Star card is drawn to represent a snapshot moment from the myth of Pandora's box, while the Hanged Man is drawn as Prometheus, ready to receive Zeus' punishment.

Morgan Greer Tarot

Loosely based on the Rider-Waite deck, these cards are borderless, full of bright, lush colors, and most characters are drawn in closeup, with features and details well-defined. This is a great deck for those who are new to the world of Tarot, as the artwork is very approachable but still intricate, beautiful, and complex. Designed and published in the 1970s, the Morgan-Greer illustrations hint at the trends of flower power and psychedelia. This is one of very few decks to use a medieval or fantasy era setting while also including racial diversity in the illustrations.

Robin Wood Tarot

This deck is inspired by Rider-Waite but leans heavily upon pagan symbolism rather than Christian religious imagery, so it is a go-to for modern-day pagans, wiccans, and secularists. The illustrations have an ethereal, art-nouveau era style, with a dark fairy tale mood, and bright colors that make the card imagery extremely easy for novices to read.

Decks for Experienced Readers, Collectors, and Tarot Lovers

Tarot de Marseilles

This traditional French medieval style deck is a must-have for any collector who loves history. It is one of the oldest deck designs still in popular circulation; its earliest version may have been produced as early as the year 1500; there is a copy of this deck still in existence that was made in 1650. In the Tarot de Marseilles, illustrations of the Major Arcana cards are somehow cartoonishly simplistic and hauntingly beautiful at the same time. The only reason this deck is not ideal for beginners is the design of the numbered suit cards; while they are beautiful and intricate, they often feature geometric designs rather than illustrations and can be difficult for novices to interpret.

Motherpeace Tarot

This is one of the most popular and distinctive modern decks around. It was designed in the 1970s to update the classic Tarot imagery to something better suited to new-wave feminist ideals, particularly inspired by the Goddess movement. The cards are round rather than rectangular; their shape symbolizes the moon and feminine energy. This is a wonderful deck for those who crave a diverse, intersectional, feminist update to Tarot imagery and symbolism. The deck even has its own unique spread of eleven cards laid out in a circular shape.

The Hermetic Tarot

Another great deck for history lovers, and those with a special interest in the esoteric side of Tarot. This deck features a great deal of symbolism from the Secret or Hermetic Order of the Golden Dawn, an occultist group that was popular in Europe at the turn of the twentieth century and still survives to this day (though it boasts lesser numbers currently). While the current Golden Dawn movement may have some unfortunate connections to fascist and racist ideologies, the Hermetic order was primarily concerned with the preservation of ancient alchemical, cabalistic, and arcane knowledge; current leaders of the Hermetic Order claim no connection or alignment whatsoever with the modern Golden Dawn movement. This deck is a wonderful tool to further your study of individual card meanings, as the images feature clues to elemental, astrological, Kabbalistic, numerical, and geomantic connections for many cards. The entire deck is drawn in only black and white, with highly detailed illustrations; you'll want to stare at these spreads for hours.

Aquarian Tarot

This deck is breathtakingly beautiful, featuring art deco and art nouveau inspired illustrations and a modern color scheme. The symbolism is a bit more complex than a standard deck, and this isn't ideal for a novice cartomancer but for a reader who has some experience with a traditional deck, it will be easy to transition into this style.

Shadowscapes Tarot

This is a gorgeous deck, with finely detailed, ethereal illustrations. In fact, the beautiful imagery is the only reason this deck might not work for beginners--it can be a distraction, and furthermore, some of it is quite abstract. This is a great deck for anyone who loves fantasy, Norse mythology, and faeries.

The Wild Unknown Tarot

This beautiful deck is gaining a large modern following. It may not be best for novices, as many of the illustrations are minimalist, featuring nature and animals rather than human characters but the artist's interpretations of card meanings are profound and inspiring.

Starchild Tarot

A perfect deck for the modern-minded wiccan, this deck uses a gorgeous pastel, new-age color scheme, and photo-collage art to create some truly breathtaking imagery. This deck draws heavily on cosmic spirituality, sacred geometry, metaphysical healing philosophies and ancient mystery schools for symbolism.

Fountain Tarot

Another wonderful modern deck, the Fountain Tarot features original oil paintings by Jonathan Saiz that beautifully capture the concepts of Tarot, updating them for the internet age while retaining a sense of mystery and appreciation for its historical legacy. It's a must-have for modern metaphysical practitioners, energy healers, and contemporary art lovers, too.

Visconti-Sforza Deck

This deck is about as old as the Tarot de Marseilles design, and another wonderful deck for history lovers, with illustrations drawn in more of a medieval style, barely hinting at the dawning of the Renaissance. The original Visconti deck is missing four cards--the Tower, the Devil, the Three of Swords and the Knight of Coins--so for modern prints, these four cards have been recreated in a similar style to the rest of the deck. Many of the original cards survive to this day, in museums and private collections; they were often created using precious materials, such as gold leaf for the card's borders, and show us not only that Tarot was valued by the wealthy and powerful but also provide us a glimpse into the daily life and value structure of the Italian nobility of the 15th century through its detailed imagery.

Chapter 2: Tarot History

The Symbolic Language of Divination

Perhaps one of the most intriguing things about the Tarot is that it seems to be a product of both human invention and divine inspiration. Unlike other forms of divination that utilize simple tools like dice, or naturally-occurring phenomena like cloud watching, Tarot is a fairly complex affair involving many different interactive symbols originating in human culture.

Yet the Tarot has no single author or "original" deck. It is a divinatory art that was developed collaboratively over centuries, through the contributions of many people. There isn't even a comprehensive set of universally accepted interpretations for each card. Nonetheless, the Tarot offers limitless possibilities for finding clarity and meaning for those who seek the cards' assistance.

The Tarot can be thought of as a "language" through which we can hear and understand divine messages, whether we're reading the cards for ourselves or for others. Just as runes, tea leaves, or the lines of our palms each have a language that can communicate specific information, the Tarot—both the individual cards and the symbolic system of the deck as a whole—can show us much about ourselves and the world around us.

And this language is also still evolving, as each new generation of readers studies the theories and approaches of those who came before them and then adds their own perspective to the tradition. This is part of the dynamic nature of this particular divinatory system.

Newcomers to Tarot often ask: Who, or what, is the guiding intelligence determining which cards you draw from the deck? Is there some kind of specific magical force inherent in the cards themselves?

The truth is, no one can answer that question for you, because it depends on your individual beliefs and the unique way in which you understand and interpret the divination experience.

The cards can indeed behave in some seemingly magical ways, such as when a single card jumps out of the deck while you're shuffling, or when you pull a series of cards that are all astonishingly accurate to your situation. But—and this is important to know—you are also part of the equation. However you ultimately define the source from which the information comes, you yourself are connected to that source. You are tapping in to the wisdom of your own higher self, in conjunction with any other energies assisting in the reading.

If you're eager to get started tapping into that wisdom, you're free to skip ahead to the end of this guide and discover the basic meanings of each card in the Tarot deck. However, for a truly rich and informed understanding of how Tarot works, it's advisable to have some knowledge of where the Tarot comes from, as well as the basic functions of each type of card in the deck. You'll find all of this and more in the discussions below.

The Origins of the Tarot

Some divination methods, such as scrying and watching the flight patterns of birds, are older than recorded history. Others, such as runes and palm reading, can be traced back at least to ancient times.

Tarot, by comparison, is a relatively new system of divination. It began to emerge in earnest in late 18th-century Europe, and was more substantially developed in the 19th and early 20th centuries. But the roots of Tarot—in terms of the structure and imagery of the deck as well as the esoteric wisdom contained within—go back much further.

Many myths, misconceptions, and scholarly debates about the history of Tarot abound today, and the full tale of its origins is beyond the scope of this guide. Instead, we'll take a brief tour of the main stages of its development, as this provides helpful context for understanding the Tarot today.

The Western Mystery Tradition

During the 18th century, several French scholars and aristocrats began to take an interest in esoteric (or "occult") subjects like divination, magic, and alchemy. Like others in Europe had done over the course of many centuries, they were rediscovering and building on older philosophical and mystical traditions, including Jewish Kabbalah, Pythagorean theory and other Greek philosophy, and Hermetic teachings.

These and other elements of ancient and medieval spiritual exploration are collectively known as Western esotericism, or the "Western Mystery Tradition," which is still very much alive today. As we will see, various participants in this tradition have influenced our understanding of the Tarot as it has developed over time.

One such figure was Antoine Court de Gébelin, who in 1781 published an essay considered to be the first known work on the Tarot as a means of esoteric enlightenment. This inspired other "occultists," as such seekers were known, to expand on de Gébelin's ideas, and a few years later another Tarot enthusiast, Jean-Baptiste Alliete (who went by the name "Etteilla"), published the first guide to reading Tarot cards as a divination tool.

Several decades later, another highly influential occult scholar named Éliphas Lévi joined the efforts. Lévi's teachings on the Tarot, particularly in terms of its relationship to Kabbalah, are widely credited as being the most significant of his time, and his influence ultimately stretched into the 20th century and beyond.

Myths and Misconceptions

The French occultists contributed much to what we now consider to be "the Tarot," in terms of understanding its symbolism and its relationships with several different threads of esoteric knowledge. However, these seekers were also laboring under key assumptions about the Tarot that later proved to be historically incorrect.

First, they believed that the Tarot had originated in ancient Egypt. This was due partly to erroneous connections made between imagery on some of the cards and certain Egyptian artifacts, and partly to fabricated evidence being circulated among occult enthusiasts. It was also fashionable at that time to be able to connect everything having to do with esoteric knowledge back to ancient Egypt, so the notion that the Tarot was Egyptian was readily received.

A related belief was that the Tarot was brought to Europe by the people known to Europeans as "gypsies," who originated in India and began arriving in Europe during the Middle Ages. These nomadic people, more correctly identified as the Roma, were also mistakenly believed to hail from Egypt (hence the name "gypsies"), which obviously didn't help dispel the Egyptian origin theories. Later scholars, having more information about history and geography than these innovators of Tarot did, ultimately dismissed these ideas.

Today, many people argue that the Tarot had nothing to do with Egypt or gypsies, but was just an invention of the 18th-century occultists, who merely transcribed their existing esoteric knowledge onto what had been a mundane pack of playing cards. Yet this isn't an accurate assessment either. Actually, it turns out that while none of these origin theories is accurate, there is some truth to be found in each one.

For example, it is true that the Tarot deck as we know it today was modeled on playing cards used by the nobles of medieval society. These were somewhat like modern playing cards, in that they had four numbered suits, each of which had its own symbol.

The suits were typically known as batons, cups, swords, and coins. Each suit contained an Ace; a card for every number between two and ten, which are often called the "pip" cards; and four "face" cards, with a Knight in addition to the Jack (or Knave), Queen, and King. These cards were used to play various games known collectively as Tarot, which originated in Italy where they were known as *Tarocchi*.

At some point during the 15th century, a fifth "suit" was developed and added to these decks, which was entirely different from the others. This new suit consisted of several illustrated, un-numbered cards depicting scenes and figures which reflected Italian society, but which also appeared to be allegorical (or containing a hidden meaning).

These cards were known as *trionfi*, meaning "triumph," because they held more power in the game than the other cards. There were many different versions of the *trionfi*, and decks could vary widely in terms of the number and iconography of these cards. Eventually, the "triumph" cards became known as "trump" cards.

As noted above, it is commonly believed that these cards were used simply for entertainment purposes, and had no connection whatsoever to the esoteric ideas of the French occultists who would later attempt to link them to ancient Egypt. However, some scholars suggest that there was more to these Tarot decks than just card games for the wealthy.

There is evidence that as early as the 16th century, at least some of the cards from Tarot decks were being used for divination purposes, and even some church leaders in the mid-15th century used the imagery on some of the triumph cards to aid with philosophical and religious discussions.

Furthermore, the iconography on many of these "playing cards" was not without occult significance. During the time that the triumph cards were first being created, belief systems like Hermeticism, alchemy, and other esoteric philosophies were subjects of interest among the populace. But by the time the *trionfi* suit was added to the Tarot deck, the Roman Catholic Church had been cracking down on spiritual beliefs that contradicted its own doctrine.

To preserve what was quickly becoming "heretical" knowledge in the era of the Inquisitions, artists frequently created iconography that could still communicate esoteric ideas without overtly defying the Church's rules. Some believe that the imagery on the triumph cards was intended at least in part for this purpose, as they contained symbolism linked to the same sources—including ancient Egypt—that were inspiring what would come to be called the Western Mystery Tradition.

As for the gypsies, while they didn't invent the Tarot deck, they are not at all irrelevant to the story of the Tarot. The Roma brought their own belief systems and esoteric traditions with them, which, while distinctly different from that of Western esotericism, no doubt laid the groundwork for the emergence of Tarot as a divination form.

They were already readers of palms, tea leaves, crystal balls and clouds. They also had other divination forms that involved symbols, numerological associations, and a randomized process (like throwing dice or drawing lots) that they were able to adapt to a deck of cards. So as Tarot cards became more widespread in the 13th and 14th centuries, the "gypsies" incorporated them into their own divination traditions. Ultimately, the European occultists began to follow their lead.

Marseille and the Making of the Modern Deck

Until the invention of the printing press in the mid-15th century, playing cards would have been relatively difficult to come by, as decks were created by hand. This is why relatively few medieval Tarot cards have survived the centuries, and why there are so many differences among the earliest decks.

As printing technology became more widely available, the mass-production and standardizing of the Tarot deck got underway, particularly in the French city of Marseille. Here, the "triumph" cards were numbered with Roman numerals, in a relatively consistent order, and were given titles, such as "The Magician," "The Lovers," and "Strength."

By the end of the 16th century, this standardization was more or less complete, and though many different manufacturers created Tarot decks, all were very similar. This new "standard model" became known as the Tarot of Marseille (also spelled "Marseilles"), and the

499

version of it most familiar to modern readers was first produced in 1748.

This was the deck that French occultists Antoine Court de Gébelin and Etteilla used as they explored the esoteric potential of the cards. As this period of discovery and innovation continued into the next century, the two different sections of the deck—the trionfi and the remaining four suits—came to be called "arcana," meaning "secrets" or "mysteries." This helped to popularize a concept of the Tarot as a divinatory art, distinct from its playing-card origins.

The Golden Dawn and the Waite-Smith Deck

Eventually, the Tarot came to interest British occultists of the 19th and early 20th centuries, in particular members of the Hermetic Order of the Golden Dawn, an organization founded in 1888 that came to heavily influence modern occultism in many ways. Here, occult scholars including Samuel Liddell MacGregor Mathers and William Westcott drew on the insights of Lévi and other earlier French occultists, but ultimately tweaked the deck to fit their own understanding of esoteric concepts and occult correspondences.

It was through this group that poet Arthur Edward Waite and artist Pamela Colman Smith came to create the most popular, and arguably the most influential, Tarot deck of the 20th century. It was based on the Tarot of Marseille, but with an important difference—it provided illustrations for the "pip" (numbered) cards. (One other known deck, from late-15th century Italy, had illustrated pip cards, and Smith drew some of her inspiration from visiting an exhibit of these cards while she was creating the new deck.)

This meant that rather than simply finding three cup symbols on the Three of Cups card, for example, one would instead discover three female figures with chalices in their hands, raising them together in what may be a ritual or a celebration. This imagery could open up more specific possibilities for interpretation than a simple pictographic image.

This was the first full Tarot deck designed exclusively for divination in the English-speaking world, and it's widely credited with popularizing the Tarot in the 20th century. It was initially known as the Rider-Waite deck, crediting the original publishers, William Rider & Son, but has more recently become known as the Waite-Smith deck, in order to give due credit to the artist responsible for the images on the cards.

The Evolution Continues

Given all of the various phases of its development, from "everyday card game" to incredibly rich and diverse divinatory art, it's probably most accurate to say that the Tarot has no single "true" origin. Rather, it has always been a work in progress, a synthesis of wisdom, symbolism, and ideas with roots in many different cultures and time periods. And that work is by no means complete. Even though the Waite-Smith is still essentially the "standard" deck in the 21st century, many variations and even departures from it have arisen over the past several decades, as we will see later on.

As these newer decks have flourished, so have new systems and methods for interpreting the cards, which may or may not align with the interpretations popularized by the French and British occultists. Traditionally, occultists have argued for a specific set of interpretations that must be memorized in order to read the cards, but 21st-century mystics see these things differently, emphasizing intuition over rigorous study. Many also argue that as society develops and changes, so do the messages available in the Tarot, so sticking with the "old" meanings and methods can limit or skew our understanding of the cards.

These are important points to keep in mind, as the Tarot has been in a process of evolution since it first emerged. However, if you're new to the cards, it's helpful to get a good sense of the basic traditions before developing your own unique approach. So let's begin at the beginning, with an orientation to the Tarot deck as it has been known for the past century.

The Modern Tarot Deck

As we have seen, the standardization of Tarot decks that occurred in 18th-century Marseille ultimately gave rise to the structure of the Tarot as we know it today: a 78-card deck, comprised of 22 Major Arcana and 56 Minor Arcana cards.

The Minor Arcana is further divided into four suits, which retain the original structure of the four-suited card decks of medieval Italy: an Ace, nine pip cards numbered 2 through 10, and four Court cards.

The cards of the Major Arcana (or "greater secrets") generally reflect aspects of the inner self, the emotional and/or spiritual growth that we encounter along the journey of life, and significant events and turning points on one's individual path. By contrast, the cards in the Minor Arcana (or "lesser secrets") typically represent the more mundane elements of everyday life, through which we discover, experience, and apply the "lessons" represented by the Major Arcana.

The meanings associated with each card can be derived from one or more of many elements: the name of the card (especially within the Major Arcana), the number of the card (especially within the Minor Arcana), the card's illustration, and other details, as we will see shortly.

The Major Arcana

The Major Arcana consists of 22 cards depicting a sequence of images: archetypal characters (The Emperor, The Hermit), celestial bodies (The Sun, The Star), objects (The Chariot, Wheel of Fortune), virtues (Judgement, Temperance), and situations (The Hanged Man, The Tower).

Traditionally, the cards are numbered in Roman numerals from I to XXI (1 to 21), with the remaining card, The Fool, either left unnumbered or given a "0." The ordering of the cards is consistent across decks, with the exception of the Justice and Strength cards (which will be explained below), and the position of the Fool, which is typically at the start of the sequence but can also be found at the end.

Various schools of interpretation for these cards have developed over time, with one approach often influencing another. However, the concept of the Major Arcana as representing a "journey" or "path" of some kind has been a recurring theme over the centuries.

In this framework, the cards may reflect the major events we encounter as we move through our physical lives, or they may represent our psychological or spiritual journey, as we experience the lessons our souls chose to learn during this present incarnation. In practice, the

Major Arcana tends to address both physical and intangible aspects of our life experience.

Probably the most commonly used interpretive system for the Major Arcana today is what is called "the Fool's Journey." This term was made popular in the late 20th century by Tarot scholar Eden Gray, but the concept is likely inspired by the work of the Order of the Golden Dawn, as well as the writings of psychoanalyst Carl Jung and mythology scholar Joseph Campbell.

In this approach, the Fool is not a silly or stupid character. Instead, he represents the soul of each human being in its innate innocence, before it has embarked on the journey of life. The rest of the cards, laid out in order from 1 to 21, tell the story of what happens once the Fool steps forward into the journey of psychological or spiritual development.

The Fool will encounter both obstacles and victories, and meet many archetypal characters who will teach him important lessons along the way. The final card in the sequence is the World, signifying the fulfillment that comes with having learned and integrated the lessons he has encountered on his journey.

Of course, life's lessons rarely follow such a linear, storybook progression. Indeed, we can find ourselves in the position of the Fool in a number of different circumstances, such as starting a new job or new relationship, or encountering an intense emotional or psychological experience for the first time. This is why the Fool is not actually part of the overall sequence of the cards. Whether he's the first card or the last, he has no actual number and can fit in at any point in the sequence, as each card can be read in relation to him.

As for the rest of the cards, the order of the sequence is not meant to be proscriptive, since the stages of one's individual journey may take any order. Furthermore, the "journey" of the Major Arcana is cyclical, meaning that every time the Fool reaches the World, it's time to start again and learn something new. So the Fool's Journey concept can be thought of as a map, helping you identify where you are in the context of your situation, but it is not necessarily a set of directions.

There is no standard, universally-accepted set of interpretations for the Major Arcana in the context of the Fool's Journey, but many guides and seasoned Tarot experts offer sufficiently similar meanings to create a general consensus. As you familiarize yourself with the cards over time, you will no doubt come to your own understanding of each one, and how it relates to you on your own personal journey.

The Minor Arcana

While the cards in the Minor Arcana may seem less significant than the "trump" cards, they actually represent the essential ingredients that make up our lives, without which, the lessons of the Major Arcana would have no context.

Each suit of the Minor Arcana is centered on a particular realm of experience: ideas, feelings, action, and manifestation. As these cards make up the bulk of the deck, they tend to be more prevalent in a reading than the Major Arcana cards.

In modern decks, the suits are most often known as wands, cups, swords, and pentacles, but some decks keep to the more traditional medieval names and symbols, while others have adapted different names and symbols altogether. The more widely used alternate suit names are listed beneath each suit description.

Wands

The suit of Wands represents the realm of inspiration, intention, and ambition. When we are feeling creative, inspired, spurred to action, and/or envisioning outcomes we are utilizing Wand energy.

There is a distinction to be made here between thought and action, however. Action is not yet dominant at the Wands stage, and sometimes this suit can remind us that enthusiastic beginnings still require follow-through. Wands also represent risk-taking and initiative, as we desire to grow, create, and expand our horizons. Because we are essentially motivated by desire—either to manifest a positive outcome or avoid a negative one—feelings of both apprehension and excited anticipation are connected to the cards of this suit.

On the whole, Wands are considered positive cards, and often show up in a reading as a sign of encouragement.

Also known as: arrows, batons, clubs, cudgels, rods, scepters, spears, staves

Cups

The suit of Cups is the realm of emotion, creativity, psychic insights, love, empathy, and matters of the heart in general. The Cups tend to represent the feelings that accompany, or arise out of, the thoughts we are having about a given situation. These feelings tend to influence our behavior, whether or not we're consciously aware of them.

A full range of emotions—both pleasant and unpleasant—is present within this suit, so some cards may appear to be negative, depending on the reading. Yet any cards that assist with getting clarity on a situation should be appreciated.

Cups can also speak to the benefits and potential pitfalls of psychic gifts and empathy. While an open and perceptive mind is generally an advantage, taking on other people's energy or getting overwhelmed by psychic impressions is not.

Also known as: bowls, cauldrons, chalices, goblets, hearts, vases, vessels

Swords

The suit of Swords represents the realm of action, movement, and struggle, as well as logic, reason, and intellect. The effort involved in pursuing a goal, which can often be perceived as struggle, is the realm of Sword energy. It can require much effort to turn our ideas into reality, but this is also where the most learning tends to occur.

Action is the result of the combining of ideas (Wands) with emotions (Cups), yet the Swords advise rationality and detachment from expectations of specific outcomes. Because of this, the cards of this suit can be perceived as cold or harsh with their messages, as they cut straight through any illusions we may be clinging to. In some cases, Swords may signify strength, authority, and power, as well as the more unfortunate elements of human nature that lead to violence and suffering.

The suit is not overwhelmingly unfavorable, but the Swords do tend to bring up the trickier aspects of a situation.

Also known as: arrows, a Thames, blades, daggers, feathers, knives, scimitars

Pentacles

The suit of Pentacles is all about manifestation, results, roundedness, and material well-being. These cards often appear in relation to issues of finances, abundance, business pursuits, and the home and family, as well as the physical body.

Pentacles represent the results of the initial inspiration (Wands), which is then responded to in the feeling realm (Cups), and consequently acted upon (Swords). While the other three suits predominantly inhabit the invisible realms of non-physical energy, Pentacles are concerned with the material, physical plane. However, they can also represent the feelings of security we all seek on the material plane, and the sense of being grounded in one's sovereignty as a person.

The cards of this suit are generally considered favorable, as they speak to the rewards of our efforts, but can also reflect fear around not having (or being) enough.

Also known as: circles, coins, discs, shields, stones, talismans

The Significance of Numbers

As with many other forms of divination, numbers are highly significant in the Tarot. From the time of the modern deck's development in Marseilles, the number assigned to each card has been considered to be important to its meaning. In decks with non-illustrated pip cards, numerological correspondences are especially important to interpreting meaning. Each of these cards bears a number between 1 and 10—the number set at the core of numerology, also referred to as "the decade."

While different Tarot traditions may draw from one or more numerological systems (such as Pythagorean, Chaldean, or Kabbalistic numerology) when it comes to interpretation, the number descriptions below are representative of common themes and associations for each number in the decade. These core characteristics can help you get a clearer sense of how each numbered pip card is distinct from the others in its suit.

One is the beginning of that which is about to form or take shape. Represented by the Ace of each suit, it is considered to hold the "seed" or absolute potential of a situation. This potential may be dormant, and may even be unknown to you, just as a seed can be either intentionally planted or arrive unexpectedly on the wind. Either way, this potential needs further action and development for manifestation to take place, just as a single point in geometry needs another in order for a shape to take form.

Two is the necessary "next step" that allows the potential of the one to become something more. In geometry, where one point has nowhere to "go," two points make a line possible. In the Minor Arcana, these cards often depict two people, but this number can symbolize aspects of duality, polarity, balance, and choices as well as relationships.

Three represents the first fruition of the balanced union of the two. It is the synthesis of inspiration, cooperation and growth. Three points are the minimum required for the first closed shape—the triangle—to form. Three is also found three times (3, 6, 9) within the decad. It represents expression, creativity, manifestation, and integration. Three moves beyond partnership into group collaboration—beyond the balanced polarity of two into something more that requires a new, more complex balance—a pattern that will now begin to repeat through the rest of the numbers.

Four is a number of stability and completion. Added to the triangle of the three, it creates the first three-dimensional shape, the tetrahedron. In this sense the four is the manifestation of the initial idea of the one into material form. It represents balance, as seen in the four legs of a table, and secure foundations. Four is also associated with justice and fair dealings (as in the expression "fair and square"). Its metaphysical significance is seen in the four elements, the four cardinal directions, and the four seasons.

Five, like the three, is a number of outward expansion, coming along to disrupt the perfect symmetry of the four so that new manifestation can occur. The cycle of creation requires change, which is often disruptive and can cause uncertainty, difficulty and even chaos for periods of time. However, this imbalance spurs new movement, which opens up opportunities for new developments that could not arise otherwise.

Six brings order to the chaos of the five. Like the four, it is a number of balance and harmony, but since it integrates every stage of the one's manifestation thus far, its structure is more complex. As the first product of an odd and even number, it reconciles differences and restores equilibrium. Six represents successful adjustments to past challenges, and can often signify a victory. It represents the qualities of compassion and cooperation, responsibility, and service to others.

Seven is a number of strong mystical significance in spiritual traditions around the world. It is found in nature in the visible light spectrum, the planets visible from Earth, and the musical tones of the scale. We live in the rhythm of the seven through the days of the week. Seven creates a new dynamic out of the six by adding the one, creating new changes and opportunities. It represents choices, mystery, uncertainty, spirituality, wisdom, and the potential for perfection.

Eight brings back the energy of balance and symmetry, now as a double of the four. The continuous line of the eight resembles the symbol for infinity. There is stability on both the material and spiritual planes as circumstances harmonize with the cosmic order of the Universe. This brings new energy and power for accomplishing goals, organizing and integrating what has manifested so far, and bringing things nearer to completion. Eight represents progress, capability, regeneration, success, and personal power.

Nine is the final single digit, and as such symbolizes the end of a cycle, but in the numerological system of the decade, the final completion is still to come. Nine appears in every multiple of itself in the form of adding the digits in the multiple, representing the patterns of perfection found throughout the Universe. It is the triple of the three, a mystical and powerful configuration. It represents affirmation, culmination, and the surety of success, as well as boundaries, limits, and strength.

Ten contains the properties of the one, but now on a new level. As the final number of the decad, it completes whatever was left unfinished or unresolved in the nine, and sets the stage for the next cycle of manifestation to occur. Ten represents wholeness, fulfillment, and reaping the benefits of persistent effort. It is a number of resolution, consolidation, and readiness for new beginnings.

Having a sense of the esoteric meanings of individual numbers can add enormous depth to your understanding of the cards, especially when it comes to non-illustrated pips. But if you don't have experience with numerology, don't worry—you can still access interpretations for all of the cards, either through this guide, your personal deck's guidebook, or other sources on the Tarot.

If you find that a certain number or pair of numbers keeps showing up in your readings, however, it's worth looking up their esoteric meanings, as this signifies that the Universe is definitely trying to tell you something.

The Court Cards

Also known collectively as the "Court Arcana," the four face cards of each suit (Page, Knight, Queen, and King) typically illuminate aspects of personality and character. They may represent actual people involved in a situation, but they often speak to the way people are *behaving* with respect to the situation, or to the personal qualities required in order to successfully navigate it.

Based on medieval European concepts of nobility, each court card has a rank within the hierarchy, with the Page at the "entry level" and the Queen and King at the top. These ranks signify various levels of experience and maturity within the domain that the suit represents—inspiration, emotion, action, or manifestation.

In this context, Pages represent younger people, who are just starting out in the realm of experience represented by the suit. For example, the Page of Pentacles may appear in a reading about a potential new job. Knights are more experienced in their respective realms, but are not always mature enough to know how to successfully channel their highly charged energy. The Knight of Swords, for example, may indicate that someone is acting rashly to achieve a goal without first considering all possible outcomes.

In regular playing cards, the King typically "outranks" the Queen, but in Tarot the two can be seen as the masculine and feminine embodiments of maturity and mastery over a situation. In this light, the Queen of Cups can represent the ideals of using emotional intelligence for the benefit of all, while the King of Wands may point to a wise and trustworthy counselor.

The Court Arcana can also refer to specific events or developments within the context of the reading. Pages, whose duties traditionally included running messages for the nobles they attended, often signify that news will be coming your way. Knights herald sudden action and/or a swift change in your circumstances. Queens represent creative ideas and plans becoming fully realized, while Kings signify a mastery of how you handle whatever comes your way.

As is the case with many other aspects of modern Tarot, not every deck uses the traditional names for the Court Arcana. Some decks substitute the Knave for the Page, while others use the Princess and Prince in place of the Page and Knight cards. This latter approach serves to balance out the gender representations, as opposed to the original face cards which contained three male roles with only one female role. Other modern decks may present Pages and even Knights as females in their illustrations as a means of creating balance.

Esoteric Correspondences

So far, we have seen that each card in the Tarot deck has its own distinct symbolic meaning based on the archetype it speaks to (Major Arcana), the character or personality traits it represents (Court Arcana), or its suit and number (Minor Arcana). In addition to these core identifiers, other esoteric correspondences were integrated with the deck as it evolved in prior centuries.

As we saw earlier, Lévi perceived structural correlations between the Tarot and the esoteric traditions of Kabbalah (which by this point had been absorbed into the evolving Western Mystery Tradition as Hermetic Qabalah, apart from its Judaic religious context). He and other occult scholars viewed the 22 cards of the Major Arcana as being connected to the 22 letters of the Hebrew alphabet, which have their own esoteric meanings, and found correspondences in both the Major and Minor Arcana with the Kabbalistic Tree of Life spiritual tradition. Later, Waite and other Golden Dawn members attributed planets and zodiac signs to the Major Arcana cards.*

Many Tarot traditions still incorporate elements of Hermetic Qabalah to various degrees in their interpretations of the cards, and there are particular spreads and even decks that center on this connection. But the subject of Kabbalah/Qabalah is far too complex for the scope of this guide, and you don't need to understand it to read Tarot cards successfully.

Should you find yourself intrigued, however, it can be a rewarding option to explore further. In particular, those who study astrology may find that the planetary and zodiac associations can enhance your interpretations of the cards. For now, we'll just focus on the most

514

significant and beginner-friendly realm of esoteric correspondences—the classical elements, which have also long been part of the metaphysical "fabric" of the Tarot deck.

The elements—Earth, Air, Water, and Fire—were seen by the ancient Greeks as the building blocks of everything within physical reality. Many other ancient cultures had similar concepts. While we now know this to be an oversimplification in the literal sense, we can still think of the elements as core energetic forces at play in our lives.

In the context of the Tarot, elemental associations can help shed further light on the situations we're asking about. Various occultists over time have assigned elements to both the Major and Minor Arcana, using different rationales and a variety of esoteric sources. As a result, these correspondences can differ from deck to deck, though there is a good deal of consistency as well.

The correspondences for the Major Arcana cards vary so widely that a discussion of them goes beyond the scope of this guide. However, the four suits of the Minor Arcana make for a natural fit with the four elements, and these correspondences, along with the numerological associations outlined earlier, can be particularly useful when it comes to the pip cards.

* In the process, they decided to reverse the order of the Strength and Justice cards. This move was not universally accepted, so today's decks may reflect either the original order of the Marseille deck or the revised order of the Waite-Smith deck.

The Suits and the Elements

In most traditions, Cups are associated with the element of **Water**, which always takes on the form of whatever contains it, and follows the path of least resistance. Water is also the realm of emotion. Cups cards, therefore, can speak to matters of the heart and/or psychic receptivity, and may advise us to open up to others or to establish useful boundaries.

Pentacles are associated with the element of **Earth**, as they relate to abundance, security, and the importance of being grounded in material reality. These cards often speak to issues related to money, career, and the home. However, they can also remind us to keep our feet on the ground in the midst of heightened mental and/or emotional activity, and to appreciate the physical experience of being alive.

Wands are most often associated with **Fire**, as the cards of this suit speak to the passion and energy that come with initiative and creative inspiration. Fire is the element of transformation, and Wands represent the "spark" of inspiration that is transformed into action and manifestation. However, some systems view inspiration as being in the realm of Air, which is also associated with thoughts, daydreaming, and other mental activity.

Swords are typically associated with **Air**, as they are seen metaphorically to cut through illusion and sharpen the intellect. They speak to using logic and reason to solve problems—all aspects of mental activity. Other traditions emphasize the *action* aspect of the Swords suit and therefore connect it to Fire, as it is ultimately action that transforms reality. The fact that swords are literally forged in fire also plays into this association.

Chapter 3: Reading and Understanding the Meanings of Tarot Cards

People also ask whether tarot cards selected from a random deck will contribute meaningfully to a person's life. It is usually not necessary to tell tarot what to do in a given situation, but instead, it provides you the choices or the various directions. There are several hypotheses about how powerful tarot can be. In this post, we will look at two of the main hypotheses behind tarot.

Synchronicity is the first of such hypotheses on how tarot reading functions. It is assumed that the cosmos would lead us through chance in the right direction. These are simply signs that say, "You're there," or "You should attempt this." Synchronicity and tarot can partly be clarified by the use of quantum mechanics. Without getting into a full debate on quantum mechanics, it is safe to say that quantum mechanics have forces that have a very real effect on physical objects. It is assumed that these powers affect the cards that it reads.

Tarot's next principle is prediction. Many people assume that we prepare our values and opinions on tarot reading and receive the outcomes we expect. In other words, you consider what you are searching for. When this tarot hypothesis is true, then tarot may be a really valuable tool. All I say is that it will help you communicate with the real desires, thoughts, and perceptions in your subconscious mind. Tarot's interpretation of our subconscious might be linked to our all-known inkblot test. At this stage, I would have to suggest that tarot allows you to learn what is inside and to communicate to your higher self.

You don't need a psychic to read tarot, but some claim that the energy they provide is stronger for a psychic. Two specific forms of tarot readings exist. The first is the tarot problem. You use the tarot read

517

here to address a particular question. You usually seek a yes or no response. Try to look at this sort of tarot as a reference to help you decide. Try to ask the question with some specificity, but not too specific, in a general overview. It is also better to focus on the problem around you when asking a question in tarot. I mean, pose suggestions on what you should do to modify the situation, enhance it, or adjust it. The easiest way to ask the query is also to be objective. Attempt not to pose the question from a specific one. It will offer you a wider variety of ideas and answers. For example, you want to remain positive in your concerns and desires when doing a tarot.

The next kind of tarot is an interactive interpretation. The aim of this form of tarot is to give you a specific summary of your life. You can get a little specific information regarding life, income, health, and relationships by reading this sort of tarot.

When the tarot is finished, the reader normally shuffles the cards. This is the time to stay and reflect on what the tarot readings can teach you. After the deck is shuffled, the person who reads the tarot must put the cards in a set. The positioning of the cards in the spread has value along with the card itself in the tarot. Depending on the nature of your query, the user, and time permitting, various tarot spreads are used.

Surprisingly, tarot can be very accurate. I firmly suggest that people seek to play with tarot interpretation. I think you may be pleased with the responses you have got and by the issues addressed.

While occultists draw the allegoric cards decades, illuminated decks are now all around. Tarot is the most popular worship rite. The inherent estheticism of this ancient art has enhanced tarot curiosity and made it a cornerstone of social media — there is only emoji tarot.

Given its ubiquity, tarot may still remain enigmatic and confounding. Exactly what is tarot? What do cards say, and how do they use them? Do not worry: the fundamentals of the tarot are understandable

How to choose a deck?

Smart, imaginative tarot decks are always at your fingertips. Hundreds or even thousands of stunning decks have been released since the mid-twenties. The elegant picture of Tarot de Marseille is a romantic French ship; Motherpeace deck is a beautiful portrait of the etheric moods of the 1970s.

Many tarot readers consider that your first deck should be earned. Nothing is more useful to reward you with the magic of divination while every love is here, so I say you should be able to select your first deck. Your special link to cards is the key element with so many wonderful choices.

Whether you buy online or personally, look at different tarot decks to see the feelings, is it fun for you? Who is it? Who is it? Were you disturbed by this? Scammy? Scammy? Trust your intuition: essentially, the interpretation of your coin dictates your careful consideration. Discover the images: are you fascinated by conventional or contemporary images? Think of the symbols: Are they attractive? Remember, no tarot deck order, make sure you choose the true deck of the spirit.

How does Major Arcana Distinguish from Minor Arcana cards?

Consider the structure of the deck and its numbers ' significance. The hermetic axiom' as above as below' is the foundation for all practices of magic–tarot, astrology, or orthographic research. In other words, in the microcosm of individual experiences, the macrocosm of the universe is expressed. Therefore, the entire universe exists within a

519

tarot deck, and every card is a person, place, or event. The icons in Major Arcana represent larger secrets as well as on Minor Arcana cards, which speak to smaller secrets.

The Major Arcana cards are significant and innovative. It's a strong message, describing movements that change lives and decide the beginning or end of times, and we mark our trips, and each is alone. These complex cards appear during major transformations and signify distinct moments of transformation. During our bigger journey through life, the cards are numbered to represent the stations, time in its chronological order.

The Minor Arcana cards, on the other hand, represent regular ties. Such cards show everyday people, like dancing, dining, relaxing or quarreling. Researchers propose conduct that can be fleeting or have little effect during subtle transformations caused by human behavior.

The cards for Minor Arcana are divided into four cards, each of which has 10 numbered and four short cards. The card number in the Minor Arcana shows the stage: the ace card in the middle, the 10 the finish. In addition, the evolution of the cards reveals our understanding of circumstances, both personality types, and of actual individuals. The Page (or Princess), Knight, Queen, and King view situations with an enhanced degree of understanding and experience.

The suits complement their special astrological and astrological features (walls, pentacles, swords, and cups). Walls symbolizes passion and inspiration (in relation to the fire element), Pentacles represent tools and physical information (in relation to the earth element), swords display mental intrigues (in relation to air elements), and Cups show emotional things (in relation to water element). Such suits demonstrate which power networks are available and which are the best way of dealing with any specific situation.

How to Start Card Reading

The Major and Minor Arcana cards together create a significant image vocabulary. It is important for all the replies we are looking for in the list that reflect an individual, circumstance, or potential result with each card. It is important to remember that Since there are no hidden mysteries or closed tarot agendas, your own interpretation of narratives will understand the meaning.

Make sure you shuffle your deck (or "clear") before reading. It should be a trance in this deliberate act. Know your cards ' physicality and visualize your question. If you read for someone else, spend this time in-depth to allow you to get to the heart of the case.

Take time. A first important move in the reading of tarot cards is deck clearing since it opens the doors to supernatural realms. Cut the cards into three and rearrange the stack, face down every time you're ready. Prepare the tarot cloth to "fall" the cards by your chosen fabric. "Three-card dispersion" is one of the most simple and efficient tarot dispersion schemes. The concepts should be updated to suit any circumstance (past, present, future, self, fellow individual, incentives, challenges, results, mind, body, soul). Without intervention, the cards and their accompanying locations show relations and interactions. Take a moment to create your own creative tale before you read every card's clear explanation. What do the cards you have drawn feel about? What are the colors and symbols? Are they facing each other or away, if there are features? Do the pictures look uniform or uniform?

Growing card has classic associations, but your intuition is the best available resource. See your emotional response immediately: your instincts tell your memory, reinforce it. Each card has a specific meaning for you to create your own systems and patterns. The Devil

521

card may represent a former lover, and the Two Wands symbolizes a new job. Your specific lexicon helps you to write such narratives that can be adapted to any given scenario or situation.

Step by step process to getting started

The three-card breakthrough is a great place to start reading the Tarot if you're a Tarot beginner! Although you are a professional Tarot reader, it is nice to quickly respond and get back to what is important.

Three cards are spread nicely to suggest any linear direction or sequence of events. For many different questions and conditions, the allocation of three cards can be used. To learn this, we need to focus on the three-card distribution that provides an overview of your history, current, and future.

Materials needed

☐ Tarot cards

☐ Handbook or manual for an explanation of tarot

☐ Optional: insight, candles, incense, etc.

1. Choose a Deck for Your Tarot

First, you must buy a Tarot deck of your own! There are many thousands of decks, so it is important that you purchase a deck that is worthwhile. Pick something that appeals to you esthetically. Nonetheless, it might be a good idea to choose something commonly known when you're new to the Tarot. The Rider-Waite Tarot Deck is a very common and simple Tarot Deck.

2. Get a cool and quiet place

Certain space and a comfortable atmosphere are required to be read. Choose any place for you and feel right! It could be like your bedroom, living room, outdoors, etc. Just make sure you choose a comfortable location and can always focus.

Even wise men, incense, crystals, stones, or candles might be ideal. This is optional, but a good way to describe and clean the area.

3. Focus on your thought pattern or your intensions

Until you start reading, you must choose a question or purpose. Tarot is an excellent tool for us to consider our areas of fear by showing different impressions of our unconsciousness. Therefore, try picking a subject you have no harm to. It should be open and available to ask questions. Concentrate on your request, particularly when handling cards.

If you find it difficult to choose a topic, remember what you would like to know by reading. Questions can be as easy as "What can I do in the coming month?"

4. Always Shuffle Your Deck

The cards can be easy to mix, but it can be difficult occasionally. Tarot cards are much bigger than normal cards, and you'll want them to stop bending. You can build your deck in various ways, so choosing what you want is up to you.

Below are some suggestions:

☐   Split the deck into different pieces, and bring them back together;

☐   Method of scrambling: spread all of the cards to a table or floor, then scramble again;

☐   Method of insertion: hold half the deck on each side. Then insert half the deck haphazardly into the other half.

Note that any "good" or "evil" ways to stack cards. Use any form of shuffling that is best for you.

When mixing your chips, emphasis on your question or objective.

5. Split your deck into 3 parts equally

Now, divide your mixed deck into three separate stacks. Place these stacks next to each other.

6. Turn over your cards

Flip over the top card from left to right on each mini stack.

7. Check your cards

Let's first consider what each card symbolizes before we translate it. In this reading, there are 3 cards:

1st Card: The Past

- Events of the past that still have an effect on you

- Events of the past that are weighing you down or have the potential to help you move forward

2nd Card: The Present

- Your present situation

- Your current problems/challenges

3rd Card: The Future

- The direction in which things are moving towards for you

- The outcome of your current situation

Note that your tarot reading is a particular question, focus, or situation on which you want clarification. Therefore, in relation to your question, your cards represent the past, the present, and the future.

8. Feel your cards

Get the mood of your card! See photos of the coin. What kind of answer do you have? Can they give you a sort of feeling? Are you connected to one of the cards directly? How are the colors, icons, and pictures interacting?

9. The words of the card reading

Now is the time for your preparation to finally understand. Tarot cards can be hard to interpret, and a great deal of preparation is needed. You need a guide to explain the meanings of your cards if you're a beginner. Most tarot decks are followed by a book or a tarot card. To enhance understanding, you can also use several online tools. See how each card you revealed has its value for a better understanding of the cards for the Major and Minor Arcana links in' How Tarot Cards' Consider how these concepts apply to your historical, present, and future questions.

Tips: It is important to remember that cards work together very much. The large picture is larger than any coin. What are the relations between the cards? Can you find some patterns?

Minor Arcana usually tends to draw attention to everyday events, people, and issues. Major Arcana, on the other hand, refers to our life's specific trends. Major Arcana always applies to our total energy.

Remember, read the tarot diffusion correctly takes a lot of time! If individual cards are seen as word recognition, combining many cards is like learning to speak in phrases.

Tarot Card Meanings

The Tarot Deck was now set to the size of 78 cards, popular in Northern Italy during the sixteenth century. Usually, the Major Arcana cards are big problems in the Querent. Such fundamental principles are life and death, ethical dilemmas, moral, and communication with others. These values are human life. The Major Arcana can be viewed by the Querent as a spiritual map for tracking his path through life and beyond. The Minor Arkana addresses the earthly and banal as well as the Querent's answer. If, however, the cards are able to interact and paint a perfect picture of life, the variations between minor and major are often flickered.

Based on many years of experience and research, the following definitions of the Tarot card are explains used by people during decades. There are no "true" or "wrong" card meanings, but these principles will help you respond.

- You can find great perspectives into your history and learn to look at what lies ahead.

- Get to Find the truth about your men.

- Remember who you can have faith. Who's going to be in the future?

- See your life clearly in every possible way: romance, financial affairs, family, career, and purpose.

- Become the focus of the parties. friends are going to challenge you to teach them.

Major Arcana Card Meanings

The 22 cards of Major Arcana are often the major cards on the deck that reveal the foundations and pillars of Querent's life. This includes universally recognized and highly symbolic archetypes that span a wide range of mythologies and faiths.

The Fool

- Carefree

- Foolish

- Important decisions

- New beginnings

- Optimistic

Meaning

The Fool is a very powerful Tarot deck card, usually a new start–and thus an end to something in your ancient life. The role of the Fool in your diffusion shows which aspects of your life can alter. The Fool embraces important decisions which cannot be made easily and which require an element of risk for you. Adopt the changes with optimism and care to achieve the best result.

Past: You faced the gamble, and the original thinking worked. You have given great potential by doing things in a new way.

Present: You are entering a new phase of life at this period. The experience of this change may seem good or bad now, but it will have a clearer influence in the future. Risk assessment is essential to make the right choice.

Future: To excel, you need to find new ways to achieve your goals. You must be prepared to cast old habits when the opportunity comes, and if it does not come, it can be time to create them for you with new methods.

Yeah / No Key Interpretation: The Fool is a new start and carefree experience. While this card may suggest nonsense, it is more hopeful that it reflects pure events and is free from the restrictions of your present life. More than certainly, important decisions will be made, and the answer to your question is yes.

The Magician

- Confident

- Creative

- Important communications

- Skillful

- Talented & proficient

Meaning

The magician usually works with smart and competent communicators. His involvement in your delivery suggests a degree of self-confidence and motivation that encourages you to put ideas into

528

motion. A practical card, the revelations it offers best apply to the pragmatic and physical aspects of your life, rather than to the theoretical or ephemeral. Your performance in future political or business ventures probably depends on your own power of will and commitment.

Past: Your trust and creativity have enabled you to realize your ideas effectively. You have achieved through intellect and professional execution.

Present: Your knowledge and skills are currently needed to influence the changes that are occurring. To make the changes effective, you have to play your cards correctly.

Future: The future ahead of you is unpredictable, dangerous, and potential. The opportunities will be influenced by your friendships and the support of those who are close to you. A victory or artistic achievement will bring you a new start.

Yes / No Key Interpretation: the wizard is symbolic of your activity and power. Its positive connotations illustrate somebody who speaks smoothly and is good in all aspects. This card indicates that you can step forward and take action using your goodwill. Your question is answered, yes.

High Priestess

- Feminine influences

- Insightful

- Mystery

- Understanding

- Wisdom

Meaning

Your association with the High Priestess shows that you have a strong intuition rooted in good judgment. She can suggest that the explanation is second to instinct. Your mind has to believe your heart's intelligence to adjust. Nevertheless, she is also aid by definition, and her appearance in certain areas of your spread may mean someone near you comes with their own instincts to your rescue. Intuition is most effective in seeing what's hidden to the senses so that the High Priestess can also come to warn you of the hidden facts or influences that are important or are important.

Past: You needed new opportunities and could step beyond your comfort zone. If you lack support in important areas of your life, consider spending time on new people and new ideas. You reach a maintenance phase, but you may need the support of someone else.

Present: you claim to show the undiscovered or repressed creative abilities. Having a spiritual guide will help you realize your mental or creative abilities. To get what you want, you will conquer the fear of commitment.

Future: You will receive real benefits, but only if you continue your discipline and motivation. If you refuse to deter you, your future will be bright. Follow your intuition, and you will be constantly satisfied with success.

Yes / No Main Interpretation: The High Priestess is a woman full of mystery, intelligence, and knowledge spiritually intuitive. A path of self-discovery corresponds with the inclusion of this card. This stands for things that are not yet present in your life, so the answer to your question is ambiguous.

The Empress

- Abundant creativity

- Fertility

- Fulfillment

- Mother figure

- Productivity

Meaning

The presence of the Empress is traditionally associated with strong maternal influence and is excellent news if you want harmony in your marriage or if you want to start a family. Any artistic efforts that you currently undertake are also likely to succeed, as this card often finds people who are exposed to strong explosions of creative or artistic energy. Nevertheless, this creative energy is perhaps not in the form of a drawing or an art project: this card often indicates a high chance of pregnancy-not actually for your own, but in the near future you may see a new addition in your extended family or a close friend's family! This card is a good portrait of you and your friends.

Past: The last opportunity you have now is to show its power. Through the company, personal or creative, your continuous effort is needed to excel in a new partnership. Note your most resourceful actions, but your consistency in particular.

Present: Before you, there could be a new beginning, and you agreed on its price. Be sensitive to the emotional aspects of life and understanding. A dear man needs a helping hand or support in the night. The job is yours, irrespective of your preference.

Future: the future will bring your emotional and physical wounds, healing, and rest. It will be more beneficial to spend time building new routes than to repair bridges. When you take care of them, the savings will pay off.

Yes / No Key Interpretation: the Empress motherly stands for everything. She refers to successful business projects or other constructive economic incentives as a caring, compassionate problem solver. She advises to step forward in order to achieve your full potential, and the reaction you are finding is yes.

The Emperor

- Authority

- Father figure

- Masculine influence

- Rational

- Stable

Meaning

Against the Empress, the Emperor implies a mighty power, usually male in nature. This may also include concepts that you consider to be historically male, such as leadership and authority, self-discipline, and stability through action. The optimistic effects indicate that you are on the road to success or advancement, but also that it may be favorable. Often a friend of those who is meant to take greater responsibility, it can foreshadow improvements or defeats that allow you to shoulder a larger burden than in the past. Whatever the motivation for improvement, it demonstrates that you may have an extraordinary inner strength, which will motivate you to move and lead.

Past: Authority has been instrumental in shaping your life. Your good position could be due to a powerful government or person. The resolution of a recent conflict is imminent.

Present: Someone in a position of authority may be offering to help you. In any case, the more seasoned hand may be more competent than yours. It is important to protect their loved ones, but leaders must be able to compromise. Beware of the excessively dependent.

Future: You may come closer to your goal by taking the initiative, but only if you are responsible for all your actions. You will be given a chance to play one of the many tasks in life. Remember those behind you who follow.

Yes / No Main Interpretation: The King serves fatherly as the equivalent of the Queen. In your existence, it is form, order, and authority. This card shows, as you move forward in your efforts, that confidence and rationality will take you a long way. Your reaction here is yes.

The Hierophant (Pope)

- Approval

- Conformity

- Consent

- Good advice

- Marriage or Union

Meaning

The Hierophant can imply many different things based on your own personality. It stands for doctrine at its root, but doctrine can come in the form of teaching and guidance or rigid authority. It is also important where it appears in your spread because it is often indicative of your own approach to global moral, religious, and social traditions. Wisely speaking, it helps to show the path to fulfillment.

Past: a desire from your past has meaning. Look at a power you might have overlooked.

Present: There is a possibility of working or studying under a superior. If the others around you can be wrong, you can.

Future: Search for encouragement to achieve success through a good organization or formal values. The acts should be driven for selfish reasons. Otherwise, they won't be compensated.

Yes, no key: The Hierophant is a sign of schooling and culture. This card proposes to seek spiritual advice or guidance in your life. This coin, often symbolic of obedience and religious acceptance, has no positive or negative significance. Perhaps the only solution is.

The Lovers

- Attachment or combination

- Conflicting choices

- Partners

- Relationships

- Union

Meaning

Your first reaction is most likely to associate this card with affection, but it doesn't hold a simplistic disposition, much like sex. Romance not only comes in many varieties, but lovers may suggest essential or complicated decisions ahead of their lives. This is not because it generally excludes one another from choices, paths to two very different futures, but it also shows that at least one of these paths will lead you to a good place. When you notice it in your diffusion, you can carefully consider it, but not be scared of it. This tells a story of complicated, perhaps unpleasant choices, but you can understand the right decision and the positive result.

Past: You will be more able to connect with others by getting more in touch with yourself. A recent conflict will soon lift the emotional burden and bring about a successful resolution.

Present: There is a tension that is developing and will test the beliefs. To advance, you have to make a choice between love and career. Nor will the choice ever disappear, but it will shape your priorities.

Future: It will encourage you to note that the opposites are two sides of the same coin. The right choice will only be made if you and others have accepted you.

Yes / No Key Interpretation: lovers suggest you're somewhere in your life at a crossroads. While this card is very symbolic of relationships, love, and unity, it can also reveal a positive partnership or teamwork to make progress. Your question is answered, yes.

The Chariot

- Journey

- Progression

- Strong character

- Success from effort

535

- Transportation and movement

Meaning

You've got to work hard in front of you. It can be resolved quickly, but the cart is a powerful card, and the job you do is likely to be long and difficult. You can face rough highways, long uphill walks, dead ends, and painful setbacks. Only with an upright card may you achieve a good outcome, but do not lose hope: this hard road will provide you with a strength of intent, the ability to overcome with organization and stamina, and the trust which only those who have achieved what they thought couldn't have accomplished. Few powers, properly harnessed, may resist such an individual.

Past: Your character was tested for its tendency to protect your own ego and interests. The war has improved you, and recent events have presented you with an opportunity to achieve your win.

Present: Good news is coming, and in a decisive victory, you will improve the opposition.

Future: Continue your fight, and you will achieve the end you have sought. Honor, applause, and appreciation, if you do not rest, are all possible results for you.

Yes / No Key Interpretation: The Chariot indicates some kind of ride. This journey is likely to be a progression of some kind, with a positive connotation. It could also be the last performance for which you played. The faith, course, and victory shown by this card indicate that the answer is yes.

Strength

- Energy

- Facing problems

- Strength

- Vitality

- Willpower

Meaning

Force is the rawest form of power, and in some way, you have it. If you fight illness or recover from injury, it is a very happy card. As can be suspected, its influence on you and the use that you use can lead to light or darkness. You are expected to bravely face the challenges and overcome them with perseverance and will. With this ability to overcome life's obstacles, however, it has to control you, and this card could be a warning to control your own actions or emotions before they harm you or the people you care for.

Past: Your power is measured, and your energy is both physical and mental. Such inner strength will drive you to test your skills in other ways.

Present: Download no offers that will change your future. Have faith in your own beliefs, and be strong enough to have confidence where you go.

Future: Your future is strong and energetic and will lead you to major changes in life. You will make the most of a great opportunity to improve your life by knowing your true value.

Yes / No Key Interpretation: The strength card shows that you have confidence and are faced with problems in your life. This indicates an individual who is able to exercise great self-control in all matters.

Patience and determination can be expected in your endeavors, and most likely, the response you want is yes.

- Change

- Destiny

- Good luck

- Life cycles

- New direction

Meaning

The Wheel of Fortune speaks to good beginnings, a symbol of life cycles. You will most likely find the predicted activities optimistic, but because they are facets of chance, they may be outside of the control and influence. Tend things you can control carefully and learn not to agonize about things you can't.

Past: Your past actions are the seeds of your success in the future. In order to make progress, you have to accept the changes.

Present: There's a positive change coming, but remember that luck is beyond your control.

Future: The future offers an opportunity to change paths of personal development and happiness. You must be prepared to change your mindset because it is beneficial whether your decisions are successful or not.

Yes /no key Interpretation: The Wheel of Fortune reflects prosperity, transformation, and a new way of life. The overall feeling of the game, while it contains ups and downs, demonstrates a significant change for the better and for the bad. The response you want is yes.

Justice

- Balance

- Equality

- Fairness

- Justice

- Law and legal matters

Meaning

Justice is a very good card to play when you have behaved reasonably and equally to others and especially if you were a survivor. It is an important indicator of a positive resolution, but how and what kind of judgment can depend on your experiences. Nonetheless, if you were unjust, coercive, or otherwise dishonest and unethical in your activities, pay attention. For the unfair, at maximum, this token is a dire warning that you can adjust your ways before you get redress and, at worst, it's a simple statement that it is already too late. In optimistic situations, it can just advise you to aim for harmony in your existence.

Past: managing your feelings will pay off your interactions and get you peace. If you find inner balance, the confusion of your life can be overcome.

Present: You must get any guidance, or you will have a debt repayment.

Future: When everything is said and done, you should get the answer that you expect. Your moral character is justified, so keep it integral and strive for balance.

Yes / No Key Interpretation: Karma, fairness, and balance are all about the judicial card in various matters of your life. This does not suggest an outcome for or against you, but it appeals to its presence to accountability, dignity, and integrity. Your question is not answered clearly.

Hanged Man

- A period of transition

- Gaining for a sacrifice

- Suspending

- Restricting

- Discontinued

Meaning

Through two somewhat different ways, the Hanged Man can be viewed. Every change is a little sort of death, for the old must die in order to create the new, and it can simply indicate a revolt or change, perhaps beyond your control, but more likely to be the decision you can not turn away from, for good or ill. The other interpretation is of sacrifice, although it is not easy to interpret whether this sacrifice is small or large. Both interpretations imply permanence, and you need to think very carefully about decisions in your life.

Past: the loss of certain things from your past has brought your spiritual life new value. What you sacrificed must be seen in a new manner.

Present: If something is hurried, it may indicate that it will delay. Be aware that helping is not more important than helping the person.

Future: You now have many things unknown, so you have to set new goals and plan carefully. You're going to move forward at the right moment.

Yes / No Main Interpretation: Hanged Man implies a kind of metamorphosis by changing habits, letting go, or moving through a transition period. Although it can mean that it has to give up to gain a new perspective, it has no positive or negative connotations. Perhaps the response is.

Death

- End

- New beginning

- Loss

- Dramatic change

- Destruction

Meaning

Death is indicative of your future change. Almost every aspect of your life can be this change, but it will almost certainly be permanent, significant, and absolute. Death implies a full void between the past and the future, and will undoubtedly be traumatic. Despite the sense of loss, death plays a major and natural part in life and eventually leads to acceptance. It is a necessary part of moving on, and if you embrace them rather than fight them, you will find it easiest. Wait for a close relationship, a job, a marriage, or even a life, but don't focus too much on the negative.

Past: You've moved into a new life phase. Over time, everything shifts, and the journey through this universe is no different.

Present: A major event approaches and comes suddenly. You're going to lose something precious.

Future: Develop a new perspective on the world to move forward. The past is behind you, and the rest of your life is before you, so continue on your journey with all your heart.

Yes / No Main Interpretation: The Death Card shows some kind of drastic change to make a new start. It often includes a kind of defeat, disappointment, or ruin. This card's overall tone is dark and not good. Your reaction, therefore, is no.

Temperance

- Capable

- Control

- Harmony and balance

- Moderation (drugs / alcohol)

- Self-confidence

Meaning

Temperance is an optimistic card to encourage you to balance your life and to address problems in a calm manner. It recognizes that opposing forces do not have to be at war in you. Take your decisions carefully with confidence that good decisions will lead to a good resolution.

Past: The lessons you have learned to work in cooperation with others are a constant phenomenon. You have been deeply influenced by the contrast of tangible and spiritual aspects of your experience.

Present: Anything you've long wanted will come to fruition. Wait for a rich partnership or marriage in your immediate social circle.

Future: Take control of your life and moderate practice. You will resolve all current conflicts and begin a new chapter in your life by remaining in balance.

Yes or No Core Interpretation: the card Temperance advocates God's interference, order, and unity. The overall positive presence of this card in your work reveals high self-confidence and control. The answer given by this card is probably yes.

Devil

- Anger

- Jealousy and resentment

- Self-delusion

- Selfishness

- Violence

Meaning

The Devil is engaged in trapping. It implies a condition where there is no exit or a path that leads to it. Pre-warning may or may not allow you to avoid the trap. Which kind of trap and how you avoid it depends on the location of the devil and the cards around it. This card does not forecast disaster, but just caution.

Past: One of your choices was wrong for you. Past: Your growth is slowing down by negative forces.

Present: There's an event that will change your life beyond your influence. Whether it's good or bad is unknown, so stop unpleasant behavior and be true to yourself.

Future: The time has come for you to find beauty within yourself and avoid future predictions. Find the courage to change your future. Your life is beyond your knowledge, but your self-delight will be defeated by this awareness.

Yes / No Main Interpretation: Devil is cynical about everything. Anger, violence, temptation, fear, and doubt are only a few of the terror of this card. This implies that you may feel trapped in an unhealthy relationship, in abuse, or in a deception. This card tells you no, without a doubt.

The Tower

- Destruction

- Dramatic change

- Loss and ruin

- New start

- Unexpected events

Meaning

Dark and predictive, the tower is the embodiment of chaos and confrontation. Not only change, but the abrupt and jarring movement caused by unforeseen and traumatic life-long events. The Tower of your proliferation is always a threat, but life is always a disaster, and you must determine if you will address it with grace.

Past: The old must be destroyed to make room for the new. The ambitions you have pursued are based on weak foundations and offer false rewards.

Present: In your life, conflict is coming to ahead. In order to maintain relationships, they will need to be reassessed and restructured.

Future: Your future will be bright with the challenges ahead. See things like you want them to be to make them so. You can give strength to know the worst behind you.

Yes / No Main Interpretation: The Tower deals with unforeseen events and shifts in your existence. The changes, however, are in line with something catastrophic, catastrophic, and generally negative. It might be linked to a kind of accident, disaster, or other damage in your life. The reaction this card offers is no.

The Star

- Calm and serenity

- Destiny

- Hope

- Opportunity

- Renewal

Meaning

The presence of the Star means for you a period of relief and renewal. This renovation could be spiritual, physical, or both. This is especially positive if you or someone near you recover from disease or injury. It is a light in the darkness that enlightens the life and your history.

Past: Go from the difficulties of the past and start your renewal. Peace will be the end of all struggles; you will depend on your inner strength and external systems of support.

Present: In order to find answers to your current problems, consider harmony and constraint. The correct amount of assistance and encouragement will bring your circles harmony and happiness.

Future: Your renewal time is near. You have chosen the right path to regain both physical and mental health. You will motivate others around you by being bold enough to choose the riskiest paths.

Yes / No Key Interpretation The star is symbolic of beauty, hope, and renovation. This indicates a time of inner harmony, joy, and constructive prospects. This card's overall feeling is optimistic and serene. The answer that his presence suggests is yes.

The Moon

- Be careful

- Caution

- Confusion

- Delusion

- Risk

Meaning

It doesn't seem anything in your career. Perhaps you can't accept a misconception or a fact on your end. It can also mean something significant that another person keeps from you. This can be a source of concern or depression in your life, and the Moon is a powerful indicator that you have to depend on your intuition to see the subterfuge.

Past: Your understanding of an event in the past can be distorted by your present perceptions. Think about your history and ensure that the pieces fit together. You will find more peace by eliminating uncertainty.

Present: A task that takes the form of a new creative idea or a dispute in relationships is coming. Your history will show you the best way to proceed.

Future: If your ideas are paired with concrete practice, your creativity will get you prosperity. The quest to fulfill your ability will contribute to many problems in your lives, but the outcomes are spectacular.

Yes / No Main Interpretation: The Moon is a confounding and elusive piece. The presence of risks, secrets, and a degree of mental confusion is suggested. It would warn you to be cautious and careful in any effort in your life. The answer you want is no. No.

The Sun

- Abundance

- Achievement

- Joy

- Productivity

- Success

Meaning

Finding the Sun as an inherently good influence is a positive development. This implies personal gain and that personal goals and happiness are within reach if you are ready to invest in their actualization. When you embark on a new personal undertaking, such as marriage or the formation of a child, the Sun has a strong impact.

Past: the achievements in the past will pave the way for potential joys. Continue to develop your line of work or field of study, and there will be incentives.

Present: There is a chance for a new friendship or a relationship that leads to happiness and pleasure. Don't give up, and you're going to succeed.

Future: You are entering a time in which your life will shift. Make full use of this moment, and you will have an everlasting future.

Yes / No Main Interpretation: The Sun is the card of happiness, pleasure, and power, as opposing the Earth. This shows productive results, successful actions, and overall good fortune expressions in your lives. The answer to your question is, therefore, yes.

Judgment

- Change

- Decisions

- Success

- Transformation

- Upheaval

Meaning

Judgment tells a transitional story, but it doesn't change suddenly or come about from luck or intuition, unlike Death or the Tower, but changes that arise from reason. This means dreams that are often lengthy to come to fruition. If it refers to the future, then it can also refer to the essence of the change; if you choose, ruminate and let your mind direct your choice. Logic is a better guide than experience in this situation. Be prepared to make an important decision in your life, which will obviously form your next book.

Past: The past is full of good practice, but the escape from these encounters is continuing. You start a new chapter in your life.

Present: The present has arrived, and the past gives up on your fate. This is the best time to change a lifestyle item.

Future: The choices will bear fruit, and you will earn what you deserve. You have a clear path at your feet and course. You'll see your true goal to the finish.

Yeah / No Key Interpretation: The Judgment Card represents a kind of change or transformation that has probably already taken place. This could imply the involvement of a divine or technical call and decision-making that contributes to your performance. Your question is answered, yes.

The World

- Certainty

- Completion

- Positive

- Reward

- Satisfaction

Meaning

The planet is an example of a massive and inexorable tectonic transition. The move is a chance for you to put the Old to an end and the Future to a good start. It shows an increasing maturity, a sense of inner balance, and a deeper understanding. It suggests that you can approach a final sense of identity and self-assurance that comes with age. This also reflects the dropping of walls, sometimes in the effusive context of the soul, but sometimes in a purely physical meaning, which signifies journeys or possible journeys.

Past: the way on which you are finally going brings you full circle. It may take a while to do so, but the journey allows you to take on new responsibilities and viewpoints.

Present: The present time gives you a need or a long-wanted shift in the world. You will consider others ' thoughts to be as true as your own to achieve fulfillment.

Future: You must find your goal. Future: Same with dreams; in order to make it happen, you must first be conscious of it. There is no guarantee of success, but your experience can fulfill your wishes.

Yes / No Main Interpretation: The World Card means happiness and success at the conclusion of a trip. Completion, rewards, certainty, and positive results are all directly related to the presence of this card. The possible answer is yes.

Minor Arcana Tarot Meanings

The 56 Minor Arcana are the antecedents of contemporary cards and are also divided into four different suits. Walls match clubs; cups match heart, swords match spades, and coins match diamonds. There are 10 pip cards for each suit (Ace to 10) and four court cards (Page, Knight, Queen, and King).

Suit of cups

The cup suit is typically emotional and correlates to the water's astrological dimension. The Zodiac signs associated with this are Fish, Cancer, and Scorpio.

King of Cups

- Compassionate

- Good advice / Helpful

- Integrity

- Mature, Authoritative Man

- Spouse

Meaning

The King of Cups is a worldly and quiet authority projection. It's probably a reference to someone else who will help you to achieve your goals. This person may appear uneasy, even distant, but his motivations are pure. Any advice they give is important to you and should be taken into account in your own deliberations. If it applies to you, it indicates an inner strength and strict control of emotions.

Past: You will be revisited by a question from your past. When you needed help, it could be a good idea to look for professional guidance.

Present: Someone who is really good should emerge in your life. Take advice, and don't wait to seek assistance.

Future: To create a peaceful state, seek advice. You won't find peace on your own but aim for a strong ally to help you.

Yes / No Main interpretation: the King of Cups ' voice of reason is loving, moist, and gentle. He is a leader of influence with deep insight and comprehensive theological understanding. This card is capable of making decisions by channeling knowledge and providing good / helpful advice. The answer is unclear, either positive or negative.

Queen of Cups

- Intuitive

- Mature, Sensitive Woman

- Spouse

- Virtuous

- Wise

Meaning

The Queen of Cups is traditionally associated with openness and affectionate disposition, the emotionally open complement of the Duke. Although she is transparent in nature, her presence is still mostly passive. Her presence is particularly a reminder for men to remain in contact with their character's emotional aspects. You should take her presence with a gentle hand to show you the strength of your inner aspects, the power of which might be obscured by its calm nature.

Past: by integrating certain facets of your personality, you have become conscious of yourself. The accomplishment you want is not yet here but will arrive if you proceed to expand your inner awareness.

Present: The influence of a powerful woman will reveal possibilities for your life. It may challenge or inspire you, but anything it does will lead you to precious insight.

Future: Seek your loved ones for help or advice, especially the feminine wisdom around you. Despite your business success, your path will be decided by your emotional factors.

Yes / No Key Interpretation: The Queen of Cups is a sensitive and virtuous woman who stands for a transformation in and of hers. He recommends a good listener and a caring therapist. As the King of Cups, her attitude is either positive or negative, so she answers your question unclearly.

Knight of Cups

- Arrival

- Creative

- Invitation

- New opportunities

- Proposal

Meaning

The Knight of Cups encourages you to keep in mind that victory is not only a practice of arms strength but also a sophisticated and knowledgeable way of thinking. He can also be provided crazy fancy rides, though, so you can also view him as a message to hold you focused. There are sure to be new initiatives in your life, and you must keep looking for new ways to achieve goals, but not losing sight of where you are headed.

Past: Your strength is your intellectual ability, and your self-determined will. It is natural for you to be caught off guard by the new direction and ideas of others.

Present: suddenly and unexpectedly, a generous offer or invitation will arrive.

Future: Keeping focused and following your most passionate beliefs will advance your goals. Through strong, meaningful relationships with others, you will find peace.

Yes / No Core Interpretation: the Knight of Cups is a charming and caring dreamer with fresh opportunities or some kind of optimistic invitation. This reflects recognition of yourself and an introduction to finding the right direction for your future. The response you want is yes.

Page of Cups

- Announcement

- Birth

- Creative ideas

- Good news

- Message

Meaning

The Page of Cups suggests an introspective nature, inclined to the art, with a kind heart, if it refers to you in your spread. You can allow your credit to pass you out of shyness. The card can also show someone in your own life who is probably overlooked and who can assist you in pursuit of a specific goal. While the website relies somewhat on its place in your delivery, it typically has good news.

Past: You have an idea that can be further developed for greater results. Your awareness of obstacles leads you to understand the best ways of dealing with them.

Present: Good news will hit you and inform you of the value of a new life perspective. See mood in life and remember laughter's healing power.

Future: Be prepared for the next opportunity. It's too easy for you if you're not ready to seize it. The internal challenges through which you travel will show you how to love deeper and deeper.

Yes / No Main Interpretation: The Cup Page is a soft, creative messenger. He brings good news and messages about new, serene beginnings with him. All dealings with this card are positive, and the answer is yes.

Ten of Cups

- Abundance

- Achievement

- Commitment

- Family

- Happiness

Meaning

When you consider the X of Cups in your chart, you should expect a long goal. Like the majority of the Cups, this card is full of emotional undertones. It can show that you once were near to mending ties with friends or family members if there has been a split. We may also consider that it symbolizes the settlement of your own inner emotional turmoil. It is usually indicative of lasting emotional ties with respect to marriage.

Past: you have been pushed forward by believing in your path and pursuing your strongest convictions. This commitment and your comfort with authority have made it possible for your life to show recognition and success.

Present: A new company is about to start. This task, event, or journey will lead to the start of a long-standing friendship. Don't miss this chance.

Future: Some aspects of property ownership may present a potential for financial success. Either domestic satisfaction is sought, or reputation is earned through public work. Despite the difficulty, it is possible to balance both at once.

Yes / No Main Interpretation: Ten cups are perfect harmony, wealth, and happiness. It suggests that personal or family dreams may come true, and a sense of overall satisfaction and safety in life. Ahead of you, positive achievements, and emotional stability; the answer you are looking for is yes.

Nine of Cups

- Complete

- Fulfilled

- Generous

- Pleasure

- Satisfaction

Meaning

This card is a very strong positive sign for you! It is a lasting or powerful satisfaction in your life. While nothing is eternal, you should hope to be truly happy somewhere along the course of your life. It is strongly connected with creative efforts and good wishes for the future.

Past: Your soul achieves a peaceful balance is the source of true happiness. Your efforts will bring your reward. Stay strong and continue to work.

Present: Your material and emotional well-being are at hand. Ask for advice and support from your peers, but know that you'll find satisfaction.

Future: The goal you set for yourself is to follow a path. Stay true, and you'll hit the goal you're searching for. Sync the heart and mind in order to find a real message.

Yes / No Key Interpretation: Nine cups show joy, satisfaction, pleasure, and overall satisfaction. His presence indicates a bright future full of good times, happiness, and a period of your wishes. The response you want is yes.

Eight of Cups

- Abandonment

- Avoiding

- Changes in lifestyle

- Leaving / Going

- Personal development

Meaning

The VIII suggests that your lives are stable and secure, but for a personal cost. Your present existence is still not completed. It could be a strong push for you to continue based on the balance of your spread and find the courage to hit in a new direction. To determine the source of your boredom, you will have to look closely at your work and relationships, and then decide whether you are willing to disregard some stability in your life so that you can find happiness.

Past: Your ability to earn money with determination and hard work is needed in the future. Your direction was uncertain, but your heart tells you to continue searching. The improvement that you are searching for can take any form.

Present: You will experience something completely new, either at thoughts or at places that travel great distances. Big changes are coming.

Future: Keep an open mind, and every journey will produce life changes. Personal success and the completion of your objectives will bring you joy.

Yes / No Key Interpretation: The 8 cups show a certain amount of lifestyle change. This carries with it feelings of discomfort, boredom, and flight. It could indicate that something in your current life needs to be abandoned, left, or turned away. The sad tone of this card does not imply something.

Seven of Cups

- Confusion

- Dreams and ambitions

- Speculating

- Decision

- Temptation

Meaning

This card talks to your inner self deeply. He tries to talk to you about your unconsciousness or the realms of your imagination. Your hopes, dreams, and unfulfilled aspirations are all fair to Cup VII. This speaks of profound misunderstanding or of the aware mind's lack of understanding of your true motivations. It is time to look at your own motivations carefully and examine your goals, but it is also a risky time to respond to your findings.

Past: You have lost a lot of time in your life, chasing the many conflicting interests. Do not be fooled by illusions and daydreams; choose a realistic purpose, and start working.

Present: For your daily intellectual and artistic tasks, you will earn a shocking incentive.

Future: The lack of decision-making will slow your progress. Being open to change will benefit, but it will also allow you to decide what is real. Be yourself honest.

Yes / No Main Interpretation: The Seven of Cups symbolizes contradictory choices, mysteries, and temptations, as justice is absent. This card reflects misplaced aspirations and poor choices. It has a sense of pessimism and disappointment. The response is no.

Five of Cups

- Avoidance

- Detachment

- Loss

- New hope

- Regret

Meaning

This symbol is an omen of gloom. Like the rest of his suit, he is emotionally bound and warns of loss and disappointment. Expect a retrogression in your career, almost definitely mental. Although this can be painful, it can be an emotionally invested effort or target. It could also refer to some positions to past events that continue to cause regret or heartbreak. Optimism is the only solution; this, too, will pass.

Past: The urge to try something new stems from your disappointment or dissatisfaction. Your current sadness reflects these unsuccessful expectations.

560

Present: Follow the ways you can find. But if you avoid the truth, sustainable satisfaction will be difficult to achieve.

Future: Your mistake will lead to a regrettable situation. Be prepared to repair the damage and, above all, to forgive yourself.

Yes / No Main Interpretation: Five cups are a regrettable card full of sadness, disappointment, and scope. It may be a sign that you don't appreciate what you have in your life or perhaps avoid something yet to come. This card's disappointment and discontent provide no reply to your question.

Four of Cups

- Boredom

- Disappointment

- Dissatisfaction

- Re-evaluation

- Tedious

Meaning

Apathy is evil's most insidious. You can lose yourself, not even realize what you have lost if its influence remains unchecked. This card is a powerful warning you need to break out of your current cycles. Look for motives or people to look after and struggle with. Make new targets and look for new paths. Now is the time to take chances, as the cost of failure is much less than the cost of failure.

561

Past: You're dissatisfied, and this is influenced by nothing. Your desire for change will be the most powerful stimulus to change the world around you. To change the situations, take a new path.

Present: Don't be afraid to start. Rather, anxiety is unnecessarily fulfilled. Search for new ways of development to new levels.

Future: Before you reach your goals, there will be long delays. Do not lose faith and meet your head. Make your plans, and don't lose sight of the exciting benefits that you want.

Yes / No Key Interpretation: Four of Cups is an indifferent card that shows a sense of apathy, forbearance, and even deception. It may mean that you have to reassess some area of your life or possibly just find yourself where you are and have missed opportunities. For now, there is no clear answer.

Three of Cups

- Abundance

- Celebration

- Creativity

- Entertainment

- Gathering

Meaning

This card is both a celebration and a cause of celebration. It tells of great happiness for you in the future, not passing happiness, but secure happiness that will last and will be shared with all around you. Commonly associated with the completion or, even more likely, a meaningful project.

Past: Long dormant talents begin to influence your life, and your work starts to influence your future. You can discover more benefits by exploring more encounters than before.

Present: Around this moment, there is an abundance of energy that means that you are approaching a new stage of life.

Future: the desire to help other citizens will greatly influence your decisions, and you will have greater joy in your community's significant role. A future of fullness, shared by those who value you, lies ahead of you.

Yes / No Main Interpretation: Three Cups bring love and joy with them. It proposes happy meetings or celebrations and successes in different aspects of your life. It is connected to loving celebrations and close relationships, meaning that the answer you are looking for is yes.

Two of Cups

- Commitment

- Friendship

- Love

- Partnership

- Relationship

Meaning

A partnership is the only focus of the II of Cups. What sort of partnership is less clear, but you are part of a powerful partnership in the past, the present, or the future. This partnership requires absolute trust and respect. It might be an emotional love affair, of course, but it could just as easily be a deep and lasting friendship. The exact nature may or may not be exposed by the remainder of the series. However, it will be a source of happiness for you, and for you, a presence in your life that you can count on at every turn.

Past: You made a friendship or partnership recently, which in the future will bring you great rewards. This relation will be important in the coming years.

Present: Soon, a loving union or close partnership will start. This friendship gives you great rewards through commitment and dedication, even though they are far away.

Future: Search for a companion who will help you achieve your objectives. It should be somebody like you, who can understand your priorities and ambitions.

Yes / No Key Interpretation: The two cups are crying out about love, positive intercourse, and unity. This implies a life full of close ties, healthy partnerships, and mutual love. This card includes all happy, positive, and loving feelings. The answer it gives you is yes.

Ace of Cups

- Abundance

- Creativity

- Intense relationship

- Satisfaction

- Success

Meaning

The Ace of Cups is the beginning of an emotionally healthy time for you. Expect ample peace, happiness, and love at this moment. Existing personal relations will improve important new ones. When marriage is on your horizon, during this period, you should hopefully lay the foundations for it.

Past: Your creative talent and ability to succeed in your work has been shown on numerous occasions. You also allowed greater productivity by being committed and intensely focused.

Present: Good news will bring your life happiness and extreme satisfaction.

Future: The problems you will face in the future will affect your emotions, but ultimately bring you great joy. You will have great rewards if you consider this natural balance.

Yes / No Key Interpretation: The Ace of Cups represents overall satisfaction in all aspects of your life. It forecasts success and abundance by using good intuition and creativity. Such optimistic experiences could be correlated with new relationships or perhaps a conception or maternity. The reply is yes.

The suit of swords

The sword suit is usually associated with intellectual activity and correlates to the astrological air dimension. The zodiac signs involved are Gemini, Libra, and Aquarius.

King of Swords

- A Mature, authoritative man

- Assertive

- Authority

- Government / Legal

- Leadership

Meaning

The King of Swords is the professional side of authority. Also connected to legal or business people, he is definitely someone who will support you in one of these areas. This person can be arrogant or even try to dominate you in the belief that they know how best to help you. Although polite, its main motivation is unlikely to be emotional.

Past: The power lies in your head. Looking ahead and taking authority into account, your collection of good ideas will become a reality.

Present: A figure of authority can assist you in initiating your plans.

Future: the ultimate goals are resisted. Guile and your superior mind will lead you through this destructive barrier. You will find fulfillment in coordinating the members around you.

Yes / No Key Interpretation: The King of Swords is a confident, professional, highly intelligent, and leadership decision-maker. This reflects major decisions to come and the need to monitor and set limits when making strong commitments to your goals. This card does not provide a clear answer, perhaps at all.

Queen of Swords

- A mature, perceptive woman

- Independent

- Loss

- Pain

- Separation

Meaning

The Queen of Swords is a very perceptive person, sharp and professionally distant. You'll most likely find her to be your help and advice, perhaps a teacher. Not necessarily female, but probably, this person should have confidence and may take an interest in you, but it is unlikely that the interest is romantic. A strong ally, respect her intelligence, and you will receive unparalleled guidance.

Past: Your strict perfection idealization can cause stress or pain. If you fail to follow this goal, you will not excel.

Present: Seek a bright knowledgeable elder who can be a lady to advise. You should preserve your freedom as you embrace friends ' support.

Future: Don't focus on your goals so intensely, as this may restrict your ability to do so. Trust your strong spirit to illuminate your larger picture.

Yes / No Main Interpretation: The Queen of Swords is a problem solver that is logical and autonomous. She puts an end to something troubling about your life, but not without a painful loss or separation. She is stoic and clever, but she does not give anything like a positive or a negative result. Perhaps the only way.

Knight of Swords

- Conflict

- Destruction

- Domineering

- Loss

- Unexpected

Meaning

If the Knight of Swords represents you or someone near you, beware. It is indicative of a strong personality that mixes zealous dedication to achievement with reckless intelligence. Nevertheless, these same qualities will build a formidable enemy, whether in the form of a friend or your own inner self. Instead, the Knight suggests that if it refers to your circumstances, you are heading towards turbulent times that you can most successfully face decisive action.

Past: The desire for change inside you has increased. Set your future goals, but leave them for yourself.

Present: A young upstart catches your interest. A problem will be solved by your assistance, but you will be ready to deal with it.

Future: A dramatic change of outlook will instantly realign the direction of your life. Search for support from your friends and loved ones.

Yes / No Key Interpretation: Swords ' Knight is dominant and destructive. It is controlling a project or situation but in a ruthless way. This card carries unforeseen loss, conflict, and the need for your own thoughts and beliefs. The negative tone of the card suggests a no reaction.

Page of Swords

- Aggressive

- Challenging

- Change

- Intelligent

- Vigilant

Meaning

If the page reflects you on the list, your attitude can appear too stubborn and reflective, but it also suggests good analytical skills and an energizing disposition. You want to define the core issues and correctly assess your own stance on them. This will render you an outstanding leader. Alternatively, if the card applies to a case, brace yourself easily for many important decisions. Trust your reason and judgment to deal with these difficulties.

Past: The skills that sleep inside are brought to the surface. The events of your past lead you to activity, and the time is at hand to develop your own path.

Present: Unforeseen coverage is on the way. You have to rely on your intelligence and ability to adapt to benefit from the changes that come.

Future: There's a profound desire for change that irritates and agitates you. The quest for true independence of mind will contribute to a clearer understanding of your inspiration and others.

Yes / No Key Interpretation: The Swords page is a smart, rational, and vigilant young person who brings with him some kind of official change news. While changes can be challenging, this card shows pretense that your life is mental clarity and inner demons. The response here is most likely yes.

Ten of Swords

- End

- Failure

- Mortality

- New hope

- Ruin

Meaning

The X of Swords is a source of fear for anyone who believes in the power of the dice, and you must plan for whatever it means. It is one of many cards that can be a disaster, but it is a disaster that can not be avoided, alone. It not only forecasts a complete failure but an inevitable one. Moreover, the failure is not small or easy to overcome. This is no fate to be altered or stopped, only endured: fresh hopes can be created from the ruins if you remain strong.

Past: In coming to terms with an often-bitter reality, you know that the most important aspect of recovery is to step on.

Present: The culmination of something important is approaching, so be able to deal with the consequences. Nothing is eternal in existence.

Future: Evaluate your direction. Be careful to follow the views of others, because this can bring you to learn your own facts. Seeing the world pragmatically balances your optimism.

Yes / No Main Interpretation: The ten swords indicate a rapid conclusion in your lifespan or a bad ending. It could mean failure, disaster, or death followed by despair and a sense of the weight of the world being shattered and crushed. This card says no, blunt and aggressive.

Nine of Swords

- Accidents

- Paranoia

- Depression

- Grief

- Mental anguish

Meaning

The IX of Swords, one of the most negative cards in your spread, anticipates or describes powerful anguish. The root of this frustration may well be in you because you are too fast to shine a negative light on your behavior or capacity. It can also be caused by paranoia. Although often unfounded, sleeplessness, fear, depression, loneliness, and isolation may take your pain. Be careful to push away those who seek to help you and find the courage to seek help. Even if these emotions are, in fact, finding a solution in your current state may be challenging. Check the other cards carefully, search for cards connected with potential sources of help and advice.

Past: You can feel unfulfilled and feel oppressed and stifled creative energy. Don't miss the moment because of your terrible disagreement with the past.

Present: You will soon be lifted from the difficulty you have encountered. It is necessary to address your feelings of depression and mental distress.

Future: The standards you have established can be unreasonable and can lead you to self-deception and disappointment. You have to be able to forgive yourself and others for going beyond your negative feelings.

Yes / No Key Interpretation: The Nine Swords symbolizes concern, grief, and fear. It could mean a time of mental anguish, a terrible accident, or many nights without sleep. A turn for the worse could take you ahead, and you should take care of depression and self-harm thinking. No, the answer given here is not.

Eight of Swords

- Constraint

- Disillusioned

- Frustration

- Obstacles

- Restrictions

Meaning

Some things in life are beyond your control, and the VIII Swords indicate that some of them actively hold you back. This can be as intimate as a bad boss or as common as international policy. In any case, the choices are likely to be limited at all turns, and you may feel can irritation and anxiety. The only thing you can control is your best course' of action: you. Take patience in this situation and be ready to move when the situation changes.

Past: Your resistance to causing someone discomfort derives from your desire to avoid conflict. This is a great benefit, but it can keep you from behaving in your best interest.

Present: The challenges are only surmounted by the bravery and endurance before you. Others ' demands lock you up and prevent you from growing.

Future: Do not be scared to use your own judgment to decide your own course. When you deny your emotions and trust others in yourself, you miss the chance of changing your life.

Yes / No Main Interpretation: The Eight Swords is a symbol displaying challenges and problems. It shows both the fear of failure and bad luck. The anger and restriction that overcomes the sound of this card show that you respond no to your query.

Seven of Swords

- Avoiding confrontation

- Failure

- Incomplete

- Theft

- Unknown opponents

Meaning

Another card that points to the forces that oppose you, the Swords ' VII, points to your frustration. This is both optimistic because you can find the source to alter the conditions and bad because this source can be conscious of you and deliberatcly sabotage you. Nonetheless, the path to your performance resides not in direct confrontation, but rather in guile. Find ways around them rather than attack the obstacles raised against you.

Past: Some of your projects may have to be placed on the back burner to give more attention to the most pressing issues. The arrangements you have made are not as good as you had expected.

Present: Diplomacy and cleverness are the best way to deal with a recent conflict. Prevent confrontations that are free.

Future: Your future success depends on your capacity to overcome opposition. The method you choose will decide whether you are failing or getting ahead. Assessing the opposition will better inform your acts.

Yes / No Main Interpretation: The Seven of the Swords is both disappointment and clear pessimism. It suggests that you can steal or not live up to your full potential, either because of unknown adversaries or because of your mental decline. The answer you want is no. No.

Six of Swords

- A journey

- Better future

- Escape

- Leftover challenges

- Travel

Meaning

Your mental focus will drive you to abandon your present challenges, leading to better times ahead. From a conceptual point of view, it is important to think through your issues. You may have issues ahead, but the worst is over.

Past: You have overcome a major obstacle while remaining true to yourself. Your understanding and objectivity will lead you to a better future.

Present: Your life will change for the better. A burden or challenge that you face can give you a new path.

Future: You will eventually overcome the obstacles you encounter. The struggles are needed to ensure that you grow in order to find a better future.

Yes/ No Key Interpretation: The Six Swords are symbolic of a journey to mental clarity or escape. It suggests a better, better future or a calm period right before you. Moving on, you might need to use your logic or natural mind, but the end result is positive. The reply is yes.

Five of Swords

- Conflict
- Defeat
- Loss
- Low self-esteem
- Separation

Meaning

This card shows conflicts in your life. Worse yet, failure is closely linked. The defeat is likely to be traumatic, and you must withdraw and regroup. Your confidence or self-esteem may be impaired, but the V of Swords is a reminder of the ability to be trapped in the process. Defeat with dignity, step ahead, and success comes to you.

Past: your failures are the result of your overview and incapacity. You must be honest with yourself to succeed.

Present: An unrealistic attitude can lead to a defeat. Your error is going to cause pain. Be realistic about your expectations to evaluate and move beyond the conflict.

Future: Taking your failure by grace and don't give up in despair; from any setback, you will build triumph.

Yes / No Key Interpretation: The Five Swords suggest conflict, disagreement, and future problems. In the near future, there might be a loss, defeat, or painful separation, with feelings of brokenness and low self-esteem. There is nothing associated with this card that is positive, and your reply is, therefore, no.

Four of Swords

- Delays

- Healing

- Rest

- Sickness

- Withdrawal

Meaning

576

In combination with the turbulent nature of the Swords, the IV of Swords offers your respite from the battles of your life, order, and stability. Peace can be fleeting, so enjoy it as long as it lasts. It can suggest a rebound from chronic illness.

Past: The plans that you have already made may not guide you properly in the coming changes. The cloud over which you feel hanging will soon pass, and the light of your life will return.

Present: Organize your reflections and analyze them in isolation. Your sleeping virtues of inner strength and reverence for yourself will lead you.

Future: Take the generous time you need to plan ahead. There's no rush to decide what's best for you and for the men.

Yes / No Main Interpretation: The Four of Swords refers to some kind of illness or abstinence. But it also provides peace, regeneration, and harmony. Certain definitions may literally be a split or a ceasefire. This card's place is rather moderate but mostly optimistic. The answer is probably yes.

Three of Swords

- Fresh beginning

- Loss

- Pain

- Separation

- Suffering

Meaning

The appearance of the Swords III in your array indicates considerable pain in your life. This discomfort is probably due to or as a consequence of confrontation, perhaps because of disrupted relationships or friendship. The suffering may be part of a new beginning, but you must truly face the pain to resolve it.

Past: You still have great emotional or physical pain. When you give up responsibility, you can take the opportunity to create something new, because something you cherished was recently lost.

Present: You're going to experience an intense emotional upheaval soon. This pain phase will bring you to a better future.

Future: The way ahead is cleared to make room for something new. You know how to take advantage of the opportunities.

Yes/No Main Interpretation: The Three of Swords depict pain and suffering, either by an emotional loss, the termination of an important relationship or by a breakup. The cognitive disorders and mental anguish that this card provides constitute a no reaction to your query.

Two of Swords

- Balance

- Conflict resolution

- Decisions

- Peace of mind

- Prejudice

Meaning

The II of Swords is, like crossed arms, a clash between powers. Not simply a shortage of combat, but an equal distribution of opposition power. It may indicate that you are capable of mediating conflict or that you are caught in a dilemma with no clear result. This state's resolution will probably bring peace for you.

Past: Honesty about your past can help you make a hard decision. The dispute you have encountered will be overcome through a new approach.

Present: There is a fight that will lock up the resources to settle it. You will take deliberate action to decide the resolution by overcoming indecision.

Future: You must overcome the difficult situations ahead of you immediately and do not delay or hesitate. Make the best possible conclusion when behaving frankly and genuinely.

Yes / No Main Interpretation: The Two Swords symbolizes the settlement to disputes and the actions to be made. The conclusions can, however, be reached through the search for inner peace and compromise. While this card shows my total peace, it does not tend toward yes or no. So perhaps the answer is.

Ace of Swords

- Achievement

- Advantage

- Mental focus

- Victory

Meaning

Like all Aces, the Ace of Swords is the purest embodiment of its suit. This means a strong element of concentration, commitment, and analytical ability in comparison to your behavior or acts. It can suggest a change by warring powers, likely within; disputes of not inherently transparent thought concerning inner awareness, remain energetic to prevail.

Past: In the name of good, you have fought to add your intense energy to an idealistic cause. The recent events have launched unchangeable events.

Present: You enter a new era of your life, and everything will change. The causes and results of this change are not certain, but you will find many things in this period.

Future: Making your creative thinking work may require some courage, but if you wish, you can overcome the longest odds.

Yes / No Key Interpretation: The Ace of Swords represents victory with mental strength and performance. This card is all synonymous with truth, transparency, and creative thinking. A brilliant idea could be at the corner, or perhaps it is a kind of divine inspiration for creativity. The answer will probably be yes.

The suit of wands

The suit of walls usually corresponds with the career and the astrological element of fire. The Zodiac signs are Mercury, Aries, and Sagittarius.

King of Wands

- Authority figure

- Financial gain

- Honest and trustworthy

- Mediation

- Professional

Meaning

The King of Wands will reflect an upcoming financial turmoil. It could also be an affiliation with male authority, a dictator, and an arbitrator. You may be helped to resolve a dispute. Open up to the guidance of the expert.

Past: The new ideas you have incorporated in the past will open up opportunities in the present. The suggestions have motivated you and helped others.

Present: If you get support spreading your proposals, you can excel. It will inspire more and more to support others around you.

Future: In your professional life, the future will bring you happiness. Good investment and conservative spending can outweigh the risks you take and give you more prospects by strong conviction.

Yes/ No Key Interpretation: The King of Wands is an authority who is voracious, determined, and confident. It represents a kind of expansion, establishment, or financial gain in your professional life. He is a positive presence that can bring positive effects. The reply is yes.

Queen of Wands

- Career-oriented

- Hard worker

- Honest

- Independent and home-loving

- Thoughtful

Meaning

The Queen of Wands has an engaging and polite attitude that shows that you are confident yet self-contained. An independent streak contrasts with your close friends and family's strong attachment. Depending on your position, this card may also be a person near you on whom you can rely.

Past: Patience is one of your qualities and helped to create comfortable living arrangements with your mates. You have made wise decisions; sound thinking will help you in the future.

Present: A loving friend will advise you. This friend may be a woman, but he is thankful and offers the favor irrespective of her gender.

Future: You will achieve success by following the advice of a close female influence. Your home will be successful and without intense conflicts. You and your loved ones are happy with your environment.

Yes/no interpretation: Sure, the Queen of Wands is a vibrant, emotional, and independent woman. No Key Interpretation. She proposes a person who is successful and career-oriented. The appearance of this token, truthful, reflective, and optimistic, indicates someone searching for positive self-development, and its answer is yes.

Page of Wands

- Adventurous

- Ambitious

- Energetic and Active

- New beginnings

- Skilled

Meaning

A key indicator, the page suggests good news from or about a young person. When the card identifies you individually, it shows that you have unlimited energy, intense commitment, and young love for learning. It may also point to a new idea that you are about to pursue.

Past: The opportunities for recent work have inspired you to search for financial gains or start new creative projects.

583

Present: Good news. Good news. It will infuse your life with joy.

Future: After an incredible flash of inspiration, a new phase of your life will commence. Such motivation comes from good reports, advancements in your profession, and developments in your life.

Yes / No Key Interpretation: The Wands page is a vigorous, vibrant and fearless young man with a can-do approach. This card is an adventurous and optimistic way to overcome obstacles and start new ideas using your expertise and bravery. The answer you're looking for is yes.

Ten of Wands

- Burdens

- Challenges

- Intense pressure

- Oppression

- Overcommitment

Meaning

If the X of Wands is on your chart, you typically work too hard or carry on more burdens. It can show both the undue pressure to accomplish or achieve your goals.

Past: The resilience that you have developed over the years can help you to overcome the current problem. The depression you recently dropped off will allow you to create a new ideology.

Present: Take the challenge and see it until the end. If you are distant from someone around you, anticipate a chance to reconnect.

Future: Focusing your energy in one direction and consolidating your efforts will make success easier. You will have the opportunity to achieve your wishes, but first, you must achieve your high goals.

Yes / No Main Interpretation: The Ten of Wands is a card strongly correlated with intense stress and strain of living in certain places. Some items that this card indicates are emotions that are trapped, abused, or unable to manage the circumstances. With an overall negative message, the conclusion is no.

Nine of Wands

- Afraid

- Cautious

- Defensive

- Impermanent Security

- Inner strength

Meaning

The IX of Wands is a bitter revelation in your series, as it indicates ahead of you both battle and the ability to overcome them. Your life is probably comfortable at the moment, but in some less critical aspects of your personal or work life, there are also likely signs of trouble. The inner strength will be required to maintain the current situation and then proceed as change is necessary for you.

Past: The difficulties you have endured have brought you some current peace. Your progress has been made easier by analyzing the responses of others, but this strategy is not a successful one.

Present: A friend's or loved one's support can help you overcome the obstacle.

Future: In the future, disputes are likely, but you can solve them. Trust your inner strength in order to succeed and do not surrender your beliefs for short-term gains.

Yes / No Main Interpretation: The Nine Walls are displaying determination and bravery under pressure. It also shows, however, the need to be vigilant and protective in combat that is yet to come. There is nothing in these matters that suggests a more positive or negative outcome, so perhaps the answer is

Eight of Wands

- Hasty actions

- Journey and Travel

- A Journey or Flight

- Motion

- End to a delay

Meaning

Stay set for an unexpected spike in your lifespan. Things will be very busy. The good news is that any projects that you start will advance quickly, you will experience a few delays, and the conclusion will probably succeed. This card is good news for marriages, even if it provides the likelihood that partnerships must be traveled. Given all, this is a good card to use in your set, as long as you are prepared to get to work.

Past: There are past goals that can't advance you. Write a transition that gives you the greatest happiness. The fight that has occupied you will go on and a short peace will follow.

Present: Exciting news will come to break your tranquility. Inconvenience is needed to remove you from your moving presence.

Future: A new enterprise will offer your future success, but in a sudden decision, you must be willing to make the right choice.

Yes / No Main interpretation: The Eight of Walls is a kind of path or road. This implies occurrences that move rapidly and unforeseen incentives. This reveals and finishes some kind of pause or blockage in your life as challenges are resolved. Your question will probably be answered, yes.

Seven of Wands

- Coping and Resistance

- Courage

- Long-term successes

- Perseverance

- Strength

Meaning

You have almost certainly great stores of bravery and perseverance in difficult times. You may not be conscious that you have these abilities, but you will definitely require them. May minor but more definitely big differences are planned. It is not known where they will emerge, but you definitely have the ability to overcome their enemies.

Past: Your commitment and continuous work will always carry you ahead, given slow progress. Don't give up. Don't give up.

Present: There's a big conflict, but don't be scared. You must conquer this obstacle with bravery and thus undergo a significant change in your life.

Future: Keep believing in yourself. The odds may be against you, but you can defeat them. You will have the courage to fight and test yourself in a bright future.

Yes/ No Primary Interpretations: The Seven of Walls has long been a hit because of its effectiveness in overcoming obstacles and taking calculated risks. Using courage to stand up and what's true with this coin. The answer you are looking for is yes.

Six of Wands

- Completion

- Good news

- Reward and Recognition

- Success

- Triumph

Meaning

If you consider the Six of Wands in your area, your past efforts are about to pay dividends. If you remember your past work or earn material rewards, the potential will be a certain level of success. If you're waiting for certain reports, this card is probably good news. Nevertheless, it is also delicate to note that your performance should be followed with magnanimity and grace. Do not let the good fortune go to your head in order to avoid losing contacts and risking revenge.

Past: The effort and inspirations of your past have made you stand now. Go on your quest, and incentives will be discovered.

Present: The good news is coming. Although this move is optional, it will greatly help you to accomplish it.

Future: At the end of your road, there is a triumph. To reach it, you will require diligent exploration and opposition elimination, but you can do everything you want.

Yes / No Key Interpretation: Six walls show victory, triumph, and success. This implies that an individual feels honored by winning and having the motivation to go forward. The general feeling in the presence of this card is good news. The reaction is yes.

Five

- Struggle

- Anxiety

- Strife

- Disagreement

- Strife

- Conflict

Meaning

The Five of Wands is never a welcoming invitation, as long as custom indicates that you are in line for battle and exacerbation. Pay careful attention to the surrounding cards to find insights into which areas of your life are subject to these conflicts. Wait for them and console yourself that a positive solution is not beyond your reach. Just be prepared for the possibility of a personal victory.

Past: The battles you faced have led you to courage. This is a valuable feature, but only moderately. Facing difficulty needs patience, so the development can feel too sluggish to meet obstacles.

Present: Confusion or confusion will impede advancement.

Future: In the future, there will be an incentive for you to curb the bravery to excel. Nobody can decide your actions but you, and therefore rely on your willingness to achieve balanced progress.

Yes / No Main Interpretation: The five walls indicate that somehow they are threatened and have to protect themselves against others. This carries with it emotions of hardship, apprehension, and general discontent with still to come internal struggles. The pessimistic prediction with this card gives an answer to no.

Four of Wands

- Celebrations and happiness

- Completion

- Harmony

- New beginnings

- Pleasure

Meaning

The Four of Walls seeks peace and security, typically in the smaller aspects of your life. However, do not allow the limited scope to underestimate the joy that simple successes can bring: this is a fresh start and a card with good endings. The involvement should be encouraged before you start a new partnership or another step, such as marriage or engagement, and it is especially good for people who are about to switch residences.

Past: The diligent contributions have been praised and fulfilled. The drive to create or build something in your subconscious has developed.

Present: Accept the support of friends and dear ones, as you can't always be strong. You're on the road to something meaningful, so don't forget that you're not alone.

Future: You can gain success by trusting in yourself and bringing positive energy to your decisions. Your future will be founded on the good deeds of your present.

Yes / No Key Interpretation: The Four of Walls is a pleasant and harmonious new beginning. It means completing something successfully in your life and brings with it feelings of happiness, balance, and progress toward good things to come. The response you're searching for is yes.

Three of Wands

- Achievement

- Fresh starts

- Long-term success

- Partnerships

- Trade

Meaning

If you are willing to bring to the table your complete imagination and inventiveness, the Wands III brings good news. You are about to reach a period where efficiency and success ability is very beneficial. Keep your eyes open and your mind free for new career possibilities. Nevertheless, the benefits that these new possibilities offer will only come in full time. You have to be patient and stay at a long distance. Therefore, search for new partners, because new companies will be most effective if they are partnered.

Past: Your actions have formed the basis for your performance. Keep your money and productivity at the heart of your course.

Present: An offer for assistance can lead to a new project or idea, so don't tarry to accept it. The ability to connect with someone with more money leads to long-term success.

Future: Being in front of you will be an emotional or analytical obstacle. You must be able to think creatively or invent a way forward to succeed.

Yes / No Key Interpretation: The 3 walls represent new beginnings, accomplishments, and positive partnerships. It can mean some sort of growth of the market, or it can indicate that you are on the right path to success. It has an overall positive message, and the answer is yes.

Two of Wands

- Achievement

- Anxiety

- Gain

- Goals

- Partnership

Meaning

The II of Wands proposes the formation of partnerships or the success of existing joint ventures in your immediate future. You will probably be able to reap the rewards of these partnerships in the form of a financial gain or promotion. On the same note, the rewards are fairly due to you; therefore, for those in fair partnerships, this is better news than for those seeking to benefit at the expense of others. The presence of this card can also indicate your underlying insecurity or concern. Such emotions may or may not be warranted on the grounds of the balance of the delivery.

Past: The research, development, and ongoing use of your expertise has led you to progress in life. Continue to look ahead and plan if you plan to reach your destination.

Present: There is a generous offer to help. This influence will help you to achieve success by analyzing and developing your ambitions.

Future: Thinking and self-awareness will lead to success. Trust your intuition, but be open to others.

Yes / No Key Interpretation: The Two Wands shows they are controlled and have advantages in their lives. On the other hand, it brings great anxiety and the chance to lose control that you once had. The dynamism predicted by this card gives no clear answer. Perhaps that's what it means.

Ace of Wands

- Birth

- Commencement

- Creativity

- Inventiveness

- New Beginnings

Meaning

Drawing the Ace of Walls means that a new business venture is usually pursued, although some view it also to imply conception. You will have to maximize the capacity for creativity, passion, and determination to thrive.

Past: re-examine your past objectives, as you may be constrained. There is a building of inspiration within you that is going to destroy your energy if you don't use it creatively.

Present: A new start is at hand. A new phase of life can take the form of a new company, a new project, or a new source of inspiration.

Future: You will think clearly and plan ahead to thrive. In your life, there is a void waiting to be filled, and it is your duty. Prepare for a transformative experience by covering this void with something to affect the new beginning positively.

Yeah / No Key Interpretation: The Ace of Wands is an imaginative, innovative card that implies some kind of thrilling marriage, hopeful new beginnings, and the emergence of something powerful and fulfilling in your lives. It may be a new project or something imaginative you're going to take on. Your query would hopefully be answered yes.

The suit of pentacles

The suit of pentacles is usually associated with the fiancee and material aspects and coincides with the earth's astrological element. The Zodiac signs associated with this are Taurus, Capricorn, and Virgo.

King of Pentacles

- Confident

- Reliable

- Security

- Success

- Wealth

Meaning

The Pentacles King embodies mature and reliable maturity aspects. Anyone with this card is expected to achieve success and prestige. Although it applies to your own traits, the Kings are the most important people in your life who can support you. You would expect the person to respect knowledge prudence because, if it is a case, it can be a financial windfall or promotion.

Past: The careful progress you have made leads you to success. The guidance you have received recently will help you achieve your goals.

Present: The idealism you showed made you confident and trustworthy, but it may be better to focus for a period on your financial security. Professional or elder consultation will help protect your efforts.

Future: Even if you are not aware of them, you have the inherent ability in the areas of financial profit and material gain. The money you earn from your own work would benefit more than material gain.

Yes / No Key Interpretation: The Pentacle King is a reliable, reliable, self-sufficient person. This displays signs of success, riches, and constant personal development. Achievement of your objectives would probably require some self-exploration and a strong commitment from you, but the result is good. Your reaction is yes.

Queen of Pentacles

- Abundance

- Financial help

- Practicality

- Prosperity

- Wealth

Meaning

The Queen is a card in the family tradition that reflects a person who is financially skillful and very pragmatic, practical, and natural. This person will come to your aid in financial matters and will probably advise you on how to manage your money better.

Past: The talents you have developed will give you the chance to create a secure environment. The assistance you give and continue to give those who are in need will be an important source of satisfaction.

Present: You will seek practical advice from a feminine presence in your life. This recommendation will help you to create plenty of prosperity.

Future: Using your skills successfully would earn you financial success. Take into account your more practical behaviors, and you will find prosperity.

Yes /no interpretation: The Queen of Pentacles is a practical, organized, and reliable multi-tasker. She has plenty of money but needs to be able to trust you and not be scared of the transition or challenge ahead, in order to achieve your goals. Sure, this card points to yes.

Knight of Pentacles

- Ambitious

- Dependable

- Faithful

- Honorable

- Thorough

Meaning

The Knight of the Pentacles symbolizes the virtues of patience, honor, and trustworthiness, and his presence in the process can indicate this to you too. An alternative, the traditional view is that it is a young man, a trustworthy newsman who will enter your life soon.

Past: Your past challenges have paved the way for a promising future. Your reliability and accountability make it a priority for you to do your work as best you can.

Present: You're encouraged by a young person. The safety you need to pursue your ambitions will come.

Future: Follow your routines to achieve the best results possible. You can achieve the heights of your highest ambitions through patience and sustained concentration.

Yes / No Key Interpretation: Pentacles Knight is trustworthy, honorable, and trustworthy. He has undeniable common sense, unbelievable determination, and diverse skills, including patience and support. The presence of this card suggests that those who remain faithful will find positive things. The response you want is yes.

Page of Pentacles

- Attentive

- Motivated

- Scholarship

- Skillful

- Studious

Meaning

The page is always an analytical card, and the suit of Pentacles is historically associated with introspection and wisdom that can be the cornerstone of your personality. When acting as a portent, you or young people, probably in the academic or financial spheres, will receive good news.

Past: Your past ambitions and idealism will succeed with your latest ideas. You are developing a new interest or occupation.

Present: There is news that the change is coming. Even if not directly, plan to assess the risks and advantages of new companies.

Future: When you stay vigilant and aware of the signals surrounding you, you can gain insight into your future. All you need to remember is now possible if you take the time to learn it later.

Yes / No Key Interpretation: The Pentacle Page is an attentive, attentive, and knowledgeable youth that is both self-disciplined and self-disciplined. He may suggest some form of advancement or, in the near future, develop a new and fun hobby. The card's overall mood is good, and the answer is yes.

Ten of Pentacles

- Close relationships

- Family

- Fortune

- Inheritance

- Prosperous

Meaning

The inclusion of this card is a good sign of your financial security and mental well-being. Nevertheless, this is only partly yours, because these positive aspects are inextricably linked in your close relations with friends and family. It can also project a legacy.

Past: By your ability to spend money wisely, you have been prosperous and a secure basis.

Present: You will receive a reward partly because of your efforts but also because of your position in your family. Evaluate your own merits carefully.

Future: There will be an unexpected solution to a difficult financial problem. The projects and ideas you are working on today will benefit future generations.

Yes / No Key Interpretation: The Ten of the Pentacles shows that stability, prosperity, and good fortune are present. All of this can be because of positive, close relationships or a tight family. You could expect a legacy or discovery of the treasure, and your answer is yes.

Nine of Pentacles

- Abundance

- Financial security

- Opulence

- Prosperous

- Wealth

Meaning

The Ninth of Pentacles represents a substantial financial reward, but one which you have worked hard and carefully planned, a just reward for prudent activities. It can also mean that a time of struggle finishes for you, and a period of a pleasant life is at hand. On a less positive note, it also suggests a lonely person, so you can still need friendship and do not have people with whom to share your benefits.

Past: Your achievements have earned the pleasure you have experienced. Although the benefits of a recent project are not yet apparent, you should earn plenty for your efforts.

Present: The solution you have sought will come and relieve you of the stress of your problem.

Future: New challenges await you in dissipating your feelings of disappointment. The hole you encounter is not remedied by the obstacles, but the incentives allow you to please yourself.

Yes / no key interpretation: wealth and financial security are the standards of the Nine of Pentacles. It may ultimately mean that you're rewarded for all your business efforts or important projects. The presence of this card could mean that you have financial and/or personal independence. The answer you are looking for is more than likely, yes.

Eight of Pentacles

- Apprentice

- Career

- Craftsmanship

- New skills

- Prudence

Meaning

If you are interested in any work that requires creative inspiration or ability, Pentacles ' VIII is a very good coin. This is twice true if you use skills that you still try to master. This is as apt as the primary work to be a passion. Unlike most suits, financial gains are not necessarily shown, but a spiritual reward. This is also not a guarantee, but rather a suggestion that success is the most likely outcome if you are prudent and organized in your effort.

Past: The skills you master will lead you on the way to success. Continue to develop, and you will hit an epiphany moment.

Present: You will excel in your endeavors by cultivating your skills. Investing in yourself will later be more rewarding.

Future: For you, the future will lead to a successful career or spiritual effort. The amount of acclaim you receive depends on how long you have invested in assessing and improving your abilities.

Yes / No Main Interpretation: The Eight of Pentacles is a card that recommends increased ability and analysis. It shows the desired career and acquires new skills only as long as you are discreet and well-balanced. This card's outlook is positive. Yeah, it's your reply.

Seven of Pentacles

- Business & Trade

- Long-term success

- Occupation

- Perseverance

- Wealth

Meaning

A balanced card, by its very definition, implies that you prevent defeat but struggle to achieve quickly. Or you can also achieve your goals, but not in the time frame that you hoped for. You face challenges, and you have to be careful to avoid becoming too reluctant or cautious to achieve. Progress can be sluggish or challenging, but it can be.

Past: Delays probably plagued you in your designs, but don't lose hope. You will be effective with your perseverance.

Present: The long time you are working hard should offer you a lot of personal development and accomplishment.

Future: The journey will be lengthy, but great rewards if you can keep going without sacrificing motivation or power.

Yes / No Main Interpretation: The Seven Pentacles is perseverance in your work or company. It is connected to performance, yet slow and steady development. This means that you have to wait a long time for your compensation, and maybe you don't function to your full potential. Here, there is no clear answer.

Six of Pentacles

- Distribution

- Donation

- Favor

- Prosperity

- Solvency

Meaning

Your life's success is linked to generosity. This can lead to your prosperity arising from your investment in others, financial investment, or a friend's advice and support. That card can also indicate the opposite that your performance comes from someone else's kindness. Both are not exclusive, of course, so drawing this card indicates that you are committed to charity and benevolence.

Past: You will flourish in the present with your fair consideration for others in the past.

Present: Your enthusiasm for life will be renewed and faith in your own talents. The happiness in supporting someone in need illuminates the larger picture.

Future: Keep in mind that the goodness of others is out of your reach, but you can offer favor. If you're searching for attention, it might be good to give to others openly.

Yes/no Interpretation: The Six of Pentacles means achievement, prosperity, and generosity. This suggests supporting people personally, providing money, and selfless welfare. There is positive favor, a sense of good fortune, and a happy future reward. The answer you are looking for is probably yes.

Five of Pentacles

- Emotional or Financial troubles

- Inadequacy

- Poverty

- Scarcity

- Worry

Meaning

The V of Pentacles that apply to financial matters, employment, or relationships, depending on your settings. Sadly, all of them have a derogatory suggestion that duplicity, job loss, and the probability of infidelity are implied. This is a time for you to carefully assess what matters in your life and determine if your work or your relationship is most important. You may have to let some of the others slip away in order to minimize harm in some areas of your life.

Past: You are heavily weighed by a recent emotional or financial loss. Do not allow your pride to lead you away from the help of others.

Present: the challenge you encounter will be resolved, so do not encourage the feelings of inadequacy or fear.

Future: The future has a necessary change to find happiness and stability for you. The transition can be guided or inspired, which tells you that all challenges can be resolved.

Yes / No Main Interpretation: The Five of Pentacles reveals the financial or emotional problems or a time of suffering exist. This card all involves worry, poverty, and setbacks. These things might be due to a lack of faith or a loss of faith. This card's overall tone is pessimistic. The answer you want is no.

Four of Pentacles

- Certainty

- Possessive

- Reliable

- Security

- Tenacity

Meaning

You may be on the path to financial and material prosperity through talent or inheritance or probably through your own entrepreneurship. This will hopefully be a good period in your life in which your emotional and spiritual needs are met.

Past: Your skill and dedication to hard work should get your material success. A new trade, idea, or business venture brings greater value to your life.

Present: For the commitment you have shown, you can receive financial incentives. You're going to win, but this triumph is empty if only you see it as a monetary benefit.

Future: To maintain your financial security, resist waste, and hold to your efficiency and resourcefulness capabilities. It is only through tremendous effort and sacrifices that you can gain leadership, power, and wealth.

Yes / No Core Interpretation: The Four Pentacles stands for health, peace, and simple order in your life. This means that you are smart and creative with what you have and stick on a strict budget but with only positive results. Progress will probably require tenacity. Your reaction is yes.

Three of Pentacles

- Excellence

- Mastery

- Satisfaction

- Success

- Teamwork

Meaning

If, in the next few months, you can maintain a clear sense of purpose, you are well placed to see that your hard work is recognized. This is not guaranteed, even if you maintain your own speed, then this will force your communications skills, as you need to depend and trust someone for the best possible result. However, this consequence is worth your effort not just to have a material reward, but also to give you a feeling of lifelong achievement.

Past: The time you spent controlling your skills was an intelligent investment. Your trust has increased, and you will succeed if you continue to nurture this self-assurance.

609

Present: The aim of your current focus is to expand and develop. Your colleagues can be a useful tool to help you achieve your objectives.

Future: The inner happiness calls for perfection and dominance.

Yes / No Main Interpretation: The Three of Pentacles is a deck that is perfection and accomplishment. These things can be obtained through productive teamwork or industrial activity. It concerns you directly as a master of your business and great career achievements. Your question is answered, yes.

Two of Pentacles

- Balance

- Fluctuating Wealth

- Juggling

- Prudence

- Transfer or Exchange

Meaning

As always, the II is linked to the forces of change and balance. Like its parents, Pentacle II can mean good or bad, but it is a potent sign of a challenge to the status quo. Your future will face challenges, but your fate lies largely in your own hands because the final result depends on how you respond to these challenges. The style of this card indicates that your best result is a conservative and thoughtful preparation strategy.

Past: You encountered the challenge of starting something new. You must learn to balance your old practices and your new practices in order to succeed.

Present: A transition for the better will be created through the information shared. You'll receive prudent advice in your fluctuating states on the best course.

Future: The persistence of your most important qualities will help you create your own prospects. If you think you find it, there's a way out of your ambivalence.

Yes / No Key Interpretation: The two pentacles indicate a shift in motion, equilibrium, and development. This offers the possibility of fluctuating income, which will probably require some form of balancing act and carry both ups and downs. The task will be high, and the inclusion of this card does not provide a clear answer.

Ace of Pentacles

- Emotional stability

- Financial gain

- Luck

- Recognition

- Success

Meaning

Aces are always a new beginning, and the Ace of Pentacles offers you a very good start. Your life is about to be really fruitful–or, at least, a moment where your efforts will be well compensated to the level of work that you are prepared to do. That time also will see most of your partnership secure, and you will be satisfied with your circumstance, given the hard work you can do.

Past: Your time has been well spent, and the success you want will eventually be achieved. The ventures you've initiated payback.

Present: You should obtain positive reports. It can help you to understand that you are on the right road to receive the recognition and material rewards you deserve.

Future: You're for a big gain. Whether financial, emotional, or personal, spiritual blessings await you.

Yes / No Key Interpretation: The Ace of Pentacles represents prosperity, financial gain, and promotion. This brings good health and emotional stability. This card suggests a positive future and can achieve your goals. The answer is yes.

Chapter 4: Tarot Spreads

There are different kinds of spreads you can use to carry out a tarot reading and gain better insight into a problem you are going through in your life. Here are some easy to practice spreads for beginners.

Single Card Spread

This is the simplest of all spreads you will ever come across, and is extremely suitable for beginners who do not wish to get into any complications and those who have trouble focusing on several cards or things at the same time. Here is how to do it:

- Think about any problem or aspect of life you would like to explore and get clarity on and then pick your deck of cards thinking about that question. This step is important for all types of spreads that you carry out and is a must-do before and during every tarot reading you ever conduct.

- Shuffle the deck of cards and then pull out a single card from it.

- Put the card down and focus on the question you asked. Make sure the question is a simple one that does not have too many options attached to it.

- Focus on the meaning of the card and explore it from different aspects to get more clarity on it. It is better to write down the aspects you explore and the answers that come to you when analyzing the card.

- Keep thinking about the answers you discover in light of the problem to get a more meaningful answer and conclusion.

You can use only the major arcana cards if your query is related to a major life event such as marrying your partner or accepting a new job offer that requires you to move to another state. If your problem is related to routine events and is not too intense, but you wish to get a deeper understanding of it, you can use all the cards or just the minor arcana cards as well.

The 3 Card Spread

This simple, self-explanatory tarot spread has been around for a very long time. It is easy to carry out and read, and gives you a good understanding of the problem you are trying to explore. In addition, it works well for big and more impactful problems as well as routine issues, and a mixture of these two problems as well. Here is how to do it:

- Shuffle the deck and focus on the problem at hand.

- Now pick out three cards from the deck and put them down on the table. Remember the order in which you pulled them out.

- The first card represents your past, the second reflects your present and the third signifies your future.

- You need to analyze them one at a time to figure out how they represent the specific period and what the card is trying to convey to you. For example, if you are focusing on your career and trying to figure out what suits you best, seeing your past card may make you realize that you should pursue your passion and viewing the present card may make you feel that your current career does not feel thriving and exciting to you, and your future card may speak to you about how good things come from following your ambitions. If you take it as a whole, the reading is likely trying to tell you to believe in yourself and follow your passion of becoming a singer and songwriter like you always wanted to do.

After you have conducted the reading, write down the findings and go through them a few times. It is best to reflect on a reading for a few days preferably a couple of weeks before carrying out another one on the same issue. You need time to think through the answers you have discovered and analyze them in detail. With many responsibilities to tend to, this cannot happen in a day so take your time.

The 3 card spread is a great reading that helps you understand the lessons you have gained over time and how things were, are right now and can be regarding a certain problem.

Mind, Body and Spirit Spread

This is another brilliant spread for beginners especially because it is simple to carry out. It is similar to the previous spread because this too involves three cards, but different in the manner that the three cards in this spread refer to your mind, body and spirit.

This spread gives you better insight into how your mind, body and spirit are working individually and as a whole, and whether you are going through a conflict between any two or all of them. Here is how you can practice it

- Pick out any three cards from the deck after shuffling it and lay them down.

- The first card points to your mind and how you are feeling about things from conscious and unconscious perspectives. You need to focus on whether you feel good about something from your mind and whether your head feels aligned to an issue or not.

- The second card symbolizes your physical state regarding a matter.

- The third card reflects the matters of your heart and whether or not you have a spiritual connection with an issue or matter.

- After you have picked out the three cards, analyze them individually one by one. As you explore the reading of a card, understand it in the light of the query you had in mind and write down the findings. For instance, you may be worrying about your deteriorating health and why you keep falling sick, and may be concerned that it is because you feel stressed because of your marriage. In that case, you need to see what each card in the spread says to you and then analyze it as a whole.

- Once you have assessed the cards individually, take them as a whole and read them collectively. If you are deeply upset about something, the 3 cards are likely to show trouble in all the 3 aspects: mind, body and spirituality. However, this may not be the case every time. You may sometimes encounter a situation where there exists conflict between your heart and mind. You may feel more convinced about something if you see it from your heart, but your mind may try to pull you away constantly from it. When using this spread, you need to see the entire matter very objectively and be clear on how you feel about an issue from the perspective of your heart/ spirituality, body and mind.

This spread works well for you when you are trying to deal with an inner conflict regarding an important decision. Also, it is a spread you can carry out as a weekly ritual just to make sure all three aspects of your being; your mind, body and heart are well connected to what you are doing in life so you live with harmony.

Horseshoe Spread

If you are concerned about a matter from different angles, and would like to get a clearer idea of how things would work out for you regarding that issue in the end, the horseshoe is the right spread to practice.

This spread enables you to understand how things may unfold and gives you a bigger picture regarding a certain matter so you become more aware of the problem at hand and how things are likely to pan out in the near future and the long-term. Here is how you to do it:

- Shuffle the deck and then draw one card at a time.

- You need to start placing the cards from your bottom left and keep putting down one card after another until you reach your bottom right and end up creating an upside-down U shape of sorts.

- You should end up having seven cards in total.

- When reading the horseshoe that you have spread in front of you, you need to analyze the situation from how it was in the past to how it is now in your present to how things will unfold in the future while moving from the left side to the right.

- The bottom left cards reflect the past events while the cards in the middle speak about your present, and the ones on the far right symbolize possible outcomes. So if you are wondering about a certain relationship or want to get more insight into why you feel depressed, the cards on the far left will tell you how you felt in the past or point to a specific event in the past that may have triggered your depression, the ones in the center will reflect your current situation, and the series of cards on the bottom right will show you how things are likely to unfold for you.

Like with other spreads, write down the findings of the reading and go through them several times to make better sense of the entire reading. This is a nice spread to practice when you have some lingering questions about a certain issue.

The Celtic Cross Spread

This complex spread gives you a more detailed understanding of a specific issue. It is a more detailed version of the horseshoe which is also referred to as the 'more modified and modern' version of the Celtic cross.

If you are a more detailed oriented person who loves to understand and get into the details of an issue, this spread is right for you. However, it will take you a few tries to get the hang of it and understand what each card is trying to tell you, but if you are persistent and keep practicing it, you will become an expert at it soon. Here is how you can practice it:

- Shuffle the deck of your tarot cards. This is a 10-card spread.

619

- Pull out a card and put it in the center.

- Pull out another card and place it on the top of the first card.

- The third card needs to go at the bottom of the first card; the fourth card should be laid on its right side, which makes it your left; the fifth card on the top of it and the sixth card towards your right, which makes it the left of the first card.

- You need to pull out four more cards and they should be placed parallel to the cards number 1, 3 and 5 in a manner that the 7th card is on the bottom and the 10th card on the top adjacent to the 5th card just like shown in the image above.

- If you cannot memorize the order of the cards, you can mark them from 1 to 10 with a soft lead pencil that can be easily erased afterwards.

- Now it is time to read the spread and analyze the answers.

- The 1st card signifies the 'querent' which in this case is you; the person asking the question. Probably it is trying to point out your state of mind or any character trait or how you feel at this point of time, or what you want from life right now or in general. Sometimes, this card can also refer to someone in your life. For instance, it may point out to someone you share a close bond with or maybe someone you are on conflicting terms with, but would like to improve the relationship with.

- The second card reflects the situation you are going through in your present. Depending on the question you asked, it could point to the matters of the heart, a financial crunch you are going through, emotional issues, relationship problems or tensions in your professional life. Sometimes, the card may not seem relevant to the query you have in mind. That is because it is pointing to the actual query, the one you should focus on. For example, you may want to know about whether or not to marry your partner, but the card may be suggesting that you are not fulfilled and content from within. This can mean that you first need to be happy from within and then find a partner accordingly because that is how you will be able to find the right partner for yourself.

- The 3rd card represents the foundation of the problem at hand. It helps you understand the different factors and elements that have produced the issue you are suffering from and are mostly related to your past. For instance, when trying to figure out why you have developed a controlling and manipulative attitude towards your loved ones, you may figure out that is because your parents treated you like this when you were younger. Remember, the cards are not going to tell you everything plain and simple, and out loud. They will obviously present many things to you, but it is you who has to make sense of the meanings and for that, you need to really dig deeper into things.

- The 4th card symbolizes your recent past, something that is associated with your past as shown by the 3rd card, but something that happened only recently. For example, if your third card reflects emotional problems, the fourth card is likely to point out the loss of a loved one or the end of an important relationship. If the reading is a positive, happy one, the fourth card is likely to symbolize happy, bright events.

- The 5th card shows the different episodes or events you will experience in the next few months or maybe a couple of years. This is from where things start to move towards the future and you get a clearer idea of how things will pan out for you. If you are going through a financial crunch, you may foresee better things coming up for you or maybe the situation may worsen.

- The 6th card indicates your current state and gives you an understanding of whether or not your problem will resolve soon enough. You get an idea of your relationship with the prospective future outcome. Continuing with the other example of a financial struggle, the card may show more emotional problems coming up if the 5th card shows your financial crunch will continue for another year.

- The 7th card symbolizes the different outside influences you are surrounded with regarding the issue at hand. You may become aware of those supporting you or those who do not back you up, and makes you aware of how different people in your social circle influence you regarding that problem.

- The 8th card is indicative of the internal influences you experience which are basically your feelings about the situation or problem you are trying to get a better understanding of. It speaks directly to you about how you feel regarding the situation you are in and the feelings could be positive, negative or a mixture of the two kinds. If the overall reading is a happy one, you may feel good, confident, peaceful, cheerful and excited, or just any one of these feelings or any other positive feeling. If the overall reading is about a grave issue, your feelings may lean more towards frustration, stress, anger, sadness or even jealousy. This obviously depends on the problem you are trying to explore.

- The ninth card represents the hopes, fears and apprehensions you nurture. While it is similar to the other card, it is more related to the different concerns you have regarding the problem you are engulfed in.

- The final card of the spread points to the long-term situation and outcomes you are likely to experience in the next six to twelve months. It is more like the conclusion of the nine cards you have read prior to this one. It talks to you about how things will unfold in another few months and prepares you for the outcomes beforehand. For example, if you get the death card as the tenth card and you are thinking about your business and the problems you are facing in it, it may mean that your business is likely to end in another few months and it is not a lucrative option for you so it is a good time to think about another option and explore it. Sometimes, the tenth card may not make any sense at all. If that happens, pull out another card or maybe two cards and place them next to the 10th card or even replace the 10th card with them. You need to then read the new cards or the 10th card along with the new card and explore the other nine cards in reference to it. You are likely to comprehend the situation and reading better then.

Do jot down the meanings and answers you find and take time to reflect on them. A single Celtic cross reading can provide you with a number of points and ideas to ponder on and it can take you anywhere from a couple of hours to even a few weeks to fully comprehend the lessons reflected in a Celtic cross reading.

You can also conduct a Celtic cross reading as a continuation of a single or three card spread. For instance, if you just conducted a single card spread about an important issue or even a routine matter but something you feel strongly about, and would like to explore it further, continue with that in a Celtic cross reading. After conducting a one card spread, explore the meaning you found out for some time and then conduct a Celtic cross reading after a couple of hours or even a few minutes after that first reading. However, it is best you take at least a day's gap between two readings to get better comprehension of its meaning and the results.

Relationship Spread

This is a nice spread to practice when you wish to explore a relationship you share with someone. The best thing about this spread is that it applies to all sorts of relationships. Here is how you can carry it out:

- After shuffling the deck, pull out three cards and put them on the left side. These cards reflect you and your feelings pertinent to that person and the relationship you share with him/her.

- Pull out another three cards and put them on the right side. These cards are indicative of that other person you wish to explore your relationship further with. The cards may also show his/her feelings related to you and how the relationship is going forward from their perspective.

- Pull out one more card and place it in the middle of the two sets. This is the advice card which points to the outcome or future of the relationship you are trying to understand, and may provide tips on how to better the bond and strengthen it.

You need to first read the cards individually and then as a whole to better understand how you feel about that person, how he/she feels about the relationship and whether or not the relationship is going somewhere, and if it is, what you can do to make it a successful venture together.

All these spreads are really helpful and can provide you with valuable insight into the different experiences and problems you are going through in life. Try your hand with each one of them depending on the issues you are experiencing and see how each works out for you. You may find yourself inclining towards a certain type of spread after you have had a good experience with it.

Now that you know the different kinds of spreads you can practice, let me share with you some tips to prepare yourself for a tarot reading and cleanse afterwards for effective results.

Chapter 5: Tips for making the most out of symbolism in tarot cards

1. Start With What You Know

I want you to come from a position of confidence as you read Tarot. For starters, if you have an interest in the meaning of Christianity, then think about what you know about it. How can you see the Tarot cards depicted? This can just offer you that degree of confidence.

Don't believe like in order to grasp the meanings of Tarot cards; you ought to know all these new things to become a master.

2. Find Common Symbols And Research Their Meanings

If you glance at the Tarot deck, you can find a few icons or pictures on the cards.

For example, in the Tarot, there are several castles, clouds and landscapes. But discovering these universal symbols can be very beneficial to continuing to gain cultural knowledge about certain symbols. What is usually a castle?

3. Explore Your Personal Connection With The Symbols

Here's where the fun falls in! You will finally develop your instincts and start communicating closer to your subconscious.

Let's use the castle as a case. The typical sense of the castle is a protected spot since the castle walls are very wide and quite sturdy. You could look at the castle and the walls and say, "Oh, my goodness, I love liberty." And it really could be worse.

It's nice to communicate with what a castle means to you. What are you looking at? And how is that distinguished from common wisdom?

4. Compare The Symbols Across Tarot Cards

We're going to stay with castles. Take out all the Tarot cards of castles. Maybe address each card's questions and analyze how they differ:

- How will the meaning of the castle change when you see it on different cards?

- Are you in the walls of the castle or are you standing on the walls of the castle?

- So how do you feel, are you included or excluded?

- Are you feeling comfortable or insecure?

- What's going on in the castle?

- The Four of Wands, for example, rejoice outside the castle, but in The Tower, the castle is bursting.

- Are castles as sturdy as you would think?

When you perform this exercise, you begin to realize that symbols will take on various definitions according to the card sense itself.

5. Read Widely

If you feel very comfortable at this point, you may be prepared to reply "Sure, you know what I think about Kabbalah but I want to find out because I want to get the extra layer of comprehension when I see Kabbalah symbols in the Tarot."

6. Create A Library Of Symbols

Even when you do all this amazing work, hold a journal of your icons and compose what they say for you.

The benefit of this is that you don't only focus on what anyone else is communicating to you as a symbol; you develop your own familiarity with these symbols.

Conclusion

Now that you've gained a basic understanding of the Tarot, you can chart a path of your own, by exploring different spreads, building on your knowledge through further resources (you'll find a list of suggestions on the following page), and just enjoying spending time with the cards.

Remember to trust your intuition along the way. Pay attention to the ideas that pop into your mind, and to the way that you feel when interacting with the cards. Don't doubt your instincts just because instructions in a book contradict what you're picking up on.

It takes time to become a fluid reader of the Tarot, but it's a fulfilling journey. Once you get comfortable with your deck and get more practice, you'll have more and more moments when the cards are clearly speaking to you directly. When this happens, take notes on your readings and go back to them later to see which of your interpretations were most accurate.

Ultimately, you'll deepen your understanding of the cards through your own experience of life. And ideally, you'll enrich your experience of life through exploring the Tarot!

Introduction

The Tarot is a pack of 78 printed cards and one clear card. It comprises of 22 Significant Arcana (or picture) cards and 56 Minor Arcana cards.

The Major Arcana cards are numbered 0–21. Each card has a title, for example, the Blockhead or the World, for instance. The Major Arcana cards depict the profound reasons for regular occasions, and, the Minor Arcana cards detail ordinary happenings. While the Minor Arcana cards may let you know of issues in your affection relationship, the

Major Arcana cards will let you know the fundamental exercise to be learned in that circumstance.

The Minor Arcana cards are separated into four suits of 14 cards each. Each suit comprises of cards numbered 1–10, and incorporates four Court cards—Lord, Sovereign, Knight and Page. These suits have various names from normal playing a card game, yet relate to each suit. They are the suits of:

• Wands (Clubs)

• Cups (Hearts)

• Swords (Spades)

• Pentacles (Diamonds).

From the outset the horde cards and their numerous varieties may appear to be befuddling. Anyway this language of images is as of now well-known to your intuitive brain, so in truth you will be recollecting the cards instead of learning them.

The Tarot is a book of images, and once you know about these images the Tarot turns into an entryway to recently concealed information and data. The Tarot is an apparatus to encourage physical, passionate, mental and profound development and learning. The Tarot can be used for anticipating the future, however it isn't restricted to that. It can likewise light up the fundamental reasons for a circumstance and uncovered the exercises to be gained from a circumstance. This is ideal delineated by the familiar axiom:

The individuals who don't gain from history are bound to repeat it. The Tarot can be used to look for the most fitting game-plan in a given circumstance, so we try not to need to repeat our exercises and once more. The above saying advises us that we are all repeating exercises and that we as a whole have the chance of proceeding onward to all the more testing choices.

Color implications in Tarot

Red:

Zest or excitement in moving toward life and its difficulties. Cards which contain parcels of red, for example, the Sovereign, demonstrate a physical or viable way to deal with life.

Orange:

An energetic or excited way to deal with life. Cards containing a lot of orange (as the Wands cards do) show an ardent or hot-blooded way to deal with life.

Yellow:

A scholarly way to deal with the current circumstance. Cards containing a lot of yellow (for example, Quality and the Sun) show mental interest and consistent idea and investigation.

Green:

Amicability and balance are symbolized in the Tarot by the color green. Not many cards in the Rider-Waite deck have in excess of a token measure of green.

Blue:

Adjusted profound comprehension is symbolized by the use of the color blue in the Tarot. It shows mind joined with a profound point of view, incorporating life's greater picture.

Purple:

Sympathy is symbolized by the use of the color purple in the Tarot. Cards which utilize purple, for example, the Darlings (sympathy for an accomplice) or Equity (empathy for outsiders), show that sympathy starts with those near us and can extend to outsiders as we develop.

White:

Immaculateness of intention is appeared by the color white in the Tarot, for example, the white blossoms in the Six of Cups (when two individuals share a delicate, private minute) or the white lilies and white tunic in the Performer, where he depends on unadulterated intentions he had in the Blockhead (appeared as the snow-topped mountains) to advance to the following card.

Chapter 1: Origin of the Tarot

Leaving the tarots card invariably evokes the illusion that old gypsy people pose before their crystal ball in a nebular room full of strange artifacts. The word "Tarot" has an aura of mystery too, for no one understands when Tarot is operating or when. While scholars are aware that the majority of recorded tarot card history comes from Italy.

Tarot may have been drawn from ancient Egyptian tablets (since there are identical silent people, who talk only in presence and image, as Egyptian hieroglyphics and some Tarot symbols), or from Hidden Texts by the Chaldeans.

Many people believe that the Tarot was carried by the Knights Templars into Europe after the cruises, while others say that it is the Gypsies who would enjoy reading the Tarot as they visited the continent in the Middle Ages.

Historians also found evidence that the Tarot decks of 78 cards were used during the Renaissance to reveal fortunes in Italy and France. Researchers believe that these early tarot decks can be a by-product of current playing cards.

In view of the various interpretations, one thing is certain: for seven hundred years, the reading of tarot cards saw the daylight as one of the most important sources of the western world's spiritual knowledge.

Some tarot historians believe that the tarot cards were developed as a game called Triumph, which today was equivalent to the game of "Bridge." The game was called "Tarocchi" (later Tarot), which spread rapidly across all parts of Europe.

The markings on the cards were quickly recognized in France and England by the practitioners of the mystic and were often used as a divination device, and eventually became a component of the occult theory.

The tarot readings were, however, still quite easy at that period.

By the eighteenth century, the tarot readers had begun to give specific meanings to each card, and in 1781 the French freemason published a complex analysis of the tarot. The hypothesis was that the images in the Tarot were drawn from Egyptian priests ' ancient mysteries and linked to the stories of Isis, Osiris, and other Egyptian gods.

In 1791 Jean-Baptiste Alliette published the first Tarot box, and curiosity in occult research quickly gained momentum as it was a popular pastime among dull high-class families.

A British occultist, Arthur Waite, and artist Pamela Colman Smith published the most famous tarot card set, the Rider-Waite deck, for the first time in 1909.

Today, reading tarot cards is very common, and more and more people depend on a tarot reading to lead them through their daily lives. Tarot readings help seekers think about themselves and others and see what their future holds. These cards can also be used for reflection and meditation. The cards are now distributed in almost infinite styles. Any deck with which the user is confident can be used.

The 78 Tarot deck cards consist of the Major Arcana and the Minor Arcana, which essentially translations into "grand secrets" and "little secrets." Once upon a time, the origin of the Tarot could be traced back to ancient Egypt, perhaps the cards representing the lost Egyptian Dead Book. This is the idea that has mostly been uncovered since the actual creation and publication of this book, but the appeal and attraction of the concept remain, and many occultists still retain it.

The first to suggest an alternative source was the Le Monde Primitif (1781), an encyclopedic paper on anthropological linguistics and Antoine Court de Gébelin (c. 1719-1784)—the Book of Thoth, another Egyptian text which he claimed was the only writing to survive the burning of his libraries and contained the pure and most sacred doctrines of the Egyptian empire. He said these doctrines were spread throughout Europe (though diluted) by Gypsies; he assumed to be descendants of the people of Egypt (a theory that has since been disproved). He found what he thought to be timeless esoteric wisdom arcane in this book of bizarre figures on 78 leaves. He also claimed that he had found hints of the true origin of the Tarot deck. Composing (falsely) the word' tar'(' way' or' path'), and the word' royal'(' king' or' royal'), he assumed it should be dictated by the Royal Path of Human Life. He assumed the wise men of Egypt were anticipating and analyzing these holy symbols for the future.

He also found clues to the Egyptian symbols in contemporary tarot cards. In his view, the Star card was the Dog-star of Sirius, who rises with the Nile flood at the start of a new year, and the Lady below, whom he perceived as Isis, Queen of Heaven who strewed water out of her vases (the tears of Isis which each year flooded the Nile). He identified the Devil card as Set, the god of darkness and chaos.

But many scholars challenged the findings of De Gébelin. Thoth's now completely interpreted book contains two charms, one of which ostensibly helps the reader to comprehend the animals ' words, and the other encourages the reader to interpret the gods. The legend of Thoth, the god of writing and knowledge, includes the book itself, which is said to be first buried near Coptos at the bottom of the Nile, and was locked into a serpent-protected shell.

Egyptian Prince Neferkaptah fought the serpents and found the book, but the gods killed his son and wife in a penalty of Thoth's theft. The Book was lost, and Neferkaptah committed suicide. Generations later, in spite of resistance from the spirit of Neferkaptah, Setne Khamwas, the protagonist of the story, steals the book from the tomb of Neferkaptah. Instead, Setne encounters a beautiful woman who seduces him to murder and humiliate his children in front of the pharaoh. He found the episode to be the dream of Neferkaptah, and in fear of further reward, he gave the book back to the tomb of Neferkaptah, and a fascinating parable. The narrative itself hardly confirms De Gébelin's interpretation of the symbols.

There are many other hypotheses, including the suggestion that Tarot originated from magical numbered cart decks that existed in India and the Far East in ancient times and could be transported by the Templar Knights to Europe during and after the Holy Land cruises. Obviously, this hypothesis is pure conjecture, like the others. If there were these games, how should we learn that they created the Tarot?

The fact is, nobody really understands from whence came the Tarot box. Its true roots are covered in mystery. Even the word's etymology is uncertain. Whereas de Gébelin suggested an Egyptian word, other historians believe that the word "Torah" is corrupt and that the Hebrew Law Book is interpreted by others as "wheel" and "rota" as the anagram of the Latin word "rota."

So, what can we say for sure about Tarot's origin?

Sometimes in Milan, Ferrara, and Bologna in Northern Italy between 1430 and 1450, the first known Tarot cards were created, perhaps when a famed four-suit player card set was developed to include additional cards trumps with allegorical diagrams. Such modern decks were originally called cartes da trionfi, trump cards, and other cards became simply known as trionfi. A written statement in Ferrara's court record, 1442, is the first textual evidence of the existence of the carte da trionfi. The earliest surviving Tarot cards are fifteen splinter decks created for Milan's kings, Visconti-Sforza, during the middle of the 15th century.

This secondary use of the cards gradually became their main function. Eliphas Levi Zahid from the 19th century (1810-1875), who studied for priesthood like De Gébelin, then switched to sorcery, mysticism, and occultism. Convinced that the root of the Tarot dates back far beyond the 14th century, he noticed connections between the Tarot and the Jewish spiritual method, known as the Kabbalah. Levi noted that the Tarot 22 trumps match the Hebrew alphabet's 22 letters. His research found many other similarities, including the similarity between the Tarot and the Tree of Life. He became actually convinced that the Tarot was a compass, a way of traveling around the Tree of Life, being divine and wise, and eventually finding the heavens.

A contemporary of Levi (Jean Baptiste Pitois, 1811-1877), the French occultist Paul Christian wrote a book called The History of Magic (1870) that defined the ritual of Egyptian initiation, related to the Tarot. The Giza Sphinx also acted as the gateway to the holy vaults, according to Christian, where the Magi performed their initiation. Corridors led to the Great Pyramid's subterranean portions. A candidate was faced with life-threatening ordeals to test his courage and intelligence. Once these tests had survived, the initiate descended into a bottomless pit on the ladder of 78 rungs and found an overshadowed opening in a long gallery, lined with 22 statues on each side and faced by pairs of mysterious bodies and symbols. At that stage, a magus called Pastophore ("guardian of the holy symbols"), according to Christian, seemed to unlock the postulant's grating. "Son of earth," he smiled, he said, "welcome. You have escaped from the pit by discovering the road to wisdom; a few Mystery aspirants have triumphed in this test; all the others have been destroyed. As your protector is the great Isis, she will lead you, I hope, safe to the sanctuary where virtue is crowned.

The Tarot has developed over the years. In the 1940s, in collaboration with Lady Frieda Harris, famous British occultist Aleister Crowley crafted a Thoth deck that incorporated several different elements, including the Jewish, Roman, Christian, and Islamic icons. Initially a member of the Golden Dawn Order, Crowley gradually split from that group and founded his own order, the Silver Star, to represent his own special (and erotic) occult brand.

Hundreds (if not thousands) of various Tarot decks have been constructed over the years. The Tarot continues to evolve while its origins remain unclear. And the root of the Tarot is perhaps less relevant than what it is. After all, the past is the past. If the Tarot will allow you to grasp your existence more fully, whether you consider universal truth in the cards, all items before this realization become meaningless, including the past of the cards themselves, of course.

Different Types of Tarot Packs

Originally, tarot cards were a kind of Italian activity. However, people took it into psychic reading, and it proved true. It remains today one of the most common worship instruments in the West, and many people trust the readings it has acquired. Several forms of tarot cards exist, and some include:

The Ator: It has a refreshing new smell, ideal for new generation psychical readings. It has amazing stories, so many people are known.

The Benedetti: Is on a gold leaf richly decorated. It is the perfect choice for readers who want to attach to their offerings a touch of class and prominence. They were influenced by the Visconti chips.

The Cat People Tarot: The cat people tarot is the best choice for people who want to see the land that is far gone. This displays the ingenuity of human beings through mystics and animals.

Column Smith Tarot: Several mental readers have adopted the abstract paint approach to their visual literacy. The column smith tarot is the perfect choice for them. The mysterious tarot is the most uncommon and least seen conventional tarot. It has strange characters that catch many's interests. It is a rare type of tarot card because readers believe it can frighten consumers.

The Golden Tarot: This one is essential for great thinkers. In the past, writers often used the ancient tarot.

International Icon Tarot: The Swiss foreign symbol tarot is accessible for a more satirical approach to tarot interpretation. It is their standard tarot reading variant.

Love Craft Tarot: This tarot is a reference to one of the ancient writers for the lovers of ancient writings.

Marseilles Tarot: The Marseilles tarot is easy to access from many shops worldwide for the highest divination among ordinary people. It was also common for people to use tarot to meditate.

The Minciante: Minciante tarot includes more than any other package of 97 tarot cards. Most people regard it as one of the most popular games. The paladin tarot deck is best suited for contemporary tarot lessons. The ability is paired with the standard tarot readings. It depicts elements of Egyptian classical sculpture admired by art lovers. The phoenix tarot is tailored for the modern tarot reader century. It is a product of the 20th century. It incorporates vibrant colors and is, therefore, really eye-catching.

Most people take tarot readings in order to predict the circumstances of their life and their fate or disasters. Fear of the unknown is the driving force for the tarot reading business. Tarot readers can choose any of the above tarot for their actions based on their choice.

Truth of Importance and Mystics Surrounding Tarot Cards

This ancient tradition has been associated with other intriguing tales, ideas, and the facts, with more than 600 years of tarot card experience. Some of them are true, and some of them are fake. None of them are real.

Below are a few vital things you need to learn as a beginner or a tarot card reader:

- The current Tarot Deck consists of 78 cards – 22 Arcana Major Cards and 56 Arcana Minor. The readings of big and miniature Arcane cards vary tremendously;

- Cards ' names varied from the current tarot in the older set. Significant Arcana as truncations, high priestess as popes, hierophants as papas, coins, staves or batons, Arcana as weapons;

- Various types of tarot card decks are available for reading tarot cards. A unique image and description are displayed on each table. The value of the tarot card remains, however, the same on each deck;

- You can use a tarot deck, called Birth Tarot from your date of birth. The cards have been customized by special tarot card readings according to the reduced number of your month, date, and year of birth;

- There are several pictures with different meanings on each card. With a detailed tarot card guide, anyone will easily understand the meaning of tarot cards;

- Each minor arcane depicts certain life issues, including cups, emotional obstruction, pentacles, monetary problems and family problems, swords, trouble and conflict, walls, and ambition;

- The main arcana cards are the major breakthroughs, improvements, happenings, and life cycles, while the tiny arcane reflects everyday life's difficulties and opportunities;

- The reading of the tarot deck is typically performed in other ways of cards known as tarot spreads. This tarot diffusion describes and recognizes a particular scenario, such that the consumer often chooses the right tarot diffusion. There are three examples of readings transmitted on Celtic Cross; True Love Read readings, career path readings, and spreads of performance;

- Minor cards appear like cards for games. - the suit contains 14 cards, 2 to 10 are numbered, and the five are knight, queen, king, as and post;

- For tarot deck and tarot card read devices, the tarot card can be used everywhere. A beginner must choose a major mystic to learn tarot cards;

- Without instruction or spiritual authority, anybody can read and learn tarot cards. You only need to tap into your instincts and link to the best guide for tarot cards

Tarot Card Essentials

The creation of Tarot Cards is a topic of speculation. Nobody knows for sure when the first tarot card decks have been invented. Some scholars believe that tarot cards were originally created in the 15th century, while others claim that tarot developed in the early 1300s. Both accept that tarot cards originating in Italy were rendered as "Tarocchi" cards and used as play cards with no direct connection to divination or contemplation. During the XVIII century, tarot cards in France became extremely popular, and the French pronunciation of "taro" with a silent "t" was universally accepted.

A Catholic priest called Eliphas Levi used tarot cards in his mystical writings of sorcery during the late 18th and early 19th centuries. Levi learned in several languages (Hebrew, Jewish, Polish, Masonic, and Cabalism), as well as many scientific studies (Astronomy, Astrology, and Metaphysics). Levi practiced in different languages. Levi developed his own tarot card deck as a teaching tool to help his students study spiritual relations and self-awareness. He was the first person to include in a tarot card deck the four elements of nature, astrological patterns, and biblical parallels. The use of these symbols has definitely stood the test of time, and many new writers still use their symbols.

The Rider-Waite deck, which was first released in England about 1910, is the single most popular deck of tarot cards used today. Rider-Waite is a mixture of the name of the company (Rider Company of

London) and the name of the author (Arthur Edward Waite). An English mystic group called the "Hermetic Order of the Golden Dawn" became actively interested in the tarot research in the late 19th century. One of his leaders and founder, Arthur Edward Waite, who was born in America and trained in England, created a series of tarot cards that could be used to predict future events. Revolutionary was the Rider-Waite deck because each card represented an image telling a story. The cards were drawn by Pamela Coleman Smith, a fellow Golden Dawn designer. Her work influenced other tarot artists who followed.

Tarot Deck Essential Components

A full set of tarot cards is made up of 78 pieces. The' Minor Arcana ' forms of 56 of the cards and the remainder of the 22 cards are the' Major Arcana.' Arcana means hidden mystery. Arcana means lies.

The 56 Minor Arcana cards address issues of significance and relevance every day. They will additionally be listed in four suits as 14 cards (Ace to 10, plus four court cards). Every suit has to do with one of four natural elements: fire, water, earth, and air.

Each fit has its own unique features:

- The masculine dimension of Fire consists of a tarot suit with' Walls' symbolizing: behavior, desire, energy, imagination, spirit.

- A tarot suit of' Cups' reflects the feminine aspect of Water, and it depicts desires, thoughts, psychological abilities, and spiritual beliefs.

- The Air masculine dimension is depicted by the tarot ' Swords ' costume, symbolizing clear thinking, intelligence, creativity, and ideas.

- The Earth's feminine dimension is the tarot suit of "Pentacles," which symbolizes: everything of Earthly existence, body, safety, and life.

There are 14 cards in each suit that have their own symbolic meaning:

- **Ace**: Fresh Opportunities, Starting

- **Two**: Balance, Partnering

- **Three**: Trinity, Sorcery

- **Four**: Foundation, Completion

- **Five**: Unrest, Chaos

- **Six**: Perfection & Beauty

- **Seven**: Study, Spiritual Quest

- **Eight**: Infinity, Stability

- **Nine**: A Magic Number

- **Ten**: Harvest, Fulfillment

- **Pages**: Learning, Exploration

- **Knights**: Movement, Action

- **Queen**: Maturity, Depth

- **King**: Strength, Power

The 22 major Arcana cards speak about issues of fundamental significance and intent. Big cards of Arcana also tell stories of one's pursuit of existence and divine consciousness. Life experiences surpass the limits of time and space, which is shown in the Major Arcana cards. Big cards from Arcana are known as trump cards.

The usefulness of Tarot Cards

Tarot cards should be seen as a method to look at one's own existence and to achieve a positive perspective. The cards have no mysterious powers and are not likely to harm you or others when properly used. Tarot cards should be used to gain positive knowledge that can be helpful in everyday circumstances and difficulties. Tarot will show a higher degree of self-confidence, a new perspective, and a better understanding of your place in the world. Many tarot readers have mentioned acquiring experiences that have helped them better understand past events and eventually have allowed them to prevent recurring errors. Some tarot readers turn to cards to forecast events in the future. Often if your mind is open to new ideas, it alone is necessary to cause a positive change in your way of life.

Tarot Deck Care

On the website, you'll find all kinds of tips for taking care of your carts. Essentially, before the first usage, disinfecting the new card deck is best; this can be conveniently done by putting the deck on a window cover for 24 hours to clean the cards from Sun and Moon. You should then season your cards with them by remaining under your pillow for a few nights. In uses, the tarot should be covered and placed in a tissue (pouch) in a velvet cloth

Getting Started

In order to start your journey as a tarot card reader, you need to make sure you have all the material necessary. The first thing is a good guide, but you can cross this one off the list: you are currently reading it. What else?

Your First Tarot Deck

There is a debate regarding one's first deck of tarot cards and how they get it. Some readers defend that the first deck a person owns should never be purchased by themselves. Instead, it should be gifted to them. A few go even further, and state that you should not purchase any of your tarot decks, be it the first, second, or fiftieth one.

This belief comes from the superstition that if you purchase your own deck, not only will it not work, but it will bring bad luck into your life. This belief might have originated when the concept of tarot reading became more popular and even people who had no idea how to read cards would own a deck.

However, this has been proven to be a myth by people who have bought their own first tarot deck and did not experience any bad luck or faulty decks. Furthermore, it is essential for your work that you use a deck that resonates with you. If you wait for someone to give you such a deck... well, you might wait forever.

So, my suggestion is that you do what feels right for you. If you wish to wait for someone to offer you your first deck, that is definitely a choice you can make. If, on the contrary, you want to purchase it, there are a few tips you should follow:

- *Hold the cards and try them out* before you actually spend money on them. Your tarot cards should feel comfortable on your hands, and you should be able to maneuver them swiftly.

- *Make sure you like the illustrations on the cards, and you can easily recognize them*. Looking at your cards and liking what you see will make your job even more enjoyable. Being able to identify which card is which will simply make the readings a lot easier and smoother, and also give the querent a good impression of your work. This is not to say that you need to be able to know each card in a blink of an eye from the beginning: it takes practice. But having a deck that makes that task easier is a good tactic.

- *Choose the deck according to the learning method you will use.* The Rider-Waite one is great for people who want to consult as much information as possible, because it is the most popular and, consequently, the one that has the most resources. Although in today's age, with the fast-growing usage of the Internet, you will most likely find information about any type of tarot deck there is. However, some are more subjective and leave the art of reading more to the interpretation of the reader, so if you are the kind of person who typically learns by trial and error and by following your hunches, decks like those might be a more fitting choice for you. Having said that, it is important to mention that a lot of experts defend that the Rider-Waite method is a good choice for beginners and that, once you are more familiar with taromancy, you can explore other decks and take on new tarot challenges.

Should You Buy Second-Hand Tarot Cards?

This is another question that is up for debate. There is no doubt that buying a used deck has a financial advantage, as you will definitely not be spending as much money as you would on a new one (although there are new decks that are very low-cost).

The argument that some readers use against the purchase of second-hand tarot decks is that you can never be sure that you will be getting a good deck. One card less or two repeated cards, and your deck is useless. You will always be taking a risk.

So, a lot of card readers opt for new decks, opening exceptions for rare or vintage decks (which can be more expensive than regular unused decks, so they don't even really count for this debate). Once again, my advice is that you do what feels right to you at this point in your journey as a reader.

Your Tarot Journal

There are two sides to every coin and tarot reading is not an exception. If each card has its own pre-assigned meaning, there is also a certain subjectivity to it. Your journal is precisely what allows you to explore the subjective side of tarot and use your personal learnings to evolve as a card reader.

I am of the opinion that every reader should keep a journal from the moment they start their path into the world of tarot.

This way, you can confirm or disprove your hunches and have a better understanding of what you need to work on in order to improve. Furthermore, you can always look back and have an overall perception of your progress as a reader. Because it is the most personal thing that you can actually keep from your learnings, this tarot journal also gains an emotional charge and, in a few years from now, it will be something you will enjoy looking back at.

Once you have your tarot journal, the most important question arises: what type of information should you write down in it? Well, in short, you should write everything that comes to you from your personal experience and interpretations when you are practicing. Specifically, a few of those things would be:

- *Notes about tarot exercises*. Again, just like in school! In the first phase of your learning process, you will be doing a lot of exercises, more than actually practicing the art form on other people. You will learn a lot of new things, possibly even things that you did not read in your guide, so it's a good idea to write them down.

- ***Your own take on the meanings of each card***. As you do readings, you will see some cards come up in circumstances where their traditional meaning does not really apply, but another version of it, a version that comes from your intuition, does. These new meanings that you create for each situation are important to write down because they allow you to create your "tarot dictionary", also these new found meanings personalize your readings a lot more.

- ***Tarot spreads***, i.e. the way you lay out the cards that come up. This is important because each position in the pattern of cards has a specific meaning and, although, there are established spreads that every card reader knows, you can create your own layouts.

Pieces to Set the Mood

This is completely optional, but a lot of readers like to prepare the space where they will be practicing tarot, just so it is special to them and inviting to others. During this first stage, when you are still learning the basics of tarot, this might not seem that important; however, once you start reading cards for other people, you should take the time to turn your tarot reading spot into a place that is comfortable both for you and your client.

A few things that tarot readers typically like to have are candles, incense, sage, crystals, and pendulums. Some people like to play relaxing music in the background, and others like to keep a window open so that the air flows inside the room. There are no rules as to what you should buy for your tarot spot: you should simply set it up in a way that oozes good energy and a positive atmosphere.

Important Concepts to be Familiar

Upright Tarot Card vs. Reversed Tarot Card

By now, you have read the two expressions: upright tarot cards and reserved tarot cards, several times, but I have yet to explain the difference between them.

When you flip a card and it lands in an upright position to you, this card has a meaning (upright tarot card). However, it can also land upside down, which changes the meaning of this card (reversed tarot card). It might seem logical to think that those meanings would be the opposite of each other, but as you will soon see, that does not always have to be the case.

Upright Cards

Upright cards are the ones that every single tarot reader knows and uses. Those who exclusively read upright cards make sure that each card on their deck is facing the same direction before they shuffle them.

Reading these cards is a lot more straightforward than the reversed ones because they give you information on more of a surface level. This means that it is easier to apply and adjust the cards' upright pre-assigned meaning to the querent's particular question(s). This is also why it is advised that new readers start by learning the upright cards and then, if they wish, add the reversed ones to their reading sessions.

Reversed Cards

Not every tarotist reads reserved tarot cards. The main reason for this is that reversed cards are often associated with negative readings (although, as you will see, this all depends on how the reader interprets them). Others simply consider that the 78 upright cards provide enough information for their reading sessions, and so there is no need to add another 78.

However, those who do read reversed cards reap the benefits; they give more depth to your readings, simply for the fact that they give you more information, therefore allowing you to get to conclusions that otherwise, you maybe wouldn't get to.

If you decide you want to incorporate reversed cards into your readings, all you need to do is change the way you shuffle your cards. A good technique is to have all the cards facing the same direction, then dividing it (around 75% of the deck on one hand and the other 25% on the other hand), turning the smaller group of cards upside down, and shuffling it well.

After you analyze the pros and cons of reversed cards, it is up to you to decide what you want to do. I believe, however, that you will never know for sure if you don't at least give it a try, so even if you don't think you will be the kind of reader who uses reversed cards, consider doing it just once or twice.

It is also important to mention that sticking to upright cards does not make you a worse reader: it is your ability to interpret cards and apply them to the client's situation, this is what determines how good you are at your art.

Your journey as a tarot reader does not always have to follow the same patterns; in fact, it probably won't! If one day you decide you want to start using reversed cards, or if you want to use them in certain readings, that is completely okay. You should follow your intuition and do what feels right whenever it feels right.

Tarot Spreads

So, tarot spreads refer to the patterns in which the reader arranges the cards. This is a very important concept in the world of tarot because each position in these patterns provides a different meaning to a card, so it greatly influences the conclusions that the reader comes to.

There are countless different tarot spreads, which is not surprising, considering the fact that readers can create their own spreads. However, some are used more often than others.

Astrology

Astrology is the study of the stars, the Solar System, and the impact that those have on people's moods and personality. So, astrologists look at what the position of those cosmic objects were at the exact time that a person was born, and from there, they are able to conclude how it has/will shape them as individuals.

Although astrologists have, at one point in history, been considered to be mathematicians, astrology cannot exactly be considered a science, since there is no actual proof of the correlation between the position of cosmic bodies and the personality of a person. Instead, astrology is commonly said to be a metaphysical study, because it deals with matters that go beyond what we can prove scientifically.

We all know our zodiac signs and we have all read our horoscopes: these are based on the astrology that those signs are assigned and this is how the predictions are made! Cohering to when they were born, people have one of 12 zodiac signs, which are divided into 4 groups: Earth, Water, Fire and Air.

So is there any connection between astrology and tarot? Yes! In fact, the two philosophies are very much intertwined, in several different ways:

- They are both based on the astral world.

- A lot of tarot spreads created when the Order of the Golden Dawn (i.e., an esoteric order that had a big focus on both spirituality and astrology) gained popularity have the shape of constellations.

- There is a Major Arcana tarot card associated with each zodiac sign; Aries with The Emperor, Taurus with The Hierophant, Gemini with The Lovers, Cancer with The Chariot, Leo with Strength, Virgo with The Hermit, Libra with Justice, Scorpio with Death, Sagittarius with Temperance, Capricorn with The Death, Aquarius with the Star and Pisces with The Moon.

- The four suits of the Minor Arcana are related to the four groups of signs.

Chapter 2: Getting acquainted with your deck

Selecting the deck

The tarot consists of many symbols derived from a myriad of human consciousness. All those decks are out there are available for you to use and have got their own unique set of symbols and system. Out of these symbols, you will be creating your personal stories in your readings. It is therefore significant and more practical on your part to choose a deck that resonates with you. For most beginners, the Rider-Waite deck is a great and easy way to start.

If you are preparing your tarot cards, it means there is something you need to know. Most people run to seek answers to many uncertainties they are facing at the moment. When using these tarot cards correctly, they could help you see and consider other perspectives so you can move towards the best possible way.

Consider what you want to learn from your tarot reading like "What's the best career move to take?" In reading the tarot cards, it's best to acknowledge that the tarot is not a tool to reveal a fixed future, but add-ons that can help you explore your unconscious inner self. It is a tool provided to project your hidden perceptions of things.

There is a wide range of Tarot decks to choose from, and many tarot practitioners prefer the Rider-Waite Tarot deck as they believe that the energy emitted by each card is more clearly compared to other card decks. For those practitioners drawn to white witchcraft and for people indulging in religion with beliefs based on nature, they can use the Tarot of the Old Path.

It is crucial that you choose a Tarot Deck that you can work comfortably with. Some superstitious beliefs are going around that you should not buy your tarot deck, but it should be given to you as a gift from someone. It, however, depends on how superstitious you are.

Reading for yourself

Creating a Sacred Space

One significant aspect of Tarot Reading is creating a sacred place where you can conduct your tarot reading activity. The area should be undisturbed and free from negative energies so you can have a better chance to resonate well with your cards.

Make sure the place which you have chosen is far from various city noises like noise from the streets, radio, karaoke, the barking of dogs or industrial sounds like someone hammering, welding, drilling, etc. Any distractions from people, things, or animals will blow away the connection you are establishing with your cards while reading them.

In designing your sacred place, listen to your perception of how it should appear and how you feel towards space, the Tarot cards, the sense of spirituality, and many more. The decoration may differ on the user as others may be using crystals, plant and silk scarves while other may be hanging New Age picture on the wall. Regardless of your choices, make sure that it coordinates with your spirituality.

Shuffle and Reset your Cards

While handling and shuffling your cards, you are in fact connecting physically with your deck. While using your intuition in your reading, you are establishing a deep connection with the cards. You may shuffle it once, but you may also shuffle it as many times as you want to get the cards "cleared." Cutting the deck into 3s enables you to reorder these cards in the pack. When you are ready, lay these cards face down.

Using tarot spreads provides you with a structure that serves as a basis for exploring answers to your queries. Every position of cards in the Spread signifies an aspect of your question. You don't have to use them in your every reading, but they can be a great way to get you started on your learning. The simplest reading spread that can help you get familiarized with the cards is the past-present-and-future spread. To start, slowly reveal each cards beginning with the card on top of the shuffled deck.

Give it a Try Using the 3-Card Tarot Spread

In time, you can develop confidence in your readings. Before trying to interpret the meaning of individual cards, scan over your cards and try to absorb whatever reactions you have to the images presented before you. Check your emotions and see how you feel towards the objects, colors, and symbols if there are any. Be openly aware of these things as you continue going through the spread.

Getting Tarot Meanings from Cards and Their Positions

While just starting out, you need a reference guide to help you get along. Usually, when you purchase your deck, it comes along with a reference guide. If you can't find it with your Tarot card, then try checking online resources to guide you in finding meanings. In this book, we have prepared a guide for your reference.

In trying to say something about the cards lying before you, then you have to consider the meaning of the cards about the question or query you are exploring. Tarot readings usually involve interpreting a random selection of events and providing them with definitions.

Rituals are essential in processing events and even if you are skeptical about this, treating your cards with respect and knowing its significance and value changes the way you perceive the world and things in it.

As you continue with the reading process, be grateful. At the end of your activity, clear your cards and store it in a safe and secure location.

How to Practice & Basic Exercises

Now that you have the material you need to start learning, and know some of the basic concepts that are typically mentioned when the topic is taromancy, it is time to actually start practicing.

Before you start doing reading sessions for other people, it is crucial that you familiarize yourself with the cards, which you can achieve by doing some exercises. When you do these five exercises, don't forget to grab your tarot journal and write down any information that you think is relevant.

5 Basic Exercises with a Tarot Deck

Exercise 1: Card Observation

The first exercise has four steps, and it could not be more straightforward. The goal is for you to really take your time to become accustomed to the imagery on each card, and to find out what each of them represents to you, beyond their pre-assigned meaning.

- Get one of the cards in your deck and look at it for 30 seconds.

- Write down in your journal the thoughts that came to your mind during that first observation.

- Go back to the card, and this time, look at it for a couple of minutes, truly paying attention to the details in the illustration.

- Create a story inspired by that card. Try to fill at least one page of the journal, to give as much detail as you can on the story and to become wiser at the end of each one.

There is no right or wrong when it comes to this observation exercise since it is purely based on your perception of each card.

Exercise 2: One Card, Several Questions

- Write down 5 questions in your tarot journal.

- Shuffle your deck and take one card.

- Use that card to answer each of the questions you wrote down.

By doing this, you will practice your ability to adjust one card and its pre-assigned definition to each situation. It might happen that you cannot seem to find a way of using a specific card to answer a specific question, especially on your first try. But, don't let it discourage you. Step away from it for a while and give it another try the next day or even a couple of days later.

Exercise 3: Negative Cards

Because the interpretation of the cards is something personal and subjective, you might get a negative vibe from some of the cards in your deck. This exercise allows you to explore that feeling.

- Take a look at all the cards in the deck and grab the ones that make you feel any negative emotion.

- Write down why you think that particular card makes you feel that way. This can be as simple as you associating the colors in the illustration to a certain gloomy emotion, or as deep as the card reminding you of a traumatic experience from your past.

- Try to think of the other side of the coin: in which type of situation could this card actually mean something positive?

Exercise 4: Connecting a Card to a Loved One

This exercise helps you understand the characteristics of each card by associating it to someone you know in real life, which can be a great way of making it easy for you to memorize the key points of each card.

- Take a card from your tarot deck.

- Write down the name of the card and who it reminds you of, that could be someone from your group of friends, a family member or even a coworker. Write down why you made that association and what the card and the person have in common.

Exercise 5: Use the Major Arcana Cards to tell the story of your life

This fifth exercise will require more time and dedication, but it can create an even deeper connection between you and your deck. What you will be doing with this is creating your own Fool's Journey (i.e., the story that the 22 cards of the Major Arcana tell).

- Think about the most relevant happenings in your life, both positive and negative, and what has shaped you the most throughout your time on Earth.

- Look at your cards, and associate them with the different stages you have gone through. You don't have to use every single card, just choose the ones that make sense.

Reading Tarot Cards: A Step-by-Step

At some point, you will start actually reading the tarot cards. You should start by practicing that process on yourself, writing down in your tarot journal what you can improve, as well as any relevant thoughts or feelings you have during your practice. This will make the whole process smoother, and it will also help you understand if you are ready to start reading other people's tarot or if you still need to train a little bit more.

After you have done it for yourself a few times, try to do a reading for someone you are close with. It has to be someone you feel completely comfortable with, otherwise, you may not give it your all during the reading, which will sub sequentially affect your performance.

After this, and if that is your goal, the time has come where you will start doing readings for strangers and maybe even profiting from it. This is a big leap, so it is important that you don't rush your learning journey to get to this point. Tarot readers don't have the best reputation and there are a lot of skeptics. You should not start doing readings for strangers simply because you want to start making money from it: you will be just another scam and it will not be advantageous for you in the long run.

So, only take that step when you feel ready and confident that you have enough knowledge and practice to be able to make every single reading session count. Each client should leave their session feeling like their money was well spent and like they have gained something that will help them solve a certain situation in their life.

Now, no matter if you are doing it to yourself, a loved one or a client you have never met before, the process of reading tarot cards involves at least 7 steps. I say at least because some readers create their own rituals and that might result in some additional steps. For now, I say you stick to these seven. With time, you might notice the need to add some of your own, but that will come to you naturally.

As usual, don't forget to have your tarot journal with you every time you do a reading.

1. Get in the right mindset

It is important that you prepare yourself before the reading and that you are in the right place mentally to accept and decipher whatever the cards tell you. A good technique to get into the right mindset is by doing some simple, but mindful breathing exercises.

You can ask for guidance while you do it or imagine everything that is worrying you getting out of your body as you exhale. As you progress in your practice, you can also add a personal touch to this first step, such as saying a mantra that resonates with you, lighting incense or playing music that calms you down.

2. Ask a specific question

Once you feel prepared to start, it is time to ask the question. What do you need help with? What do you want to know at the end of this reading?

As a beginner, you should try to ask specific questions, so that it is easier for you to look at a card and gather what your intuition is telling you. The clearer the question, the easier it will be for you to understand how the card relates to it. With time, you will be able to tackle more general questions. To exemplify, a specific question would be "Should I take the new job opportunity that has been offered to me?" while a broader one would be "What impact would the acceptance of this opportunity have in my life?"

3. Shuffle your deck

During this first phase, I suggest you read upright cards only, so you should shuffle your cards as you would with any regular ones. A lot of decks are bigger than the regular playing ones so it might take you a while to get a hold of the technique. However, practice makes perfect! Once you master the regular way of shuffling your tarot cards, you can move on to more complicated techniques.

Shuffling your cards will remove any energies from the other readings that were stuck in your deck, and that is extremely important for the current one to be as accurate as possible.

4. Cut the deck

The way you cut the deck will depend on which spread you will use for the reading. For your first few sessions, go for a simple 2-card spread:

Put your shuffled deck on the table, with the cards facing down.

Divide it into two piles and place them next to each other on the table. Some say that you should do this using your left hand because it is closer to your heart or because this hand is controlled by the right side of the brain. Others state that you should do it with your non-dominant hand, since you don't have as much control over that hand, it is less likely that you will use your conscious mind to impact the process. Just like with a lot of other choices you will have to make in your tarot journey, I say you use the hand that feels right to you.

Once you have these two piles, turn over the top card on the right pile.

5. Notice what you first feel when you see the card

Now, the actual reading begins. What did your intuition say when you first saw the card that came up? In your journal, you can write down some key words that came to your mind the moment you turned the card over and saw which one it was.

6. Observe the card in more detail

Once you wrote down your first impression of the card, it is time for you look at it in detail. Observe the colors, shapes, characters and the action that is taking place. Write down what each of those things makes you feel, and how they possibly relate to the question.

7. Close the tarot reading

You shouldn't end a reading session by simply putting the deck aside and moving on with your day. A few things you should always do; shuffling your deck one more time, thanking your cards for the guidance they provided you with and carefully putting back the deck in its package, making sure you don't damage it and that it is properly protected.

This is another step where you can create your own rituals, with a closing mantra or some mindful exercises, for example.

Chapter 3: Beginning the Minor Arcana

It can certainly be tempting to spend all your time studying the Major Arcana cards, but seeing as they are vastly outnumbered by the suit cards in the deck, collectively referred to as the Minor Arcana, the chances that you'll encounter suit cards in any spread is quite high. Within the context of a spread, the cards of the Major Arcana can be weighed more heavily, or viewed as more important to the ultimate interpretation; you might think of them as major plot points within a story, whereas the cards of the Minor Arcana make up sub-plots and contextual histories. Still, the Minor Arcana cards cannot be ignored or disregarded; they help to translate the meanings of the Major Arcana cards from generalized concepts to useful and specific advice for the querent.

Luckily, there are some tricks you can use to decipher the meanings of the fifty-six cards in the Minor Arcana that will spare you the trouble of having to memorize each and every one. Regardless of the deck's style, whether it includes unique illustrations or simply abstract designs, each card in the Minor Arcana will have a suit and number. The suit's each correspond with an element, and the numbers all bear their own significance. By combining them, even novices can make some sense out of a suit card without having any preconceived notion of its meaning.

The Suits

The four suits of the Minor Arcana are Cups, Wands, Swords, and Pentacles. There are fourteen cards within each suit: an ace, two, three, four, five, six, seven, eight, nine and ten, as well as four Court Cards.

Bear in mind that the suits may be defined differently, especially in older decks. Historically, as tarot cards were used during the oppressive rule of the Roman Catholic church, which would not condone symbols of paganism, mysticism, or the occult, a suit of coins would be typically found in a tarot deck, in place of pentagrams, and you'd be much more likely to find a suit of staves, batons, or even polo clubs, rather than wands.

The Suit of Cups

All cards in this suit can be associated with the element of water. They largely correspond to our fluid emotions, feelings, and relationships.

The Suit of Wands

This suit is associated with the element of fire and represents action and passion, both creative and destructive in nature.

The Suit of Swords

These cards are correlated to the element of air and represent intangible ideas, truth, intellectual conflict, and physical, moral, or mental anguish.

The Suit of Pentacles

665

This suit is connected to the element of earth; having formerly been represented by coins in place of pentagrams, the cards concern practical matters such as finances, work, home, the body, and the essentials for living (sustenance, shelter, and safety).

How to Interpret Numbers in Suit Cards

It's important to remember that these meanings correlate to all of the numbers within the deck, not just the suit cards; these interpretations don't necessarily need to be applied to the cards of the Major Arcana, but with further study of numerology, Tarot readers can gain an even deeper understanding of all cards.

Furthermore, the direction of these cards and placement within a spread can impact meaning. For example, while a Four card would typically represent stability, if it is reversed, this might indicate just the opposite, and reference volatility or a weak foundation. Alternatively, if an upright Seven card usually represents a difficulty or challenge, a reversed Seven could indicate that something the querent expected to struggle with will actually turn out to be fairly easy.

Numbers

The Ace, or one, card means a new beginning or a fresh start. It may reference an opportunity, new relationship, or birth.

The Two card represents duality, division or union, choice, and dichotomy. It can point to relationship issues, forks in the road, mirror reflections, or repetition.

The Three card is related to creativity and growth. One obvious example of this is reproduction, or birth, turning a couple into a family; but this can also reference artistic creation, building, or personal development.

The Four card indicates stability, strength, and a steady foundation. It often references institutions, such as schools, churches, or even family units.

The Five card is about volatile change, conflict, or difficulty. Think of a person who feels like a fifth wheel on a double date; their presence creates tension in what would otherwise be a comfortable, stable, predictable situation.

The Six card means harmony, peace, balance, and contentment. It can also point to abundance, fulfillment, and satisfaction.

The Seven card signifies a challenge, hurdle, difficulty or struggle. As compared to the Five card, this signifies a problem that is more complex, without an easy solution. While the Five represents a state of discomfort that prompts change, the Seven refers to a lasting struggle that prompts introspection. It may help to think of Five as a representation of institutional problems, or group issues, while Seven references a problem that is personal to the querent.

The Eight card represents works come to fruition, manifestation, achievement, and accomplishment. It can also signify forward momentum, progress, and satiety. It is not only a representation of success and positivity, though; it can also point to situations that the querent once recognized as disasters waiting to happen, finally resulting in catastrophe, as expected.

The Nine card speaks to endings, both positive and negative; it can mean successful completion or devastation in the form of loss. Either way, it typically references an ending that leads to some form of isolation (in the Rider-Waite deck, every Nine card features an illustration of a solitary figure), heightened awareness of the self, and reliance on personal strength, wisdom, and resilience.

The Ten card also references endings, though it speaks to more permanent, conclusive endings than the Nine card. It can represent an ultimate manifestation or culmination of work, total completion, finality. It might help to think of the Nine card as representative of the negative or pessimistic side of an ending, while the Ten card represents positivity and optimism of a new beginning; see Nine as the grief of loss or death, while Ten holds the promise of rebirth.

Combining suit and number for a formulaic interpretation

Novice cartomancers can get a rough feel for the meanings of numbered suit cards by combining the significance of the card's suit and number. Let's try a few examples below.

Two of Cups - The number represents duality, union or division, and choice. The suit references emotion and love. Layered together, these elements point toward a loving relationship or strong emotional connection between two people. The context of the spread and the querent's prompt will help the reader to discern whether these references a romantic, platonic, familial, or professional connection. If the card is facing upright, it will likely denote some positive development in the relationship; if reversed, this card may imply a division, conflict, or split.

Four of Swords - The number represents stability and fortitude. The suit is associated with intellect and conflict. Combining these notions, we can see that the card signifies intellectual strength or mental stability, possibly in the face of a challenge or hardship. The true meaning of the card takes this interpretation a step further; by reading the illustration of the card, which portrays a figure laid to rest in what appears to be a church, we can discern that this card points to an extended period of thought and introspection that is involuntary, probably prompted by physical incapacitation. This is precisely why novices will be able to learn more from illustrated decks like Rider-Waite Tarot, rather than a deck that uses abstract designs for the numbered suit cards.

Seven of Wands - The number signifies strife and hardship, while the suit implies passionate action, and creative energy. When we put these two concepts together, we can see this card represents an individual who is rolling up their sleeves to tackle a problem, ready to think outside of the box to find a solution, prepared to work hard to fix whatever is broken. It may also imply courage under fire.

Nine of Pentacles, and Ten of Pentacles - The numbers both represent completion in a sense; the Nine references an ending for the individual, while the Ten represents the total culmination of efforts. The suit, in this case, symbolizes practical matters, finances, physical health, and values. So we might then discern that the Nine of Pentacles symbolizes a person who has finally earned enough money to afford a vacation, retreat, or day of self-care; meanwhile, we could interpret the Ten of Pentacles card as a representative of a jackpot or windfall, company bonus or lottery winning. The Nine of Pentacles points to an individual who is pausing to enjoy the fruits of their labors, while the Ten of Pentacles points to a collective accomplishment that results in abundant rewards for all parties involved. Once again, the illustrations of these cards help to clarify the distinction.

The Court Cards

The specific titles of court cards can vary greatly from one deck to the next. The Rider-Waite deck includes a Page, Knight, Queen and King for each of the four suits, but by contrast, Crowley's Book of Thoth deck recasts them as a Princess, Prince, Queen, and Knight, in respective order of status. The Page is sometimes referred to as the Knave in older historical decks. Many modern decks aim to use gender-neutral titles for these cards or to invert traditional gender norms by making the Queen the highest status card, for example, or replacing all four characters with female titles. Regardless of their titles and genders, though, each Court Card is meant to represent a certain archetypal character, or personality type, that exists within the querent's life.

There are several different ways to read the Court Cards, which is where the personality, experience level, and intuitive gift of the reader factor into the interpretation of any spread. Many experienced cartomancers agree that the Court Cards usually represent specific people in the querent's life or archetypal characters. Interestingly, there are sixteen Court Cards in the Tarot deck, and they appear to roughly correspond to the sixteen different Myers-Briggs Personality Trait Indicator (or MBTI) types--though this is hardly an exact science, and opinions on card-MBTI connections vary.

While the Court Cards are typically drawn as detailed characters with distinctive features, it helps to bear in mind that they represent types of personalities, which can come in almost any physical form. A Queen of Cups card could easily represent a man, just as the King of Swords could denote a female in the querent's life.

Perhaps the easiest way to develop an understanding of the Court Cards is to think of them as formulaic combinations; they are each defined by their suit's element, their rank or status, and their masculine or feminine energy.

The four suits correspond to the four elements: swords to air, cups to water, fire to wands, and earth to pentacles or coins.

Each rank also corresponds to one of the four elements: Kings are linked to air, Queens to water, Knights to fire, and Pages to earth.

The elemental energy of air is control. A person ruled by the air element is usually clever, philosophical, and eccentric; carefree, optimistic, and charming; they may also be independent, selfish, and callous.

The elemental energy of water is understanding. A character ruled by water can be deeply emotional, compassionate, and intuitive; merciful, passive, and flexible; kind-hearted, introspective, and selfless to a fault; but also fickle, irrational, and deceptively powerful.

The elemental energy of fire is action. Someone ruled by the element of fire is typically bold, passionate, and charismatic; creative, adventurous, and courageous; lustful, irritable, and volatile; sometimes even violent and destructive.

The elemental energy of earth is acceptance. A person ruled by the earth element is usually practical, level-headed, and rational; emotionally stable, consistent, and responsible; respectful, humble, and sometimes a bit dull-spirited; open to learning and ready to do hard work to achieve end goals.

We can also correlate the Court Card ranks to their degree of maturity or experience. This is not a direct reference to literal age--the old can be quite childish, while the young can be wise beyond their years.

Additionally, we can link the masculine and feminine identities of the Court Cards to their yin and yang energies. The masculine Court Cards (Kings and Knights) can be thought of as active and assertive, while the feminine Court Cards (Queens and Pages, even if the Pages are drawn as men) can be considered passive and receptive.

Take the Page of Pentacles, for instance. The Page's rank correlates to the elemental energy of earth (practical, rational, eager to learn, accepting); his rank also implies that he is inexperienced, with a youthful spirit; finally, though he is portrayed in the Rider-Waite deck as a man, we can associate the rank of the Page with feminine energy, meaning he is passive and receptive. So without even knowing his suit, we can discern that this character is probably a hard worker, and due to his inexperience, a dedicated learner, open to receiving whatever wisdom the universe can offer him. Since his suit is Pentacles, or Coins, which often pertains to financial matters, we can look at the Page as a student or entrepreneur on the verge of success. He is a sign of good fortune soon to come, and he is able to receive it and put it to practical use.

Furthermore, you can deepen your understanding of the court cards by encapsulating the above formula within the suit element. For example, the King of Cups has elemental energy defined by his rank (King=air), a high level of maturity or experience, also due to his rank, and will tend to be assertive due to his gender. Typically, we might look at this formula and imagine a powerful person who is cocky, impulsive, perhaps even insensitive and selfish. But if we remember that this formula is also impacted by the suit element, we see that this personality exists within the context of water; this powerful, experienced, assertive personality is influenced by emotion, intuition, introspection, and passivity. The King of Cups can then be seen as a mature, authoritative, and bold person who has chosen to use his (or her) power for love, compassion, and selflessness.

These formulas can always be useful for cartomancers who prefer not to rely on strict memorization or rigid definitions of cards, as they leave a great deal of room for the reader to exercise their personal judgment and intuition. When there are no illustrations to rely upon, readers may fail to grasp the nuance of their meanings, or easily lose track of the contextual implications that influence the card's interpretation.

The Suit of Cups

All cards within the Suit of Cups are correlated to the element of water, and reference emotion, love, relationships, compassion, and intuition. Both the Suit and its corresponding element are typically considered feminine, but this does not mean that these cards couldn't represent men or non-binary individuals.

In any spread, it's important to stay mindful of the fact that the cards of this suit reference feelings--they don't necessarily reflect behaviors or objective truth. As an example, a querent asking the Tarot deck for guidance in a romantic relationship might become dejected after receiving the Five of Cups and Seven of Cups, implying a change of heart and a conflict, as well as the reversed Two of Cups, implying a choice and division. Cumulatively, these cards point to a schism in the relationship. Perhaps a lover is tempted to stray from their partner in favor of a new love--that seems like the obvious interpretation, doesn't it?

At this point, though, the reader should recognize that these cards are all within the Suit of Cups, and may only signify feelings rather than actions. If none of the other cards within the spread support the idea of infidelity or a breakup in the near future, it's entirely possible that these cards are simply pointing out the querent's fear of losing their love to someone else. They may be warning against a self-fulfilling prophecy; if the querent fears adultery and allows this fear to impact their behavior, they may unwittingly end up driving their lover into the arms of someone else. Alternatively, these three Cup cards may explain that the querent's partner is physically committed to the current relationship, but struggling to integrate it with a change of heart in another walk of life: say, for instance, that the querent's partner wants to follow a job opportunity to a new home on the other side of the world, and doesn't know how to do this while maintaining the relationship. This story fits the three aforementioned cards just as well as a story of temptation and faithlessness.

Finally, depending on how many cards are included in your total spread, you may want to count up the number of cards laid from each suit. If the spread is overwhelmingly dominated by upright Cup cards, this can indicate that whatever the situation or prompt, the querent will need to connect deeply to their emotional body and trust in their intuition moving forward. It may also be a sign that the overall outcome will be determined by emotional reactions rather than rational thought or practical decisions. By contrast, if the spread is overwhelmed by reversed Cup cards, this might warn the querent that their emotions about the situation at hand will ultimately prove to be inconsequential, or that emotion is getting in the way of progress and resolution.

Always remember: context is key.

The Ace of Cups

Upright - A new emotional beginning; new love or a relationship progressing to another stage of intimacy; creativity.

Reversed - Emotional blockage or repression; unrequited love; creative stagnation.

Symbolism - This card shows a hand reaching out of a cloud, a symbol of divine gifts. A single cup rests in its upward facing palm, representing the Holy Grail--the ultimate symbol of love, devotion, and creativity. There is a dove above it, dropping a communion wafer into the chalice; the dove is a symbol of hope, peace, and healing, while the wafer references transformation. The hand and cup float above a pond with lotus flowers floating upon the water's surface; lotus flowers are a symbol of renewal, growth, and beauty.

Two of Cups

Upright - Mutual attraction; committed partnerships; strong love (romantic, platonic, or familial); stable union.

Reversed - Conflict; distrust; miscommunication; self-absorption; discord; schisms, splits, and breakups.

Symbolism - Two figures (a male and female) stand opposite one another; each holds a cup in one hand and reaches for the other with their free arm. Above them between the cups, is the Caduceus symbol, which references the staff of Hermes; it is also a modern symbol to represent western medicine, so it points to the healing powers of love. Above Caduceus is a winged lion's head, a representation of passion, courage, justice, and majesty.

Three of Cups

Upright - Joy and celebration; playfulness and creativity; gatherings and collaborations; "the more, the merrier" attitude; sharing happiness and spreading the love; supportive community.

Reversed - Overindulgence; hangovers, both literal and figurative; broken friendships and disjointed social circles; craving solitude.

Symbolism - Three women in bright colored robes dance together in a circle, each raising their cups high in the air. They wear floral wreaths, which denote victory and accomplishment. They are surrounded by grape vines, fruits, and a pumpkin, all of which represent a harvest, the reaping of rewards, and bountiful gifts from the divine.

Four of Cups

Upright - Solitude and introspection; emotional unavailability or withdrawal; apathy; disinterest; closed-mindedness; rejection.

Reversed - A comeback; seized opportunities; optimism, open-mindedness, and enthusiasm.

Symbolism - A young man sits at the base of a tree, arms crossed over his chest and eyes pointed towards the ground. You can tell by his body language that he is not open to giving or receiving love at this point in time. Before him, three cups are lined up and sit untouched, perhaps symbolizing that he has already emptied them, or that he has no interest in their contents. A fourth cup is offered to him by a phantom hand reaching through the clouds--a divine gift!--but he appears not to it.

Five of Cups

Upright - Melancholy; heartbreak; loss; regret; disappointment; anguish; sorrow; grief.

Reversed - Forgiving yourself; accepting losses; surrender; letting go of the past and moving on.

Symbolism - A solitary figure stands in a black mourning cloak, back turned towards us as he stares down at three spilled cups on the ground, either oblivious to the two upright cups behind him or willfully ignoring them. There is a castle in the distance, on the opposite side of a river, and a bridge leading there, symbolizing long-term goals, and the fact that this tragedy will eventually be a distant memory; in time, everything becomes water under the bridge.

Six of Cups

Upright - Childlike attitudes; pleasant strolls down memory lane; nostalgia and joy.

Reversed - Stuck in the past; holding grudges; rigidly following traditions with no room for playfulness, innovation, or experimentation.

Symbolism - Two children play in a garden beside a house; the older boy offers the younger girl a cup that holds a blooming flower. The house behind them represents stability, safety, and security. Behind them, a guard patrols the city, protecting them from external dangers and enabling their carefree playtime. The flowers symbolize youthfulness and growth.

Seven of Cups

Upright - Choices and decisions; wishful thinking; lofty ambitions; day-dreaming; abundant opportunities.

Reversed - Urgency of choice; if you do not pick one option soon, you may forfeit all of your opportunities.

Symbolism - A figure stands with his back to us; before him are seven cups, each spilling over with a different symbol: a face, which symbolizes either youth or love; a castle, symbolizing security and power; a wreath, representing victory; a snake, representing intrigue or temptation; a wyvern or dragon, standing for wrathful power; a pile of golden coins, symbolizing wealth and riches; and a shrouded figure with arms splayed wide, signifying spiritual enlightenment. These seven options may correlate to each of the seven deadly sins referenced in the bible.

Eight of Cups

Upright - Satiety, exhaustion, or boredom; walking away or moving on; abandonment, escapism, and wanderlust.

Reversed - A return; inability to let go; giving it one last shot; overstaying your welcome; biding time.

Symbolism - Eight cups are stacked upon a shoreline as a solitary figure ventures off, walking stick in hand, leaving the cups behind. The moon hangs overhead, a symbol of fluctuation and the cyclical nature of change. The figure seems to be heading towards mountains in the distance, implying that they are ready and eager to tackle challenges; change is often an uphill battle, but in this instance, difficulty is preferable to the sense of ease, comfort, and boredom being left behind.

Nine of Cups

Upright - Personal success and satisfaction; contentment; wealth and luxury; self-care; wishes fulfilled.

Reversed - Be careful what you wish for because you might get a whole lot of it; overindulgence; dissatisfaction; desire as a bottomless cup.

Symbolism - A man sits with his arms folded and a broad smile on his face; behind him, nine cups are lined up in a row upon an altar. His crossed arms show us that he has all needs and cannot receive anything more; his smile tells us that he is satisfied, and his feathered cap is a testament to his ambition, hard work, and well-deserved success.

Ten of Cups

Upright - The rewards you've waited your whole life for; true love; blessings; triumph; homecoming; joyful unions; alignment, coincidence, and synchronicity; bliss; spiritual fulfillment or nirvana.

Reversed - Missed connections; misalignment and misunderstandings; familial and romantic discord; deep social schisms. This can also reference the feeling of having everything you ever wanted, and still feeling incomplete or dissatisfied.

Symbolism - A family stands on a grassy plain beside a river, beneath a rainbow of cups. The mother and father each have one arm wrapped around their partner while the other arm reaches up towards the sky in gratitude and appreciation. The rainbow symbolizes glory, beauty, and divine blessings. The parents' collective stance displays both romantic and spiritual love. Beside them, their two children hold hands and dance joyfully, symbolizing innocence, hope, new beginnings, and the notion of coming full circle.

Page of Cups

Upright - The page is young and inexperienced, but deeply attuned to his emotions and intuitions. He is creative, curious, romantic, sensitive, naive and idealistic. He aims to spread the message of love, truth, and happiness. This card signifies new opportunities and new relationships.

Reversed - Hypersensitivity, immaturity, and refusal to be rational. This reversed card can also point to a failure to listen to or honor one's intuition.

Symbolism - The page stands with one hand on his hip; on the other hand, he holds a chalice with a fish peeking out over its brim. Much like the crayfish in the Moon card, this fish represents subconscious knowledge rising up from the murky depths and breaking the surface. Listen to your inner voice!

Knight of Cups

Upright - This character may have been the inspiration for the Prince Charming in your favorite fairy tale. He is romantic, noble, bold and valiant, and extremely charming. This card doesn't just reference love--it points to a romantic journey, or spiritual quest, as the Knight's rank is associated with active energy and inexperience. He's going places and winning plenty of hearts along the way.

Reversed - The reversed Knight of Cups calls to mind the feeling we get when something that once seemed too good to be true turns into a veritable nightmare. The Knight appears perfect and ideal on the outside, but just below the surface, there is jealousy, anger, moodiness, and emotional instability. This reversed card signifies a disconnection from reality or an illusion that masks an ugly truth.

683

Symbolism - The Knight rides a white horse, a symbol of the purity of his intention. He holds a cup up in offering. He wears a winged helmet, which references Mercury, a divine messenger; this indicates that he is silver-tongued, able to charm anyone with the beauty and eloquence of his communication style. He stares straight ahead, spine straight as a rod; he seems to know that he is being watched and admired.

Queen of Cups

Upright - This card represents the ultimate state of emotional balance. The Queen of Cups has been learning from her intuitive and emotional sensations for a lifetime. She is experienced now, an expert and authority on matters of the heart and soul. She is clairvoyant, creative, sensitive, emotionally mature, and a natural healer. Her compassion is like a beacon; others are drawn to her energy, inspired by her, comforted by her presence, and eager to accept her advice and guidance.

Reversed - Too much of a good thing can be really, really bad; emotion, intuition, and creativity are no exception. When this card is reversed, it implies that a potentially compassionate and emotionally mature person has instead become melodramatic, manipulative, obsessive, or dishonest. Most likely, they've lost touch with their empathetic drive, as their own extreme emotions and desires have grown to overshadow their perception of other people's needs and feelings. This can point to extreme narcissism disguised as love, or alternatively, to codependency.

Symbolism - The Queen sits on a throne at the edge of the sea. She wears a jeweled crown and holds an enormous and ornate cup, decorated with crosses, crescent moons, grapes, and other symbols; this represents spiritual wealth, or divine wisdom. She holds all the secrets of the universe in her palm. Her throne is decorated with seashells and cherubs who gaze upon her lovingly, with admiration. She is cradled both by the sea below and the heavens above.

King of Cups

Upright - This card combines the power of rationality with emotion and intuition. The King of Cups is a sign of love that has lasted the test of time, even after lust and novelty have faded away. He signifies commitment, compassion, generosity, benevolence, diplomacy, and peacemaking. He also stands for well-managed sensitivity; he feels things deeply, but never allows his emotions to overwhelm him or spur impulsive, volatile actions.

Reversed - Much like the reversed Queen of Cups, this card points to emotional instability and manipulation, but with a more forceful bent. The reversed King of Cups may be using coercion or emotional blackmail; he may be drowning in his addictions and unable to see through the fog of his emotions. He can also represent someone who fancies himself a powerful authority figure, blind to his own emotional immaturity and inconsiderate behavior.

Symbolism - The King sits upon his throne with a cup in one hand and a scepter in the other. He stares into the distance with a serene expression that implies emotional strength. He is alone, though, with his throne resting upon a platform floating in the sea; in the background, a ship passes in the distance, and a fish leaps from the water. The ship is a symbol of navigation, while the water symbolizes emotion and the subconscious. The leaping fish is representative of emotions and intuition rising to the surface. The grey stone platform upon which his throne sits symbolizes stability and fortitude.

The Suit of Wands

Wands aren't exclusively portrayed within this suit; like the other suit items (Cups, Wands, and Pentagrams) they show up in the Major Arcana illustrations as well, held by the Magician, and the princely warrior in the Chariot; the woman on the World card holds two!

In Tarot, Wands are symbols of manifestation, creation, passion, and action. They represent raw energy, ambition, determination, and transformation. The Suit of Wands is correlated to the element of fire, which, likewise, is a symbol of passion and energy, but also represents sexuality, volatility, expansion, release, and purification.

When a spread is dominated by the Suit of Wands, this is a sign that the querent should be focusing on turning possibilities into realities. Wands are the tools we use to project our thoughts and ideas into the external world, and when you encounter a large number of them in a Tarot spread, it's likely that the universe is calling you to step up to the plate and create something. The Wand is like a microphone and speaker box; this tool only amplifies and projects what is already inside of you, and your unique mind will manifest authentic creations with your unmistakable signature. What this means is that you do not need to be a creative type in order to heed the call of the Suit of Wands; you may create a business, create a family, or create a spiritual practice if these options make more sense to you than painting, writing, or dance. The point is innovation and invention--this suit is not necessarily geared toward artistic enterprise.

In esoteric Tarot decks, the Wand is connected to a mysterious energetic life force known as Qi, or Kundalini, in non-western metaphysical healing practices like Reiki and Chakra work in Tantra. This life force is a form of vitality that animates all living beings and drives them to fulfill their personal destinies. All the cards within this suit can be received as a call to action from the universe; this is not the time to rest on your laurels, or get caught up overthinking things. You are ready to solve problems, generate new ideas, bring people together, and put your plans in action. Set your sights on a goal, take hold of your wand, raise it high in the air, and manifest, manifest, manifest!

Ace of Wands

Upright - Ace cards generally represent new beginnings, and this card is no exception. This card denotes a new creative project or business venture; inspiration, invention, and opportunities that are just too good to pass up.

Reversed - This usually means that even if your latest project started out strong, it's falling flat, losing steam, or petering out. Distraction; procrastination; setbacks and delays; indecisiveness; poor planning.

Symbolism - A divine hand reaches out of the clouds holding up a wand that is sprouting leaves. Some of the leaves are falling down to the green earth below, where trees are growing--this symbolizes new possibilities, and seeds taking root. There is a river in the background, as well as a castle upon a distant hill. The river represents motion and momentum; the castle represents stability and security, but it is pretty far off, meaning that in order to create, you may have to embrace instability and get comfortable with vulnerability.

Two of Wands

Upright - Short term success; a first step in the right direction; planning and progress; discovery and achievement.

Reversed - Don't hesitate; if you act quickly, you can still seize this prime opportunity, but the moment will soon pass you by. This card can represent poor planning, self-doubt, fruitless anxiety, and fear of risk.

Symbolism - A cloaked man stands upon a balcony, holding a long Wand (technically a staff) in one hand and a globe in the other. There is another staff behind him, planted in the ground and standing on its own. He looks over the trees, grass, water, and mountains in the distance with a sense of longing. The fact that he holds up one staff while the other is planted signifies the fact that his initial success has only stirred up more ambition within him; he is ready to move on to the next venture. The walls of the balcony symbolizes security, stability, and comfort; he gazes beyond them, showing that he is beginning to wonder if these things are holding him back, rather than simply protecting him. Is it time to take a risk?

The globe in his hand references the phrase: "The world is your oyster." Everything he needs is at his disposal; he needs only to grasp the right tools, and take a bold step forward.

Three of Wands

Upright - Expansion; travel; progress; forward momentum; stepping out of your comfort zone.

Reversed - Getting too comfortable as a big fish in a small pond; stagnation; failed plans; travel problems.

Symbolism - A man stands on the edge of a cliff, with his back turned towards us, looking out over the sea and distant mountains. He wears a similar outfit to that of the Magician in the Major Arcana. He stands by three planted staves, which represent past successes; with his hand on one, he sets his sights on the next leg of his journey. A few ships are sailing in the distance. He might be waiting for a shipment to come in, or he may be ready to board one and sail away.

Four of Wands

Upright - Celebration of hard-earned rewards; relaxation; stability; harmony; joy and relief.

Reversed - Still positive, but muted joy; tainted happiness; something puts a damper on your celebration.

Symbolism - We see a party, but from a distance; in the foreground of the card, four tall Wands are planted and floral garlands are strung up between them, creating a canopy. This denotes victory--a battle hard-fought and well-won! Women with floral wreaths dance behind it, holding bouquets of flowers overhead; behind them stands a castle, a symbol of security and authority.

Five of Wands

Upright - Competition; creative tension; disagreement; a test or rite of passage; sportsmanship, sparring, performative debates or physical fighting.

Reversed - Battling inner demons; healthy competition turning vicious; passive aggression; conflict avoidance; breaking rules for a chance at victory.

Symbolism - Five male figures stand and fight with their Wands as though they are Swords. Some of them are smiling, though, and none of the Wands are pointed directly at any of them. This is a play fight, one in which some of the players have yet to get the hang of how to use a pretend-sword--one character holds it over his shoulder like a baseball bat, while another thrusts his Wand straight up into the air. This represents a competition as a learning experience.

Six of Wands

Upright - Triumph; public recognition; optimism; confidence; victory within reach.

Reversed - Humiliation; betrayed expectations of success; a fall from grace; a failed endeavor; a leader in decline; private recognition; a personal victory unnoticed by others.

Symbolism - A male rides on the back of a white horse with a yellow cloak through a cheering crowd. The man wears a red cape. The color of the horse symbolizes purity of intention; the yellow cloak represents optimism; the red cape denotes boldness and passion. He wears a floral wreath, and carries another wreath on the end of the Wand he bears in his hand--this means a major victory.

Seven of Wands

Upright - Overcoming obstacles on your own; perseverance; personal fortitude and resolve; fighting for what is right; standing alone against many enemies or challenges.

Reversed - Weakness and exhaustion; losing resolve; cowardice; defeat.

Symbolism - A figure stands on the edge of a cliff, with his back to the ledge. Six of the Wands in the card are pointed at him in a threatening manner; he grips the seventh with both bands, not as a Sword, but as a shield across his torso. He wears a shoe on one foot, and boot on another, which may reference indecisiveness, but also may point to the usefulness of distraction tactics, or the strength of character needed to stand apart from the crowd and break the mold.

Eight of Wands

Upright - Swift action; progress achieved at an extraordinary pace; endeavors nearing conclusion; rapid change; air travel.

Reversed - Delays and detours; a lack of progress; deep frustrations; resisting change.

Symbolism - This is one of the few cards in the Tarot deck without a single human character in the illustration. Eight wands soar through the air, soon to land on the ground. Their proximity to earth represents culmination or manifestation; what was once airborne and immaterial will soon become a physical reality.

Nine of Wands

Upright - Tested faith; goals just out of reach; last-minute curveballs or setbacks; resilience and persistence;

Reversed - Giving up; dejection; losing faith; defensive attitude; a person pushed beyond their limits; broken or unacknowledged boundaries.

Symbolism - A figure stands before eight of the nine wands, peering over his shoulder at the others while he holds the ninth in his hands, leaning on it. He wears a bandage on his head and appears exhausted. The bandage represents a wound to the head or ego. He's come so close and yet he still might not make it; he's in danger of becoming too dejected to complete this project, despite all the time and energy already invested in it.

Ten of Wands

Upright - Hard work; carrying the weight of the world; extreme burdens; one final push to complete a major project.

Reversed - Relief; delegation; collapse under pressure; completion; release; responsibilities given up.

Symbolism - A man carries a bundle of ten Wands in his arms, plowing forwards towards a house in the distance. He is building something, and it's nearly complete--but is his enthusiasm to finish leading him to bite off more than he can chew? He looks down at his feet and the Wands block his view of the house in the distance; he is so focused on forward momentum that he can't see how long this journey is, and that he might not make it if he can't find someone to help him carry this load.

Page of Wands

Upright - The Page of Wands is passionate, creative, enthusiastic and charismatic. He is also impulsive--a thrill-seeker who isn't frightened by risk or danger. He is full of new, innovative ideas, and loves the pursuit of discovery. He's a free spirit who won't be tied down or caged in; always moving onward and upward!

Reversed - Immaturity combined with boldness and a love of risk can be a dangerous mix. The reversed Page of Wands is rebellious and impetuous. He wants to unleash his creative energy to the world, and blames others for standing in the way of his potential; what he fails to realize is that he is the one standing in his own way, preventing his own emotional growth.

Symbolism - The Page stands alone with his Wand as a walking staff, glancing up towards the sky, implying lofty ambitions and a daydreamer's attitude. He wears a feather in his cap, which is usually a sign of accomplishment or victory in battle-- but considering his inexperienced rank and lack of correlation to warfare, perhaps this feather is a sign that he has a bit of a chip on his shoulder, or has an overinflated sense of personal capability.

Knight of Wands

Upright - The Knight rides a galloping horse, engaged in a relentless pursuit. He's got his eye on the prize, and enough bravado and confidence to convince obstacles to leap out of his way. He implies an adventure, a chance taken, or a goal pursued without hesitation. He also represents impulsiveness.

Reversed - Step on the breaks; your head and heart are ready to tackle this challenge, but you may have forgotten your physical or material limitations. This card implies that inexperience or lack of planning and preparation can lead to a failed mission. It can also suggest a hot temper, recklessness, or destructive impulsivity.

Symbolism - The Knight rides full steam ahead on an auburn horse. He wears bright red feathers in his helmet, which signifies the passion that drives him forward.

Queen of Wands

Upright - The Queen of Wands comfortable upon her throne. She is satisfied with her lot in life and confident in her abilities. She is independent, but diplomatic and well-liked by others. Finally, she is quite comfortable in her skin.

Reversed - When this card appears upside down, it often references self-serving behaviors. These could be mild and harmless, like introversion or harnessing self-respect, but these behaviors could also be taken to an extreme and serve to create conflict. This card represents the attitude of wanting to have your cake and eat it, too, even if the rest of the world is starving. Think Marie Antoinette.

Symbolism - The Queen sits on a throne holding a wand and a sunflower, symbols of creative power and optimism. The throne is decorated with lion statues, which stands for regality and courage; the throne's back has an ornate pattern and extends up beyond the edge of the card, representing sky-high aspirations and limitless potential. She sits with her knees played open, emitting a calm but inviting sexual energy. If you wish to accept her invitation, though, tread carefully; her black cat sits before her, guarding her with a sneer and a warning hiss.

King of Wands

Upright - This character represents the kind of ruler who can affect positive, lasting change. He is a visionary, a builder, a gifted and moving speaker, and a charismatic leader. Beneath all of that, he is also honest, kind, and genuine. Like Arthur in medieval legend, this man was born to rule.

Reversed - Ruling is tough work; this reversed card can imply impatience with the level of responsibility a leader has been carrying for a long time, or the developed habit of taking shortcuts, cutting corners, or even treating other people as though they are disposable. Perhaps a once honorable leader has grown into a despot or dictator.

Symbolism - The King sits upon a similar throne to that held by the Queen of Wands, decorated with a lion motif. He also wears a lion pendant around his neck. Courage, power, and majesty are clearly very important to him. On the ground by his feet is a salamander, an alchemical symbol of transformation. The King of Wands wants to change the world for the better--or, if he cannot do that, he will at least leave a lasting mark upon it.

How Can I Use Tarot Cards?

Tarot is great in helping you make choices, manifesting goals, writing a book planning a business, coaching others, meditating—you name it. Tarot card reading enables you to:

Pay Attention to Your Intuition

Tarot card reading is an extremely personal endeavor and the meanings locked within the cards vary from person to person and from one query to another. The same card could hold an entirely different meaning for you than what it had for your friend because you are different people with different identities and intuition. This is the beauty of tarot cards; it talks to you about yourself and your life. This is how it helps you become more intuitive and understand the amazing power of your mind.

Better Comprehend Threats and Opportunities

There will always be threats and opportunities waiting for you in life. While the ideal scenario would be to avoid the threats and embrace the opportunities, not all of us are conscious and insightful enough to do that. Often, we discard opportunities perceiving them as threats and welcome threats expecting them to bring us good news and fortune. Luckily, this can change for you and tarot reading is the way to go about it.

Tarot cards enable you to have better awareness of your past, present and future as well as your behavior and personality so you can better understand whether a certain person, thing, idea, event or situation is a threat or an opportunity for you, which will ensure you make wiser decisions accordingly.

Stay on Guard and Take Risks at the Right Time

You should definitely enjoy your life to the fullest and take risks too, but it is important to know exactly when to take the plunge and when to play safe. This is how you can make informed decisions and have most of the things in life, work out well for you, because nothing works out 100% ever.

If you learn to read tarot cards, you can soon become equipped with the power to understand and explore the hidden meaning associated with things so you know when to stay on guard and when to do something uncertain that can yield great results for you.

Dig Deeper into Your Genuine Aspirations

Many of us claim that we know who we are and what we want, but sadly, this is not true. Many of us remain oblivious to our true self and our genuine aspirations, which is why we end up making poor decisions. We are stuck in meaningless jobs, bearing the pain of burdensome and cruel relationships and battling the depression associated with living a pointless life only because we do not know what we want.

Luckily, tarot can change things around for you. The cards based on your desire to know yourself and your heart's deepest desires can give you meaningful answers about who you are and what you should really be doing so you can then pursue exactly what you want and add more structure to your boring life.

Make Sense of Your Purpose in Life

As you start becoming more aware of what you want in life, what you should do, the threats you need to avoid and the opportunities you should grab on to, you start to make better sense of your life and your purpose in it. What is next then? Well, you then simply find out meaningful ways to go about that route so you can fulfill your purpose and live each day with meaning and happiness.

Chapter 4: Basic Tarot Interpretation Tips

Often when people start practicing tarot, it's rather simplistic–you know the definitions of each deck, pick, place a few in a lovely pattern and create a cogent interpretation. It is not until you get a little more into how intricate the tarot system is. Here are some suggestions for testing taro meanings and getting you a stronger reader.

1. Learn the Basic Meanings

Surprisingly, I have met many people who feel that knowing the meaning of each card is needless. We suggest to me softly, "Hey, I don't need to know all of this, I'm intuitive." Maybe this is because, for a truly talented person, it can work. But they're few and far between. This helps in a way to understand a popular tarot. In other terms, the card's underlying sense is identical. Know the fundamentals, then.

2. First Reactions

Never let go of your first emotional response when you see a card. It's always real. Unfortunately? Disappointed? And research the document carefully. Scary? Scary? Check ALL the words-many of you are shocked.

3. Look at the Images

Understanding a deck will imply that we start taking pictures for granted. Try to look at them with a fresh eye each time. You must learn to apply the picture to the problem in this way. Look at everybody's juxtaposition of cards. Are they speaking with each other? Turning away from each other? Turning away? Avoiding the eyes of each other? What about the weather? What about the weather? What's the color of heaven? Are the trees whipped by a gale of autumn? How could this impact the card's interpretation?

4. Analyze for Pattern

Expect to see the same card in tests, even for others? And realize that you, the listener, think about it. Take some time to take a closer look at the token–it has personal significance for you. What if three or four cards of the same number come up–and don't forget to count Majors too? Why could the number five rule in a lecture? Or how about the Queens three? What could that mean for your customers? Even if most of the cards in the sale are blades or cups? How would the card perception be affected?

5. Incorporate Elemental Dignities

See Primordial Dignities, as Paul Hughes-Barlow illustrated on his blog Super Tarot. This is a fascinating topic, which explains how suits help or hinder one another. For example, in a three-card reading where two Cups and one Wand occur, then the fire is controlled by water (emotions). The Wand card is reduced, however powerful it is.

6. Incorporate Numerology

The understanding of divine numerical development is always valuable in the analysis of tarot. In the above tip, where I mentioned number 5 more than two cards numbered five (including the hierophant), the person who is looking for a great number of challenges, or even a major challenge, which shadows all other aspects of his life. If the result card is 10, the current phase is over, and another reading is required. Understanding your figures will greatly help you.

7. Find the Story Thread

Each piece of tarot tells a story, even a one-card reading. Some cards can offer you a more complicated tale, and it's your job to find and pull the string. It can be rough until you have a lot of reading under your belt. I find it helps to involve the client — they often give a clue almost accidentally. The Celtic Cross is a great narrative.

8. Use a Journal

If you have an idea, a revelation, or learn a new feature of your card– write it down. Whenever you have trouble hearing, write it down. Believe me; these brief remarks are very useful for your future self. For reading, document, and evaluate, use a tarot book.

9. Understand the Archetypes

Major Arcana is focused on archetypes–basic forms that exist in all cultures and societies and go back to Plato's period, when they are first described. Several experiments have demonstrated time and time again that they are indeed a valid concept. The archetypes of the tarot are the life phases from which we all travel. There isn't enough room for this fascinating topic, but you would do well as a tarot reader to assimilate some archetypal information. You may never need to talk about them in your studies, but knowing the Majors can add a lot to your perceptions.

10. Symbolism

Each tarot deck has a symbolism. An icon is a pictorial illustration of something else (think traffic signs)–but you don't really realize what it is. Many tarot images have been focused on very grim myths or metaphysical ideas. Some of the more common ones, including color, the presence of birds, plants, livestock, etc. are worth exploring.

11. Traditional vs. Modern

Tarot readers of the days gone by had a different understanding of the meaning of tarot cards. It also depended on which occultist had the greatest influence at the time. Sometimes obviously change, and so some of the old meanings have no place today. Nonetheless, it is interesting to go back to time and evaluate old and new, so set aside a study period and do that. It is always helpful to have another layer of meaning.

12. Delve Into Your Own Life

As you get older, your life experience improves. If a card or set of cards reminds you of a scenario in your own life, then use your reading experience. You don't have to show your consumer the root. Likewise, other readings you have done in the past can reappear. Many human experiences are universal, i.e., other individuals have also experienced things that have happened to you. Be careful when a memory bubbles– it is important.

Whether you use just one or two of these ideas or integrate them all into the tarot analysis, your success can increase as a reader with every degree of understanding. Never stop learning; never stop knowing.

Steps to Use Clarifying Cards

The last card tells you what to do or do to avoid loss. This indicates the direction you can follow if it's a good card or alarms you if it's a poor card.

Clarifying cards can provide more information and details in reading for those who choose to encourage the cards to run. We can also pose certain concerns and help you to understand cards that are just not important.

Many writers, of course, use clarifying markers. Others use it only to refine a forecast to gain additional knowledge if the card becomes uncertain and how it could refer to a particular situation.

Since every card has as many interpretations as possible, clear-cut cards will allow the user to find out what meaning(s) are better.

Here are some of the methods I use. None of them are methods I've mastered from a book or a teacher; they've all been organically created for over 20 years.

See how they work for you and how you can build certain strategies!

1. Use a clarifying card to explain a card that is particularly confusing. Speak quietly to the player when you see a card that is pointless and ask, "What do you try to say to me?" or "What are you talking to?" and take another card from a stack. Place the clarifying card next to the ambiguous one. See if the question is answered by the clarifying coin. Which happens if you combine the clarifying card definitions with the original token?

2. To dig deeper into the issue, use a clarifying coin. If the card has already answered the question, but you would like more information, ask a more specific question.

3. Use a second, smaller spread with another deck to reach clarity, details, and key points. Do not interrupt the initial spread. Pay particular attention when you see exactly the same coin!

4. Ask specific read questions such as: "What's the best way to do this?", "What should my mentality do?" or "Where can I be helped?" or "What's the divine purpose?" Draw a card or tiny card for a query.

5. Spread the last card, to sum up, the read: not every speaker or every user has to be answered. But if you find these strategies

right, seek to see what happens. You may be shocked by the information and consistency that you can achieve!

Chapter 5: Tarot Rituals

The rituals here are not the types you see in movies where you have to draw mysterious signs on the ground, wear a hooded robe, place candles at specific spots and then begin to recite incantations while waiting for a huge, scary gust of wind to blow. As fascinating (or downright petrifying) as that would have been, tarot reading does not involve fetish ritual proceedings in any from. 'Ritual' in this context is a set of actions that you carry out before a tarot reading to help calm your mind and 'activate' your intuitive capabilities.

To cope in the real world, your analytical mind needs to constantly be at work; you need to analyze how much you have spent on gas, how many more years you have left to pay off the mortgage, how many calories you have consumed in a day…the list is endless. But for an effective tarot reading, you will need more than just your analytical mind, you'll need your intuitive mind on board. The rituals are just a process of helping you clear your mind, and usher in your intuition to lead you through the reading.

It is essential to note that carrying out a ritual is not a compulsory prerequisite for an effective tarot reading session. If you feel you can utilize your intuition efficiently without needing to prepare your mind in advance first, then by all means, do so. But over the centuries, most people have found it extremely helpful to have a specific routine that helps them get prepared to engage their intuitive capabilities before carrying out a tarot reading.

Your ritual should preferably be a consistent practice. It can be as simple as taking a few deep breaths and closing your eyes to enable you to calm your mind, to using velvet, silk, crystals, candles and incense to create a specific type of atmosphere you feel helps you get in touch with the deepest recesses of your mind. When it comes to tarot rituals there are no specific standard procedures. It's all about figuring out what works for you and harnessing it to the fullest to enable the delicate balance between your analytical mind and your intuition to be established. Once you feel you have reached that state of delicate balance, then you may proceed with your tarot reading session.

It is very important that your ritual procedure be a series of steps you are completely comfortable with; both mentally and physically. If you are allergic to something, it doesn't make sense to use it because you think it would let you be at peace. If something scares you, then it doesn't make sense to include it in your ritual routine either. You want to be clear-headed, not apprehensive while carrying out your tarot reading.

However, as long as you are comfortable with a particular series of steps, then by all means, carry on. Even if it is carving out specific signs on sand and lighting candles and saying whatever incantations come to your mind, as long as the ritual process makes you feel at peace and unlocks your intuitive capabilities, by all means, fire on.

A great part of most people's tarot rituals is saying prayers. If you believe in God, or the existence of a supreme supernatural entity, then you can ask Him for guidance and direction as you prepare to proceed to seek answers to your burning questions. Communicating with an invisible divine entity not only helps to calm you down and improve your intuition, it also allows you to be collected enough to frame your question properly. When you are praying, you are likely to say your question out loud; to ask God for help. Therefore, praying helps you to frame your question right without any ambiguities.

Another key part of most rituals is deciding exactly how many times you would shuffle the tarot deck before carrying out your reading. The amount of times you shuffle the deck will eventually have a direct impact on what your final reading will be, so it is extremely important for you to be clear-minded as you decide exactly how many times you want the cards to be shuffled.

During the process of preparing your mind to carry out the reading, it is also important for you to decide whether you as the reader will be the one to shuffle the tarot cards, or if you will be doing it with the querent, or if only the querent will be responsible for the shuffling. As stated earlier, there is no absolute right or wrong way to do these things; it all comes down to personal traditions, and of course, intuition. While carrying out your ritual, it makes sense to visualize the tarot reading in your mind in advance, and decide exactly who will be doing the shuffling of the cards.

It is believed by a lot of tarot experts that a unique, temporary and mysterious bond exists between the deck of cards, the reader and the querent during the process of the reading. The open-minded atmosphere helps to connect them, and as the reader and querent open up their minds to the possibilities of the reading's results they find themselves working together on a subconscious level to find a solution to the querent's problems

Chapter 6: Enhancing and Expanding Your Tarot Reading Prowess

Tarot is an art form. No matter how many spreads you have mastered or how many card meanings you have memorized, there will always be another step you can take to improve your practice and deepen your understanding.

Set goals and intentions for your readings to work towards steady improvement. Track your progress in a Tarot journal, and stay open to experimentation. Your progress may not always follow a straight, direct, forward facing line; you might have to take one step forward and then jump a few steps back to re-examine ideas that you once thought you fully understood but now see deeper layers or hidden complexities within. There is no shame in unpacking and relearning the basics that you've already got under your belt.

Masculine and Feminine

You might also try reading spreads while keeping an eye out for the balance of feminine and masculine cards; as a whole, does this spread lean towards the assertive, active, and rational? Or does it lean in favor of the emotional, passive, and receptive? You could instead focus on elemental energies; upright and reversed cards; you might even read Minor Arcana cards as changing circumstances, while Major Arcana cards reference the constants or immovable realities of life.

Astrology and Tarot

Symbols from the zodiac signs are incorporated into illustrations of several Major Arcana cards, and they are intertwined with our understanding of the four elements and the four suits that reflect them.

The world of astrology is very complex, with vast amounts of information available for interpretation. To incorporate astrology into your Tarot practice, start simple. Below is a list of the twelve signs and the cards of the Major Arcana that they are linked to, as well as their respective elements.

Aries - The Emperor - Fire

Taurus - The Hierophant - Earth

Gemini - The Lovers - Air

Cancer - The Chariot - Water

Leo - Strength - Fire

Virgo - The Hermit - Earth

Libra - Justice - Air

Scorpio - Death - Water

Sagittarius - Temperance - Fire

Capricorn - The Devil - Earth

Aquarius - The Star - Air

Pisces - The Moon – Water

The rest of the Major Arcana cards are linked to single planets or celestial bodies, rather than entire constellation signs.

Uranus - The Fool - Air

Mercury - The Magician - Air

Earth's Moon - The High Priestess - Water

Venus - The Empress - Earth

Jupiter - The Wheel of Fortune - Fire

Neptune - The Hanged Man - Water

Mars - The Tower - Fire

Earth's Sun - The Sun - Fire

Pluto - Judgement - Fire

Saturn - The World – Earth

There are further astrological correlations for all of the numbered suit and Court Cards, which can be overwhelmingly complex without a solid foundation of astrological study. Read up on the twelve zodiac signs, their seasons, and the personality traits they relate to; this information can help you make sense of confounding spreads, identify particular characters as representations of real people, and incorporate a sense of timing into your predictions.

Suits and Seasons

If you feel overwhelmed by the astrological associations of Tarot, one way to simplify the concept is to group the zodiac signs by their houses, or seasons, and correlate those to the four suits. This can allow some readers to forecast timing in a reading--for instance, alerting their querent that the resolution of their issue may not come until the next winter season hits. Some readers are not comfortable using the cards in this way, as seasons are recurring--they may be wary of getting someone's hopes up for the coming autumn, when the cards are pointing to an incident that will occur during the autumn season several years away, or even in the figurative autumn season of one's life (middle age). In that case, the seasonal implications of suits can simply be used to color the mood of it. Summer cards can imply easiness, carefree attitudes, and emotional warmth. Autumn cards may imply the brisk winds of change or the sense of manifestation that is embodied by the harvest season. Winter cards can point to conclusions, endings, and death, while spring cards may reference rebirth, survival, overcoming struggle, and moving on.

The suits and their respective seasons can also be connected to the four corners of the earth, though opinions on these links may vary from one cartomancer to the next. They each have correlated colors, as well.

- The Suit of Wands - Spring - Fire - South - Yellow

- The Suit of Cups - Summer - Water - West - Red

- The Suit of Pentacles - Autumn - Earth - East - Green

- The Suit of Swords - Winter - Air - North - Blue or indigo

Numerology and Tarot

Numerology is the study of symbolism and meaning in numbers.

This method can be further applied to the cards of the Major Arcana, and govern the relationships between cards within the context of a spread. For example, in a spread that features the Fool, and the Magician, as well as a Ten of Wands, the numbers one and zero in the Major Arcana could be connected to the Ten card, implying that all three cards are a part of the same narrative arc or theme. A spread that is dominated by the number ten is primarily speaking to culmination, finality, and conclusion, and since so many of these cards feature wands, you might determine that a creative endeavor is about to pay off big time.

The number zero does not factor into the interpretations of Minor Arcana cards but it still holds a great deal of significance within numerology and the Major Arcana. It signifies freedom from responsibility, expectation, and limitation.

Addition, multiplication, and division factor heavily into this study. If you're interested in incorporating the theories of numerology into your Tarot practice, it would be wise to study numerology on its own first, and then proceed to merge the two methodologies.

Geomancy and Tarot

Geomancy is another complex and ancient divination practice. It concerns the physical alignment (or lack thereof) of items or lines in spatial relation to one another. The term "geomancy" is derived from Latin, ancient Greek, and Arabic roots, translated from words meaning "earth foresight" or "sand science."

The art of Feng Shui is an example of Geomancy; so is tasseography (the art of reading tea leaves), crystal scrying, the I Ching, Kumalak, and even rune casting. Historical evidence suggests that the earliest Geomantic methodologies arose in Africa, or possibly in ancient Arab civilizations; these methods used handfuls of dirt thrown into the air, analyzing the patterns in which they would fall, or alternatively, lines and dots drawn in the sand with the sharp end of the stick.

Crystals, Cooking, and Creativity

If astrology, numerology, and geomancy leave you feeling boggled, numbed, or stressed, it may be time to return to the fun and carefree side of Tarot for a while.

Crystals can help to lighten the mood of your Tarot practice, as well as protect your deck from negativity. And even better--they're gorgeous! You may want to start collecting crystals with the intention of decorating a sacred space or altar in your home; they can be wonderful for meditation, yoga, reiki and chakra healing. They can also be fun to use in crafting or to wear as jewelry.

As adults, we tend to forget how we filled our days as children; without work, taxes, dating, commutes, errands, or other adult responsibilities, most of us had to get inventive and learn to entertain ourselves. We played pretend, with or without toys and costumes, and allowed our imaginations to run wild.

Both Tarot cards and crystals can be seen as toys to inspire adult play. Awaken your inner child. Throw the rules out the window. Do you feel drawn to a crystal because of its metaphysical properties, or simply because its sparkly, pretty, and you feel good when you hold it? Maybe it's the latter but if who cares! Do you need a better reason?

Attraction is a fundamental form of intuition, so aim to stop questioning your impulses and desires. It's entirely possible that you like the things you like for a good reason. Whatever crystals (or bones, petrified wood, dried herbs, essential oils, or other organic materials) you find yourself drawn to are potential sources of divine inspiration. Lean into that attraction; honor it, respect it and let it guide you.

To restore some carefree fun into your Tarot practice, you might want to dabble in using the cards to source creative inspiration. Some easy examples are through cooking, painting, or creative writing. Shuffle your deck and draw cards at random to prompt your next steps-- whether that dictates the ingredients you throw into a dish, the colors or shapes you choose for a blank canvas, or the characters and plot developments you use to move a fictional story forward. Some people also find Tarot cards helpful for free-writing (writing as a form of therapy, rather than writing done to create a complete narrative arc). Whatever practice you choose, you'll be amazed at how easily Tarot can reinvigorate your creative drive, helping you to think outside the box, innovate, and skip right over artistic blockages.

Chapter 7: Meditation And Mindfulness With Tarot

There is a reason the game of *tarocchi* became so popular that it evolved into the Tarot of today: each card, from the Page of Pentacles to the powerful Hierophant, is steeped in layers of meaning, energy, and magic. Tarot cards make excellent focal points for manifestation during meditation. Here are several methods and cards to use if you want to get started.

Personal Power and the Magician

In life, it's easy to feel down on one's self, as if other people have taken your power, from time to time. It can be frustrating to the point of distraction when we wonder how to get our power back? Firstly, power is infinite. You don't get robbed of your power, merely, other people or situations drain you of it. What you need is a fill-up from the universe.

Before you begin your meditation, make sure you're dressed comfortably and seated in a quiet place. If you don't feel comfortable sitting on the floor you can sit on a chair, as long as your back is straight and your feet are flat on the ground, hands palms down on your lap. The card should be in front of you so that you can see it clearly.

- The Magician card's place in the major arcana is One. Think about how you'd like the opportunity to start anew, on a fresh, new path.

- Think of the four elements represented by the cup, sword, wand, and pentacle. Imagine your emotions, intellect, spirit, and ego glowing with life, power, and energy.

- Focus on the infinity symbol. Allow the infinite energy of the universe to refresh your personal power and vitality.

Manifesting Long-Awaited Goals – The World Card

When it seems as if you've been adrift on a calm sea in life for too long, you can use this meditation to bridge the gap towards a goal you've wanted to achieve for a long while. The World card is all about completion, and the great satisfaction that comes from achieving a long-awaited success.

- First, imagine your sacred space filled with purple, healing light. Purple holds great energy as the vibration of psychic power and intuition, as well as being the favored color of royalty in ancient times.

- Feel the World card's connection to the Magician card—the same wand exists in both. That is because it is *your* personal power that has propelled you towards completing this goal.

- Imagine the feeling of satisfaction and pride when you achieve this goal. Imagine others congratulating you.

- Gently feel the energy of new beginnings unfurling within your spirit even as you complete this goal; when one thing draws to its completion, so does life's cycle renew it to begin something else in its stead. This is because growth and learning are infinite.

Healing and the Star

A good card to meditate with when you feel run-down, or are losing hope, is the Star. It will act as a beacon for you to focus your thoughts upon, and it's clear, calming symbolism can help rejuvenate your spirit.

- Focus on the seven white stars and know that seven brings luck and the aid of the divine feminine to help lift you from your troubles.

- Next, concentrate on the eight-sided yellow star. Eight brings relief to those in financial need, or those who are battling fatigue or hopelessness.

- As the figure in the card pours water onto the soil, focus on the life-giving water of the universe refreshing your soul.

- Give yourself permission to let go of anything that's no longer serving you and make a pledge to honor yourself and your spirit in the days to come.

Balance and Temperance

In this high-paced world, it can be easy to find ourselves overworked, stuck in hyperdrive mode, unable to slow down, or else fixated on the mindset of *more*. We buy new things to make ourselves feel better; we eat more and drink more to calm our unstable emotions. When you feel as if you need a spiritual reset, meditate with the Temperance card a while.

- To begin, focus on the triangle and square embroidered on the angel's robe. This represents the connection between humanity and nature. Have you gotten out of touch with your natural side? Feel both the serenity and wildness of the world ease and soothe your frantic spirit. Imagine the sounds of ocean waves lapping at the shore, or of the wind coming over a high mountain meadow.

- Focus next on angel's halo crown. Remember that you, too, are connected to the divine and to the universe. Feel yourself reconnect with your particular, unique spiritual journey. No one can dictate this to you, nor take it from you.

- Breathe in the scent of growing things, such as the daffodils and lush, green grass of the card's scene. Heal the gentle gurgle of the flowing stream.

- Just as the angel balances the water from each cup, imagine the balance inside you restoring itself.

- Finally, focus on the rising sun in the distance, and feel the stress and worry leave your body and mind.

Love Meditation and the Lovers Card

True love is a goal shared by most of us, yet it is often difficult to define, let alone find. The best way to find true love is to let it find you. How do you accomplish this? By making yourself *ready* for love, in spirit, heart, and mind. When you're truly open to love, it will be apparent to everyone you meet.

Many of us in hindsight have looked back on a failed relationship and notice something about how that relationship began: on a whim, when we were least expecting it to. What can we learn from this? Simply that love will come to us on its own terms, but when it does, we *can* be ready for it. Ready to receive it, ready to give it, and ready to honor it in our words, actions, and promises.

- Focusing on the figures in the card, know that true love doesn't hide anything. It stands unashamed of itself, respectfully true, honorably authentic.

- Realize that love is an action, not a state of being. You choose to show up each day in love with your partner, whether that day is challenging or peaceful.

- In order to bare yourself to someone else, you first have to make peace with, and even love, yourself.

- The best love is a combination of spirit, heart, mind, and body.

Chapter 8: Develop Your Intuition through Tarot

The Tarot can be a fabulous method to build up your instinct, Inner Wisdom, Higher Guidance or anything you desire to call it or give you the certainty to confide in your instinct.

In a perfect world, you need to arrive at a spot where your instinct naturally kicks in at whatever point you need it and you don't need to consider it. You simply realize that something is correct or wrong and you confide in it totally.

Tarot can likewise help you securely investigate potential alternatives before you concede to settling on a choice and can give you direction in any part of your life.

What is Intuition?

It is a method for knowing something or getting to data that isn't quickly evident to the five faculties of sight, contact, hearing, smell and taste.

This may be an inclination that something is extremely off-base and you should be cautious or a feeling that something is ideal for you and you ought to feel free to do it. It might be a voice in your mind or an image or a practically instinctual response.

This may likewise be in connection to an individual and whether you can confide in them.

It is regularly a first response and may really appear to be very unreasonable and silly to you as it initially jumps out at you. Anyway it will for the most part be correct.

Your instinct or premonition is there to help all of you of the time. Once in a while you have so a lot of gab going on in your mind thus numerous emotions in your body that you can't hear or believe or see your calm, all knowing truth. It is essential to figure out how to recognize the unhelpful personality babble from the real Intuition.

Instinct resembles any muscle. The more you use it, the more it will work for you and the more it will be there for you when you need it.

The Power of Pictures

Your mind think in pictures and the Tarot comprises of 78 color pictures and images, a large number of which are antiquated, which makes it one of the most dominant methods for interfacing legitimately with your subliminal personality.

Pictures are the most seasoned type of educating and learning, as they recount stories and tap straight into the correct side of your mind, which is about innovativeness, creative mind, motivation, thoughts and bits of knowledge.

The more you can trigger the can trigger the correct hand side of your mind, the more you can take advantage of your instinct or hunch.

The photos, hues and images talk straightforwardly to your subliminal personality to offer you the responses that are directly for you. This is the reason various individuals can look at similar cards and give an alternate understanding on the grounds that the cards address everybody independently.

Sights, sounds and Feelings

When using tarot cards to build up your Intuition, it is significant that you know about any sounds, voices, contemplations, feelings, pictures or vibes that surface for as you pose inquiries and look at the cards. These are probably going to be significant.

When you look at a card, do you hear any words or voices? What is said? What is the tone and volume of the voice? Is it inside your head or outside of you?

What feelings do you get when you look at the card?

Where in your body are the feelings? – Heart, head, legs, stomach zone, back, other?

Where are the photos? - Inside your head, before you? Is it true that they are color or highly contrasting, still or moving?

Are there any sensations in your body and if so where are they? Do you get any photos streak through your psyche?

Trust those first answers as they will in all probability be the correct one's for you.

Try not to look at the card for a really long time in light of the fact that your coherent personality will most likely begin to break down and may wind up normally convincing you not to acknowledge those first bits of knowledge.

When you figure out how to perceive the sign that your instinct is using to speak with you, you can distinguish them all the more rapidly in another circumstance.

With a touch of training you can before long recognize the appropriate responses from your instinct and the rationale of your explanatory personality.

Both are significant and the systematic personality can be very valuable once you have assembled all your inventive bits of knowledge.

When you are prepared, unwind, quiet your mind and pick another card.

Activities for Developing Intuition

Instinct will generally work in two different ways and those of 1) attempting to caution you of risk, so you don't accomplish something or you quit accomplishing something and 2) to alarm you that a person or thing is great and will present to you a constructive result.

Some of the time the emotions related with Positive or Negative can be altogether different and effectively unmistakable. Once in a while, nonetheless, they can be difficult to recognize in light of the fact that you might be feeling apprehensive, which can be extremely near dread, or your intelligent, diagnostic personality may have promptly kicked in to let you know not to accomplish something – for a wide range of legitimate reasons – when in actuality that activity may end up being great for you.

This might be where you have a solid tendency to reach somebody, as it could prompt something bravo, however you delay and you don't get the telephone since you fear that individual's position, or apprehensive they won't converse with you or apprehensive that they will dismiss you.

WICCA WITCHCRAFT AND TAROT MASTERY

Once in a while, so as to exploit something great, you need to step out of your usual range of familiarity and go for broke past what you would typically do and, by then, dread and rationale become an integral factor and openings can be missed. The dread is regularly that the activities won't bring the ideal increase and rather will bring torment, misfortune and suffering.

A natural streak, and in all probability will, occur in a moment and it is very not entirely obvious the message. This is the reason it is essential to know ahead of time what intuition looks like, sounds and feels to you in both negative and positive circumstances.

I would imagine that you have had circumstances throughout your life where you have had a premonition or a natural blaze about a person or thing.

Here and there you will have tuned in to it and pursued the intuition, regardless of how nonsensical it may have appeared. Different times you will have overlooked it and done what appeared to be an increasingly sensible strategy.

I would dare to state that the occasions where you have pursued your Intuition, you have been correct and this has prompted a positive result and the occasions, as a general rule, where you have overlooked your instinct, things have not filled in just as they could have done.

Instinct isn't designated "premonition" in vain, as your body appears to know precisely what is correct or wrong for you.

Here are two or three activities to get you in line with your instinct. This will likewise help you when you when you are posing inquiries of your cards and expecting to get quick, dependable and accurate answers.

We are going to look at the sights, sounds, emotions and sensations related with admonitions and furthermore those related with beneficial things.

These will be diverse for everybody since everybody has various recollections, circumstances and affiliations. The activities are intended to assist you with taking advantage of your own triggers, so you recognize what they are really going after by and by.

Tuning in to your Intuition

The most dominant activities to accomplish for your Intuition both attempting to caution you and to energize you are where you tuned in to your Intuition, made a move and had a positive and awesome result.

In any case, know that your psyche may hurl the occasions when you didn't tune in to your Intuition and things went poorly well for you. Try not to utilize these activities as an instrument for thumping yourself since that isn't generally the purpose of them.

If your brain throws up negative recollections for you, then I have incorporated a few activities for you to clean up the negative feelings and feelings connected to them.

Exercise One – How to perceive when your Intuition is attempting to caution you

This is an activity in mindfulness and not to harp on things from an earlier time, particularly if you believed you committed an error or you have whipped yourself over it since.

You have presumably had circumstances throughout your life where your Intuition attempted to caution you of threat or not to believe somebody or that something awful may occur. If you tuned in to your Intuition, you most likely felt entirely great about yourself thereafter, particularly if things turned out well for you.

If you didn't tune in to the alerts and things turned out badly for you, then there might be still be feelings of blame, fault, lament or recrimination towards yourself or others.

As you consider Developing Your Intuition and negative contemplations and feelings or agonizing recollections come up, then it is critical to clear those before you start, as they can affect your capacity to tune in to your instinct. The exact opposite thing you need is an unhelpful voice whispering in your ear, with remarks along the lines of "recall what occurred the last time we attempted to caution you."

You can utilize some the Clear Limiting Beliefs sound unwinding, which is incorporated with this bundle, to clear that pessimism or perhaps it is useful to just gone to a position of harmony with the occurrences and blunders of judgment of the past.

If that is the situation, you may get a kick out of the chance to tune in to the Acceptance Audio Relaxation, which is accessible from my site.

Your Higher Guidance doesn't have hard feelings of resentment. It doesn't quit furnishing you with helpful data, since you have overlooked it or not tuned in to it.

Perceiving Warnings

Take a full breath, quiet your mind and think about a circumstance in your past where your instinct attempted to caution you about a person or thing antagonistic.

This should be possible as two activities. One is the place you tuned in to the admonitions of your Intuition and one is the place you didn't tune in.

You can decide to recollect either circumstance. It doesn't generally make a difference.

Return yourself to the circumstance. Attempt to recollect yourself being in the circumstance, seeing who else was there, what was being said and what was happening.

Sooner or later in that experience, you presumably settled on a choice or made a move. Return yourself to the guide only PRIOR toward settling on that choice. Notice any sights, pictures, sounds, voices, feelings, body sensations or anything that may have unobtrusively changed in a moment. This would be your Intuition attempting to associate with you to caution you against going any further forward or managing the individual before you or about something that was bad for you somehow or another.

Keep in mind this occurred in a brief moment and it would have been extremely not entirely obvious in the moment it occurred. Or then again maybe you didn't miss it and you heard or felt the instinctive prompts and you acted in an unexpected way.

Attempt to reconnect with those sights, sounds, emotions, sensations BEFORE the choice and attempt to truly see them. What were they? Where in your body did you experience them? Is it true that it was an image or a blaze of looming fate? Is it true that it was an uproarious voice? If it was a voice, what sort of tone did it have that made you halt abruptly and change your choice?

From my experience, voices cautioning of risk will in general be uproarious, clear, telling and regularly utilize your name.

Did you hear something different? If you were at home, possibly your entryway ringer began to ring or your telephone all of a sudden rang.

A companion of mine disclosed to me that when she met new individuals at Networking occasions, she would heard a voice in her mind that plainly said "NO" when that individual would not be a decent individual for her to start a new business with.

The voice was in every case directly as she found to her a cost a couple of times when she didn't hear it out!

Did you get an inclination in your body that something was wrong? If so what was it? Where was it? Many individuals report prickles running up their back or a chilly sensation. What was it for you?

If you overlooked the admonitions of your Intuition, did you get a prompt voice or feeling of "Ought not to have done that or ought not to have said that?"

The more grounded your instinct is for the most part, the simpler you will disspread it to utilize tarot cards to increase natural bits of knowledge. Further on we will discuss using tarot cards to create instinct.

You would then be able to repeat this activity with another memory and check whether the sights, pictures, sounds, voices, emotions, sensations and encounters were the equivalent in an alternate circumstance where your Intuition was attempting to caution you.

Attempt it in a circumstance where you were managing an individual and your instinct cautioned you that they were dishonest or that something awful was going to originate from the experience. Once more, you can look at circumstances where you tuned in or you didn't tune in and your intuition was proved right.

This isn't an activity in judgment - it is an activity in perception. If these recollections have raised negative feelings, for example, lament or recrimination, then it is critical to do some clearing activities to separate that energy and to relinquish them.

Clearing Negativity

If you disspread negative feelings and recollections rising to the top because of this activity, it is critical to STOP and CLEAR them at the time they emerge.

You could attempt the accompanying as Quick Energy Clearers:

- Wave your arms and cut round yourself in a triangle shape from the highest point of your head to under your feet as though you are cutting up the negative energy and discharging it into the Universe.

- Utilize the Blue Flame of St Germain. Imagine you are remaining inside a blue fire of light, which is cleaning up anything negative and changing it into positive energy.

- Utilize the sound reflection of Acceptance to relinquish the negative passionate charge that is joined to occasion and view it with the nonpartisanship of "what is" or "what was." The occasion occurred and that cannot change, anyway your feelings about it can change.

- Wave a lit sage stick around to clear negative energies.

- Inhale profoundly and discharge negative feelings out into the Universe.

- Take a full breath and as you breathe out, remove all the let some circulation into of your lungs and afterward snicker profoundly as Ho, Ho, Ho to discharge significantly increasingly old, stale air from your lungs.

Exercise Two - How to perceive when your Intuition is attempting to support you

When your Intuition is attempting to support you or bolster you or urge you to push ahead or make a specific move or trust somebody, the experience might be unique. There might be a surge of euphoria or prosperity or an unmistakable realizing that everything will be good or some other positive musings, feelings, sights, sounds, feelings or sensations.

However, it may not be so natural to perceive as the Intuition may go against coherent, levelheaded conduct. It might totally negate the messages that you are getting from your different faculties – especially those of sight and hearing. There might be this inward clash going on inside you of "Indeed, pull out all the stops!" and "No, don't do it!" This regularly comes about when you have considered something and your intelligent personality has had opportunity to make its commitment or your "battle or flight" system has started up.

This is the place picking a tarot card can be very valuable as you additionally have a quick visual portrayal of the solution to your inquiry.

Put it all on the line!

Repeat the activity above. This time, think about a circumstance where your Intuition was attempting to urge you to take or to settle on a choice or to go for broke or to confide in somebody.

Take a full breath, quiet your mind and think about a circumstance in your past where your instinct attempted to support you about a person or thing pessimistic.

This should be possible as two activities. One is the place you tuned in to the prompts of your Intuition and one is the place you didn't tune in.

You can decide to recall either circumstance. It doesn't generally make a difference.

Return yourself to the circumstance. Attempt to recall yourself being in the circumstance, seeing who else was there, what was being said and what was happening.

Sooner or later in that experience, you most likely settled on a choice or made a move. Return yourself to the direct only PRIOR toward settling on that choice. Notice any sights, pictures, sounds, voices, feelings, body sensations or anything that may have inconspicuously changed in a moment. This would be your Intuition attempting to associate with you to you to go ahead or exhorting you that managing and believing the individual before you was going to prompt something incredible and magnificent.

Keep in mind this occurred in a brief instant and it would have been exceptionally not entirely obvious in the moment it occurred. Or on the other hand maybe you didn't miss it and you heard or felt the instinctive prompts and you acted in an unexpected way.

Attempt to reconnect with those sights, sounds, emotions, sensations BEFORE the choice and attempt to truly see them. What were they? Where in your body did you experience them? Is it safe to say that it was an image or a glimmer of brilliant hues or a positive result? Is it safe to say that it was a voice? If it was a voice, what sort of tone did it have that made you feel great to go ahead with something?

Did you get an inclination in your body that something mysteriously energizing, great, extraordinary and stunning was going to occur?

You would then be able to repeat this activity with another memory and check whether the sights, pictures, sounds, voices, feelings, sensations and encounters were the equivalent in an alternate circumstance where your Intuition was attempting to support you.

Attempt it in a circumstance where you were managing an individual and your instinct was attempting to direct you to believe that individual, regardless of whether your different faculties were not in understanding.

This isn't an activity in judgment - it is an activity in perception. If these recollections have raised negative emotions, for example, lament or recrimination, then it is imperative to do some clearing activities to separate that energy and to relinquish them.

Lament can regularly come as "I wish I had purchased that stock or those offers" or "I wish I had purchased that lottery ticket" or "I wish I had believed that individual" or "I wish I had said something to that individual."

Well, it is imperative to clean up any negative emotions related with those recollections. Those specific chances and individuals have gone and can't be brought back. It is essential to open up the space for new ones to come into your life.

Using Tarot Cards to Develop Your Intuition

Tarot cards can be a fabulous method to build up your Intuition further. They can go about as scaffold among you and your Higher Guidance. They can offer you a prompt response in the structure of picture.

I have done innumerable readings where a customer has taken a gander at the image on a tarot card and said "that is actually how I feel!"

When using tarot cards, it is critical to move beyond stressing over what the cards mean, as they are probably going to mean various things in each reading. Utilize the cards as a trigger for your Intuition and your Inner Guidance.

Moment Reaction Exercise

The principal practice is an INSTANT REACTION exercise to assist you with starting to confide in your Intuition and the primary responses that you get.

Take a full breath, unwind and clear your brain. You are going to deal with the cards and rapidly place them into two heaps. These are heaps that incite a prompt negative or positive response for you.

Your responses might be founded on the hues, regardless of whether the cards are light or dim, whether your prompt impression of the image is that it is cheerful or dismal, whether you get a quick feeling about a card or whatever it might be.

This doesn't make the cards fortunate or unfortunate and it doesn't make your recognitions positive or negative. This is an activity occurring in this moment and it might be that your decisions are hued at this time by what else is going on in your life. It additionally doesn't imply that the cards will consistently have that equivalent significance for you.

A few cards will give an a lot more grounded response than others. That is OK. Do whatever it takes not to contemplate it. This is a quick response work out.

When you have completed, you can look at the cards in each heap in more detail and notice which ones you have picked. It is particularly important to see the cards where you had the most grounded response, both positive and negative. Make a note of any of the subtleties of any of the cards that jumped out at you, as these may have a significant message for you at this time.

You may wind up testing your own view of the cards.

For instance I as of late drew the DEATH card, which is a card of progress and change. Generally the Death Card is regularly seen in a negative light, anyway I had been experiencing a time of stagnation and dissatisfaction, so I saw that card and said "Much obliged! Expedite it! The sooner the better!"

Moment Answers

When you have an inquiry, unwind, take a full breath, and figure your inquiry in a way that is going to offer you the best response (see segment on posing inquiries), clear your psyche, mix your cards and pick 2 or 3 cards.

Trust that these cards will be the ideal cards for you and that the appropriate responses you get will be the ideal one's for you at this time.

Notice your prompt response. Trust that. It will offer you the clearest responses. When you start to legitimately dissect the card, then the intensity of that instinctive brief can rapidly be lost.

Notice what you can see, what the hues, images and pictures are on the card, see whatever jumps out of the card at you. Know about any quick musings, emotions, words or impressions.

You can look into the implications in a book if you might want some further bits of knowledge or qualifications, despite the fact that I would firmly prompt that you don't do that since you may weaken the intensity of the appropriate responses that have originated from your very own oblivious personality or Higher Self or your own Inner Wisdom.

Chapter 9: Tips to ensure a good reading

1. Preparing a Peaceful Environment

Believe it or not, the atmosphere in which you read tarot will affect readings greatly. Not only can you be influenced by the world as a tarot reader, but it can also influence the story. It is always important to put away your own personal problems and concerns while reading tarot. The development of a comfortable room that lets you stay focused and relaxed can help you stay rational and impartial when reading. Rituals like candles or incense burning will allow you to get into the mood as well.

2. Select a Signifier Card

For tarot reading, significant cards reflect either the individual being read or the condition they inquire about. If you use the signature card to represent the person, most tarot readers prefer to use the courtroom card either by comparing the physical characteristics of the inquirer to one of the court cards or by associating their petroleum sign with one of the courtroom cards. If you choose a card to show a particular situation, you can become as imaginative as you like. You can either choose a card from the main arcana or from the minor arcana, based on the severity of the issue. The key arcana cards are used for essential problems in life, whereas the minor arcana cards tend to focus on things every day.

The important card always allows you to focus on the user you are reading about. The important cards are located prominently in many tarot spreads. It allows the tarot reader to view the cards and to recognize the main issues concerning the questioner.

3. Choosing the Right Tarot Spread

Tarot Spreads are card patterns in a particular pattern. Every card location has a specific meaning within a set. Once individual tarot cards are placed in a tarot set, their significances can be used to shape a kind of plot. The tarot reader then interprets the cards according to their location and relationships.

As a tarot reader, it is necessary to pick a tarot spread that correlates appropriately to the query. Of starters, if the issue is about love, then you will possibly want to use a spread of love. You may want to create your own tarot spread in some situations. This can be especially useful if the topic concerns more than one problem.

4. Framing the Question

How the inquirer constructs or asks a question before reading may affect the overall utility of reading significantly. The more personal the questioner is with, the higher the probability that the tarot reading can answer his dilemma in a specific way. It is also helpful to keep the topic accessible. Open questions can reveal hidden or ignored problems that could otherwise have been missing. Open-ended questions can also help the tarot reader uncover key problems or other factors that could impact the user.

5. Shuffling the Cards

There are a number of ways to match cards while reading tarot. This is usually the way the reader actually touches the cards (although some tarot readers allow nobody to treat their money). When you want to let the inquirer manage the money, you will ensure that the issues at hand are answered while they are being shuffled so that this focus can be passed to the cards. Different approaches to "cutting" cards are also available; the most common is that the inquirer three times slices the deck with his left hand.

6. Knowing Your Tarot Deck

Until I read some tarot, I still encourage people to take time to really appreciate the tarot deck with which they are dealing. Not only does this allow you to get acquainted with the games, but it also improves your comprehension of their definitions and how they communicate with each other. Needless to say, those who get a tarot read from you will still pick up your relationship to your own cards. If you don't recognize the deck for which you're operating, it will probably happen while tarot reading.

Practice Makes Perfect

Daily Practice

In order to get good at a skill, especially in the case of divination and Tarot reading, the most obvious first step is to practice daily or as close to daily as you can. You will most likely just start with personal readings, as it is easier to see how cards relate to you than to others.

After you get more comfortable with the cards, the next step would be to try readings for other people. It is best to try this with people you know well at first before branching out to people you may not know as well, and eventually offer readings for near complete strangers. At each of the stages of this step, make sure you are extremely comfortable with the readings before advancing to the next stage. Take baby steps. If you dive into the deep end before learning to swim, it is most likely not going to end well.

New Meanings

In any given reading, or even between readings, you may feel inclined to give a new meaning to a card based on what the Divine places in your heart and mind.

This is not to say you completely ignore the card drawn and come up with your own meaning on the spot every time. The card was drawn for a reason. The reason may not be the pre-set meaning, but it will have something to do with the card.

Habit Forming

Part of this is practicing daily, but a lot of it is making a divination ritual. Maybe you have a specific area in which card reading is made easier.

Incorporating the Cards in Your Life

Do: Use the Cards Often

This is how you develop a knack for reading them in the first place. Without frequent usage, even on mundane things, proficiency, much less mastery, will take a long time to achieve.

Do not: Rely Too Heavily on The Cards

They are not meant to be used as an absolute. By taking the cards literally or expecting things to happen exactly as they laid out, you put yourself on a path of failure and disappointment. Some things laid out in the cards may not ever come to fruition. This is because, even subconsciously, you know the outcome of your current path and work to make it the most desirable outcome possible.

Do: Try Different Spreads

When doing readings, you want to choose the spread you feel will most thoroughly answer the question. There's not really a one-size-fits-all spread that will cover every situation. As such, you should practice multiple spreads to fill your repertoire. Even if you think you know enough different spreads, you may find a new favorite that is more useful than any of the spreads.

Do not: Get Discouraged

If your readings aren't 100% accurate, do not worry. Few actually are. Keep practicing your readings and interpretations. They will get better with time and effort. Many beginners will quit their attempts after a few failures. By failing, you only learn how to achieve in the future. Practice makes perfect in most aspects of life, and divination is no exception.

Do: Keep a Journal or Notebook

This journal can be used for anything related to Tarot. You can write down readings and interpretations along with the date and question and keep track of how your accuracy improves. You may write down personal meanings to cards. This is especially helpful if you've re-defined most, if not all, of your deck. You can also keep track of your favorite spreads, noting the patterns and meanings of each card.

If you own one, this journal could actually just be your Book of Shadows or Grimoire.

Do not: Use the Cards Solely as a Fallback for Rough Times

Hopefully, you won't have many major problems in life to use the cards on. That being said, if you only use the cards during these times of turmoil, you won't be getting much practice, and you can't depend too heavily on your readings and interpretations to be as accurate as they could be. Even mundane readings, such as a one card answer to "Should I get a burger or a salad?" provides practice to your interpretations.

Conclusion

As you reach the end of this book, you would somehow realize that learning to read Tarot cards is more than fun and excitement. If you have mastered it the right way and applied it to change or enhance your present situation in life, you will realize that it is the best tool one should have. It may take time to memorize meanings but note that these tarot cards can connect to your inner mind.

The inner mind holds your spiritual knowledge and wisdom as well as your intuition and your inner critic. It's your inner consciousness that takes control of your life. By mastering how to use them to your advantage effectively, you can take control of your inner mind and use it to make better decisions to achieve your goals for a better and happier life.

Astrology and Numerology Academy

CPSIA information can be obtained
at www.ICGtesting.com
Printed in the USA
LVHW060828160421
683976LV00018B/35

9 781801 130653